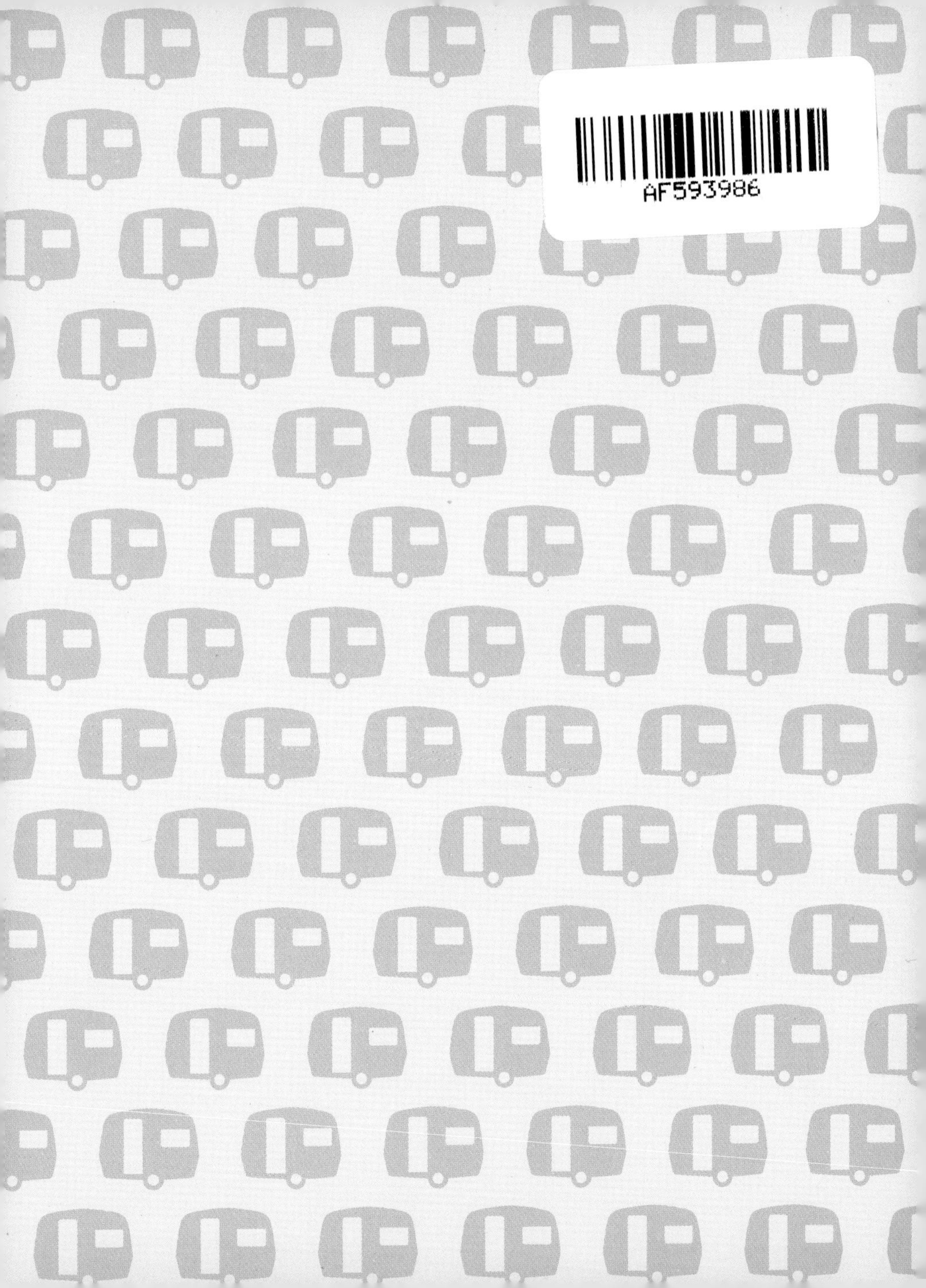
AF593986

Distressingly perceptive, beautifully absurd, seriously thought-provoking. Lovely work, somehow all so familiar and strange. Bloody brilliant!!! The most intriguing art gallery I have ever seen! The extraordinariness of ordinariness – be seduced and enthralled. Opens one's eyes to the beauty and squalor of everyday life. You're never going to run out of material are you? Love the smut. Only in Britain... It's worrying. Commendable contemporary cultural consensus caravan. Fantastically accurate depiction of contemporary Britain. Fantastic – never heard so many people laughing in a gallery space. Brilliant, funny, poignant – captures the humour of Britain perfectly. **Welcome to Britain** Lots of cool weird stuff. Truth is stranger than fiction. I want to win meat in a raffle. Still the best show on the road. Can we really be like this? There should be a caravan art gallery in every town and city in the UK. Completely inspired – makes me proud to be British. Great to see some joy in the middle of the High Street. Pure dead brilliant!!!! Get some pictures of the deep-fried creme eggs in Glasgow. We are crackers aren't we really? Certainly worth driving 60 miles to see. Extremely extraordinary. Makes us want to go back to the Museum of Gas in Fakenham. Totally caravanic. Refreshing like salad.

Dedicated to the staff at the Department of Hepatology, Southampton General Hospital, and Addenbrooke's Hospital Transplant Unit, without whom this book would not have been possible.

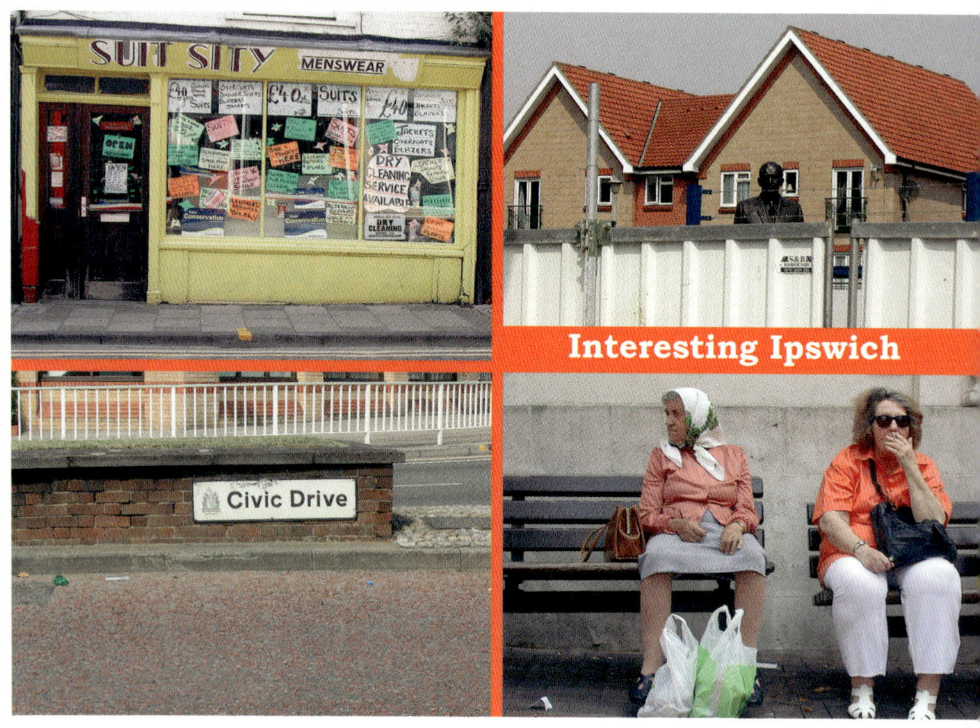

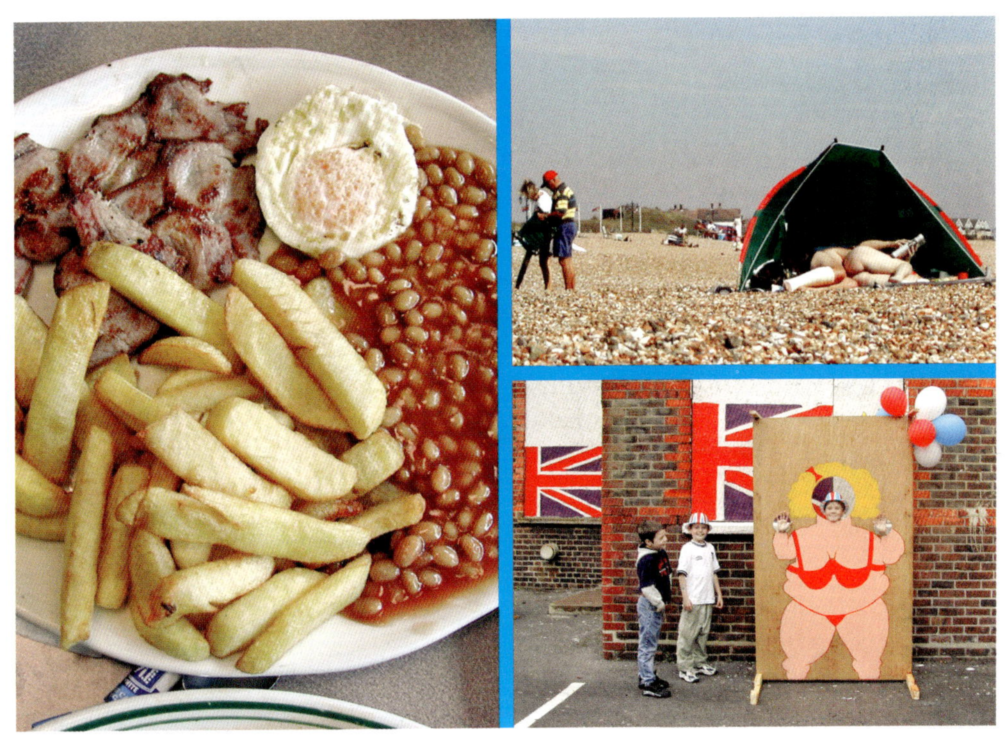

Welcome to Britain

A Celebration of Real Life

Jan Williams and Chris Teasdale

The Caravan Gallery

teNeues

Acknowledgements

We would like to thank everyone who has helped The Caravan Gallery on its way, whether wielding paintbrushes, providing parking space, giving publicity or simply taking part in 'The Caravan Gallery Experience' as a visitor.

Thanks to all the galleries and venues, festival and event organisers who have invited us to pitch up – or, at least, allowed us to gatecrash – and to all who have provided support, especially the former Southern Arts, Arts Council South East and the Scottish Arts Council. Particular thanks to all our friends and colleagues at Art Space Portsmouth and Aspex Gallery, Portsmouth, and to random Caravan Gallery fans in various parts of the world. Thanks also to The Lovely Ian at YCUK for peddling our postcards so splendidly.

Thanks to all at Headline and to Dan and Emma at Perfect Books for having faith in us and being so great to work with.

A massive thank you to assorted friends and family, especially Our Pat, Our Henry, Our Paul and Our Rachel Williams and to Maryrose and Henry Merritt, all cremeux and delicioso, forcopious amounts of love and support.

For the second edition we would like to thank all at teNeues – Bridget for the initial contact and Alexandra for following up, Rina for sterling work getting the book redesigned and printed, and particularly Hendrik for giving 'Welcome to Britain' a whole new lease on life.

Finally, thanks to Great Britain for being so photogenic.

Design and editorial by Perfect Books Ltd

Design Production by Jenene Chesbrough,
teNeues Publishing Company
Editorial Coordination by Maria Regina Madarang,
teNeues Publishing Company

Published by teNeues Publishing Group

teNeues Verlag GmbH + Co. KG
Am Selder 37
47906 Kempen, Germany
Phone: 0049 / (0)2152 / 916 0
Fax: 0049 / (0)2152 / 916 111
Press department:
arehn@teneues.de
Phone: 0049 / (0)2152 / 916 202

teNeues Publishing Company
16 West 22nd Street
New York, N.Y. 10010, USA
Phone: 001 / 212 / 627 9090
Fax: 001 / 212 / 627 9511

teNeues Publishing UK Ltd.
P.O. Box 402
West Byfleet
KT14 7ZF, Great Britain
Phone: 0044 / (0)1932 / 40 35 09
Fax: 0044 / (0)1932 / 40 35 14

teNeues France S.A.R.L.
93, rue Bannier
45000 Orléans, France
Phone: 0033 / (0)2 / 38 54 10 71
Fax: 0033 / (0)2 / 38 62 53 40

www.teneues.com

For more information on The Caravan Gallery, visit
www.thecaravangallery.co.uk

Bibliographic information published by Die Deutsche Bibliothek. Die Deutsche Bibliothek lists this publication in the Deutsche Nationalbibliografie; detailed bibliographic data is available on the Internet at http://dnb.ddb.de.

This is a revised edition of a work first published in 2005.

ISBN 978-3-8327-9281-7

Printed in China

teNeues Publishing Group
Kempen
Düsseldorf
Hamburg
London
Munich
New York
Paris

teNeues

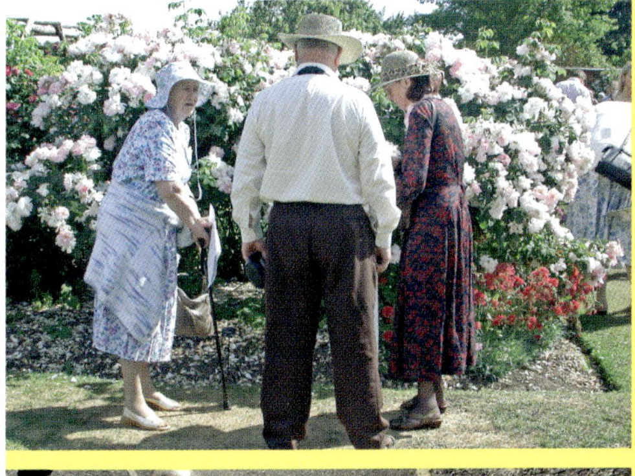

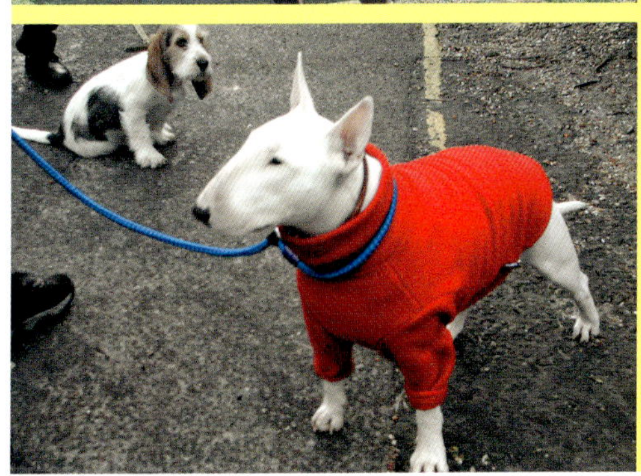

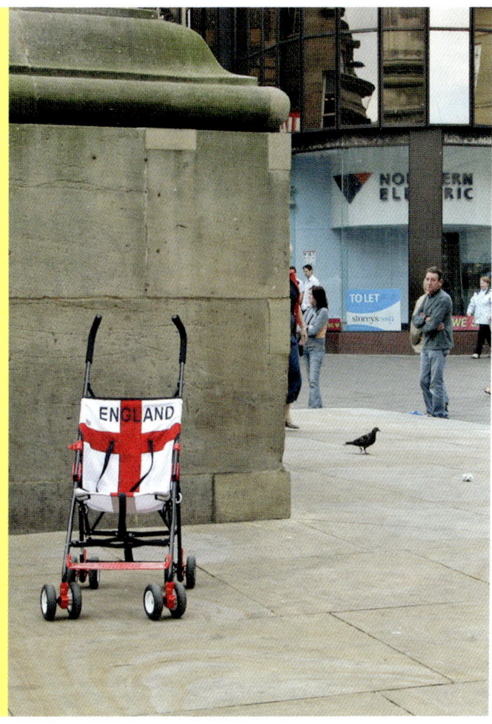

Contents

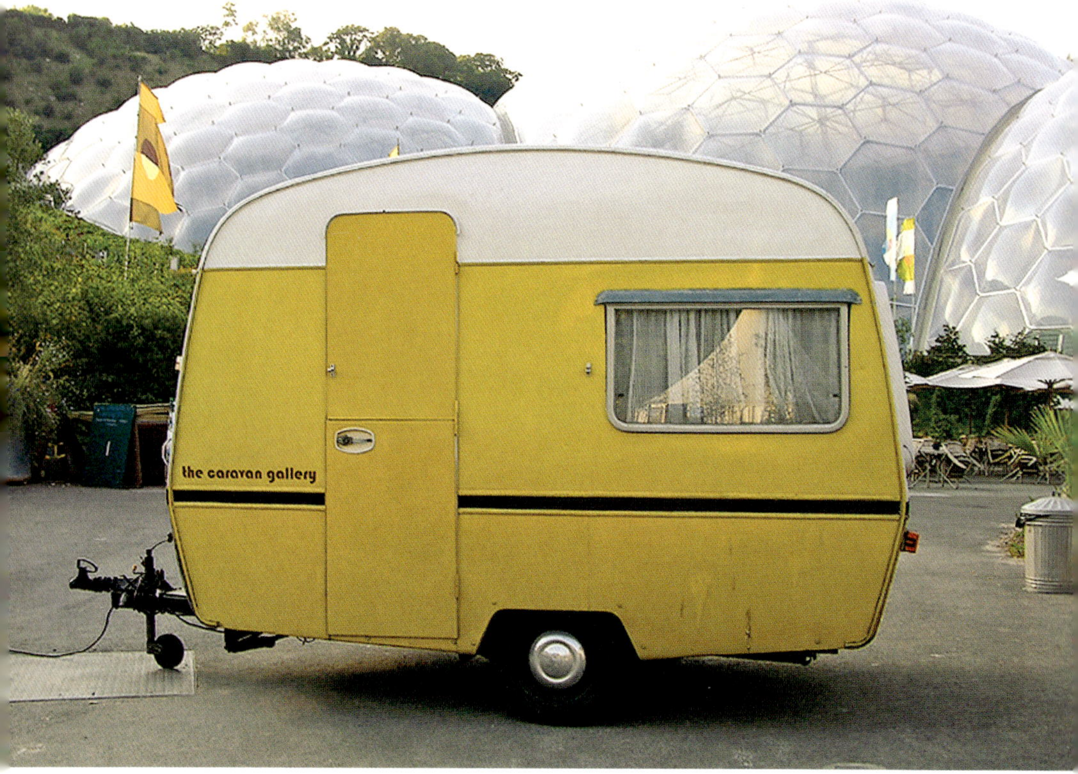

Introduction

For a number of years now, fields, car parks, villages, towns and cities around Britain, from Land's End in Cornwall to Alloa in Scotland, have been treated to the unexpected sight of a small mustard-coloured 1969 caravan sitting on its own, surrounded by tables and chairs, postcard racks, umbrellas, and dead conifers in plastic urns.

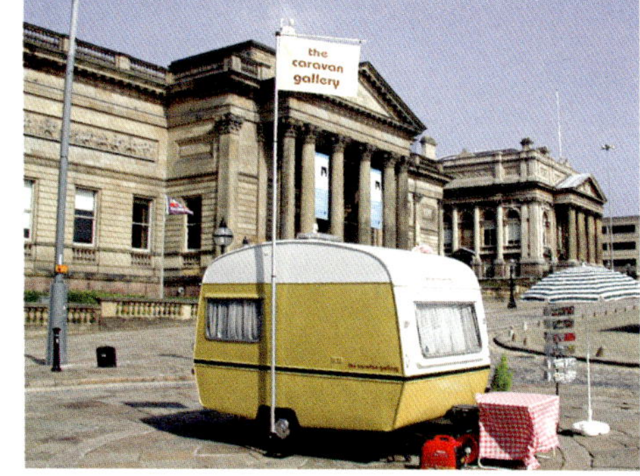

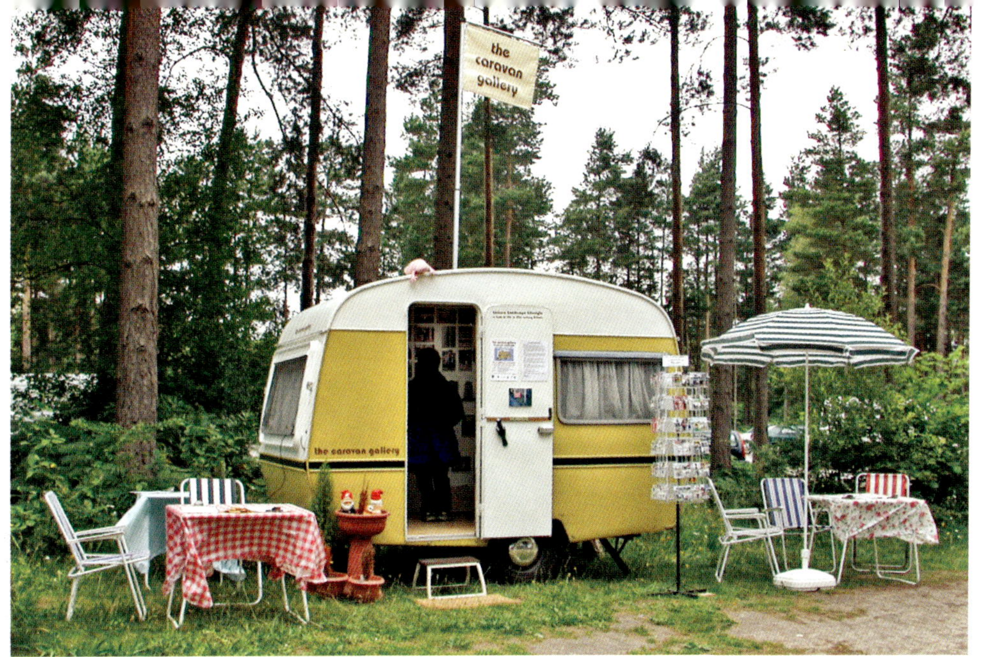

What's great about Britain?

It's the best country in the world

What's not so great?

Britain was great until they got soft

Within this unlikely setting lies a 'proper' art gallery with white walls and beech floor – and brown velour curtains: a perfect exhibition venue for the drawings, photographs and specially-made postcards produced on our mission to record the mundane, yet extraordinary, details of life in 21st-century Britain. It is called, unsurprisingly, The Caravan Gallery. A quintessential symbol of the British at leisure, it would be difficult to think of a more appropriate vehicle for displaying such an archive. 'Bobble' (our nickname, describing the Caravan's egg-like shape) reaches people that other galleries can't!

How many grand buildings have a spectacularly dead conifer outside? What is happening to our concrete car parks? Why is chicken everywhere? How many small shops are closing and why have so many churches swapped God for laminate flooring? How do people make ends meet and what does it really mean to be British? In photographing the everyday and familiar we are celebrating the overlooked details of life in Britain today. By exhibiting the results we show that there is life beyond the brown signs and Tourist Information brochures and how, by looking hard enough, unexpected delights can be found in the most unpromising situations.

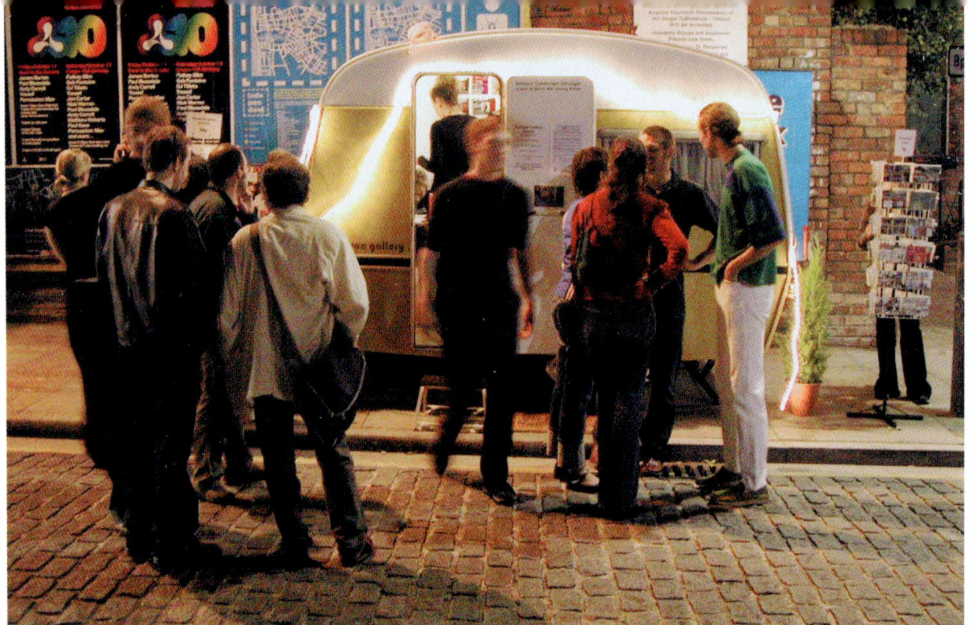

As we travel around we invite visitors to The Caravan Gallery to share their views by filling in a survey about their locality and lifestyle. With questions ranging from the serious to the frivolous, our 'subversive surveys' have always proved popular and yielded fascinating results. Other feedback comes from information left in our comments book, a fine collection of anecdotes, confessions and recommendations of places worthy of investigation.

Although we have travelled many thousands of miles and 'fetched up' everywhere from outside major art galleries to garden centre car parks, we have not, as yet, been able to cover the whole of the country (although the quest goes on). This book, therefore, serves more as a snapshot of life in Britain today, rather than a comprehensive survey, and is organised by the recurring themes that crop up wherever we happen to be. We have explored our national obsession with gardening and al fresco living, looked at curious shops and enterprises, and photographed everything from peculiar signage to knitted baked beans. We particularly enjoy recording Britain's changing architectural landscape as regeneration fever grips the

What do you collect?

Anything with cats on

Miniature shoes

Bookmarks and sugar packets

Signed drumsticks

Wives (three)

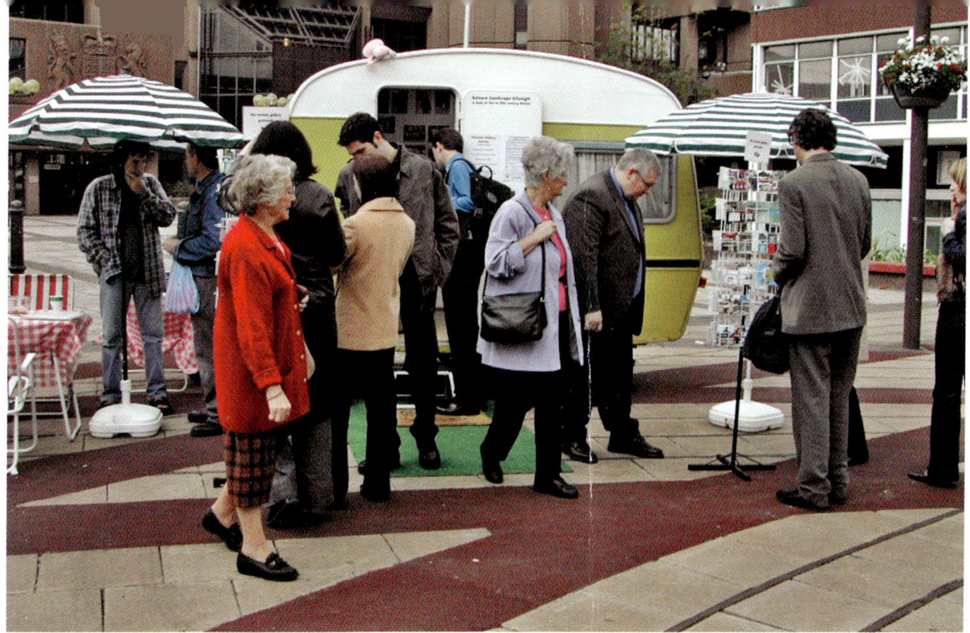

What do you think of as 'typically British'?

Seaside postcards

Thinking you're funny

It's quite chilly from time to time

White socks and sandals

nation, resulting in a heady cocktail of slick modernity and endearing shabbiness.

The photographs – many of which, by necessity, were taken at inclement times of year, in the dark, or from a moving car – need little comment from us but we have added statistics gleaned from our survey results (57 per cent of people manage to kill houseplants without even trying), answers to questions from the surveys (Q: What is great about Britain? A: Cornish pasties), and comments from the visitors' book (Can we really be like this?) to give a flavour of life in contemporary Britain.

Visitors to The Caravan Gallery often say, 'I've lived here twenty years and never noticed that.' We hope they are encouraged to look at, and appreciate, their surroundings more as a result of our efforts. They also keep asking, 'When are you going to make a book?' Well, here it is – an affectionate, pictorial documentation of the incongruous, banal and unloved, the all-too-familiar or downright bizarre features of the British landscape and people.

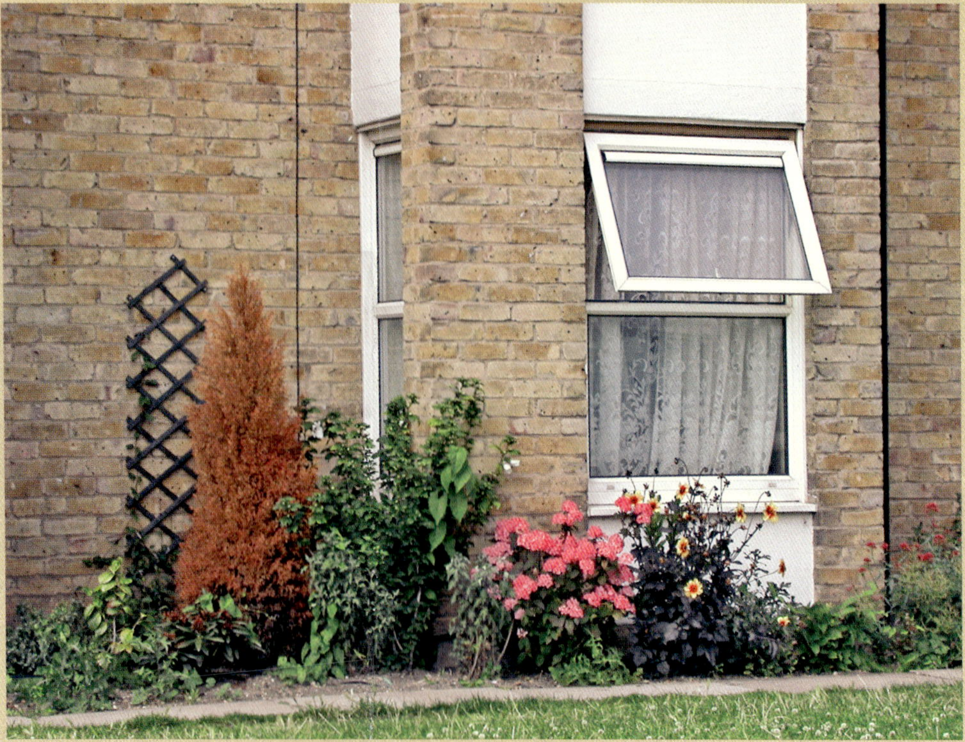

Conifers (dead)

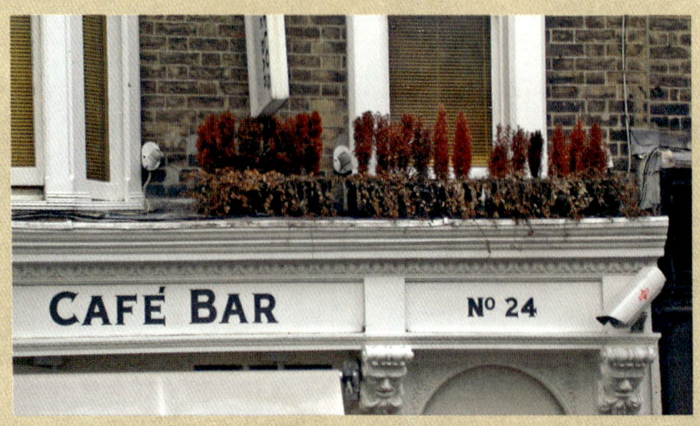

The dead conifer was adopted as The Caravan Gallery's motif because it is so ubiquitous in Britain – virtually every garden or forecourt seems to have at least one.
The dead conifer is ideal for low-maintenance gardens as it is so much easier to look after than a living plant.

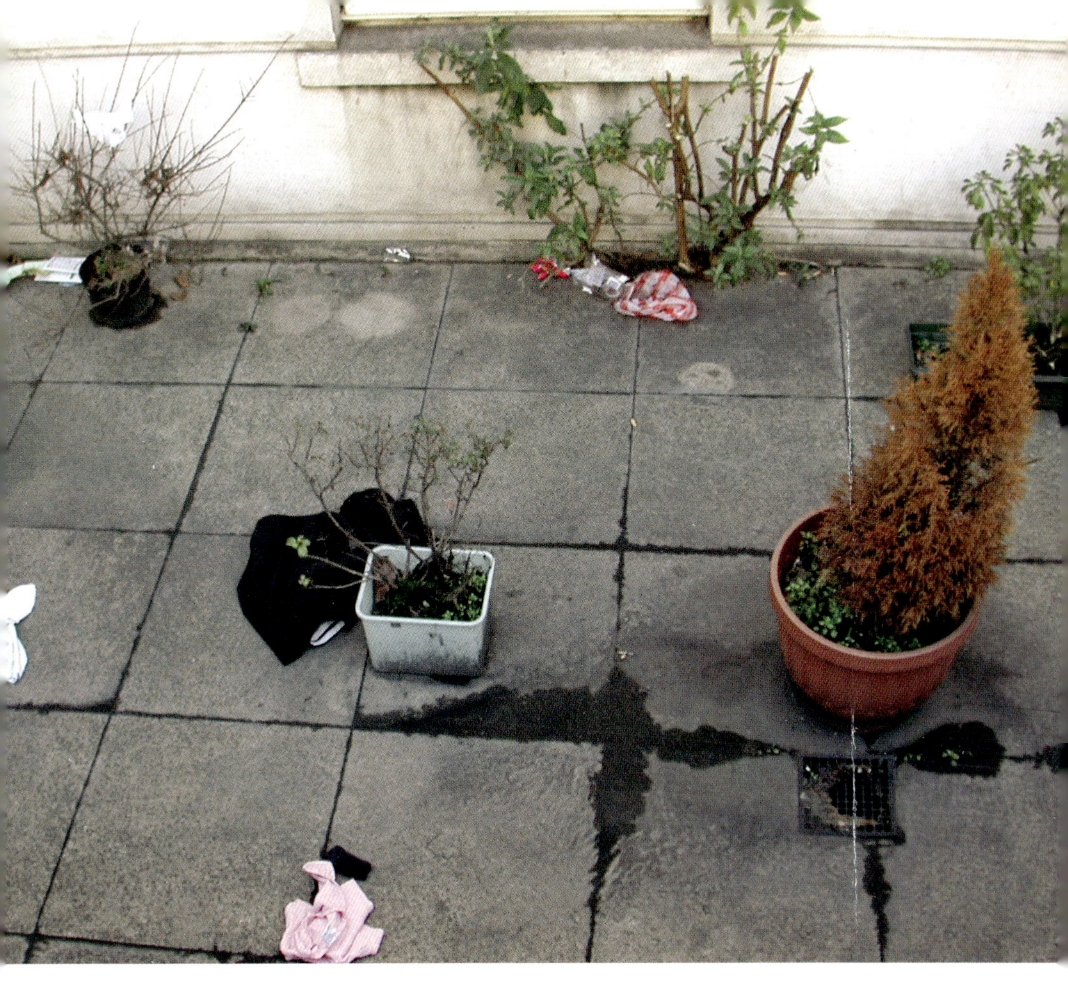

Dead conifers are everywhere. We've found prime specimens from Glasgow to the Isle of Wight, often lurking in otherwise well-tended plots. You can also pretty much guarantee a good collection in every student garden, along with a few stray items of clothing.

Only 15% of people admit to owning a dead conifer

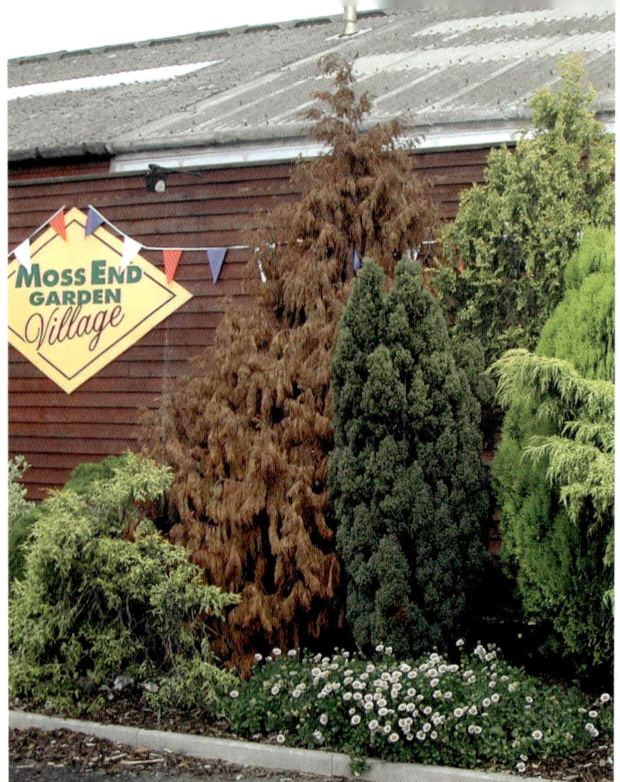

Some dead conifers stand proud as specimen plants, others try to hide in a border, while small desiccated conifers in plastic urns guard our homes.

What's great about Britain?

The green parts

What's not so great?

Net curtains

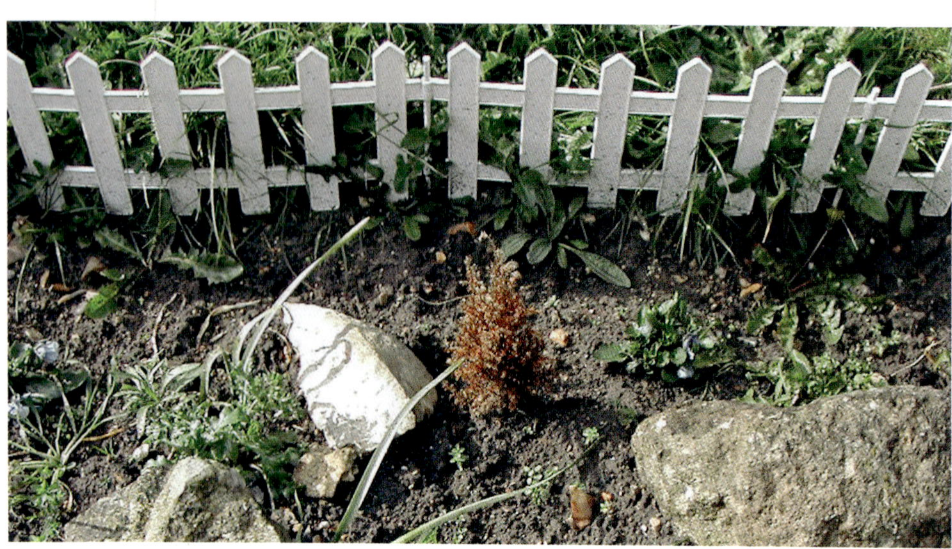

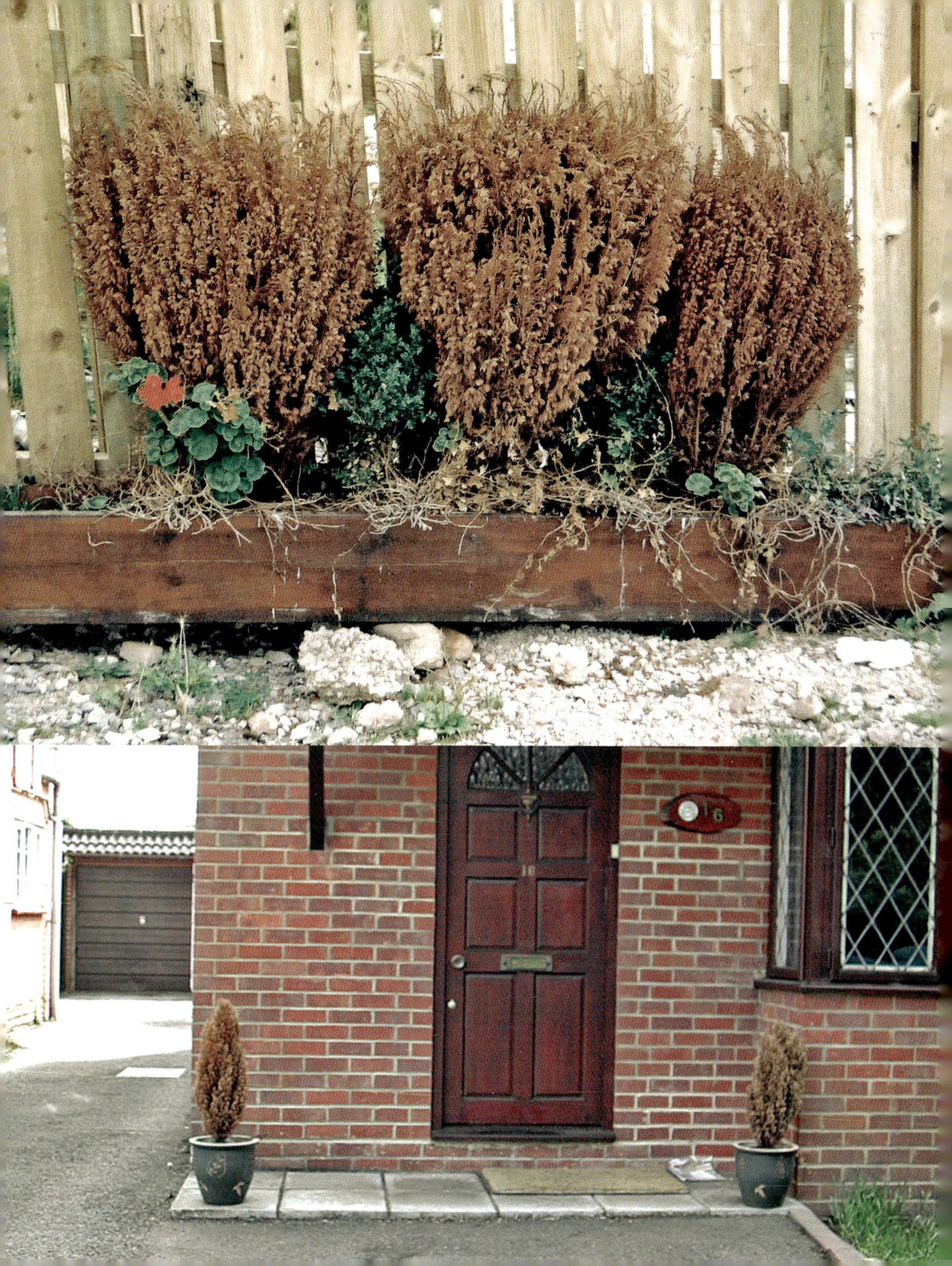

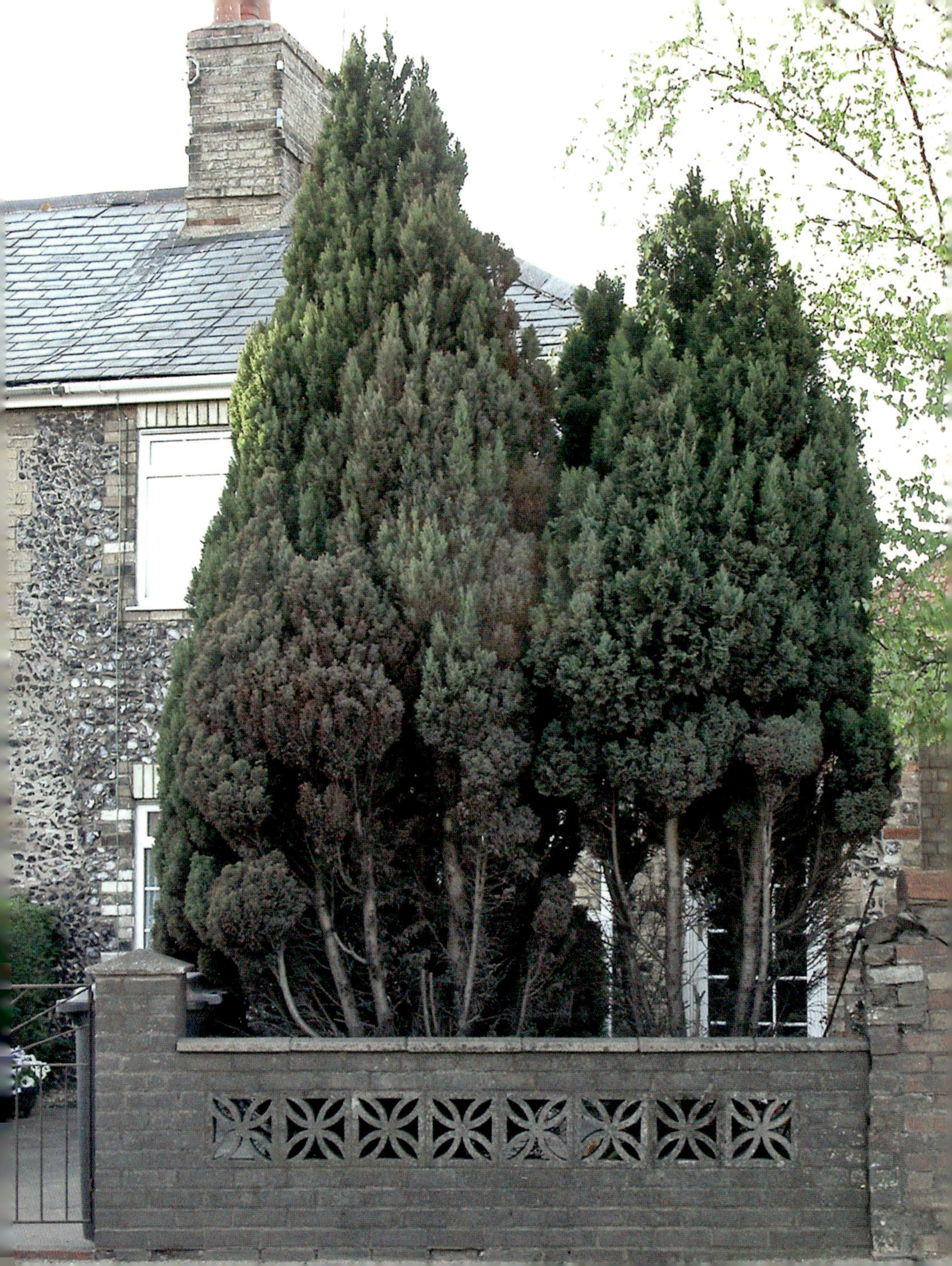

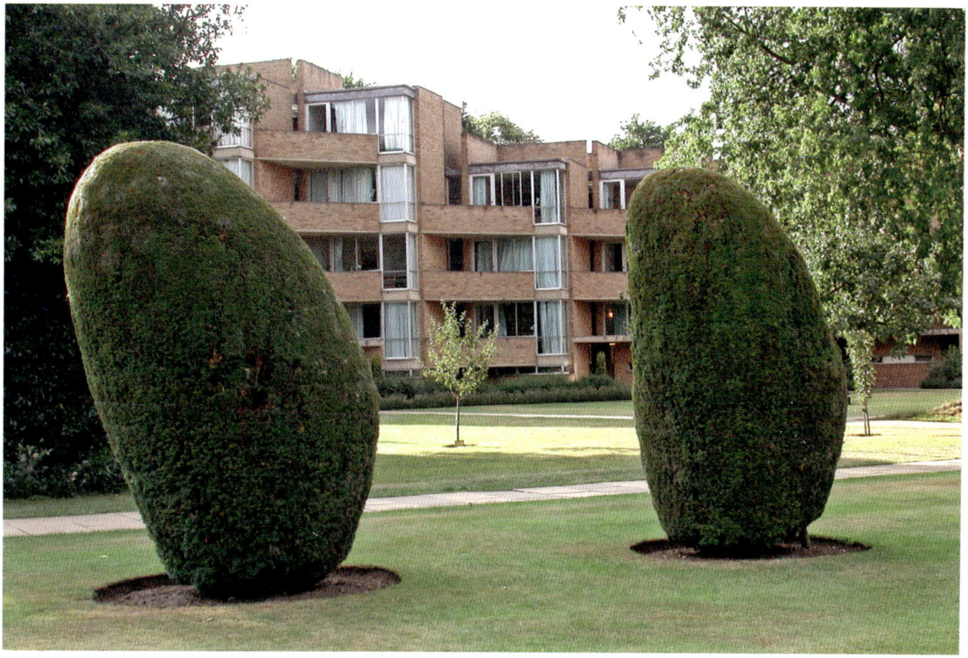

Conifers (thriving)

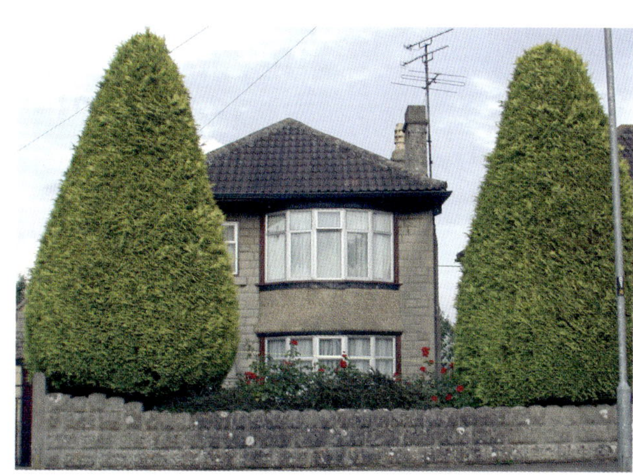

When conifer life is maintained, the results can be surprisingly spectacular. Some people feel naked without a wall of conifers (dead or alive) to hide behind, whilst others enjoy fashioning them into curious shapes.

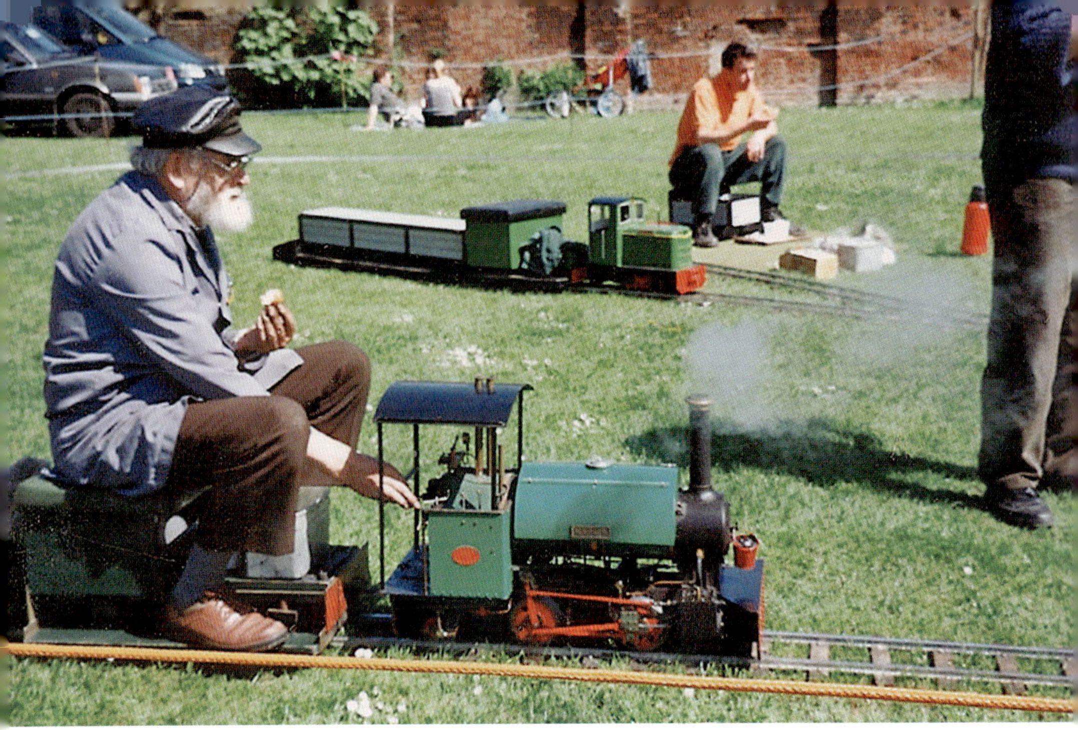

Little trains

The timeless pleasure of driving a small train over newly mown grass on a summer's day. Throw in a sandwich and a peaked cap – what more could a steamy gentleman require? Some drivers, however, may have to rely on their own steam.

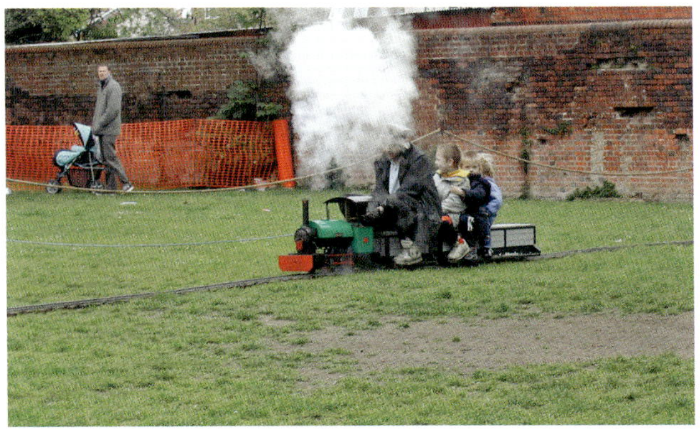

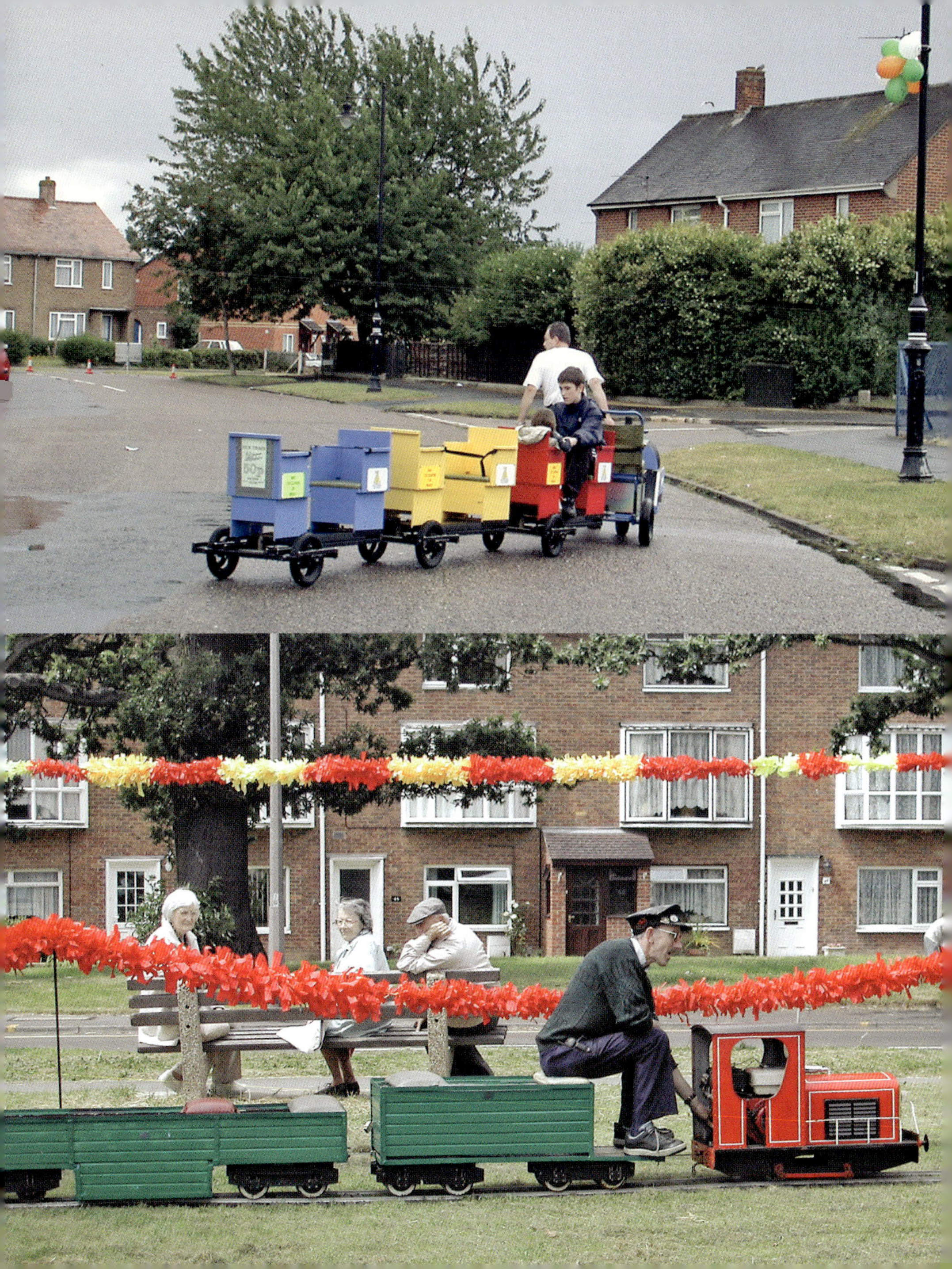
60p

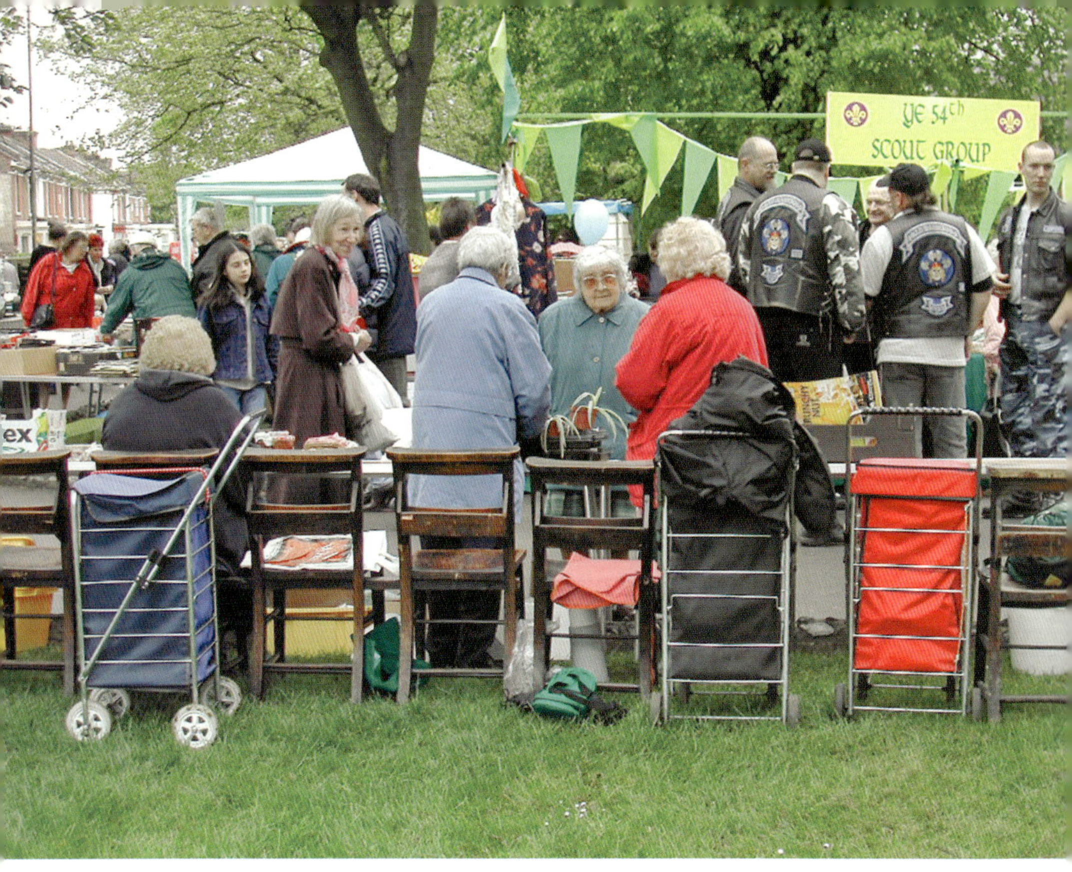

ALL TEA AND
COFFEE SERVED
IN PROPER
MUGS.

Markets

'Come on girls, get yer designer thongs here!' Victoria sponge, bramble jam, bath cubes and Battenburg cake. Gents' sports socks, Mills & Boon romances, toilet rolls (bumper packs) and designer handbags. You can get anything you want at Britain's markets, even if you don't want it. And you can always find a nice cup of tea.

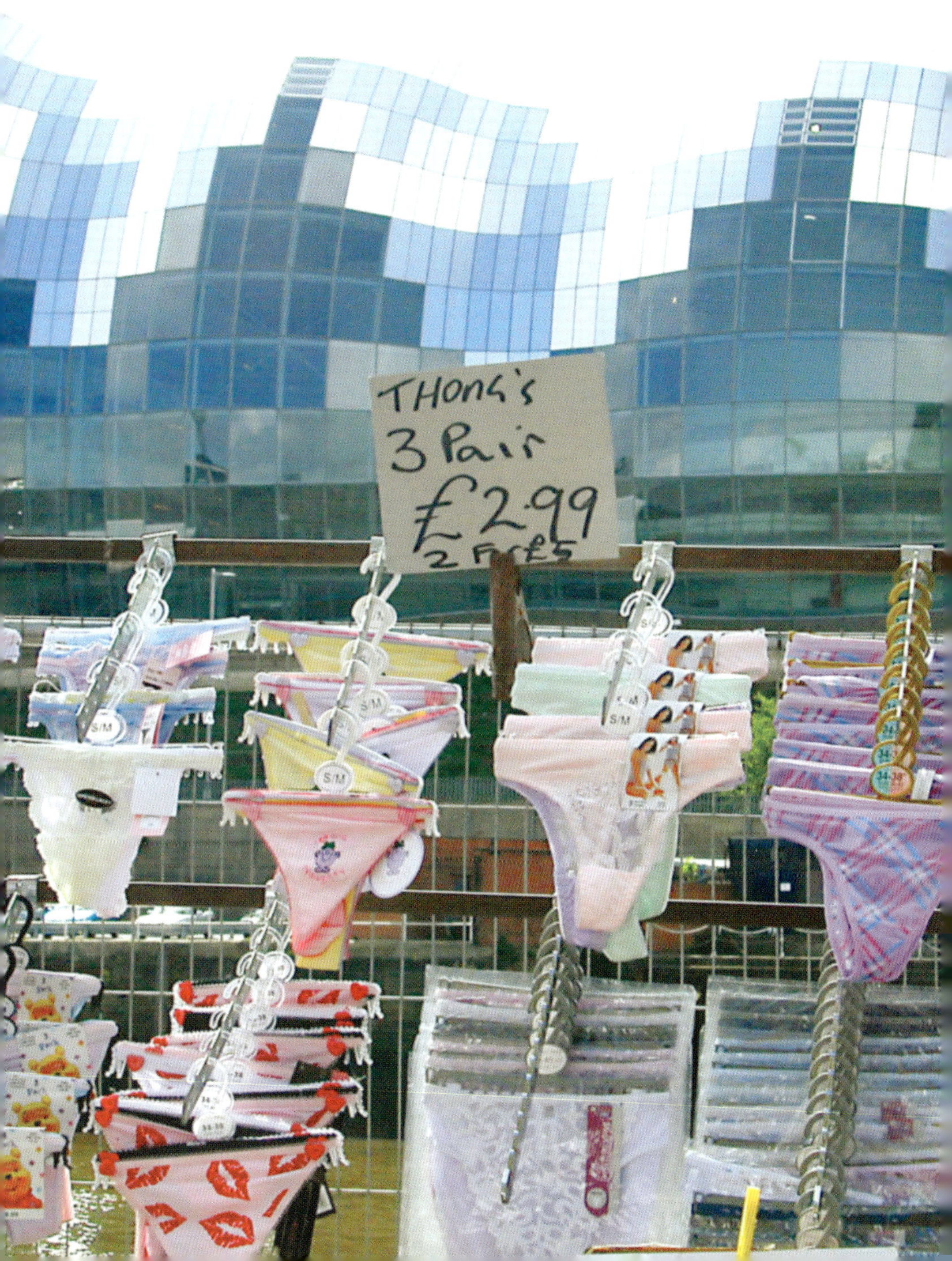
THONG's
3 Pair
£2.99
2 FOR £5

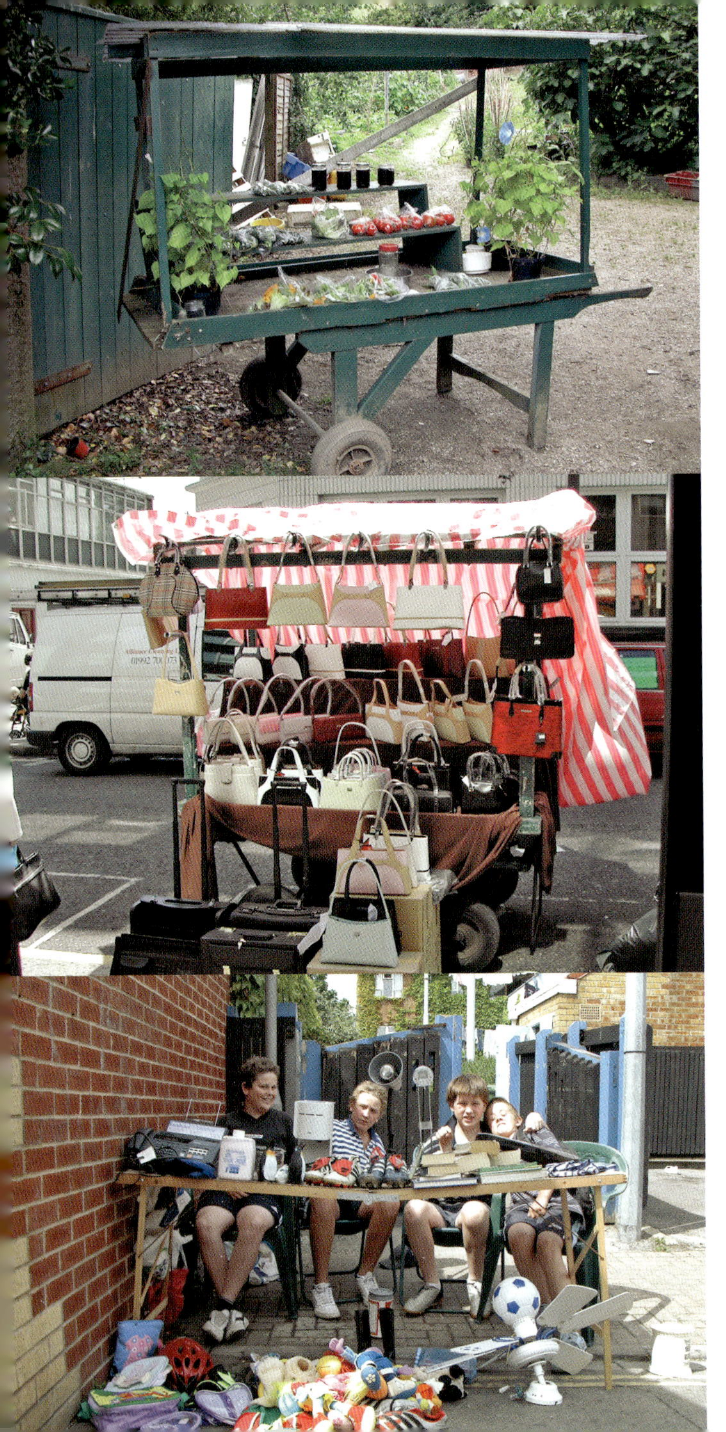

While some traders enjoy the luxury of purpose-built barrows, other resourceful entrepreneurs press spare clothes rails and sagging wallpaper tables into service.

What's the worst present you have ever received?

A horrible cup

A plastic hook set with cast plastic teddy bears

An ironing board

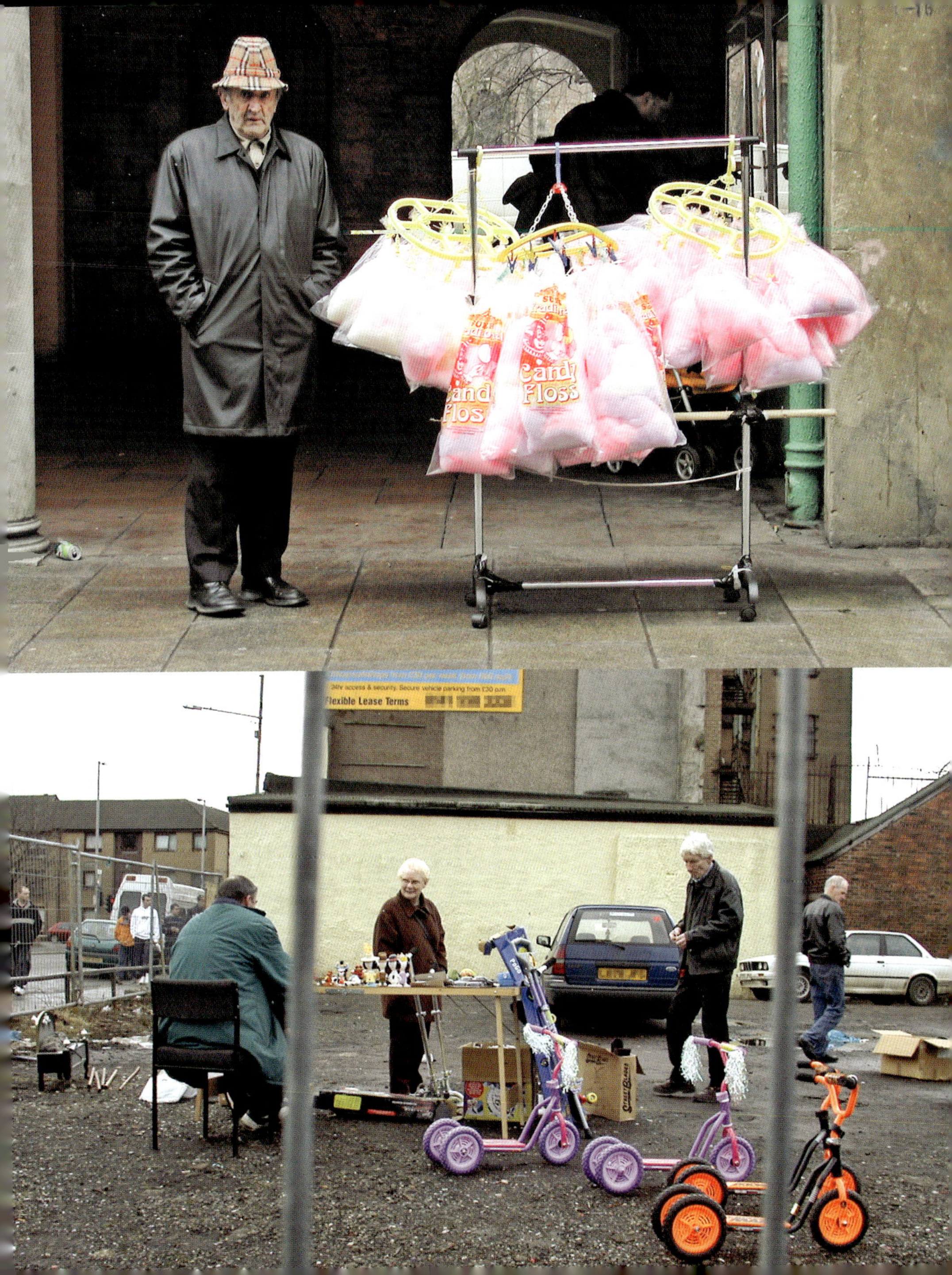
Candy Floss
Flexible Lease Terms

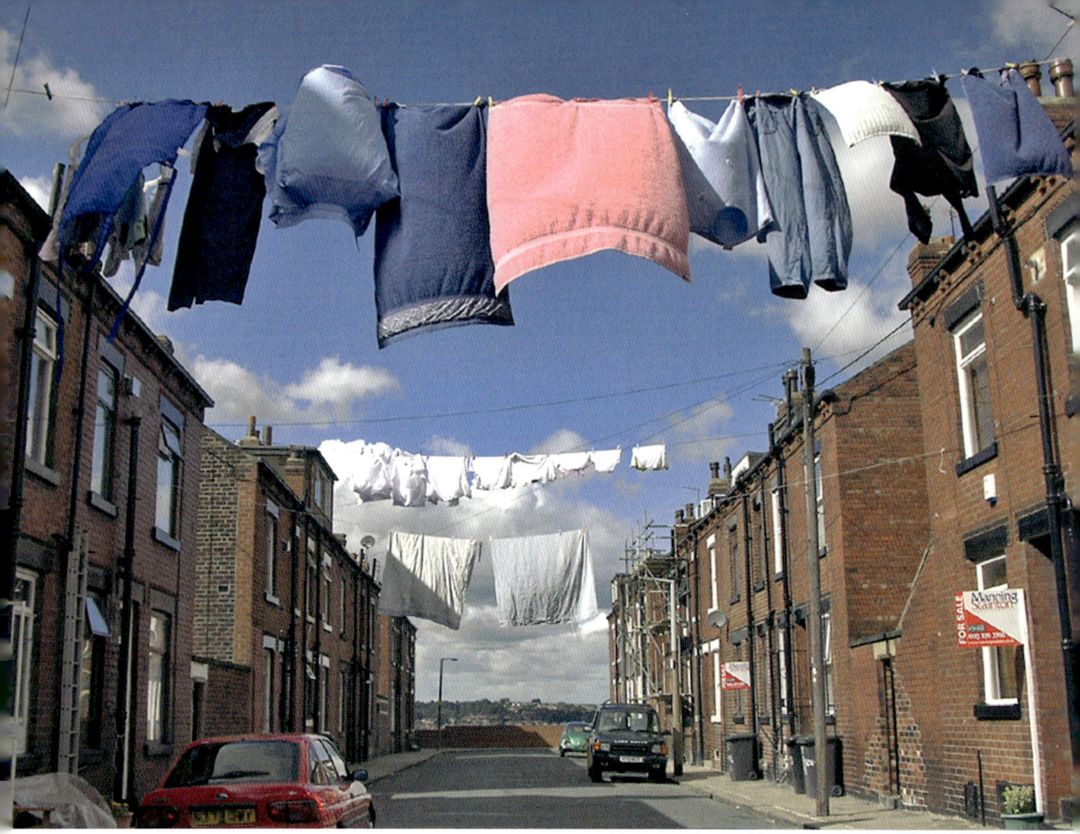

Homes

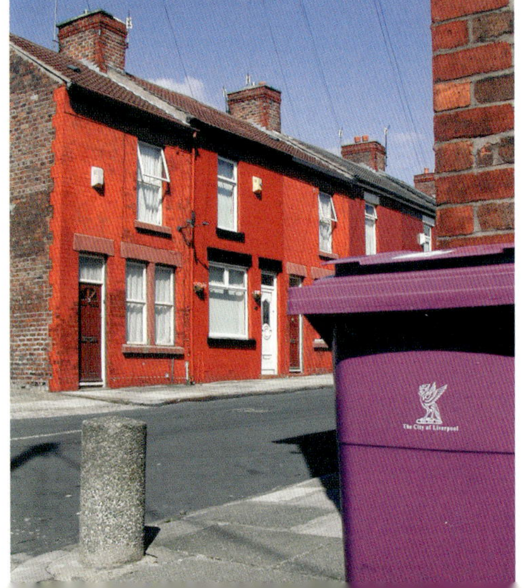

My place or yours? We live on a small island and space is at a premium, so many of us in Britain live closely packed together. And when you're living on top of each other, it helps to get on with your neighbours.

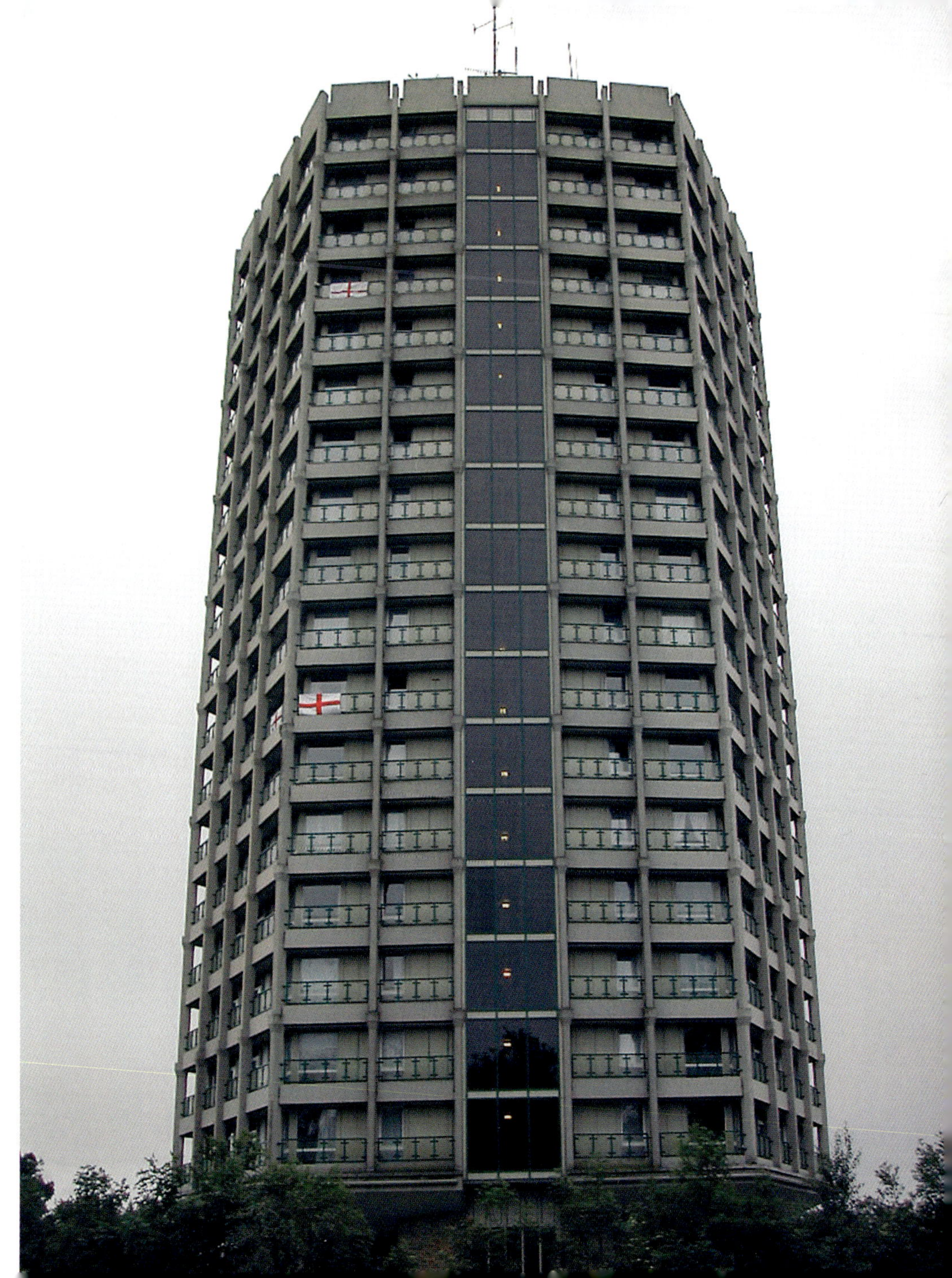

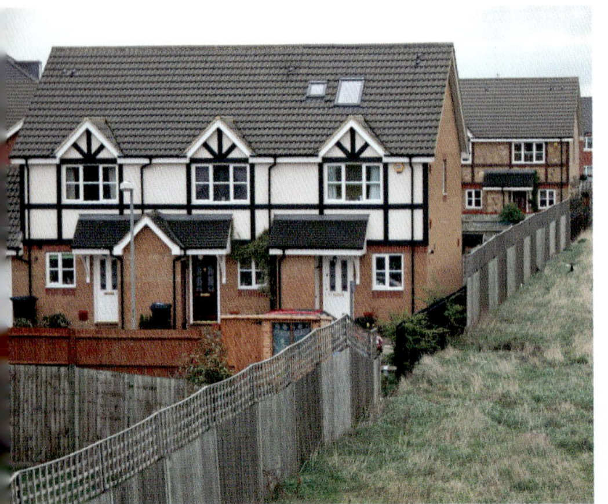

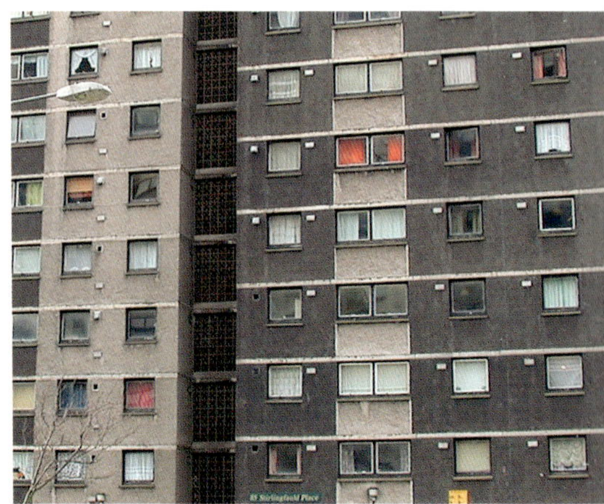

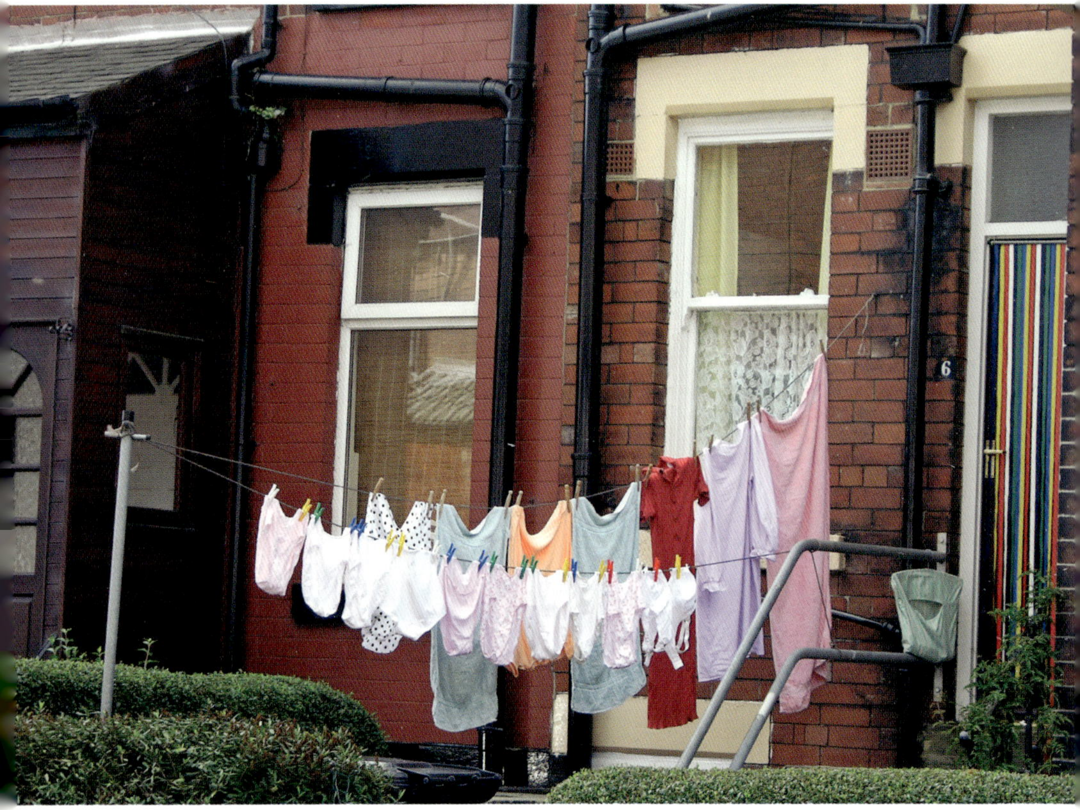

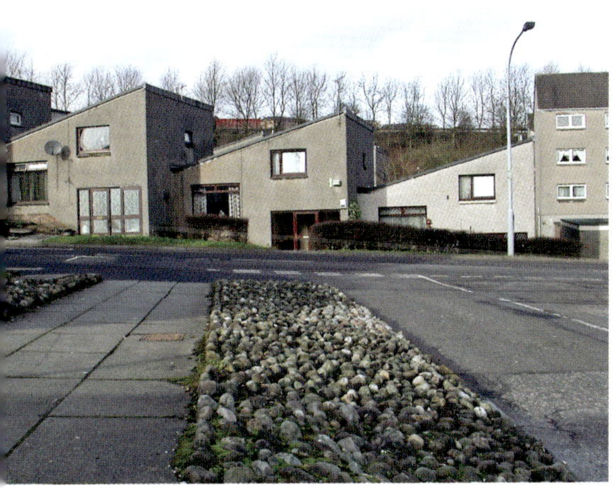

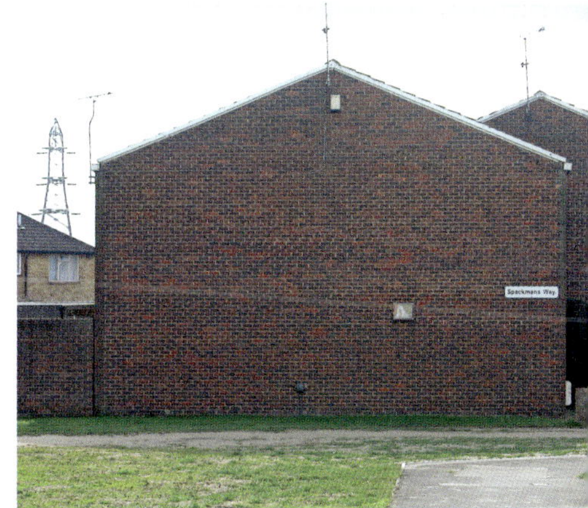

Whether it's stick-on Tudor in Slough, high-rise with multicoloured nets in Glasgow, pebble-dash in Cumbernauld, a neat red terrace in Liverpool or a cute Cornish stone cottage, there are many housing styles to choose from. Some are more unusual than others.

I wouldn't live anywhere else

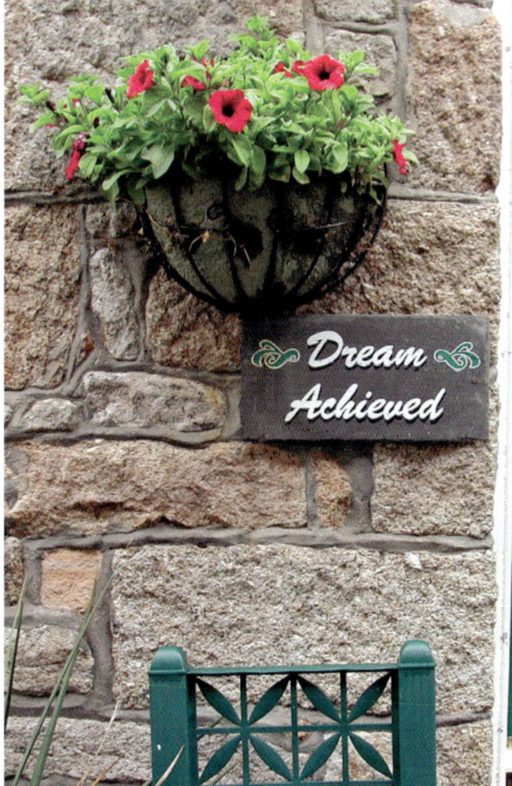

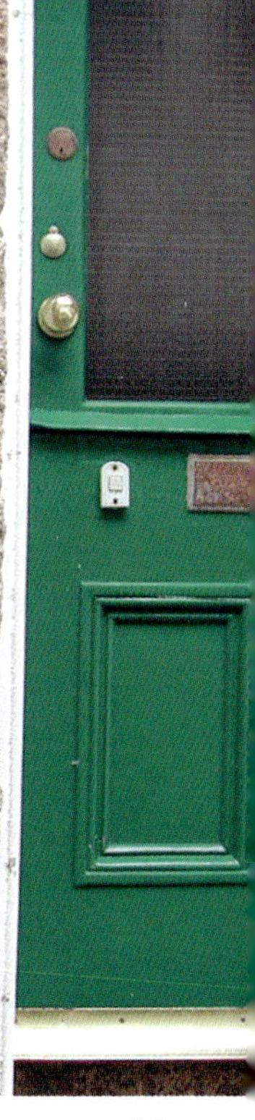

What's great about Britain?

Variety and tolerance

What's not so great?

We make bad neighbours

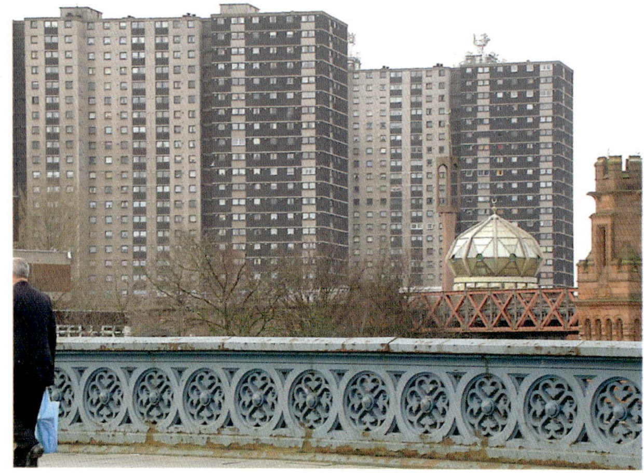

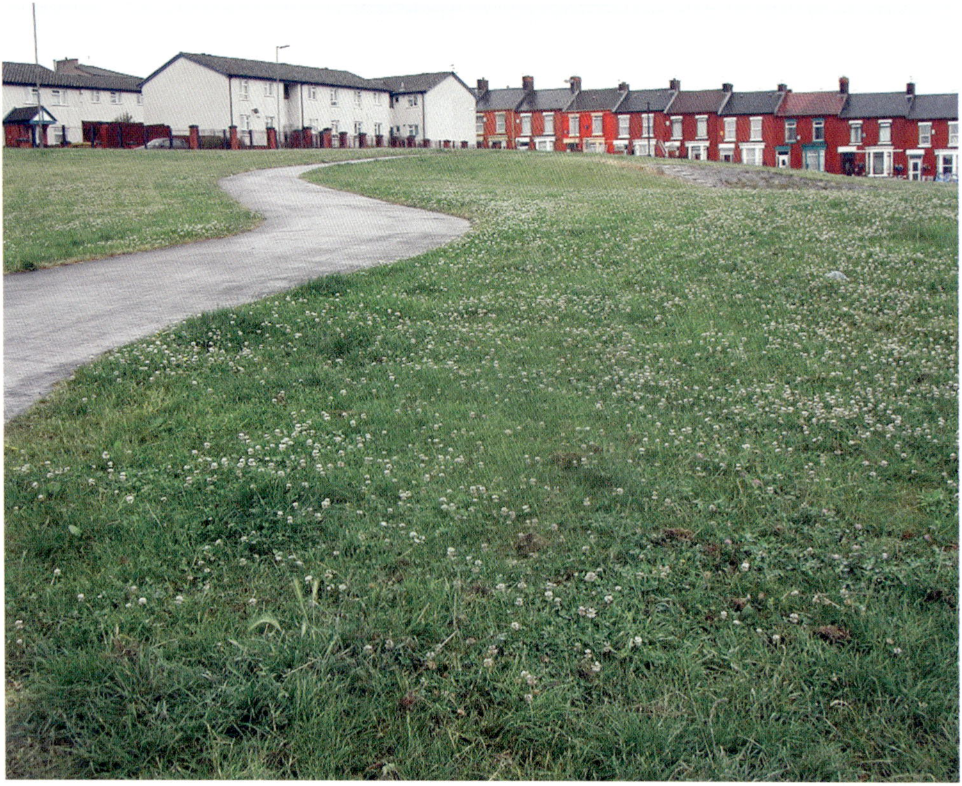

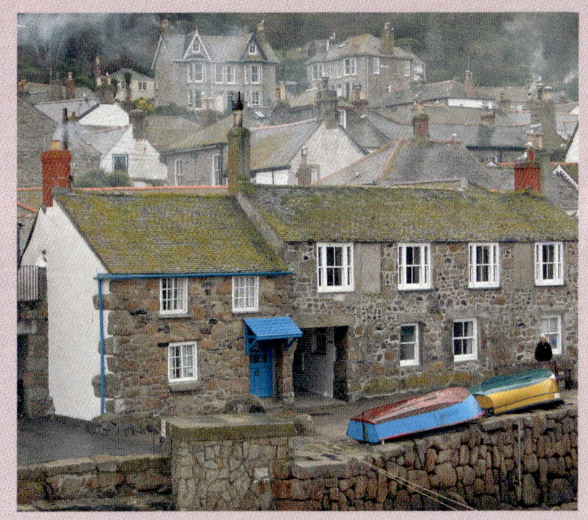

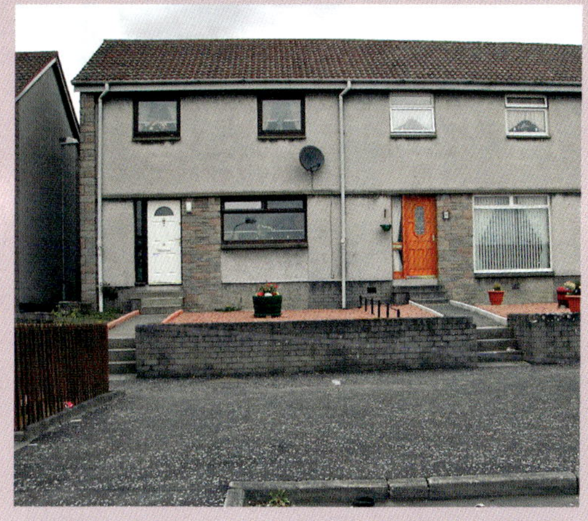

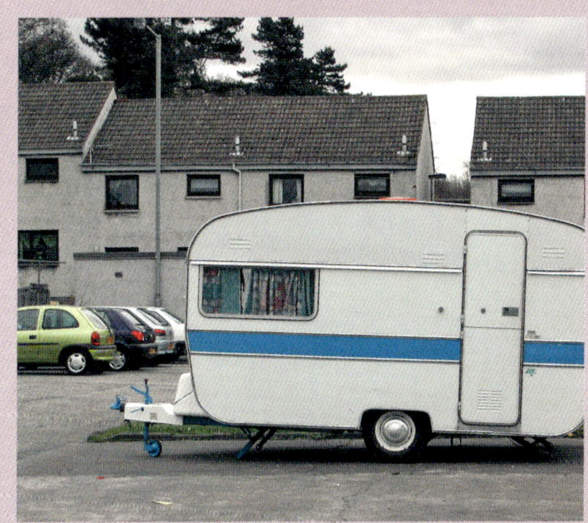

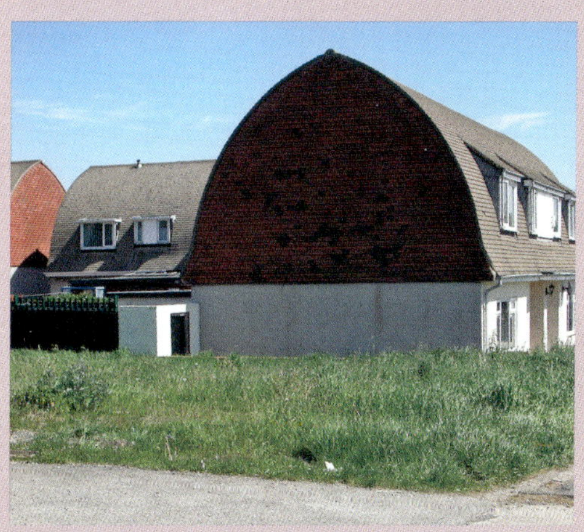

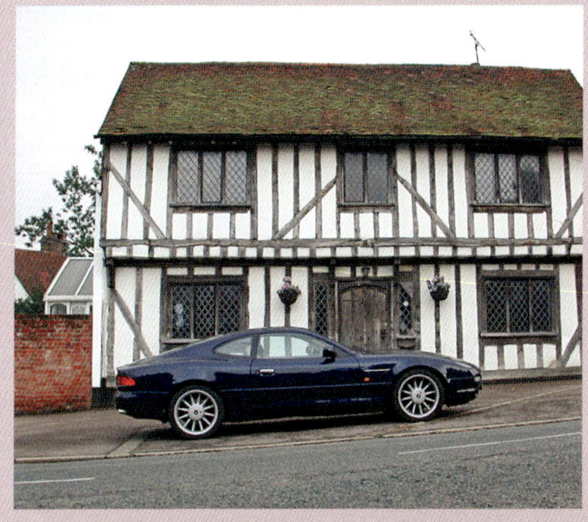

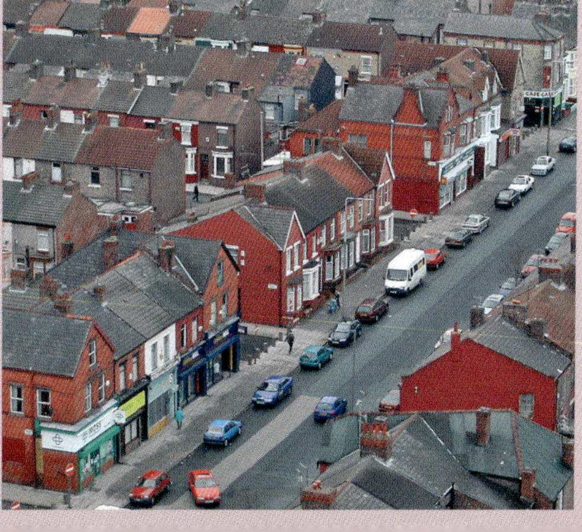

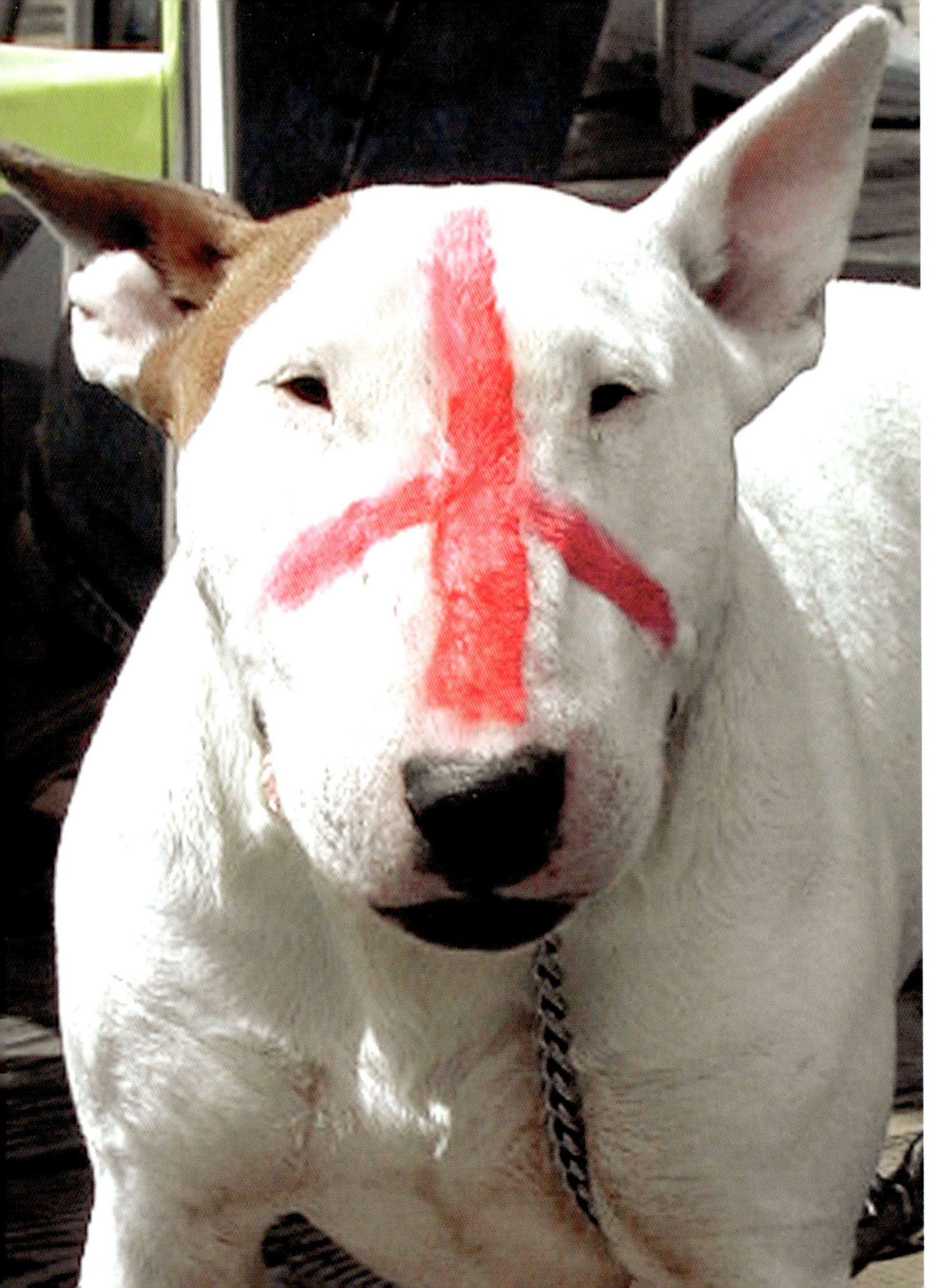

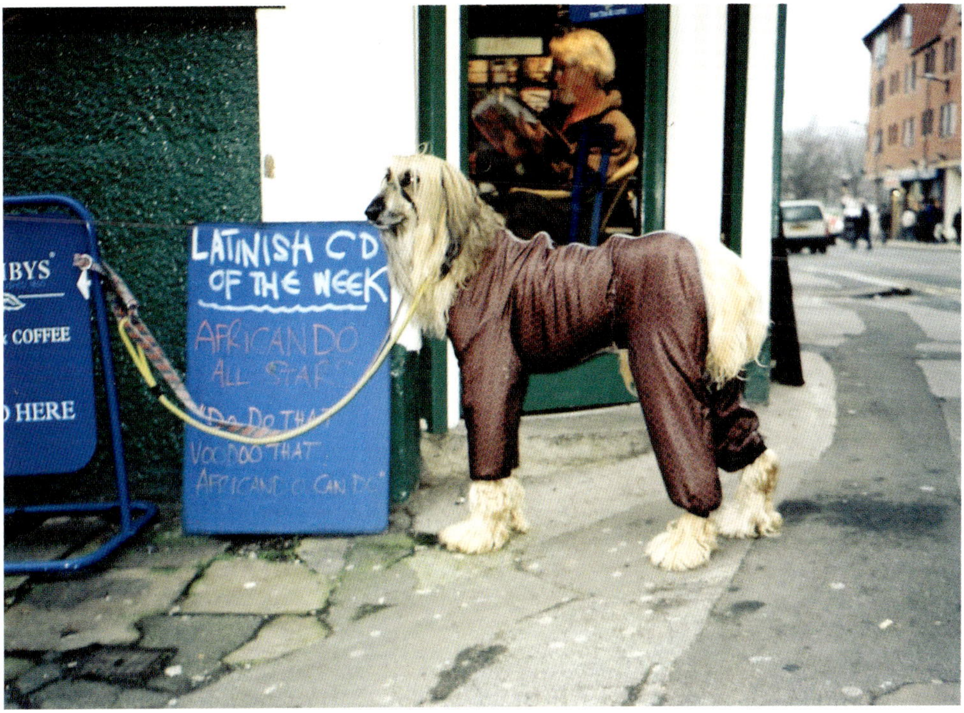

Dogs

Have you got a dog? Does it look like you? Would you go out dressed in a brown shellsuit? No? Thought not. Unfortunately, dogs have no influence over their doggy style and have to rely on the good taste (or otherwise) of their owners. Occasionally, dogs may also find themselves implicated in acts of protest.

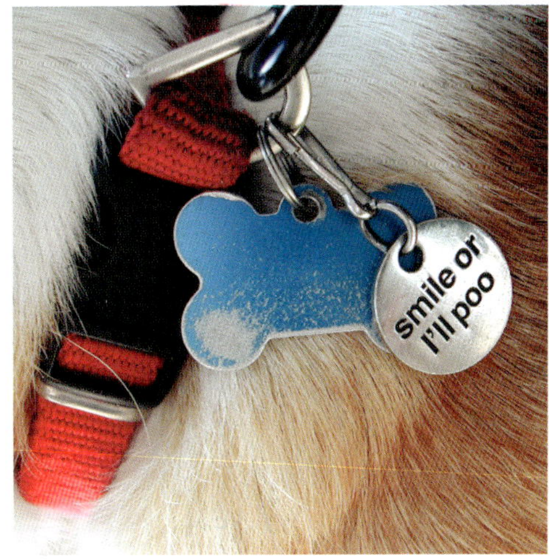

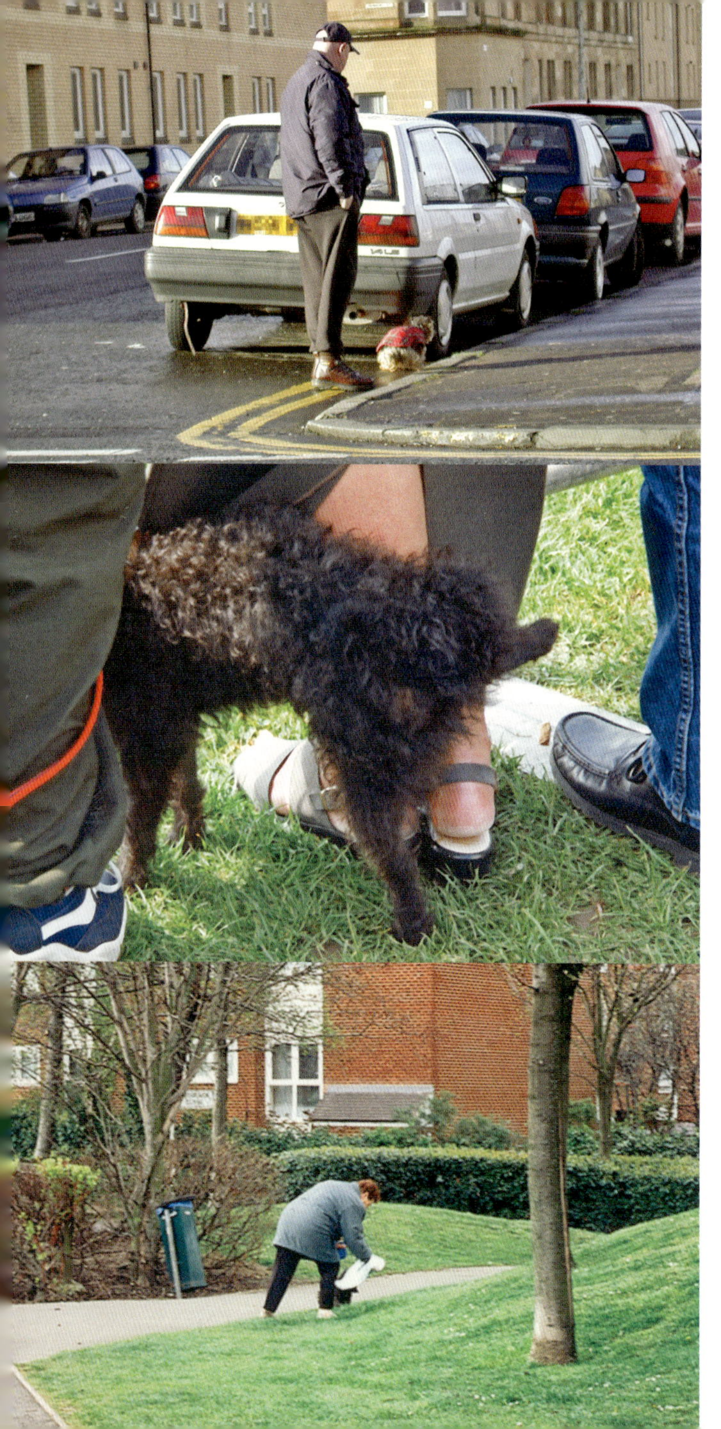

What do you think of as 'typically British'?

Rain lashing down and people waiting behind dogs with small plastic bags

What's great about Britain?

You never know what's going to happen next

What's not so great?

All the rain and too many dogs

16% of people have stepped in dog's mess in the last few weeks

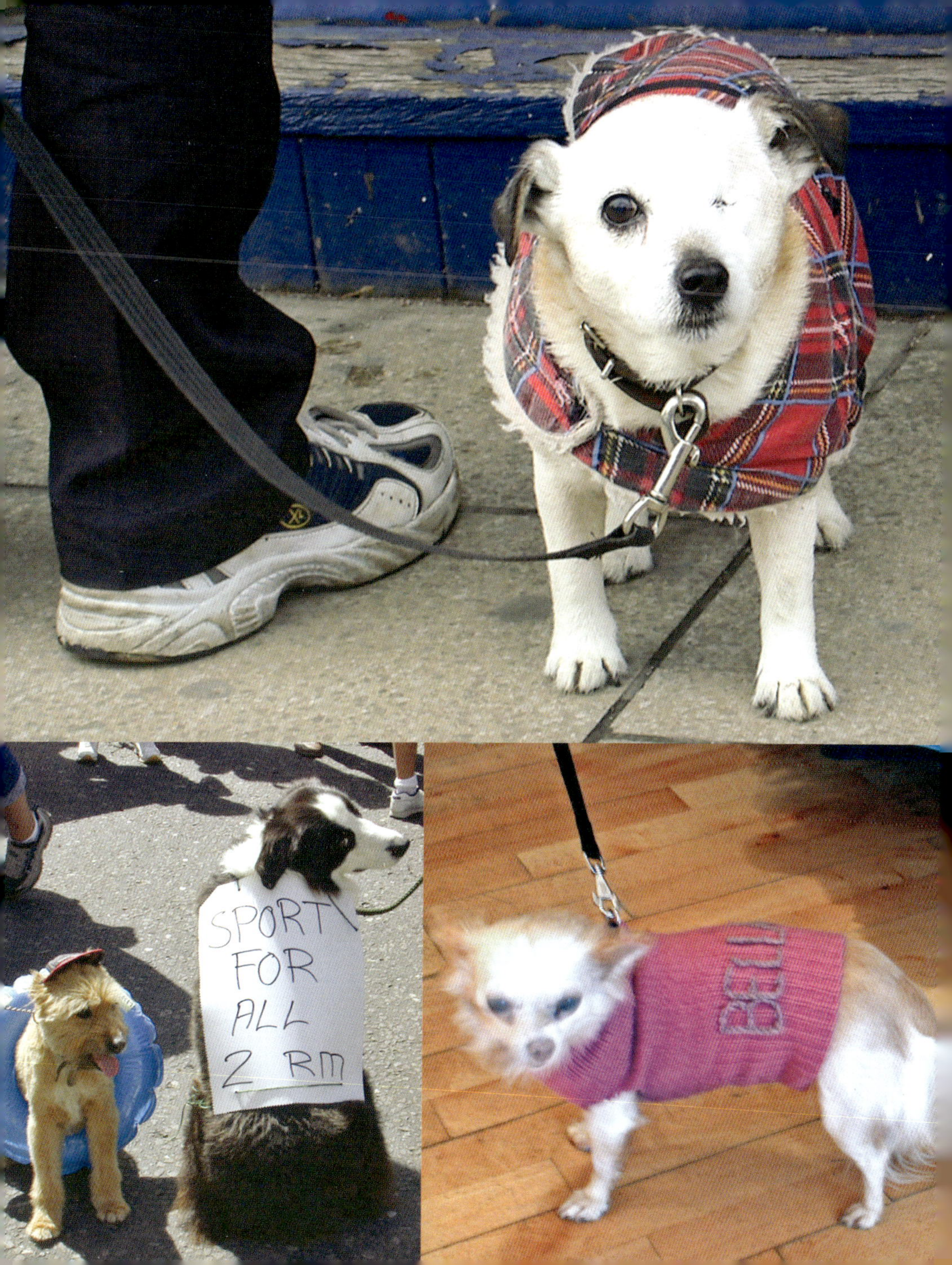
SPORT
FOR
ALL
2 RM
BELL

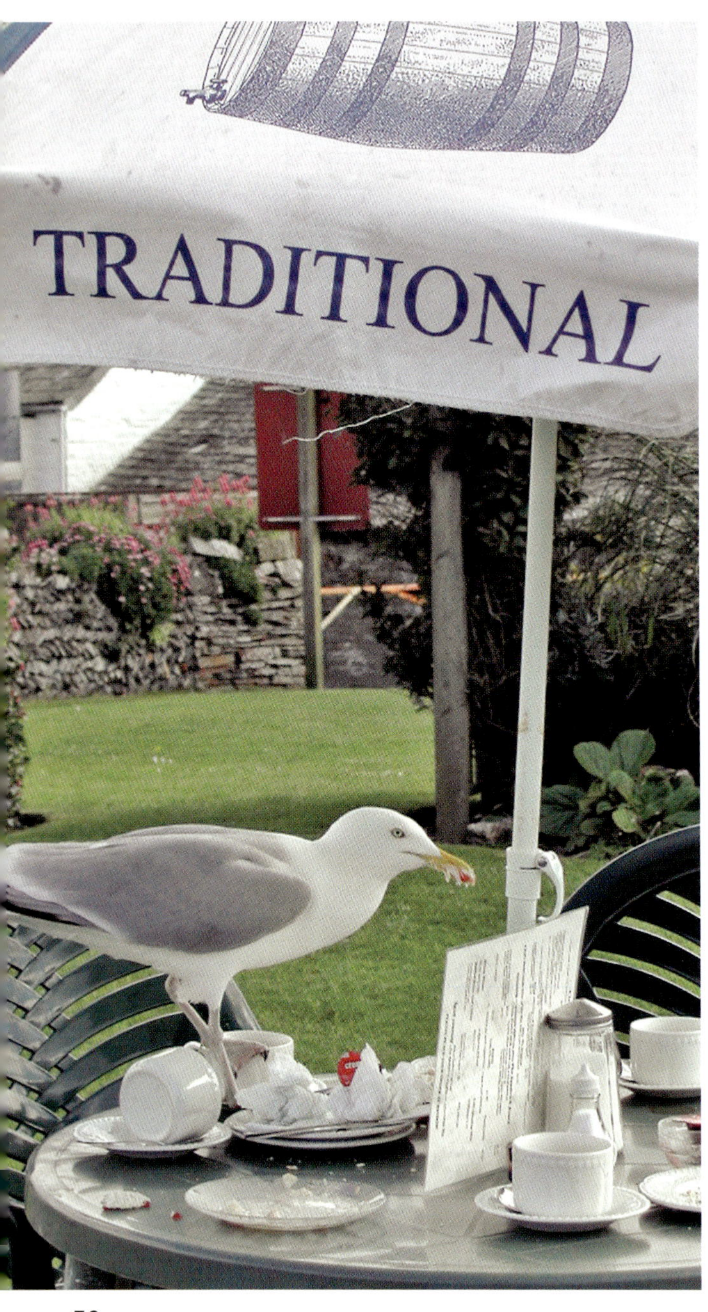

Birds

Just like the human residents, British birds enjoy cream teas and meals out, day trips with the kids and the glorious summer weather.

How do you feel about seagulls?

I shouldn't tell you but I shot six of 'em this mornin'

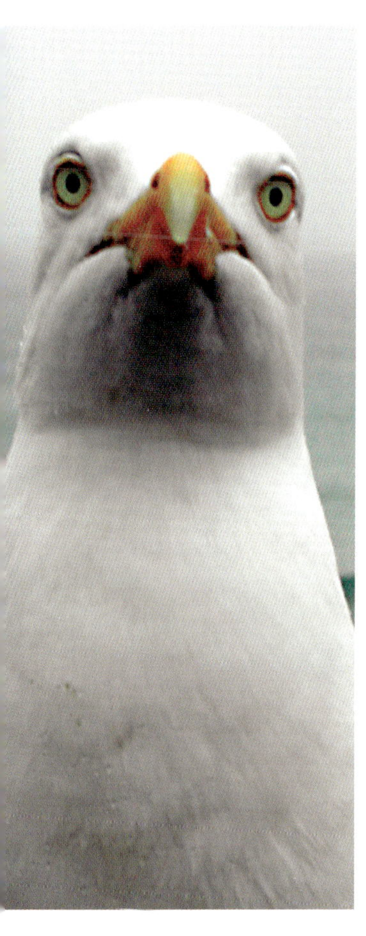

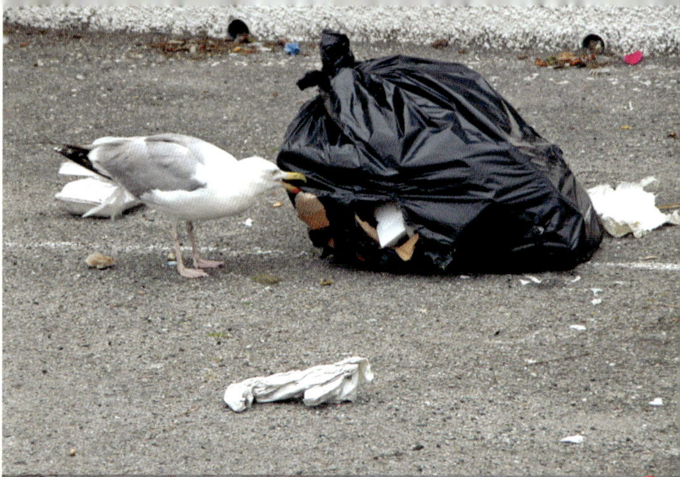

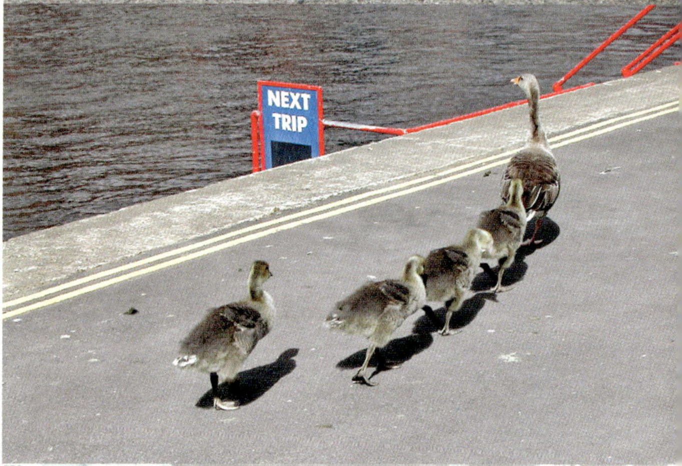

What's great about Britain?

I love the familiarity but hate the rain

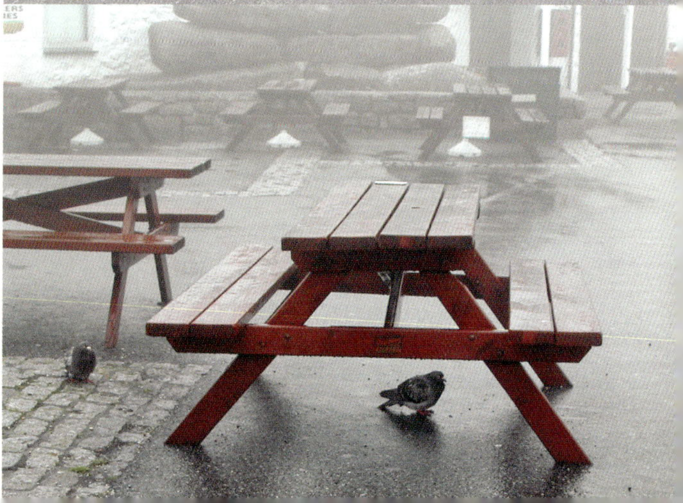

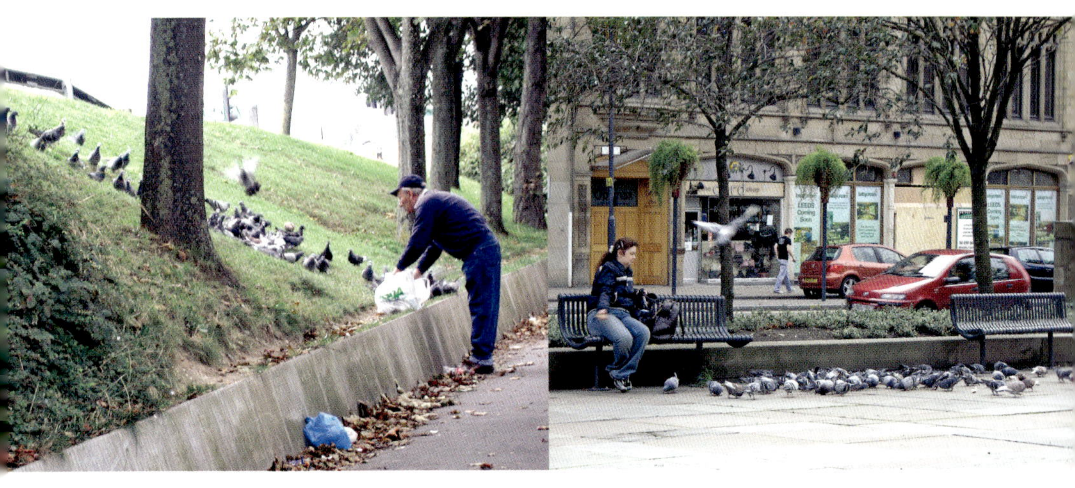

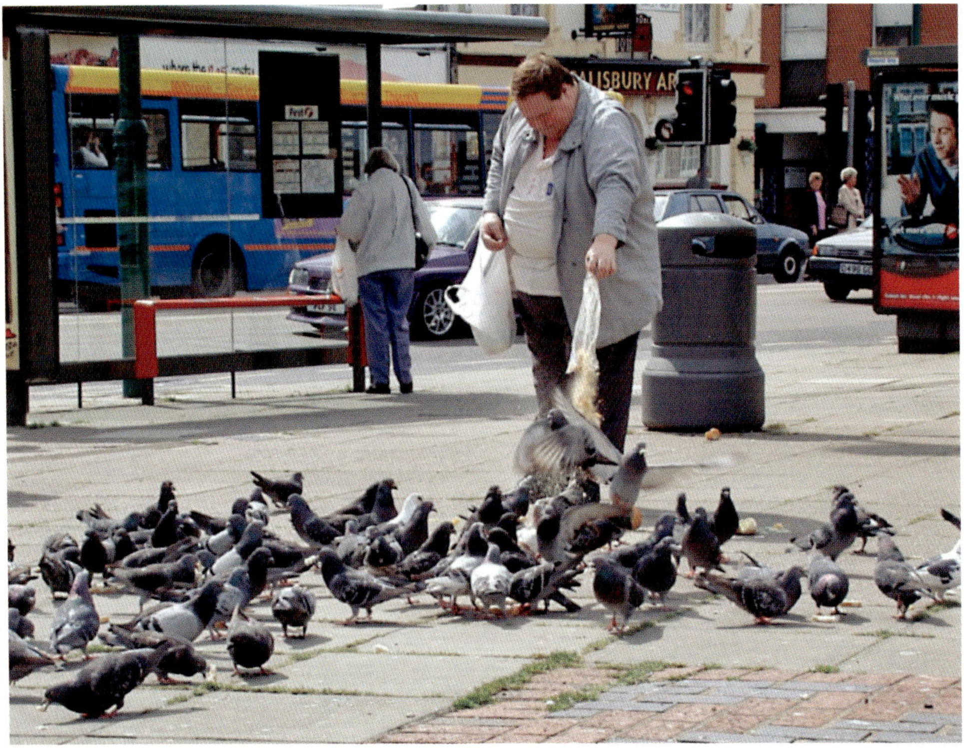

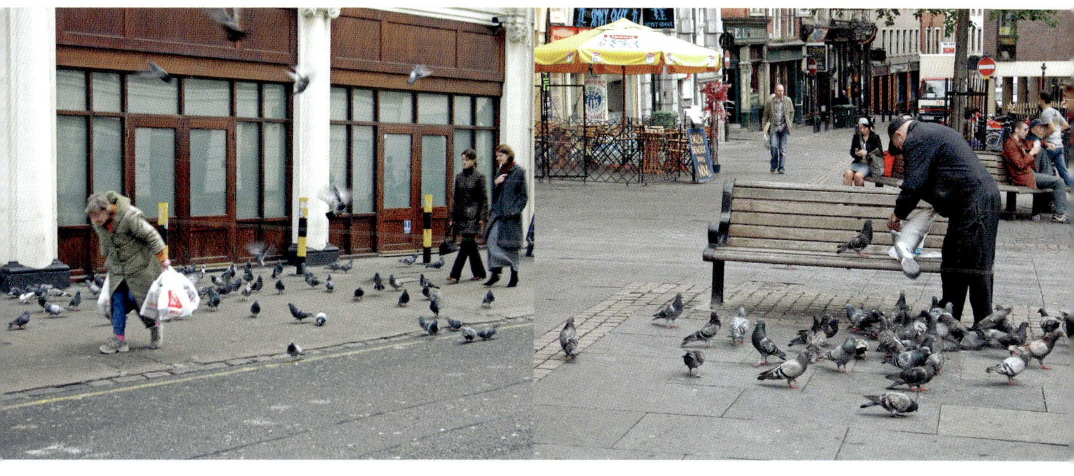

Pigeon people

Despite the signs asking us not to, there are always one or two people determined to feed the pigeons 'because someone's got to'. Every town has its pigeon feeder with a carrier bag full of old bread and an established patch for this daily ritual.

How do you feel about pigeons?

I love pigeons!

Best under pastry

I worry where their babies go

Rats with wings

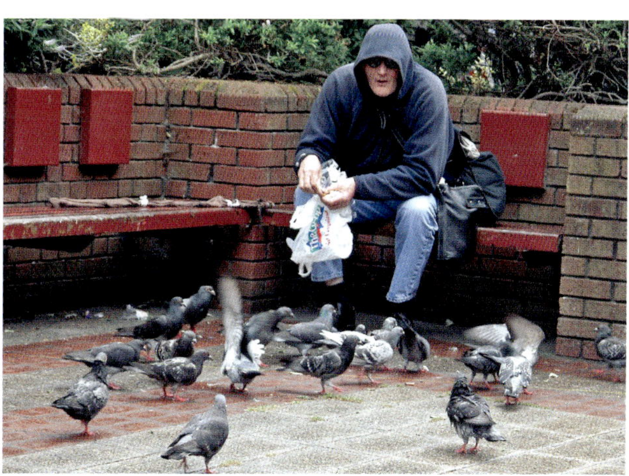

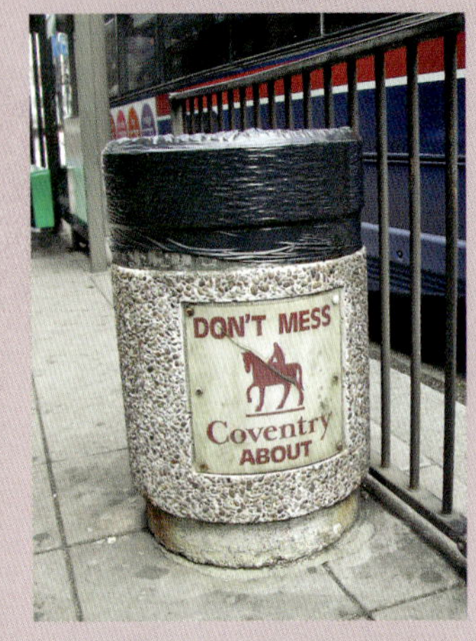
DON'T MESS
Coventry
ABOUT
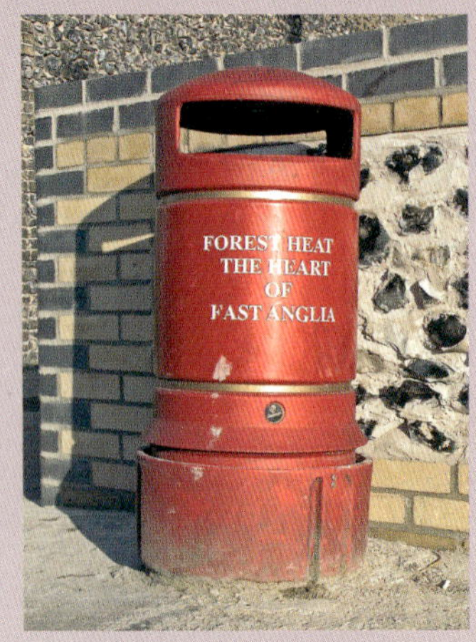
FOREST HEAT
THE HEART
OF
EAST ANGLIA
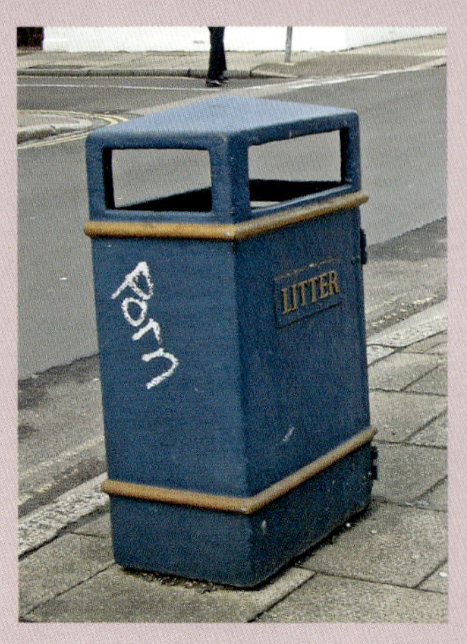
Porn
LITTER
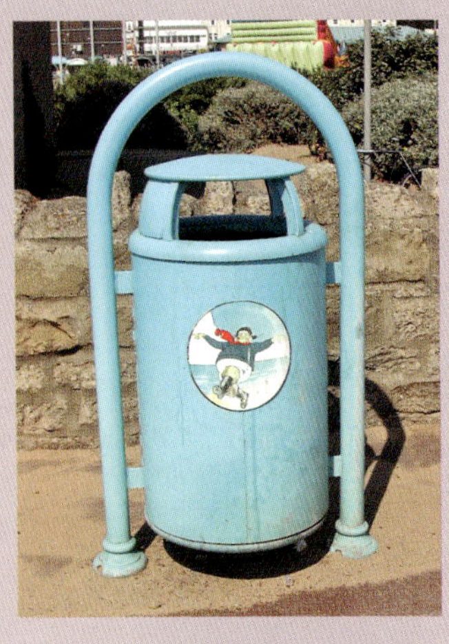
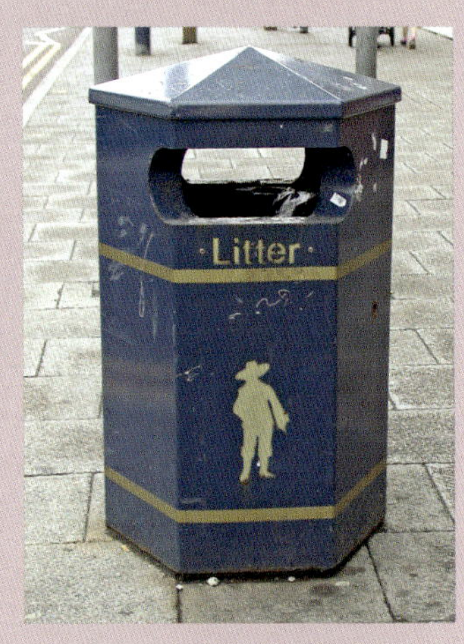
Litter
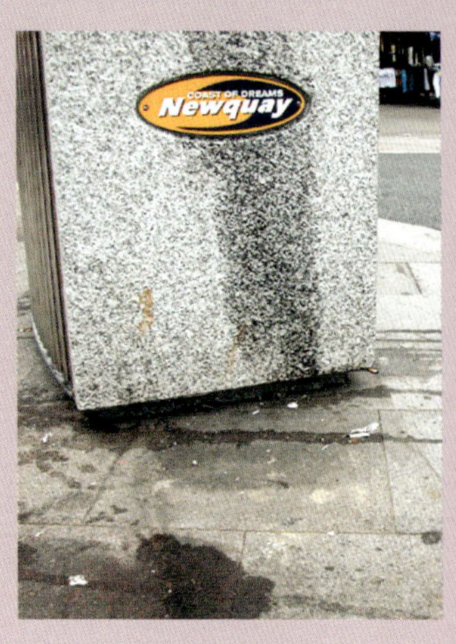
Newquay
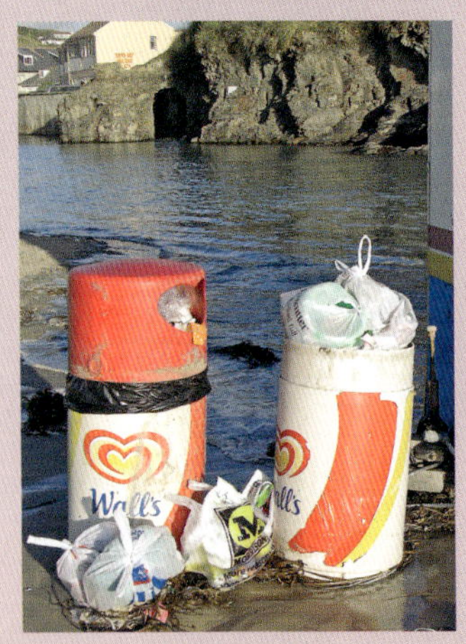
Wall's
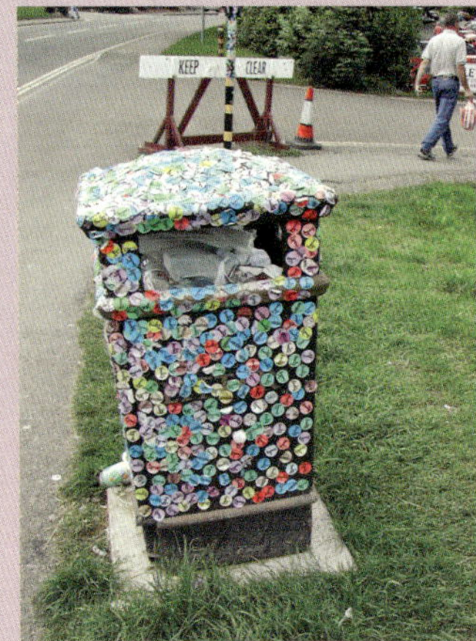
KEEP
CLEAR
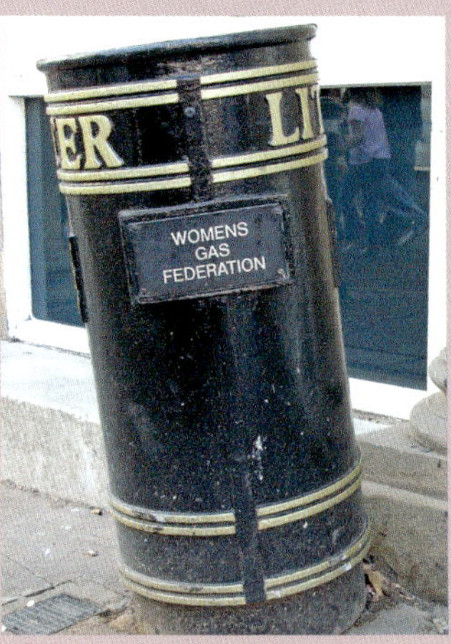
WOMENS
GAS
FEDERATION

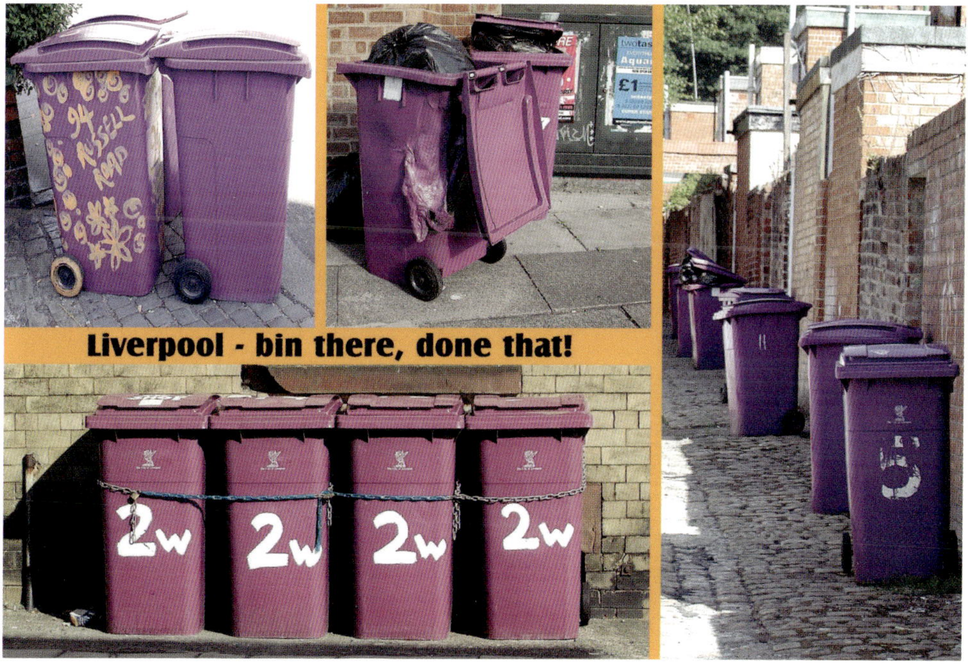

Liverpool - bin there, done that!

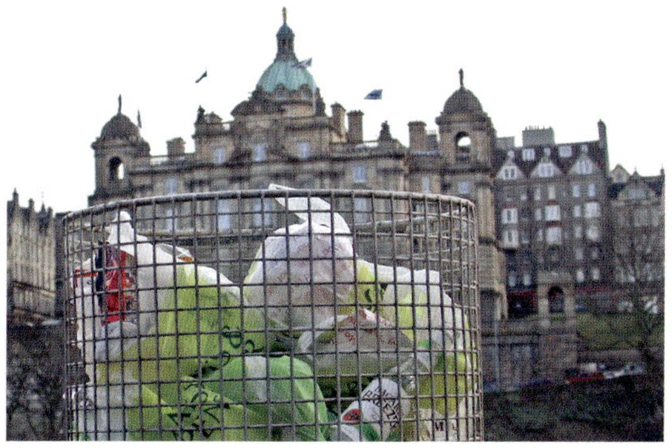

Bins

If you want to try and understand the character of a place, check out its bins. They can be an effective marketing tool for local councils although further 'customisation' might not always give the desired impression.

What's great about Britain?

Tea, cheese and Eddie Izzard

What's not so great?

The filth

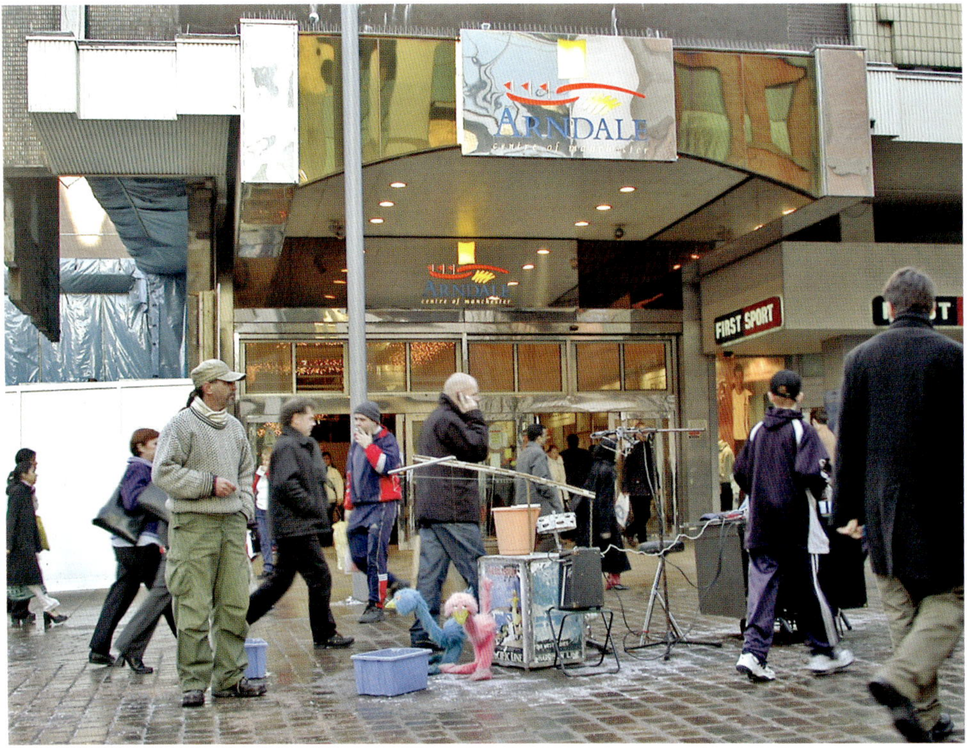

Street entertainment

In Britain people do all sorts of peculiar things on the street in exchange for money.

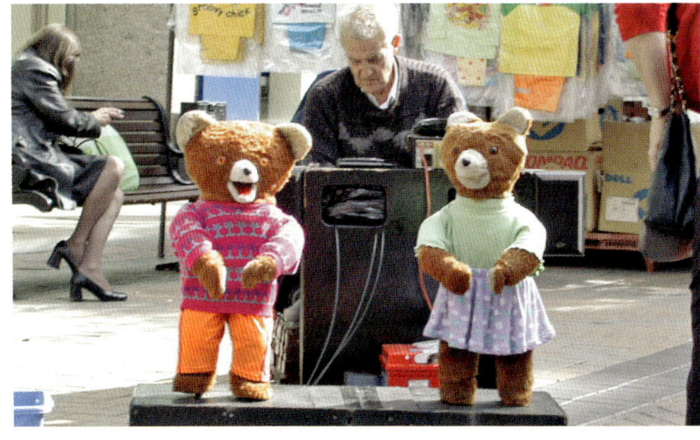

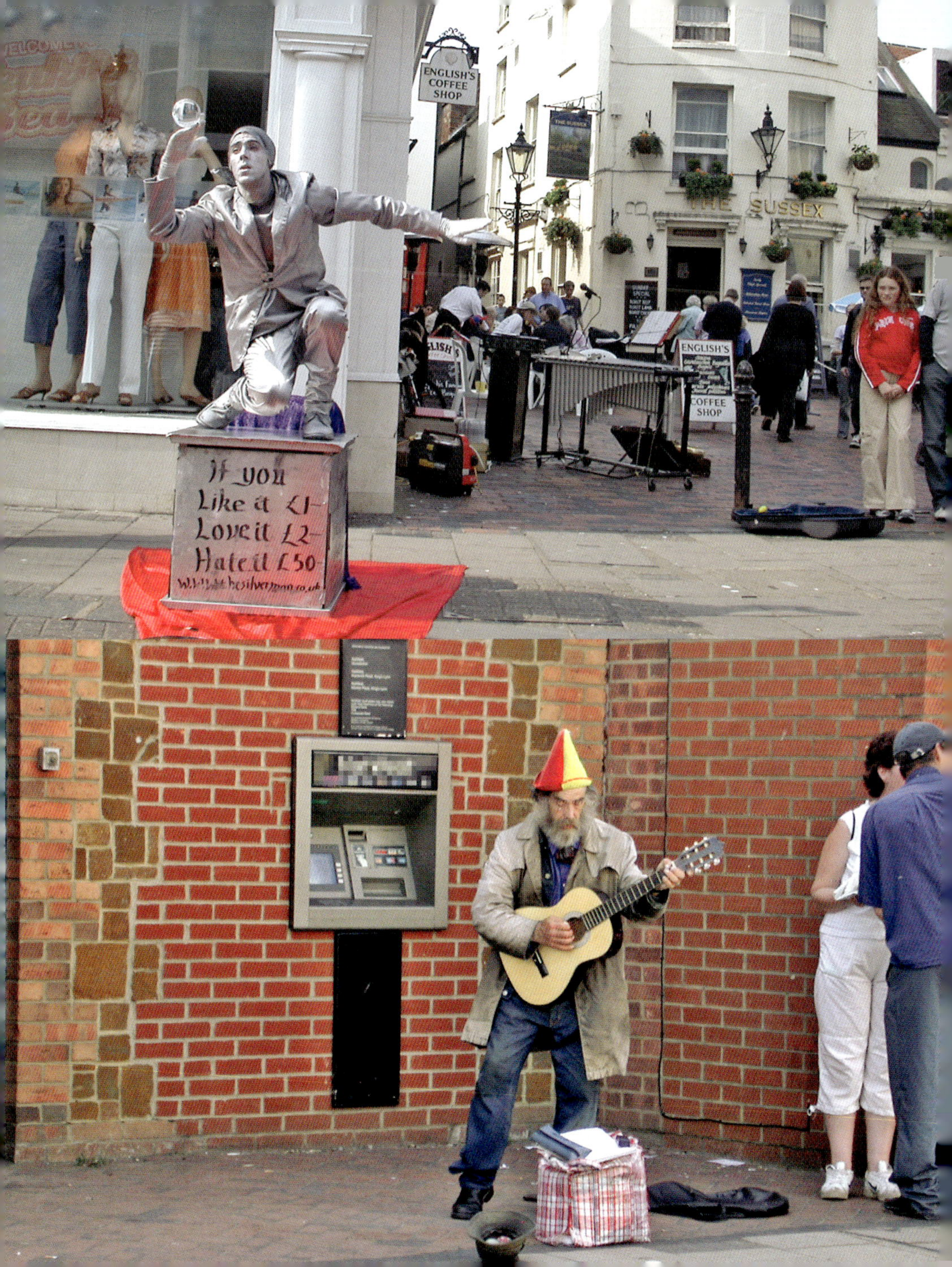
ENGLISH'S COFFEE SHOP
THE SUSSEX
If you
Like it £1
Love it £2
Hate it £50
ENGLISH'S
COFFEE SHOP

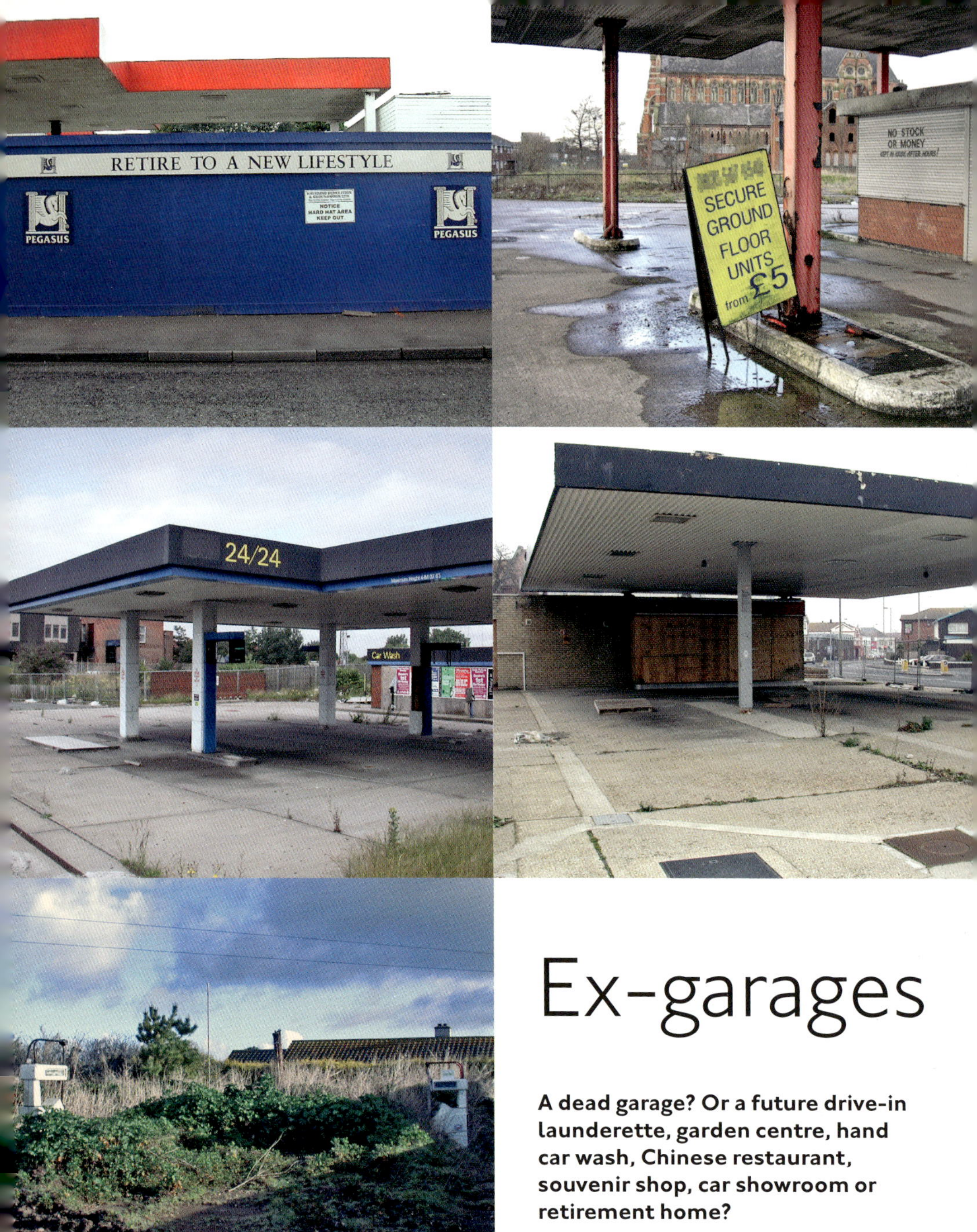

Ex-garages

A dead garage? Or a future drive-in launderette, garden centre, hand car wash, Chinese restaurant, souvenir shop, car showroom or retirement home?

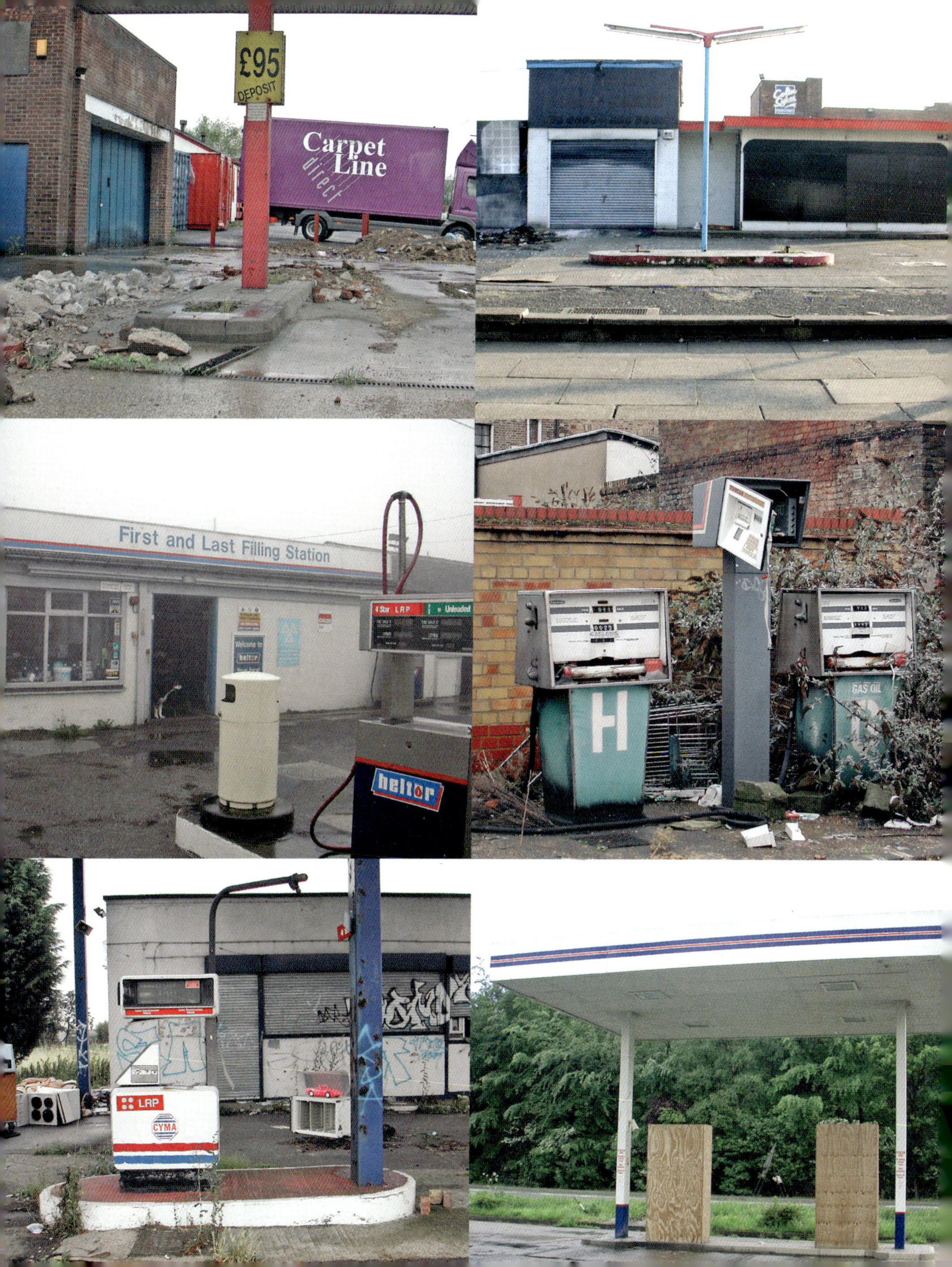
£95
DEPOSIT
Carpet
Line
direct
First and Last Filling Station
4 Star
LRP
Unleaded
heltor
H
GAS OIL
LRP
CYMA

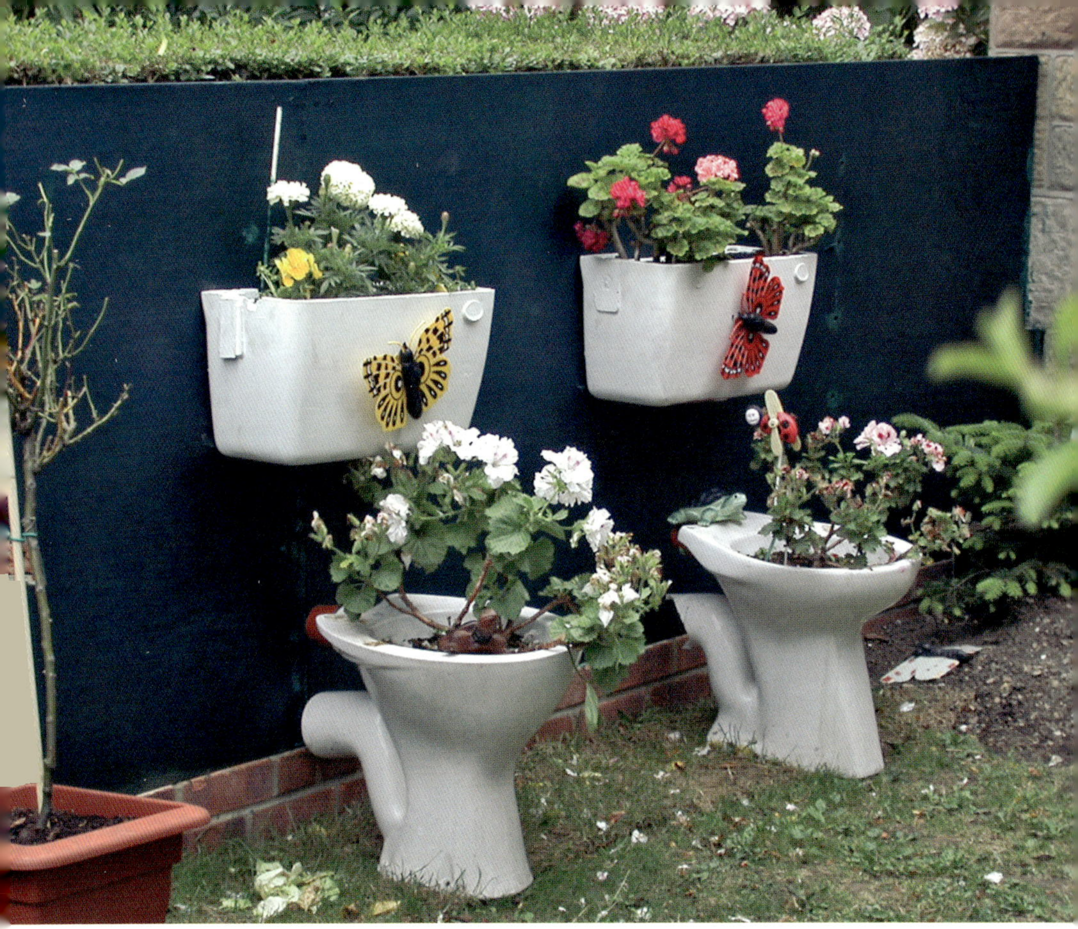

Gardens

From the humble toilet garden to the dazzling displays in our municipal parks, we British love our gardens. We all have our own ideas when it comes to creating our little bits of paradise. Some go for the low-maintenance look, using slabs and more slabs, while others prefer to use plants.

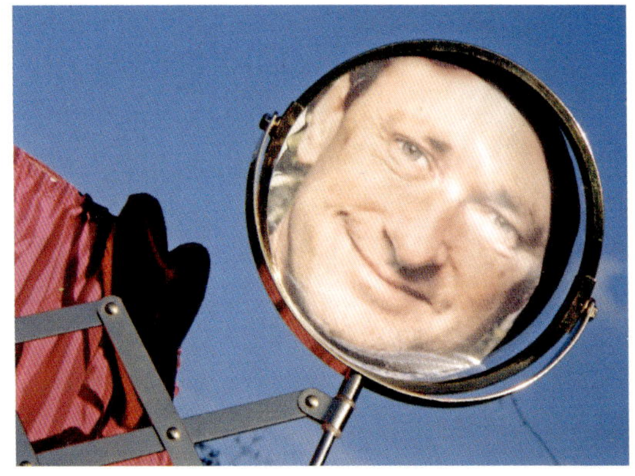

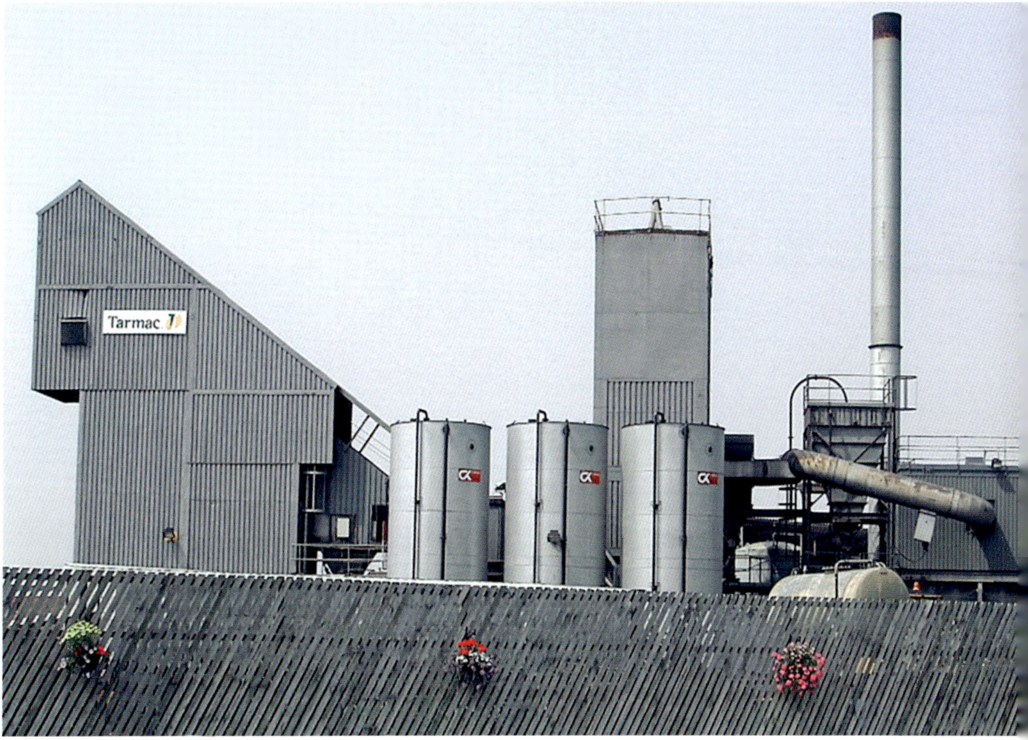

Are you influenced by home and garden makeover programmes?

Absolutely!
I turn them off as fast as possible

Love 'em, never do it though

I'd like to marry Alan Titchmarsh

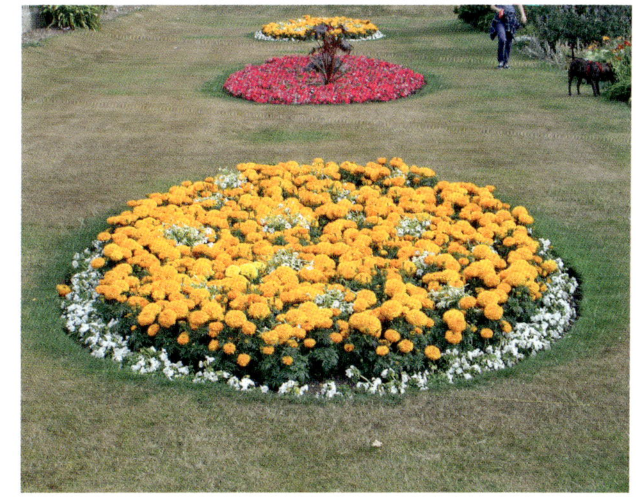

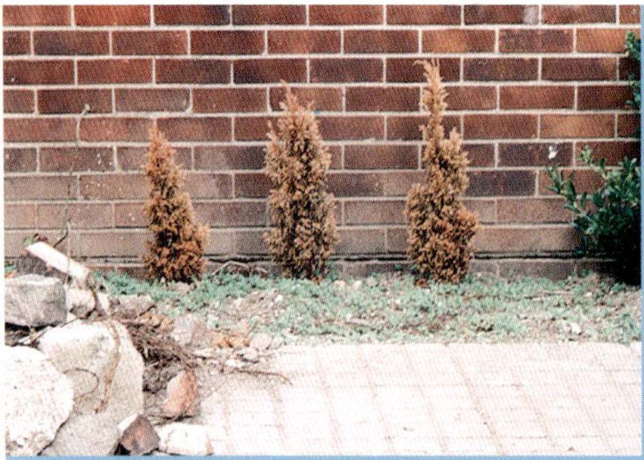

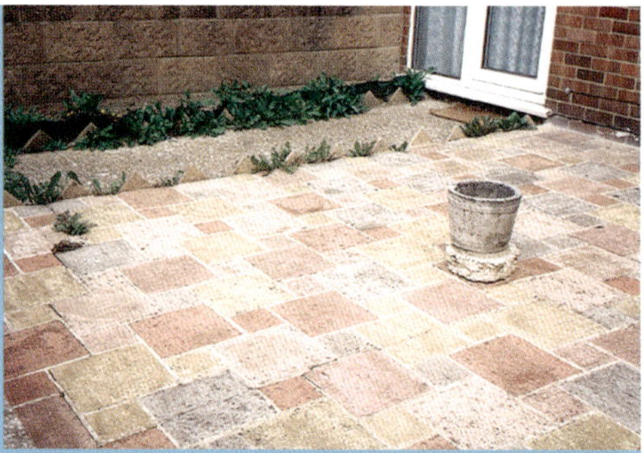

GARDENS OF ENGLAND

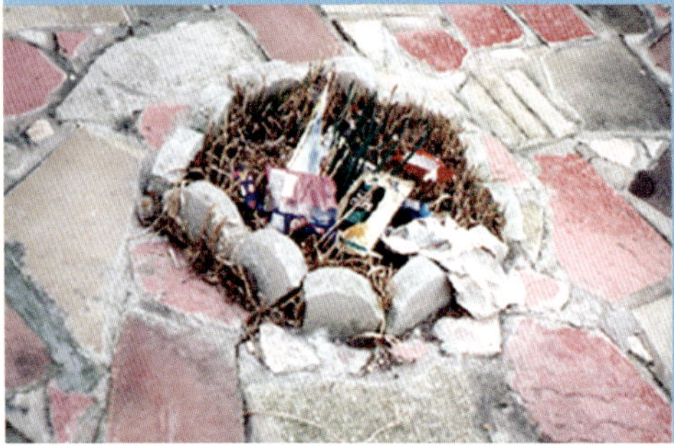

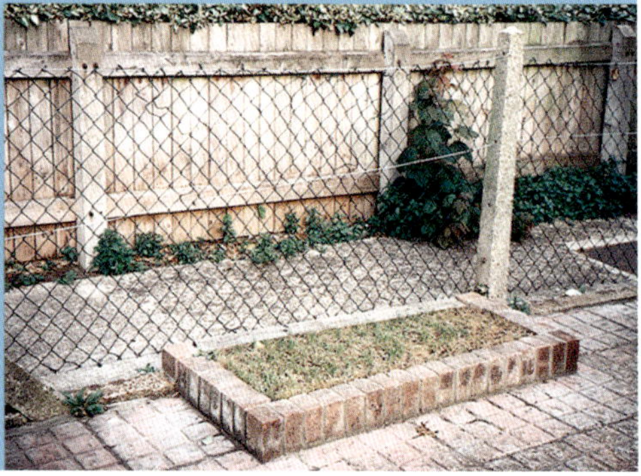

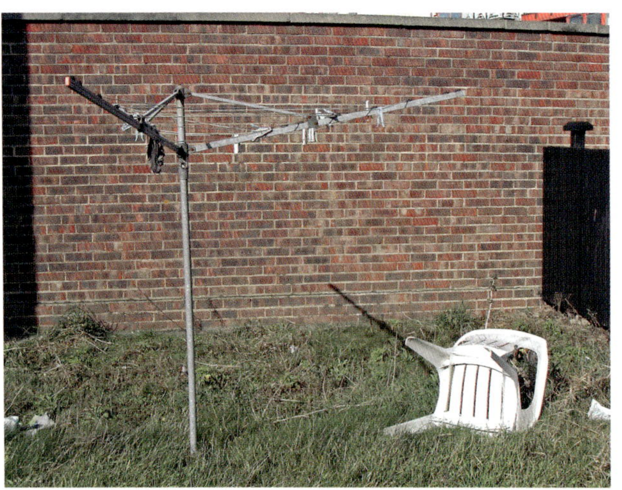

57% of people manage to kill houseplants without even trying

It's important to have a focal point to catch the eye in a garden. It could be a concrete heart, a bold display of Kniphofia uvaria or just a simple arrangement of a rotary clothes drier and plastic chair.

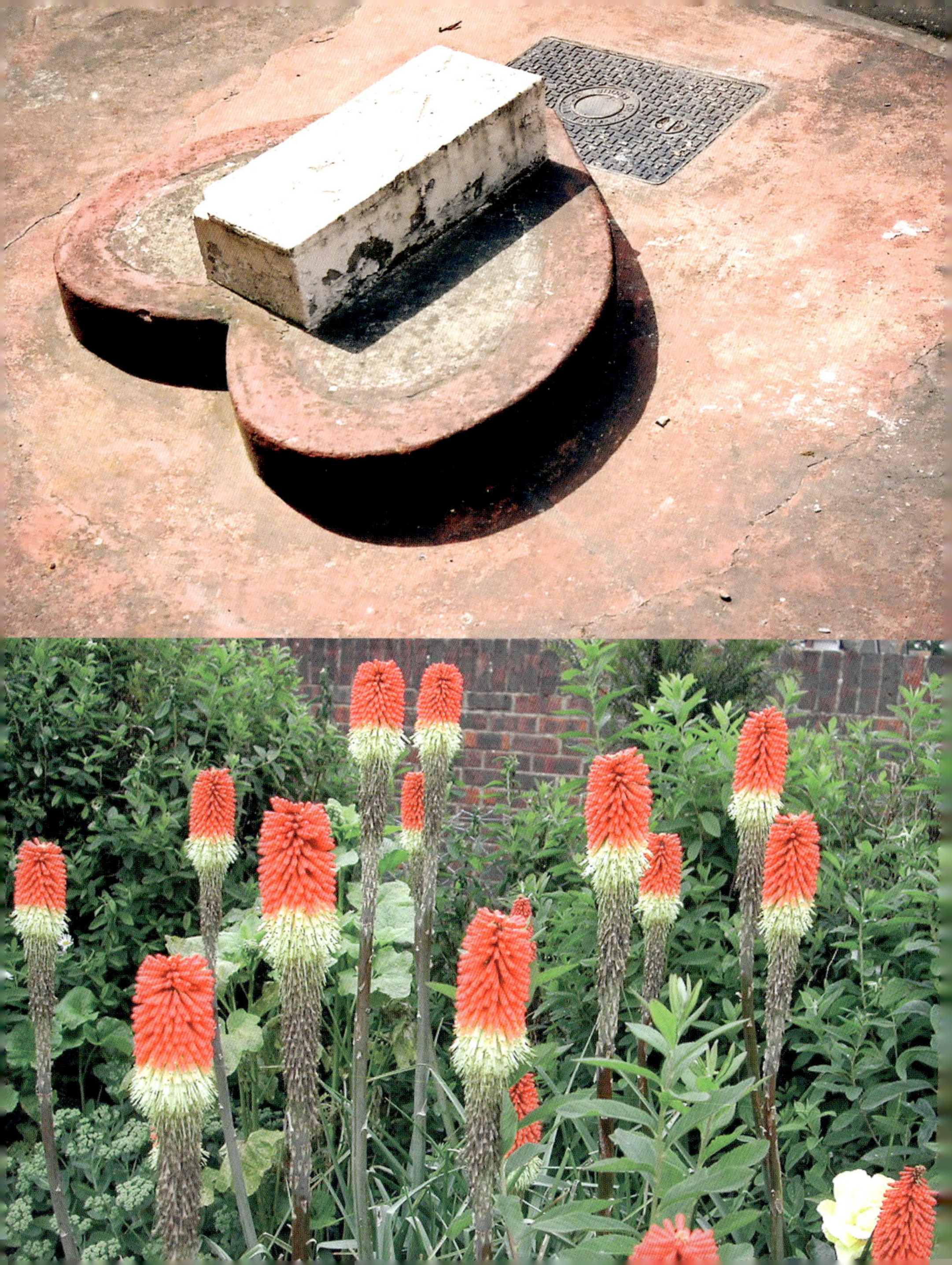

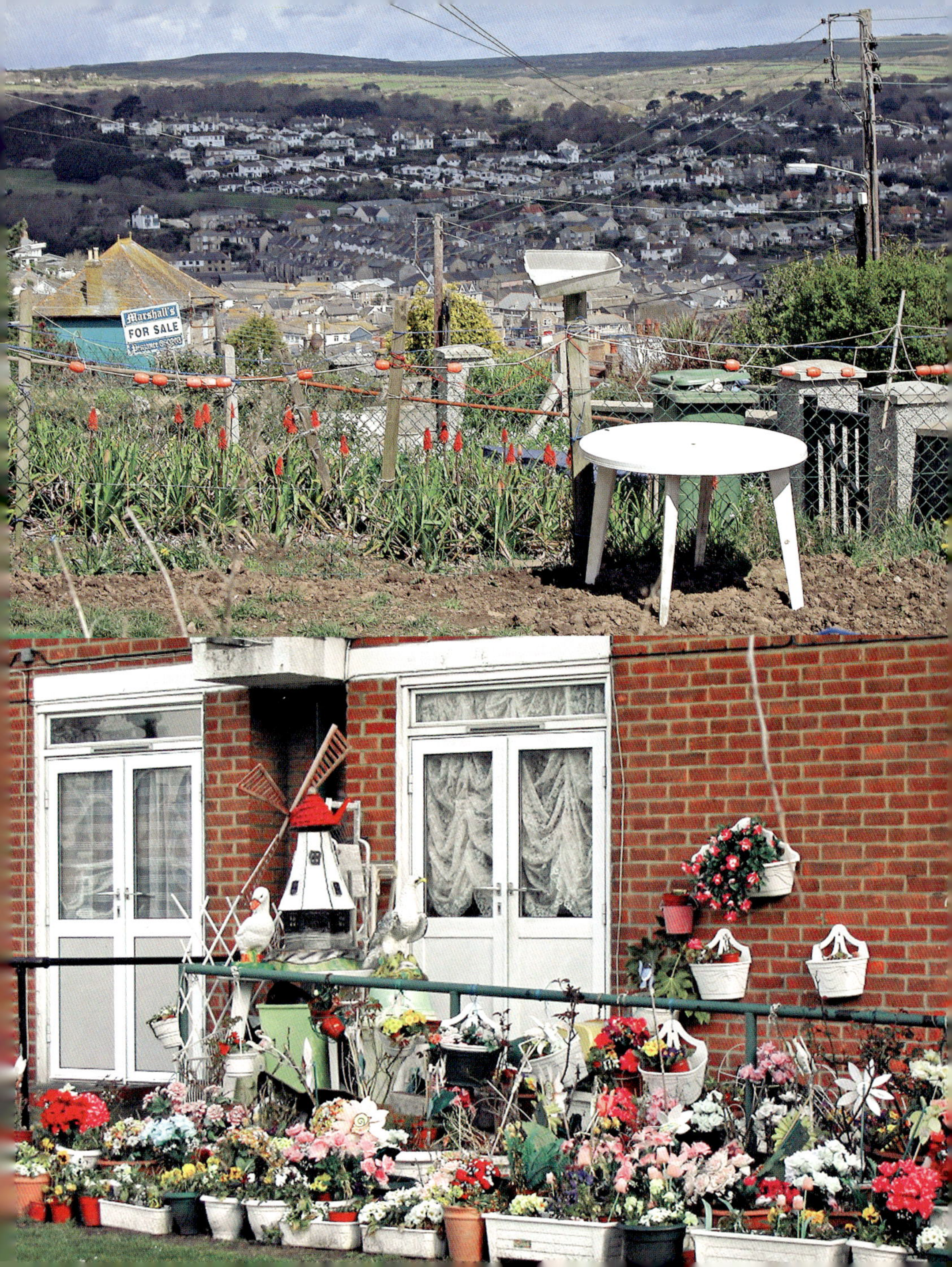
Marshall's
FOR SALE

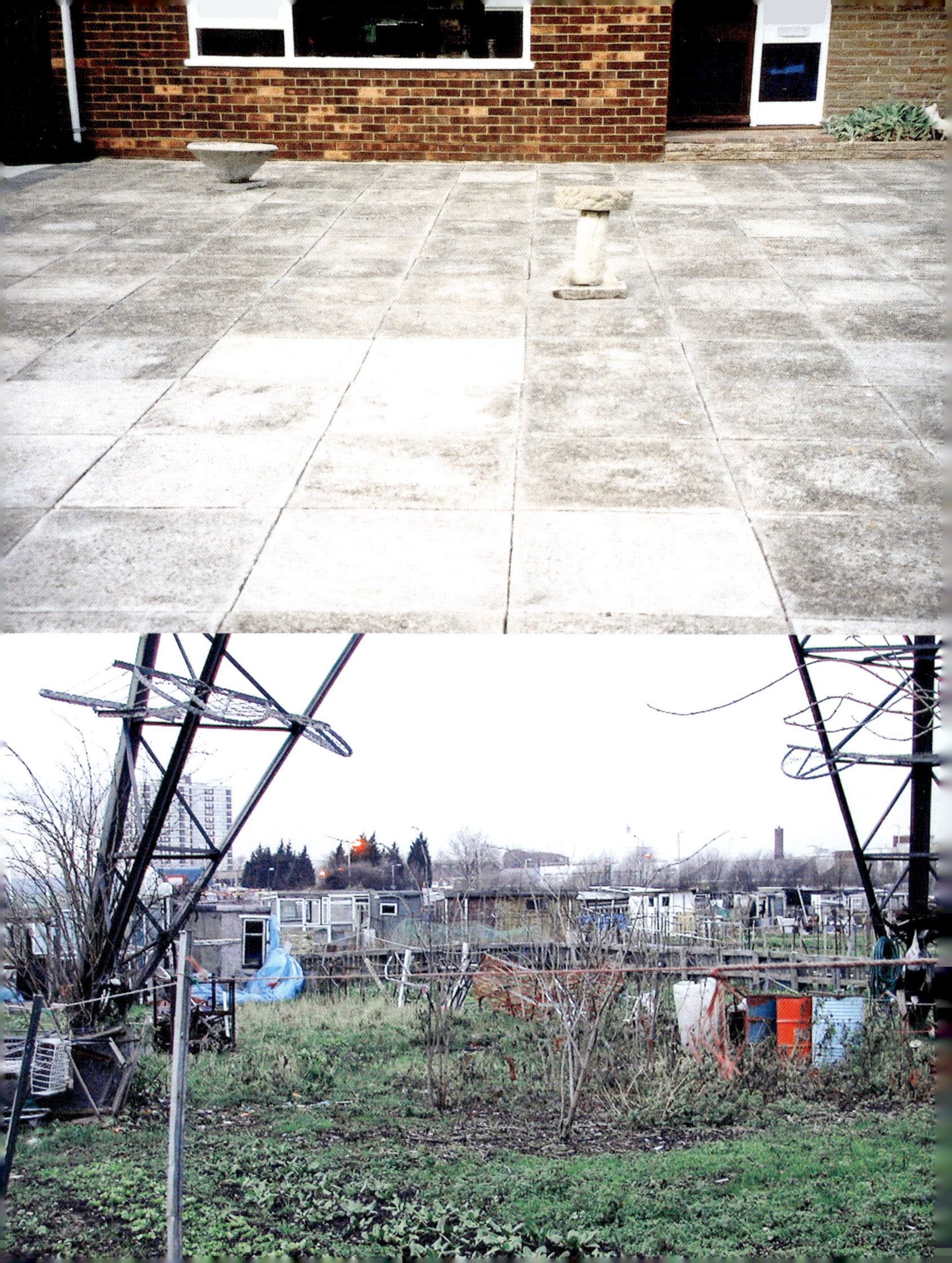

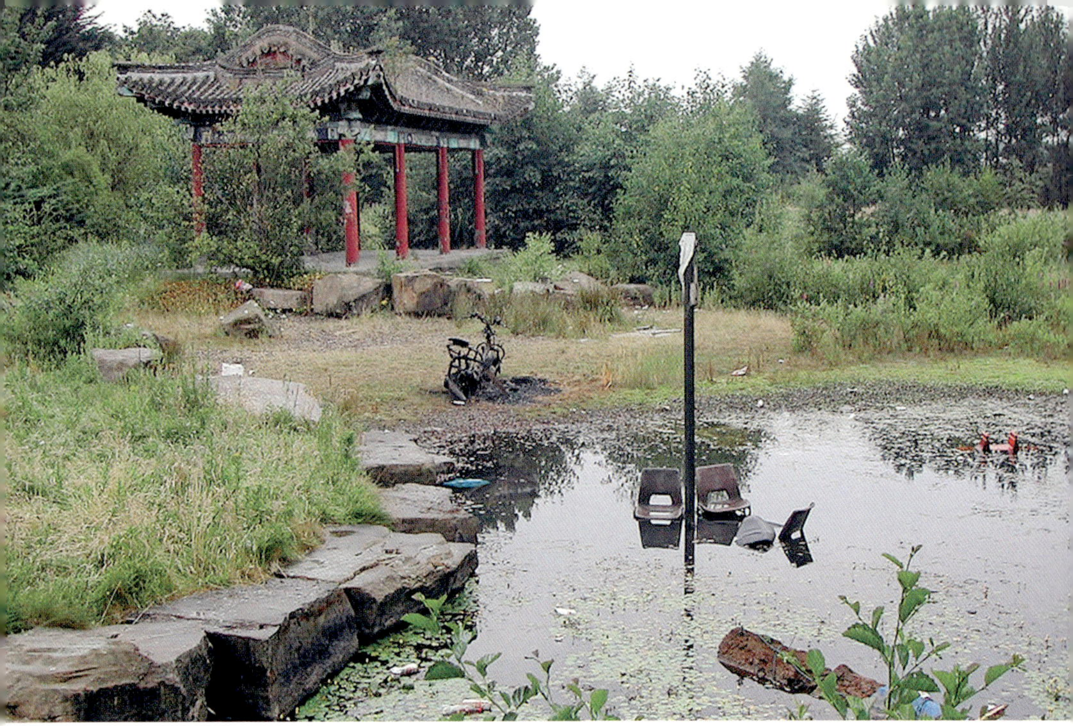

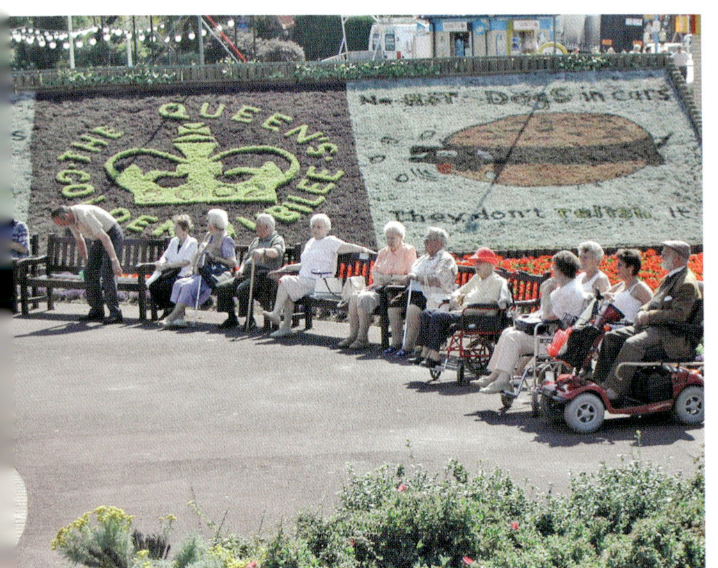

With their bright floral displays, British parks can provide a riot of colour (and useful public information) for the local bench-dwellers, but twenty years on, the International Garden Festival in Liverpool, above, is well and truly over.

What's great about Britain?

It's very green

Embracing being eccentric

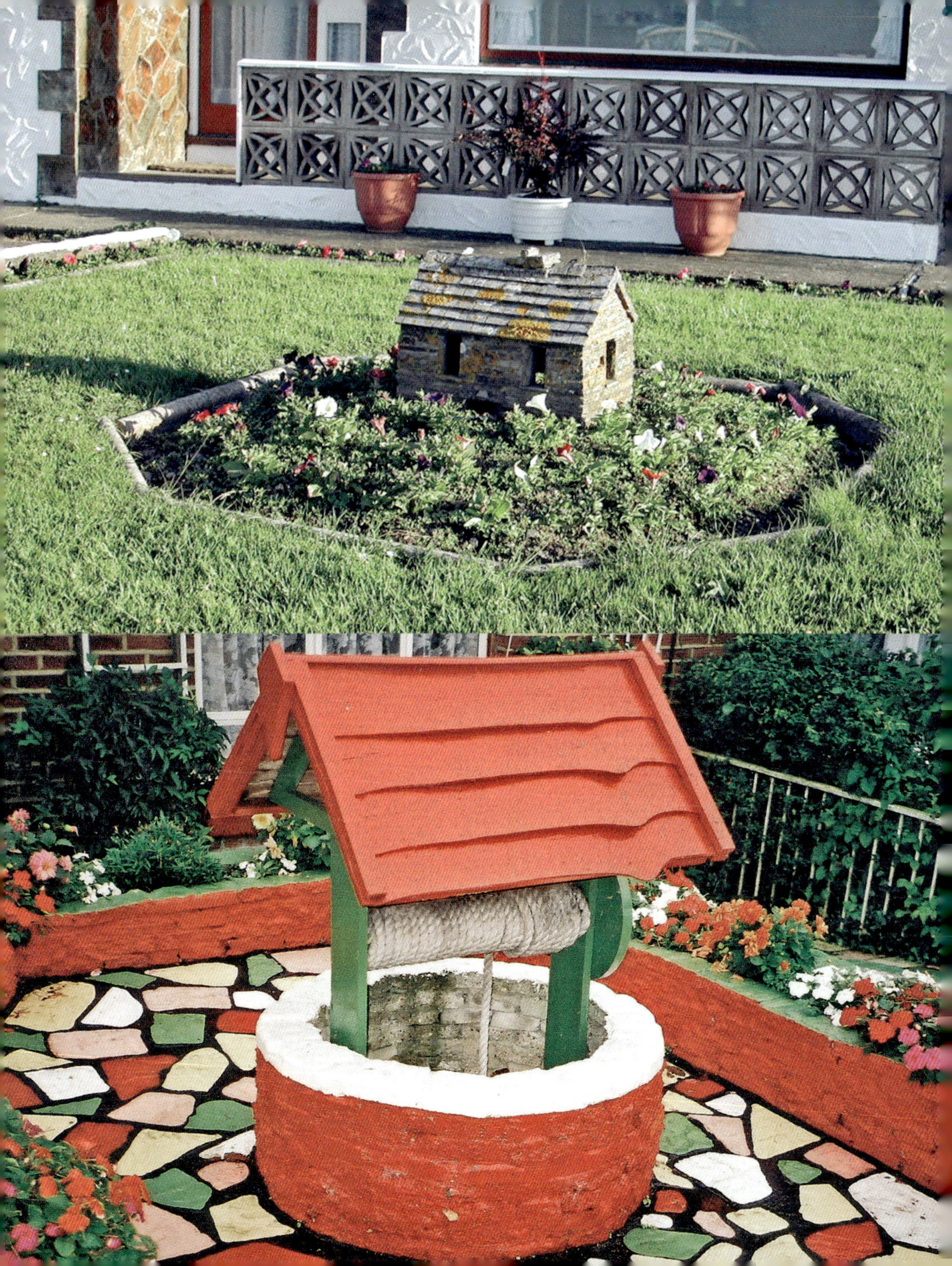

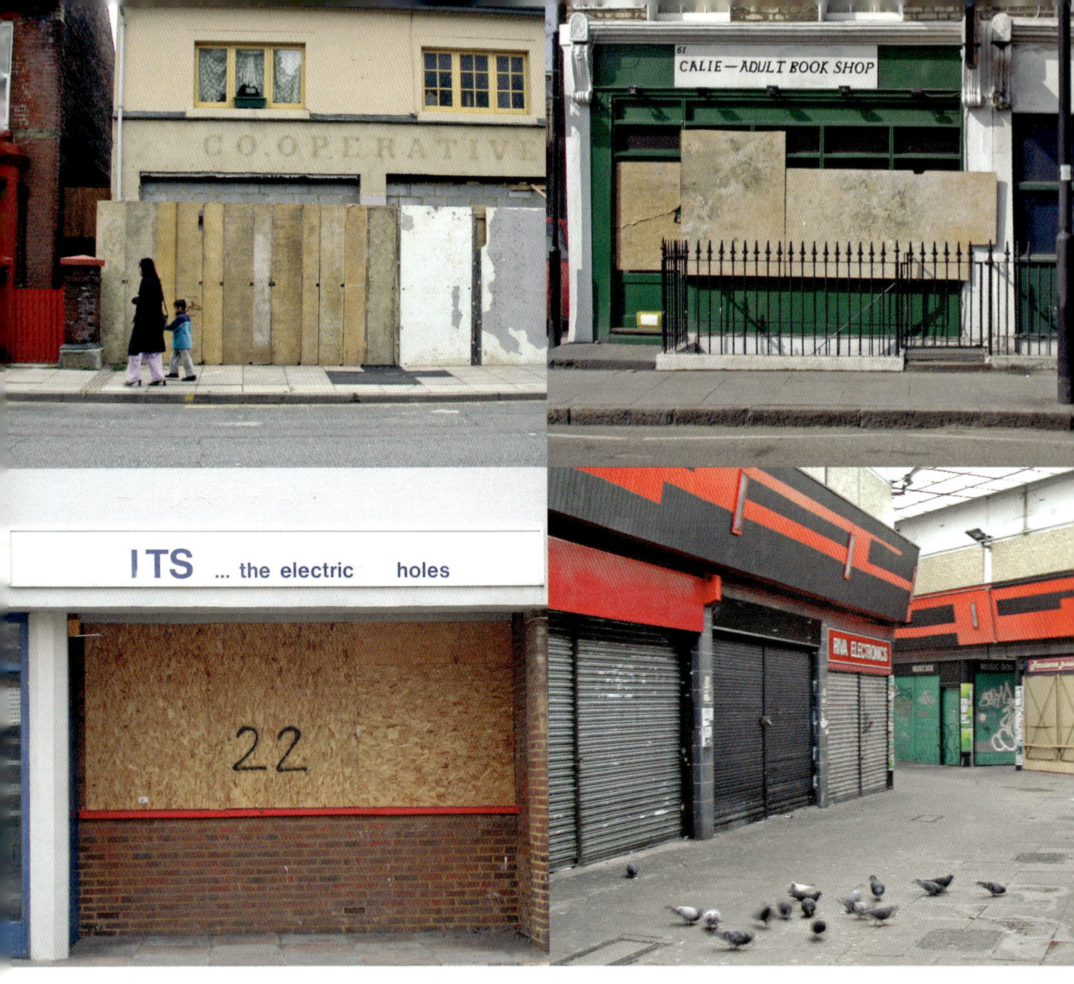

Closed

Yesterday's corner shop, today's development opportunity. Use it or lose it; it's not supermarkets that force smaller shops to close, it's the people that shop in supermarkets.

What's your personal motto?

Look on the bright side

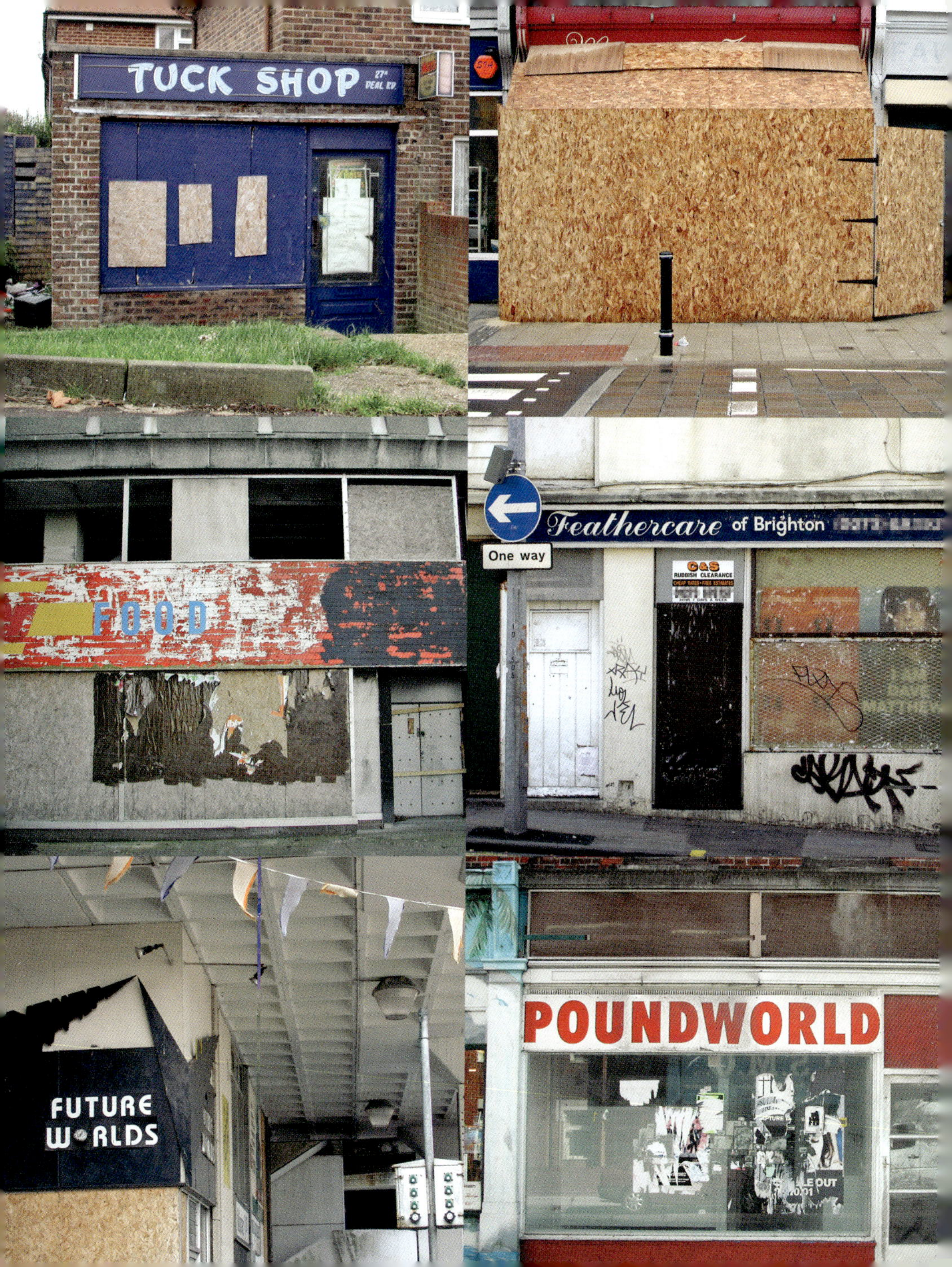

TUCK SHOP
FOOD
Feathercare of Brighton
One way
C&S
RUBBISH CLEARANCE
FUTURE
WORLDS
POUNDWORLD

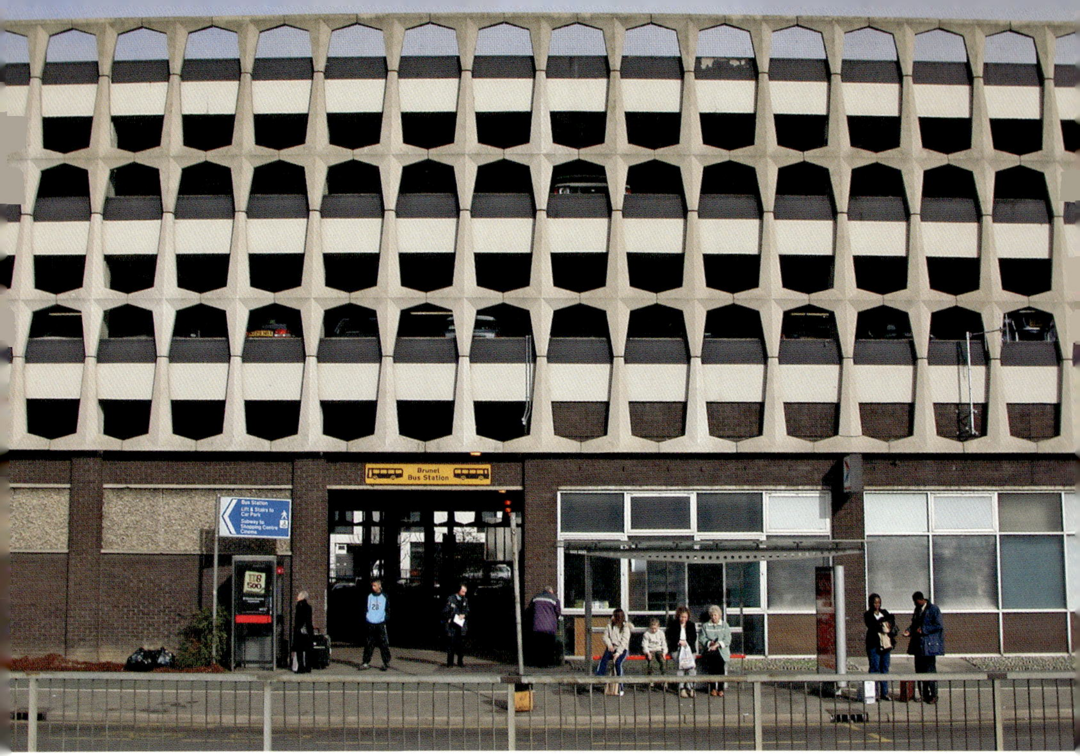

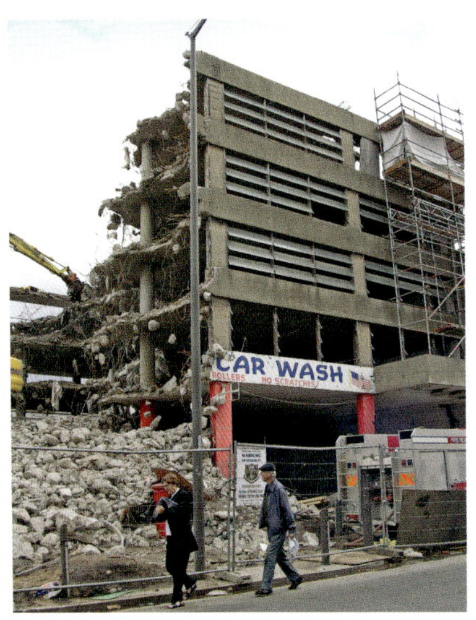

Concrete

Concrete is a dominant feature of our urban landscape. Love it or hate it, people get really worked up about big concrete car parks and shopping centres, many accusing them of being dull and depressing. A few people actually think they're rather splendid.

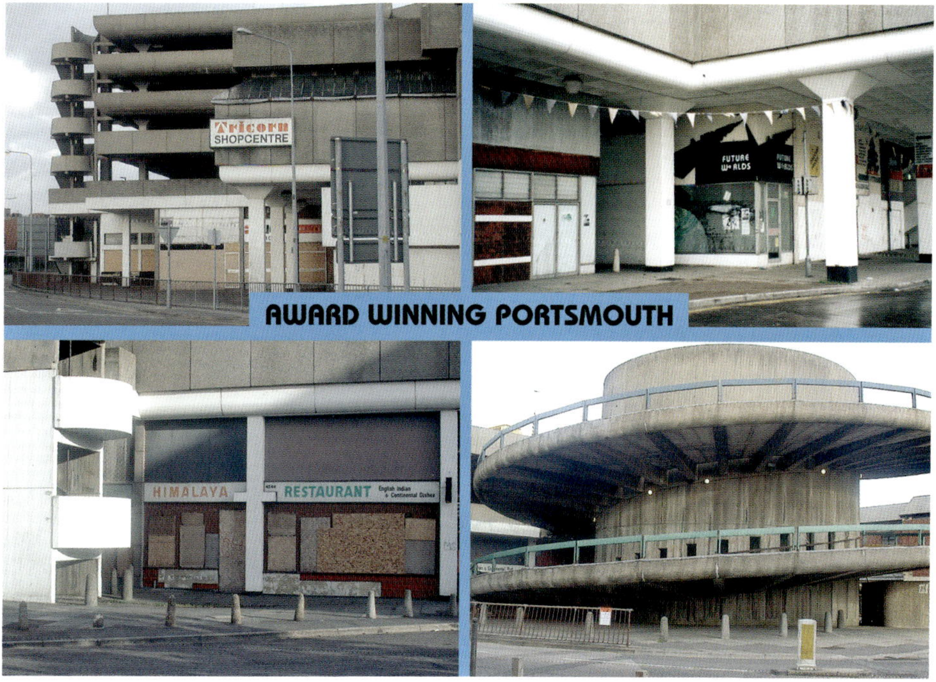

AWARD WINNING PORTSMOUTH

The Tricorn in Portsmouth won an award for being one of Britain's best examples of modern architecture. One year later, it was voted one of the worst. Like many other concrete monoliths The Tricorn has now been demolished.

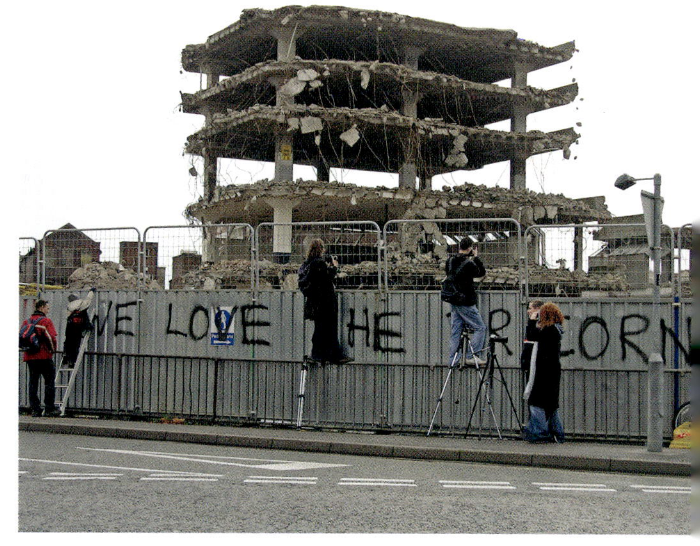

What's not so great about Britain?

Concrete

Grey days and grey days

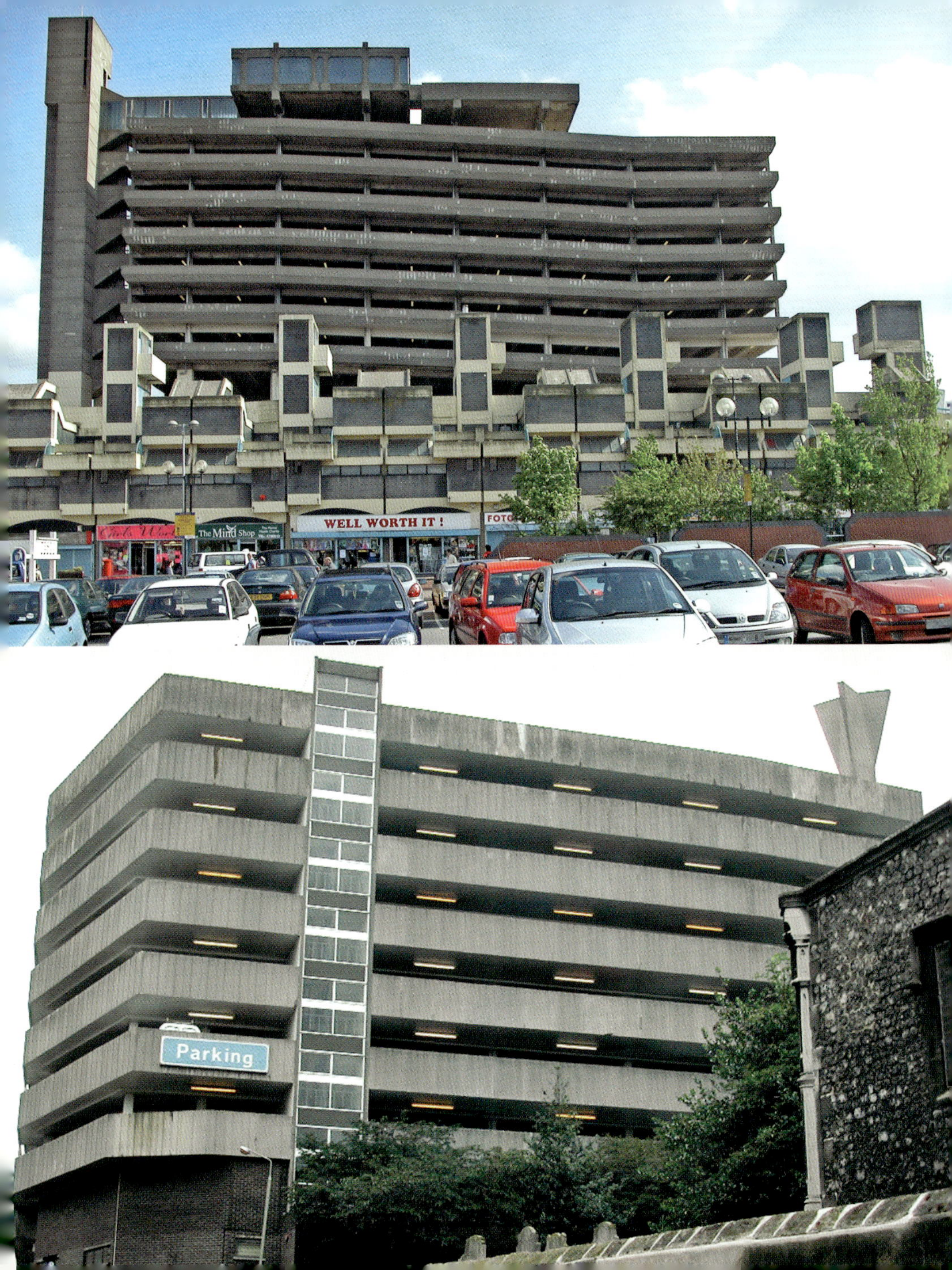
WELL WORTH IT !
The Mind Shop
Parking

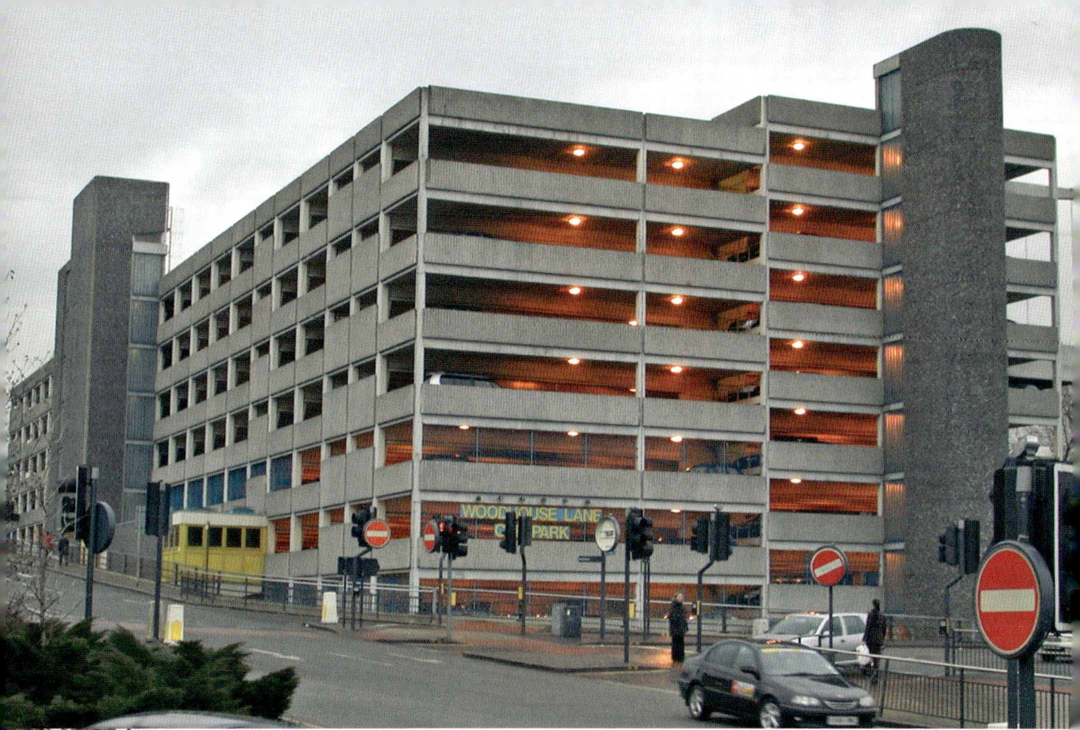

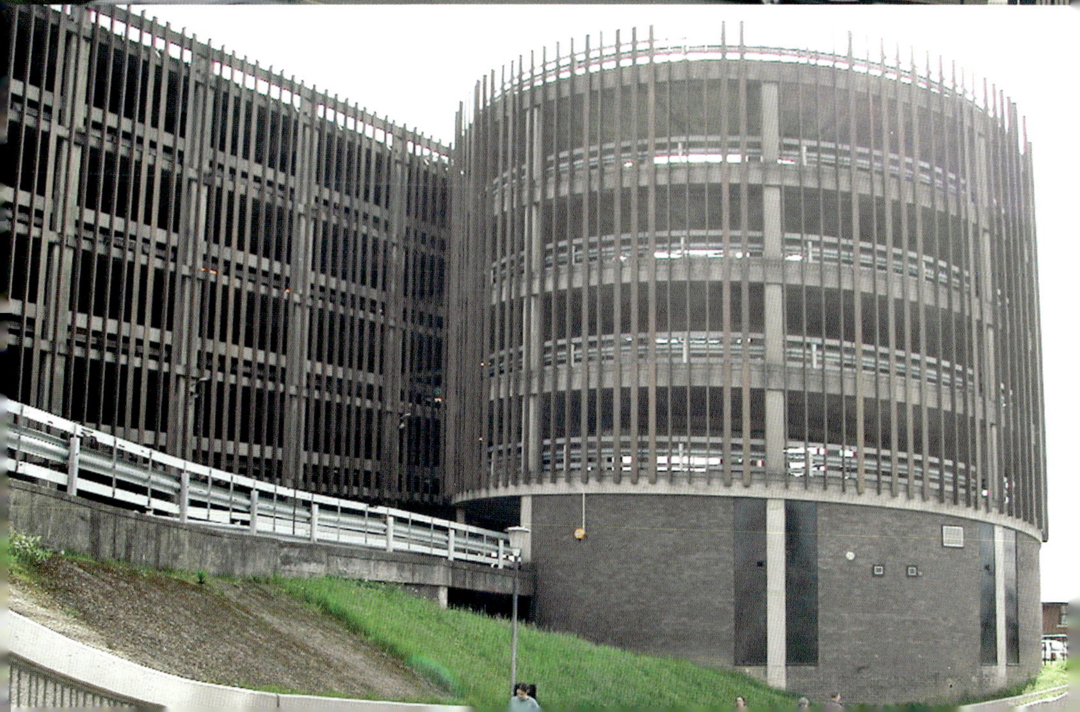

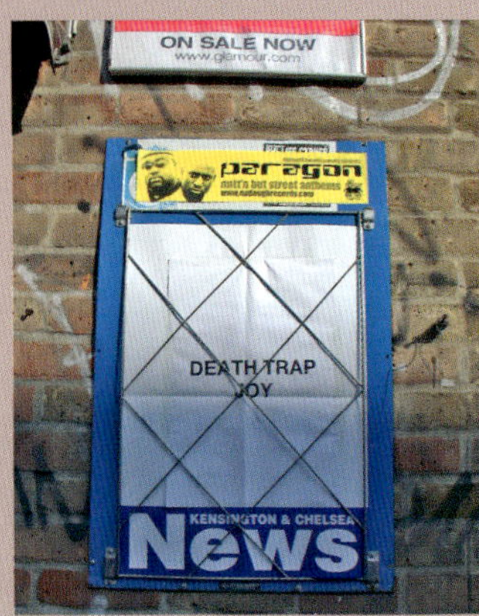

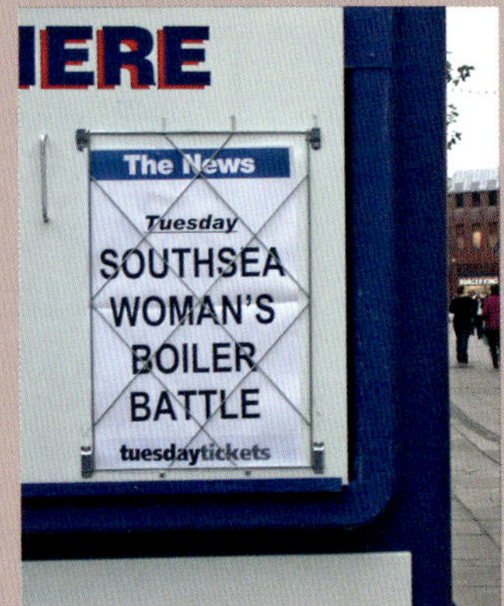

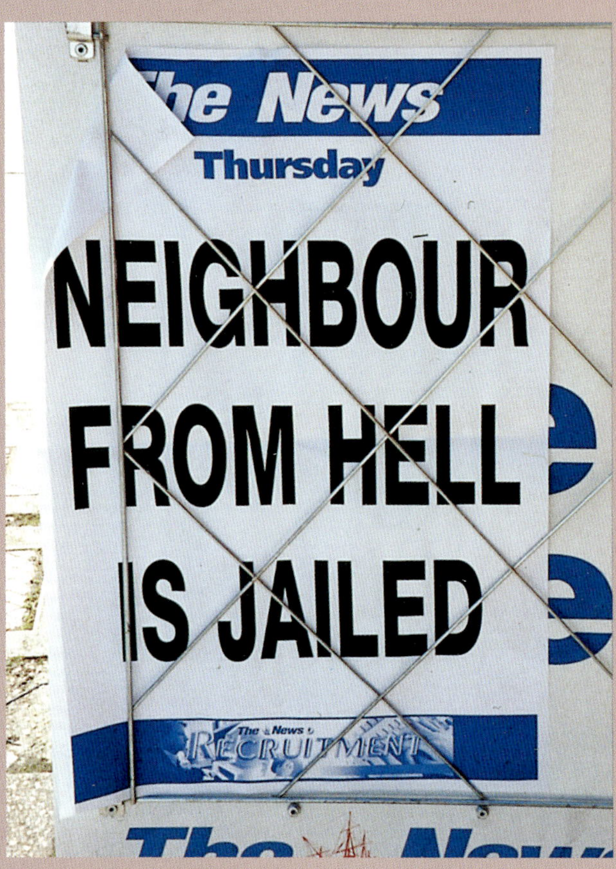

Today's news

Boiler Pervert Yob Dash Hell – screamingly over-the-top or downright bizarre, the posters on newspaper stands provide a poetic insight into our crazy world.

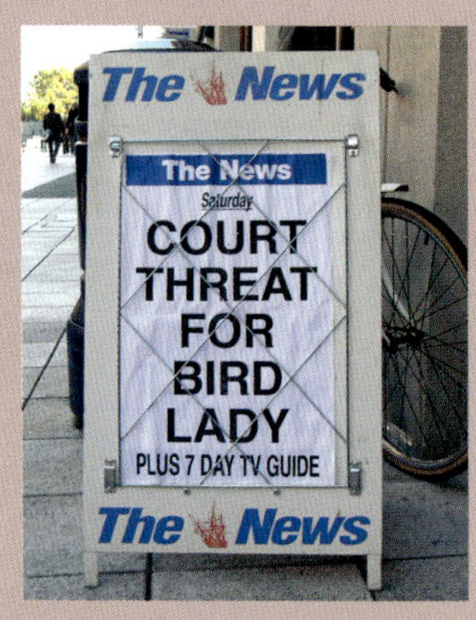

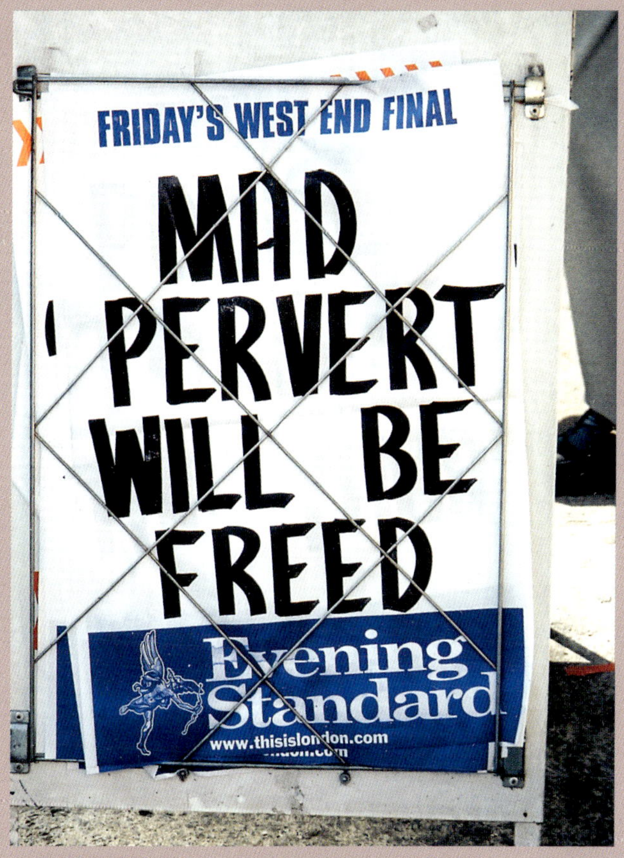
FRIDAY'S WEST END FINAL
MAD PERVERT WILL BE FREED
Evening Standard
www.thisislondon.com

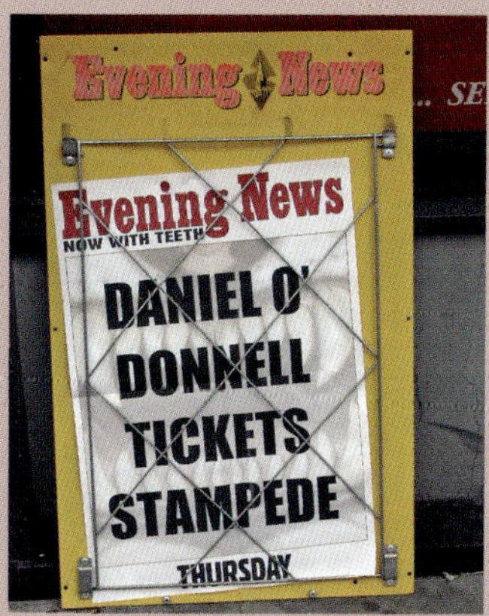
Evening News
Evening News
NOW WITH TEETH
DANIEL O' DONNELL TICKETS STAMPEDE
THURSDAY

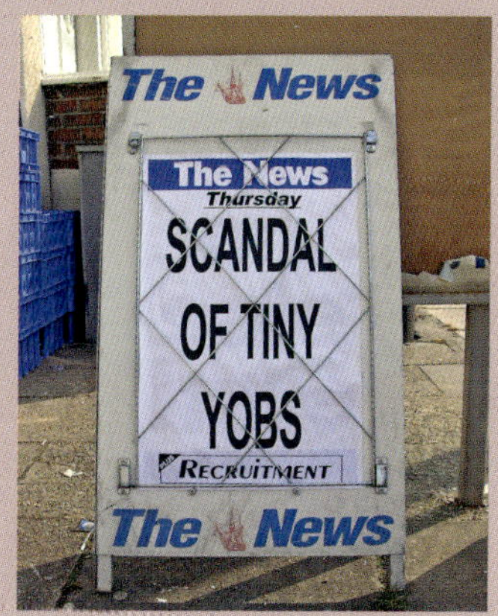
The News
The News
Thursday
SCANDAL OF TINY YOBS
RECRUITMENT
The News

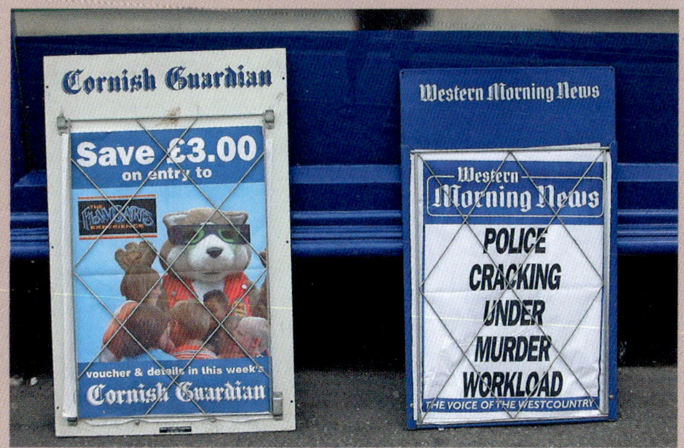
Cornish Guardian
Save £3.00
on entry to
voucher & details in this week's
Cornish Guardian
Western Morning News
Western Morning News
POLICE CRACKING UNDER MURDER WORKLOAD
THE VOICE OF THE WESTCOUNTRY

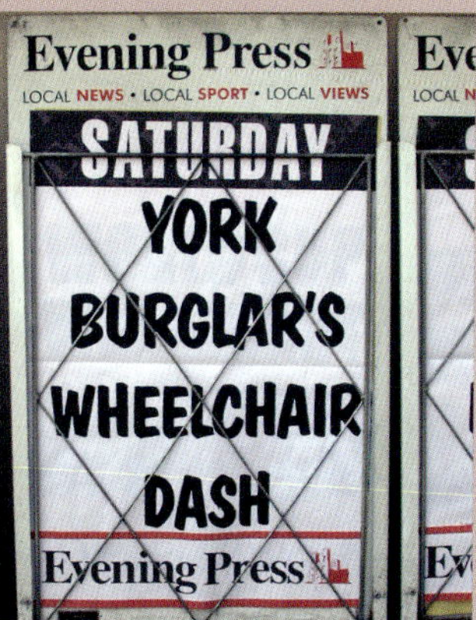
Evening Press
LOCAL NEWS • LOCAL SPORT • LOCAL VIEWS
SATURDAY
YORK BURGLAR'S WHEELCHAIR DASH
Evening Press

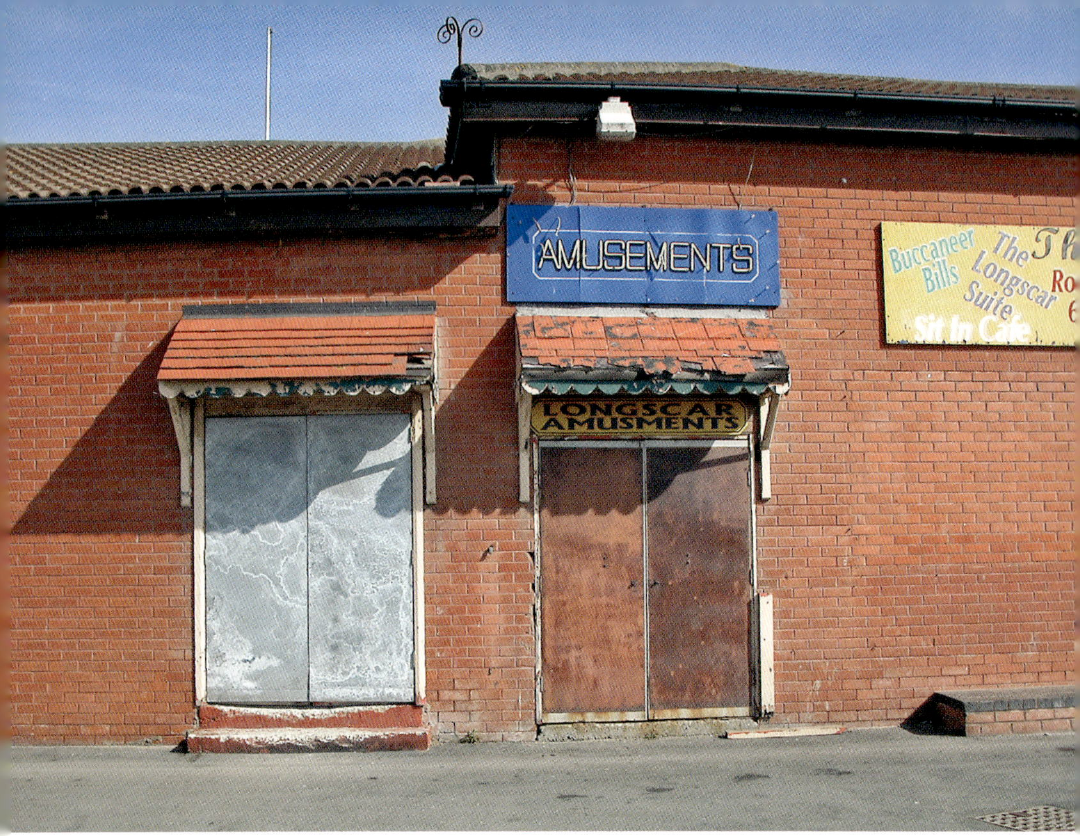

Amusements

In Britain we are expected to have fun whether we like it or not. Our coastal towns boast a wide range of amenities provided for this purpose. Fortunately, many of them are undercover – which is just as well given the high possibility of a bank holiday downpour.

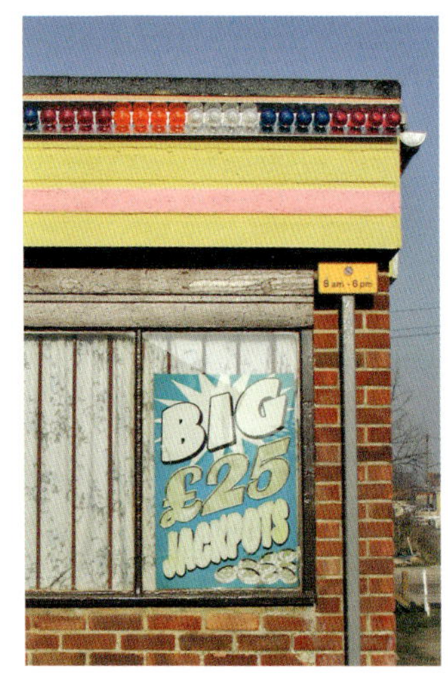

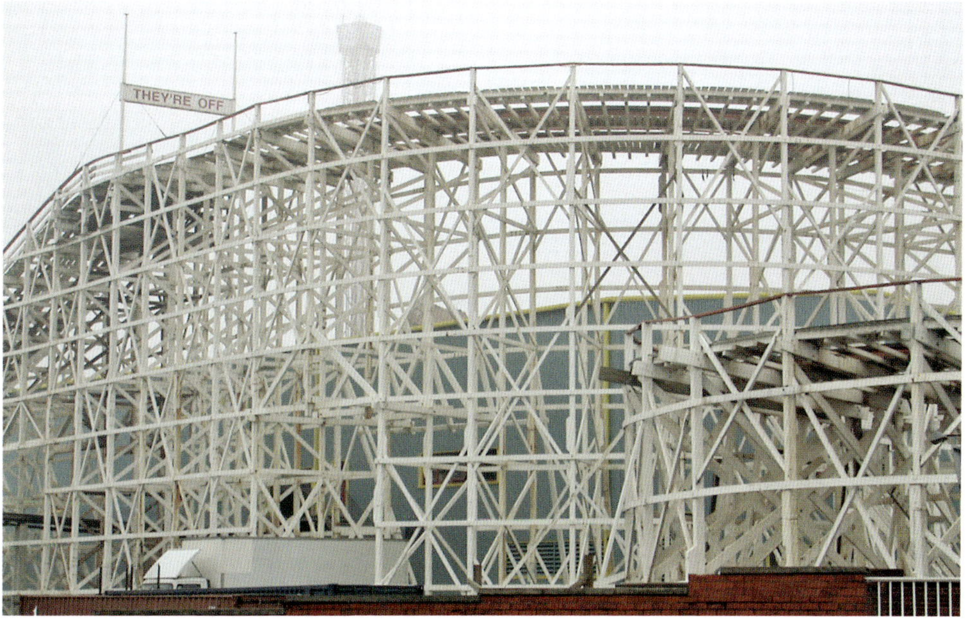

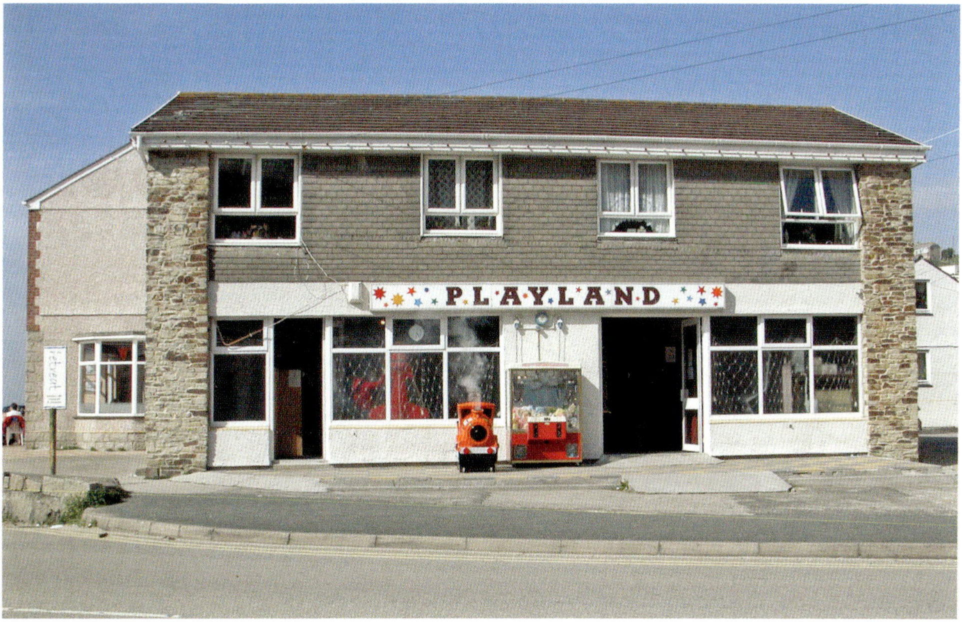

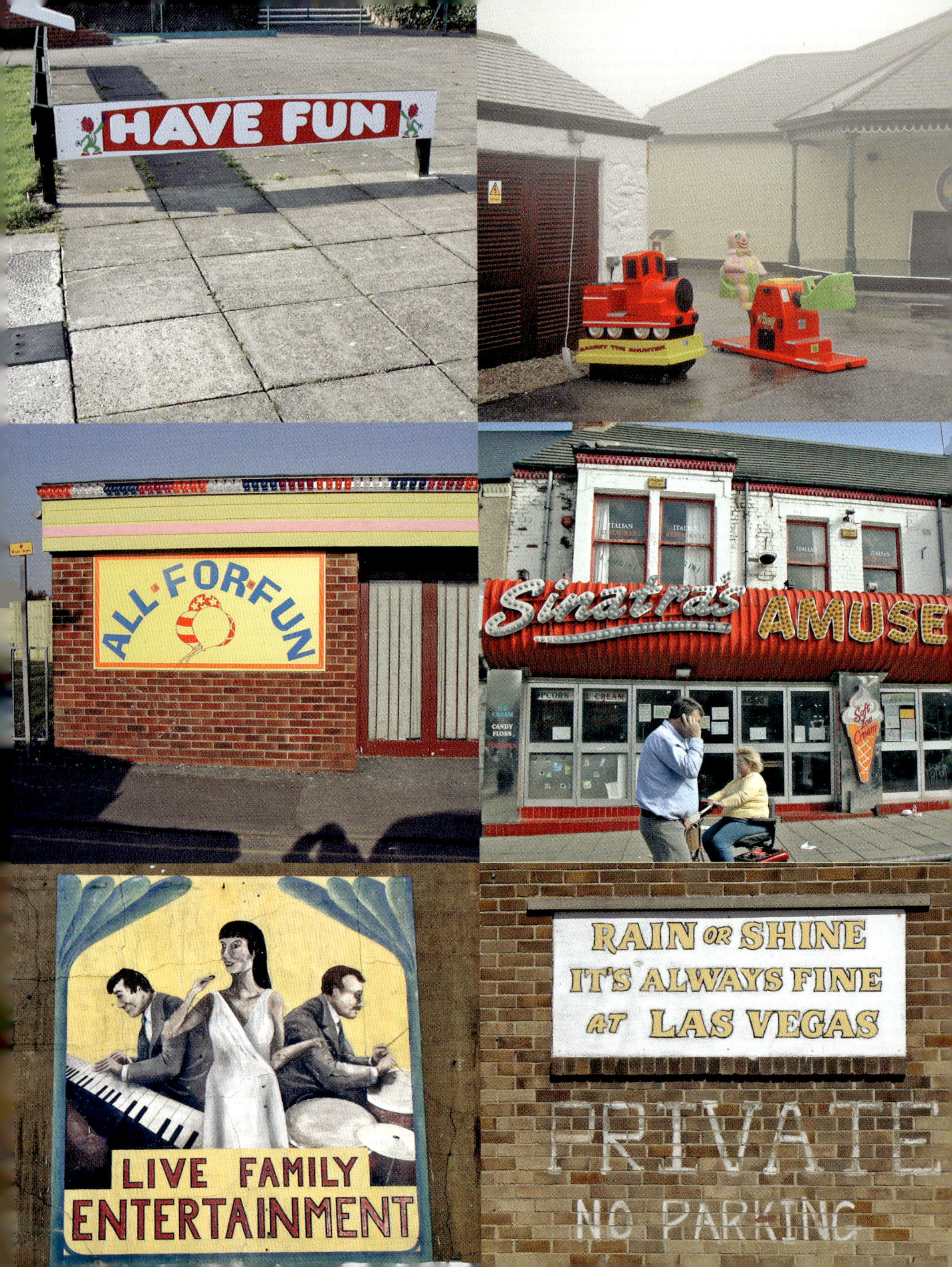
HAVE FUN
ALL·FOR·FUN
Sinatra's
AMUSE
Soft Ice Cream
LIVE FAMILY
ENTERTAINMENT
RAIN OR SHINE
IT'S ALWAYS FINE
AT LAS VEGAS
PRIVATE
NO PARKING

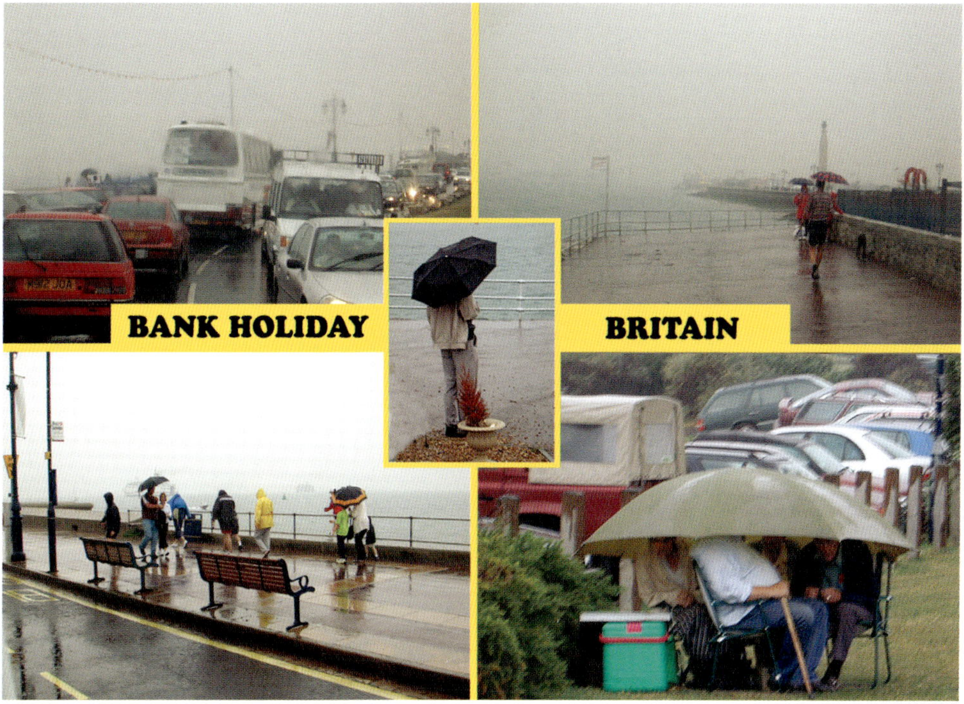

BANK HOLIDAY BRITAIN

What's great about Britain?

Chips, curry and piers

What's not so great?

Nothing, I love old England

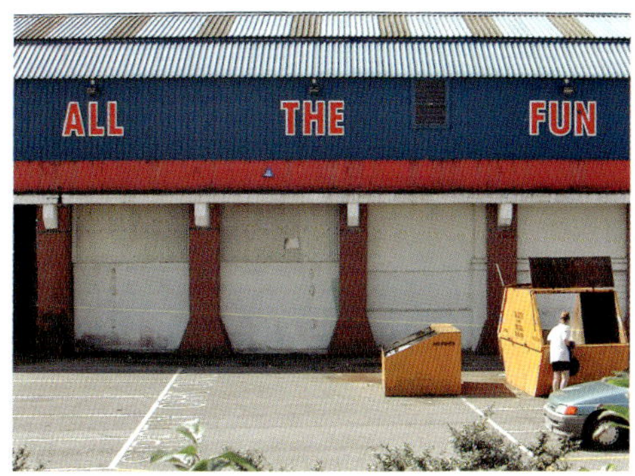

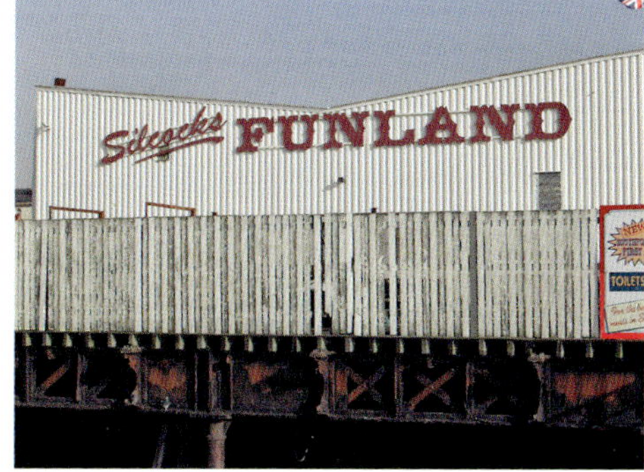

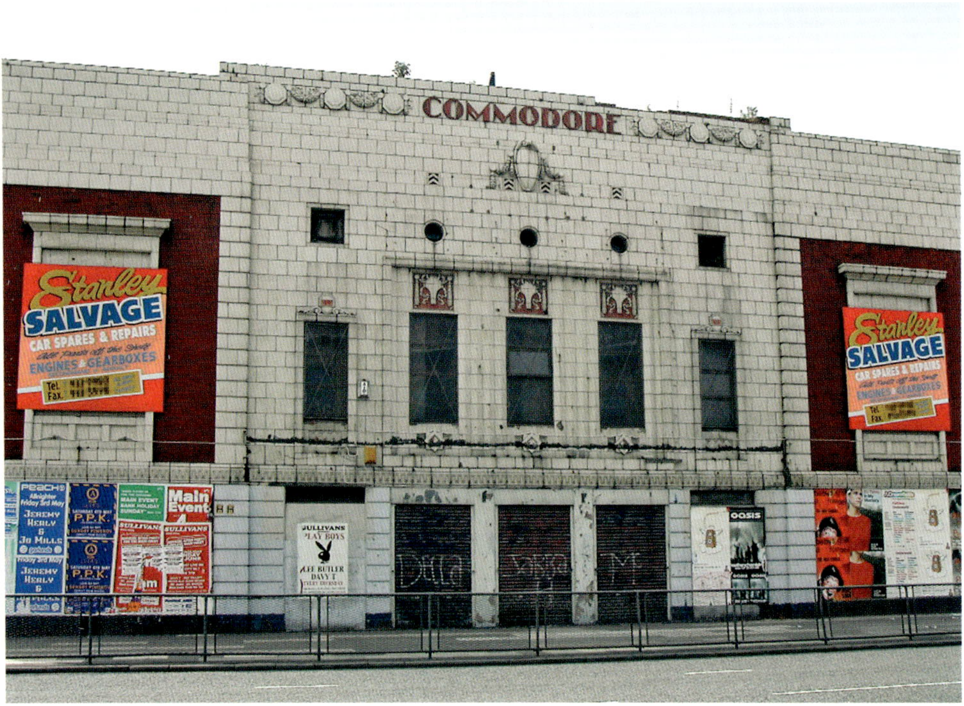

Cinemas-cum-churches

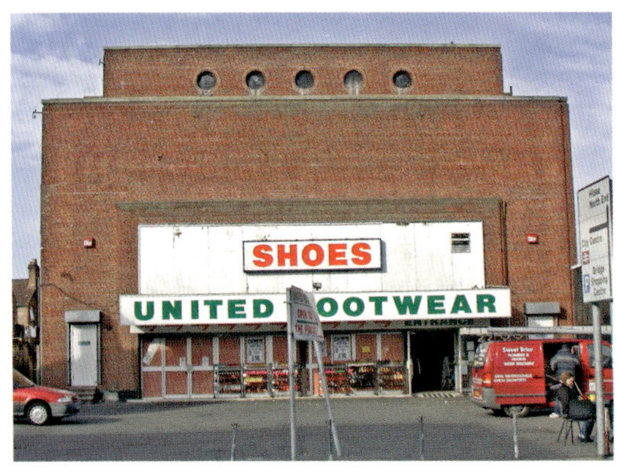

Want to buy shoes or pan scourers? Need a carpet or a beer? Fancy a game of Bingo? Chances are there will be a church or cinema near you offering these services. With features such as aisles, ushers and organs in common, it is hardly surprising to find cinemas reincarnated as churches, while churches now offer a variety of secular facilities.

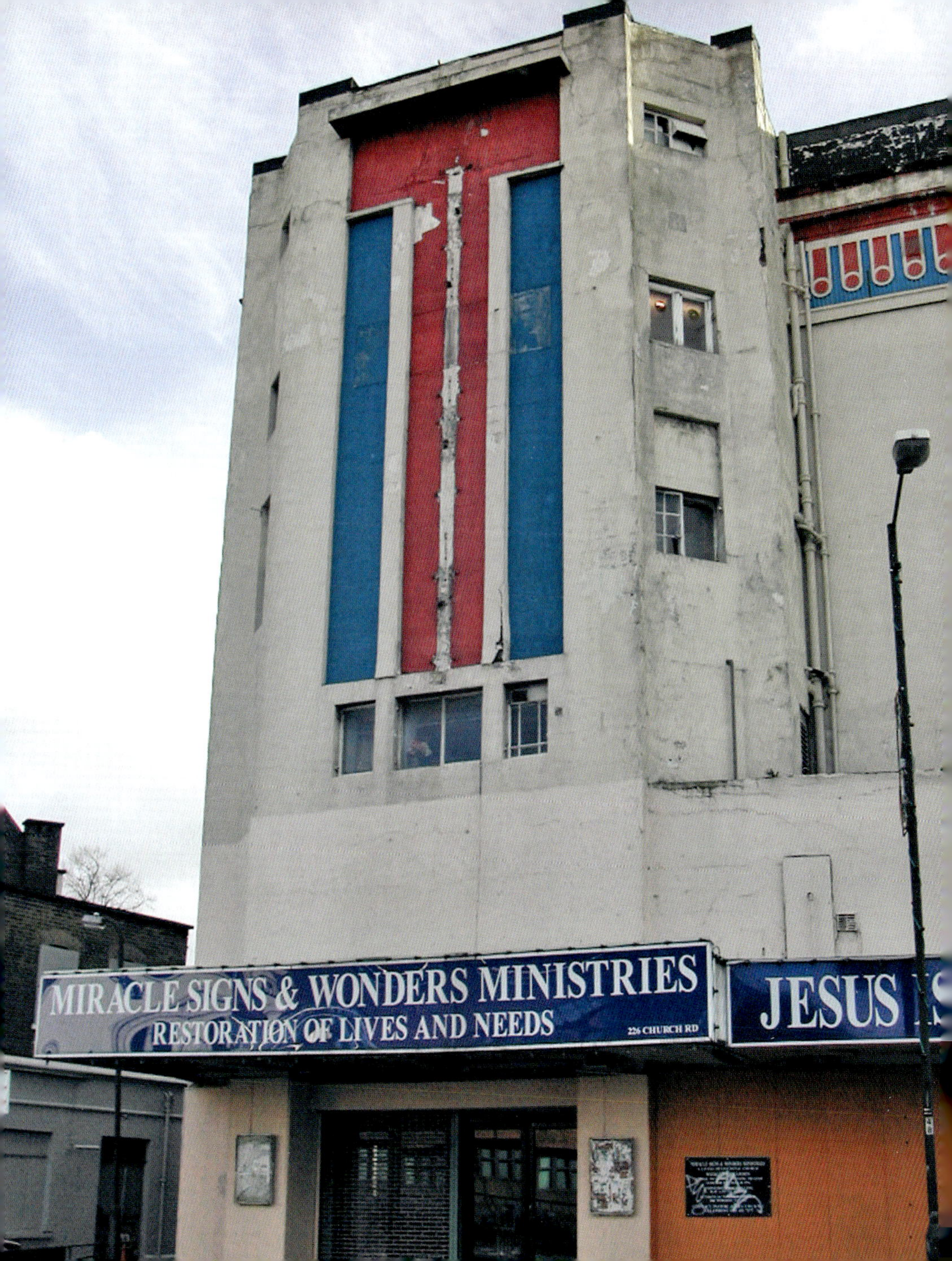
MIRACLE SIGNS & WONDERS MINISTRIES
RESTORATION OF LIVES AND NEEDS
226 CHURCH RD
JESUS

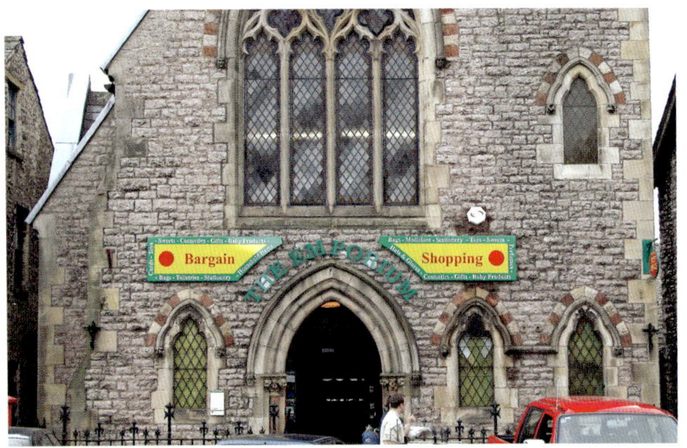

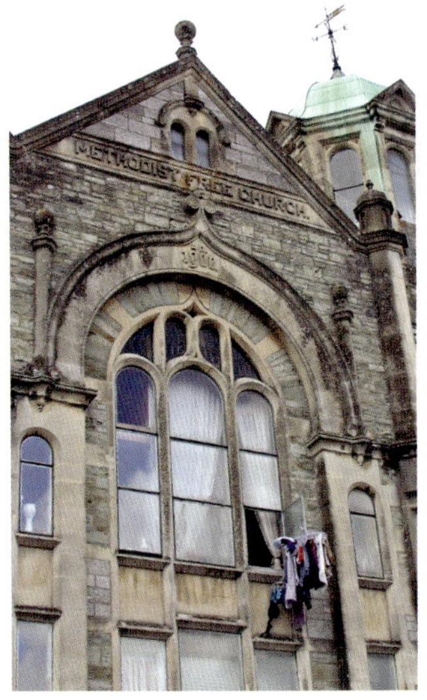

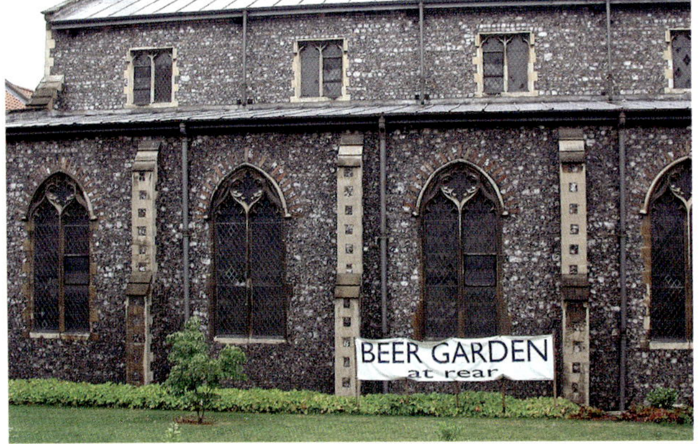

Many churches have diversified to provide accommodation, retail or pub services; those that retain their congregations find that investment in security helps to keep their prayers safe.

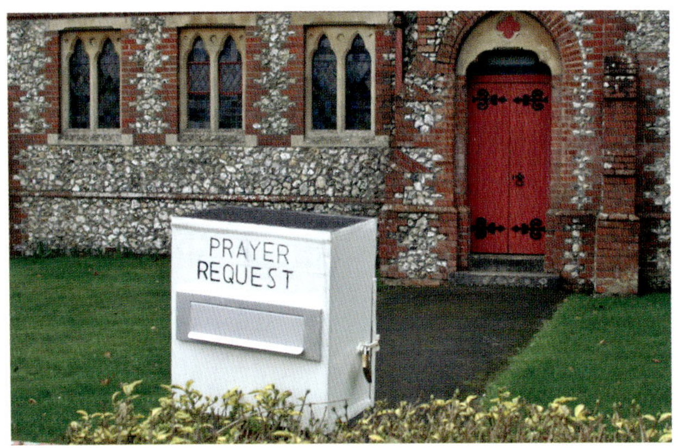

99% of people would rather die than arrange a pre-paid funeral

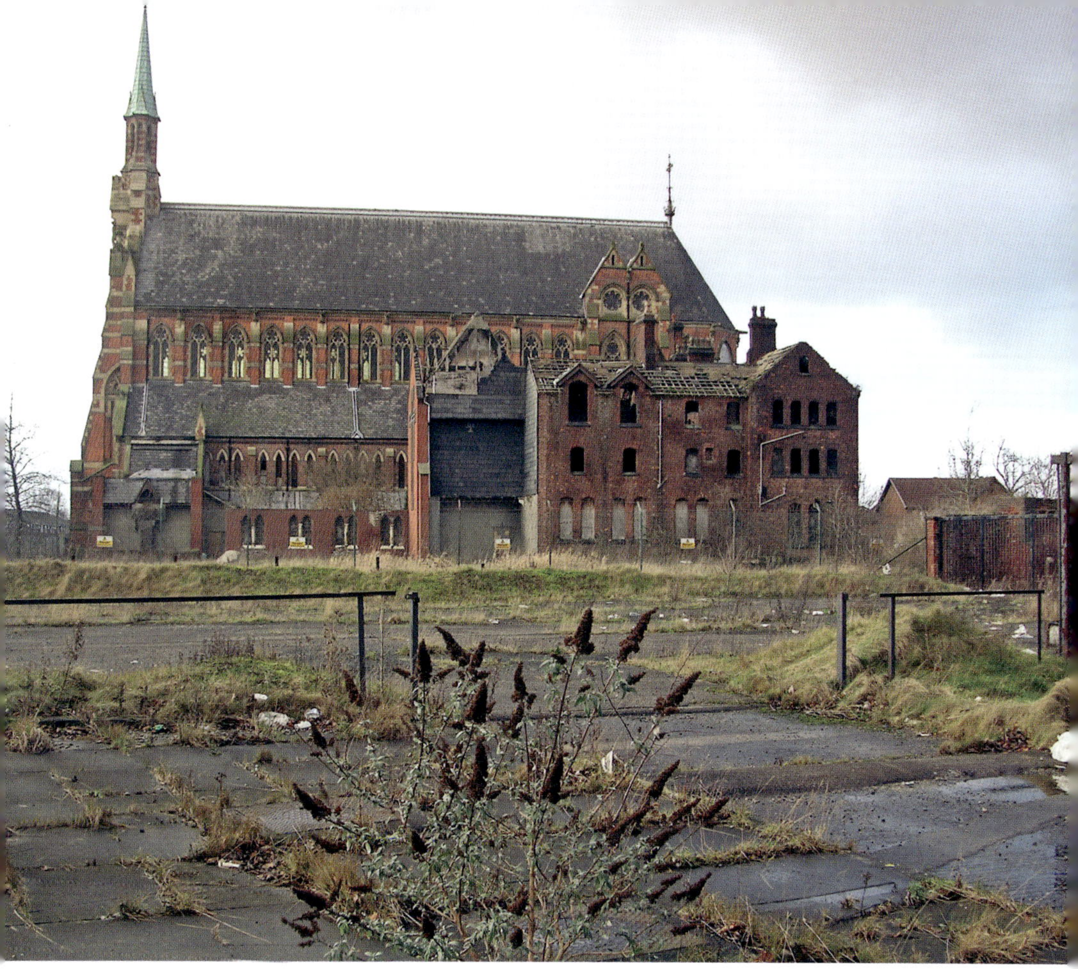

The huge edifice of the Gorton Monastery in Manchester – the 'Taj Mahal of the North', above – is on the list of 100 Most Endangered World Monuments, along with the Valley of the Kings and Machu Picchu.

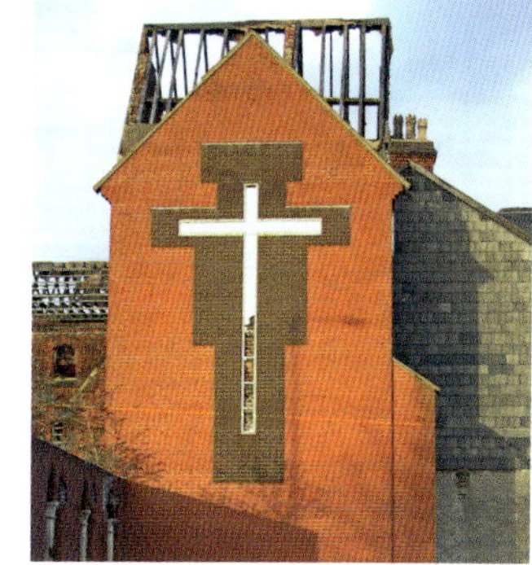

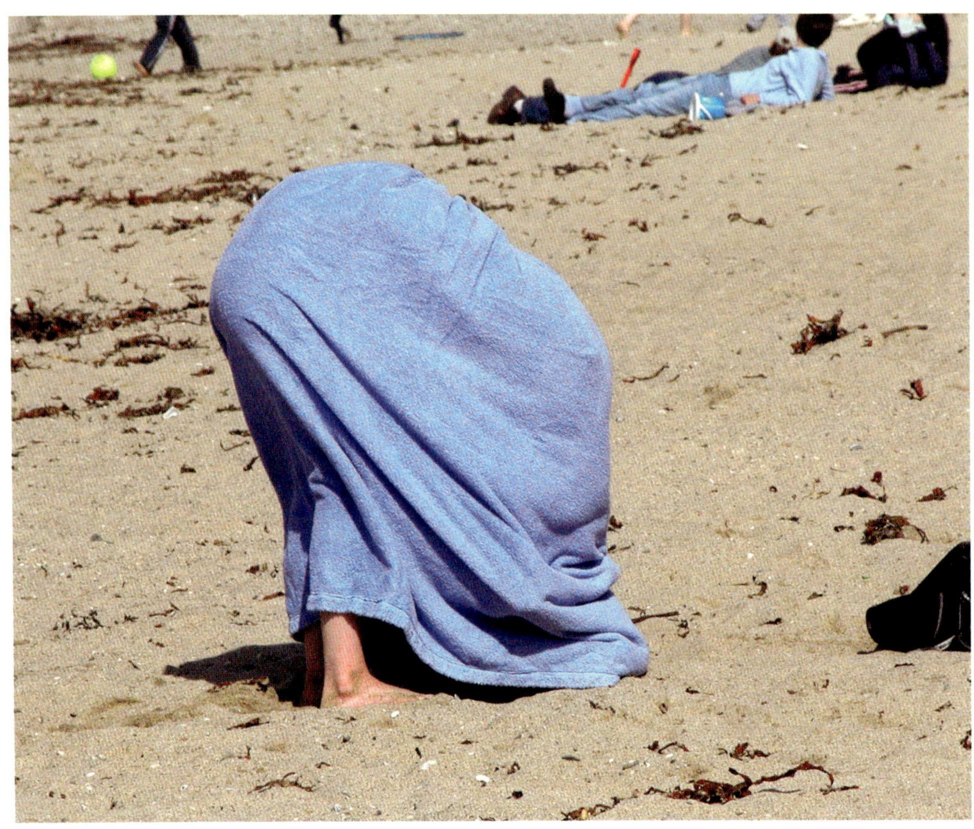

Seaside

The ideal place to park up, read the paper, have a nap and a flask of tea, all without leaving the comfort of your vehicle (except to purchase an ice cream to enjoy whilst gazing out to sea through the windscreen). Some people go to the seaside to drink lager and eat chips. Other beach-lovers arm themselves with tents, windbreaks and other accoutrements so they can be private in public; the more bashful avoid drawing attention to themselves by clever use of a large towel.

What's great about Britain?

The reticence and modesty of its people

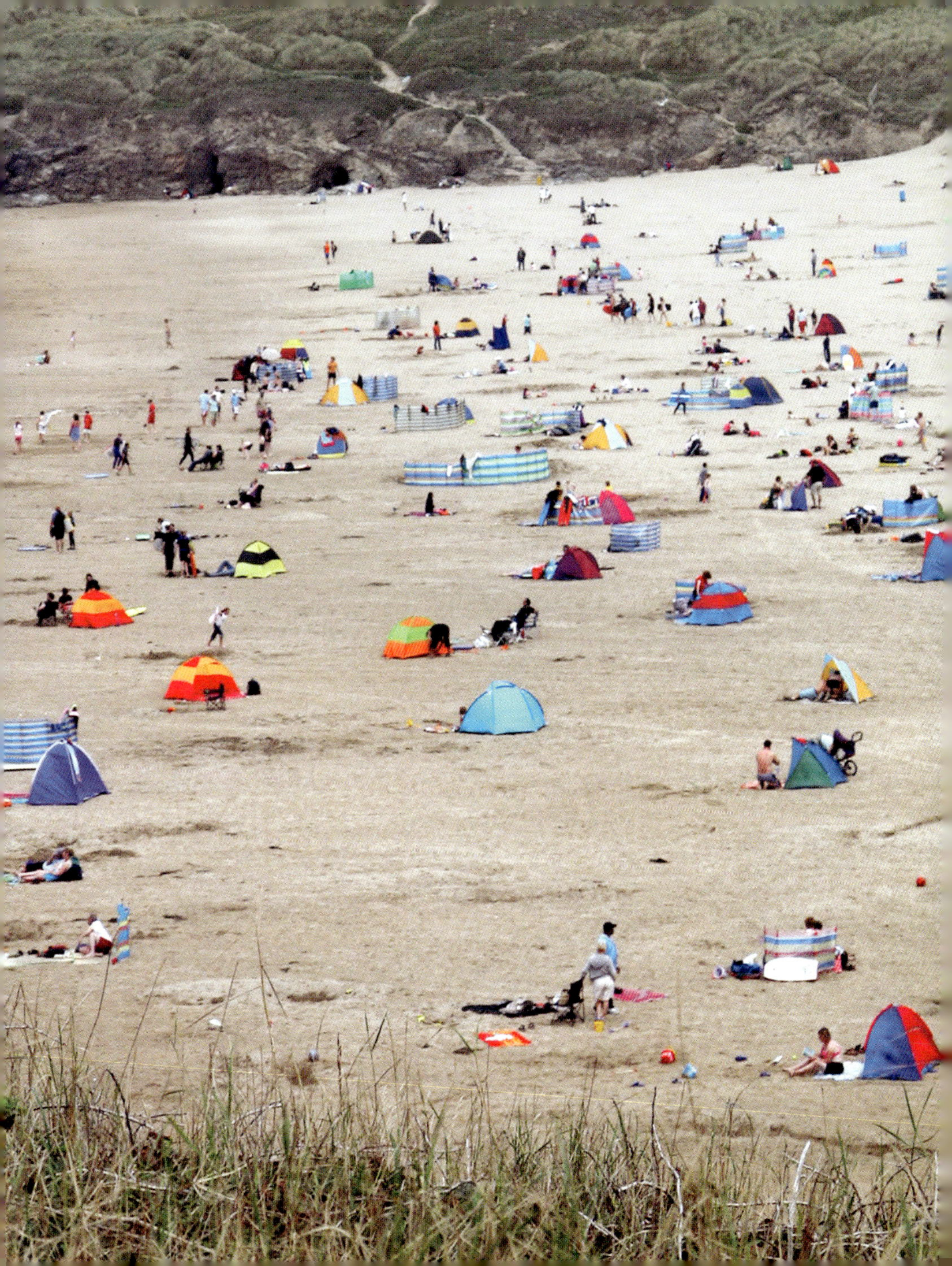

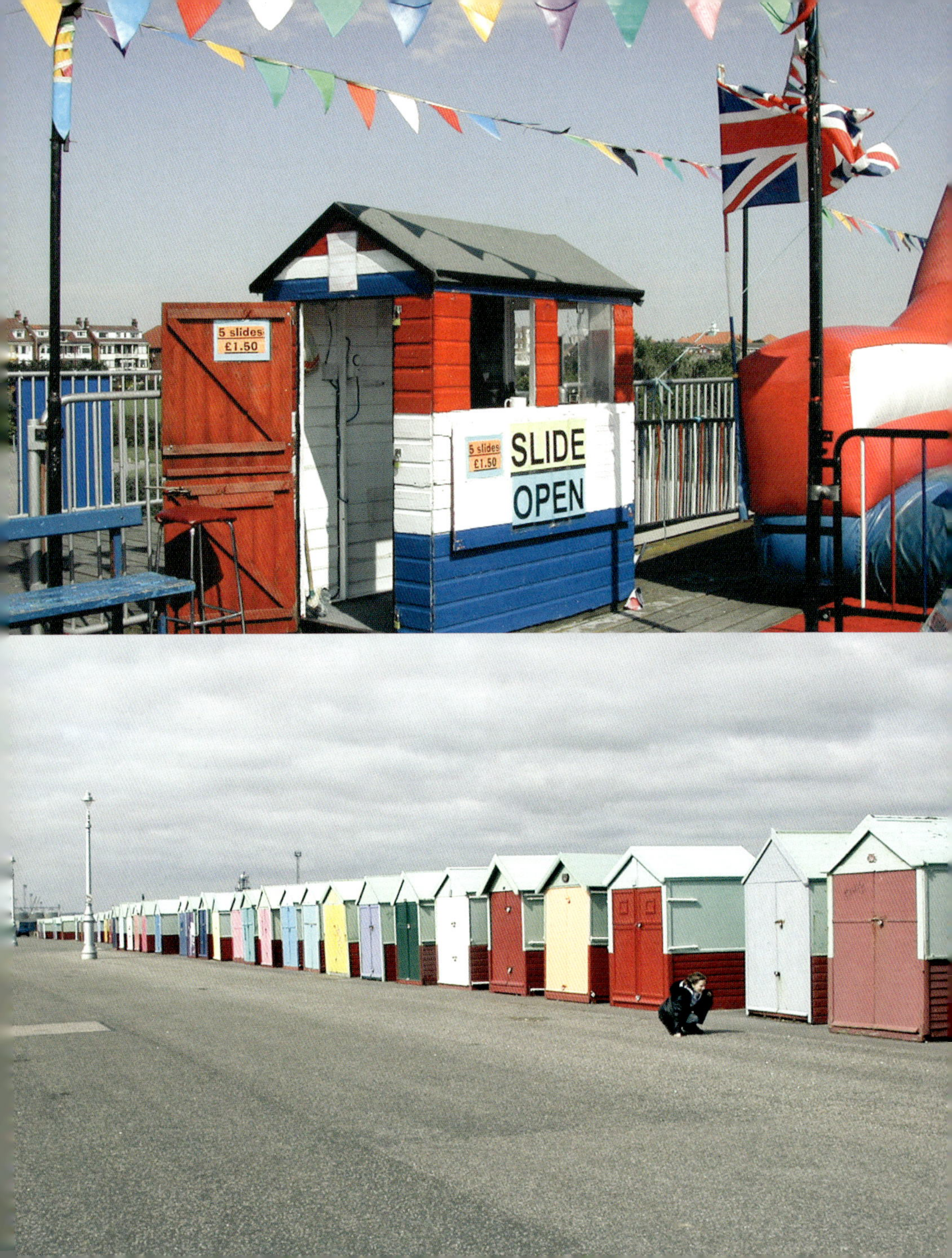
5 slides
£1.50
5 slides
£1.50
SLIDE
OPEN

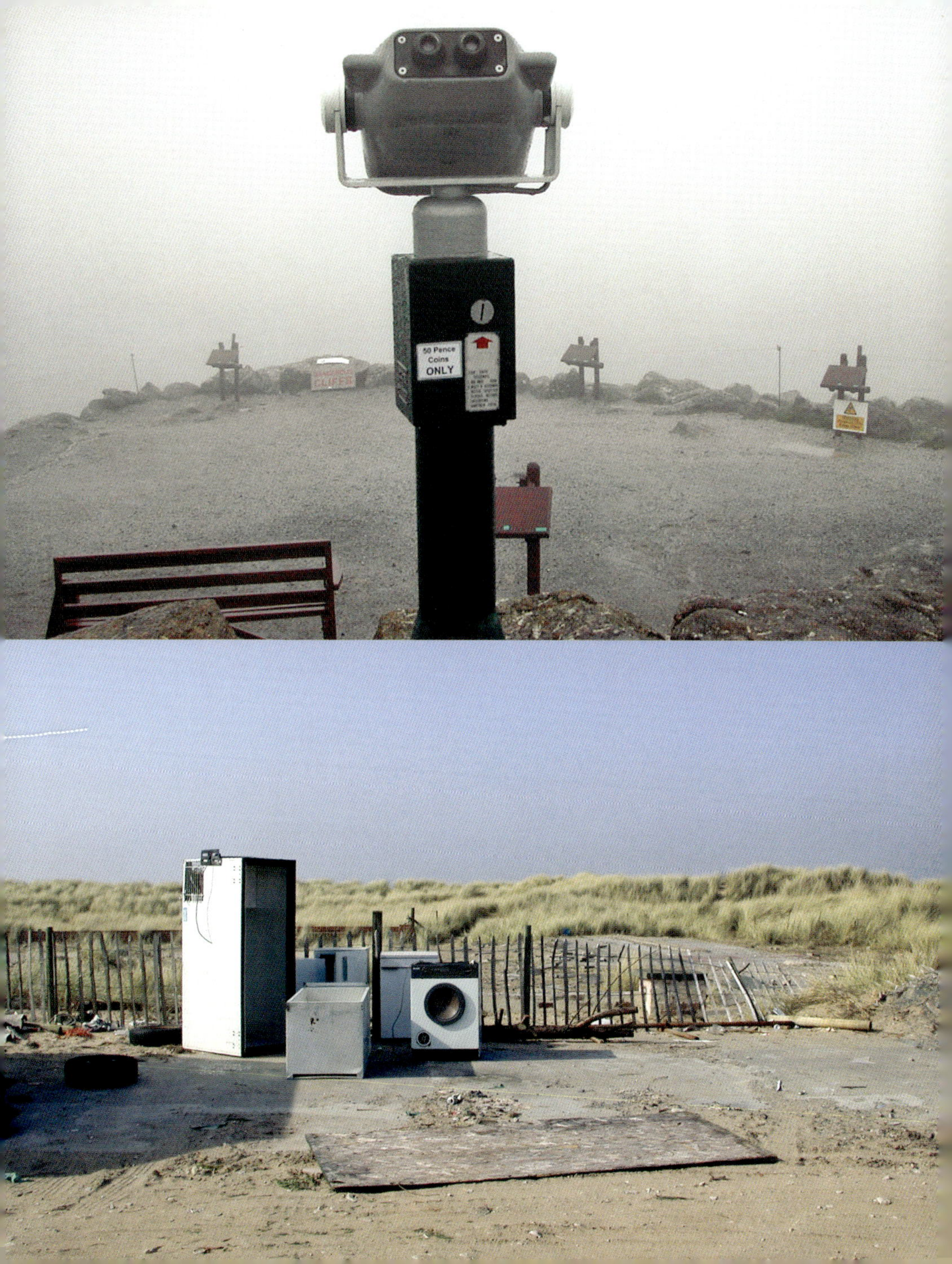
50 Pence
Coins
ONLY

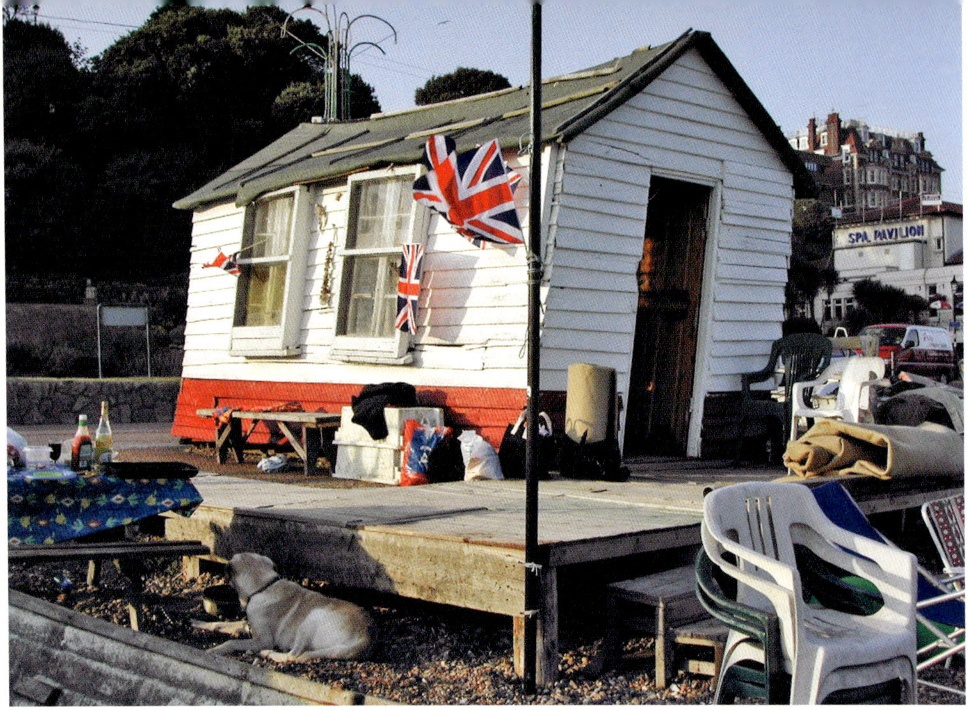

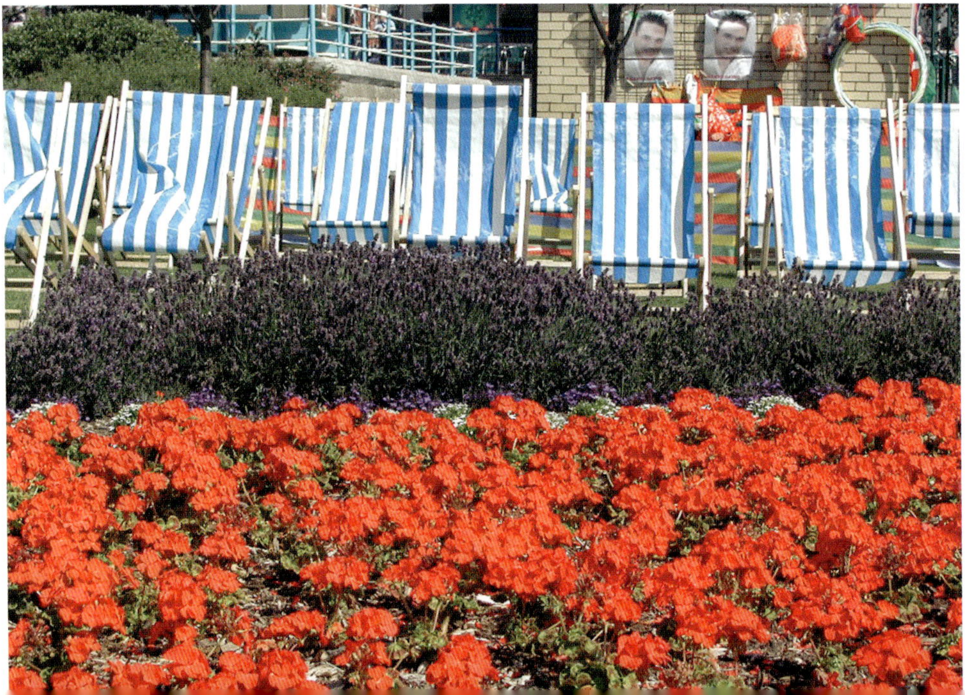

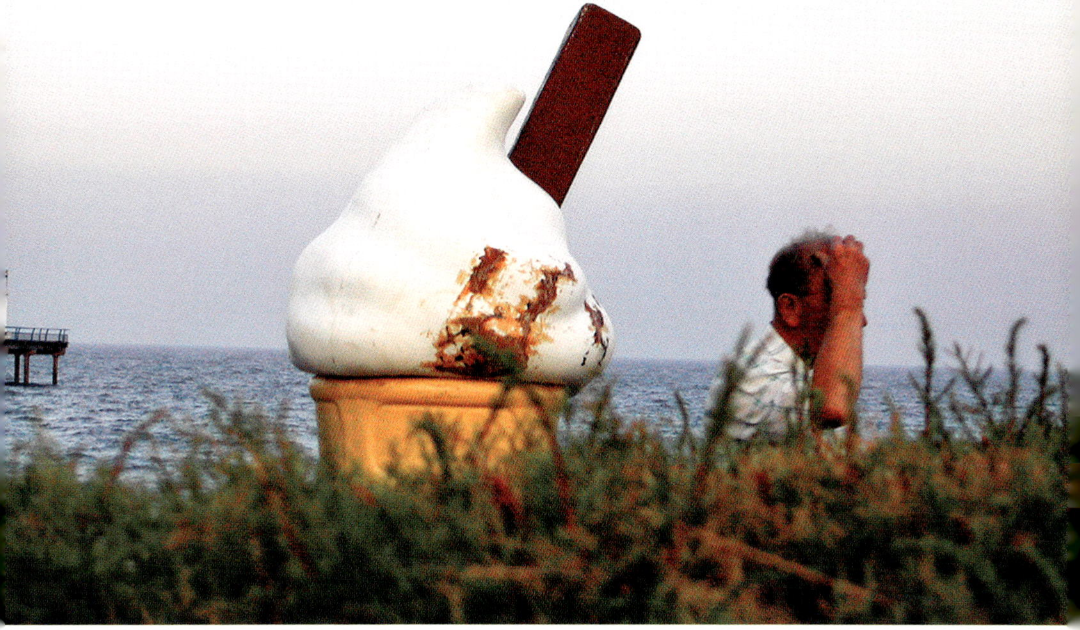

What's great about Britain?

The edges

What's not so great?

The middle

I love being British abroad; at home I would rather be French

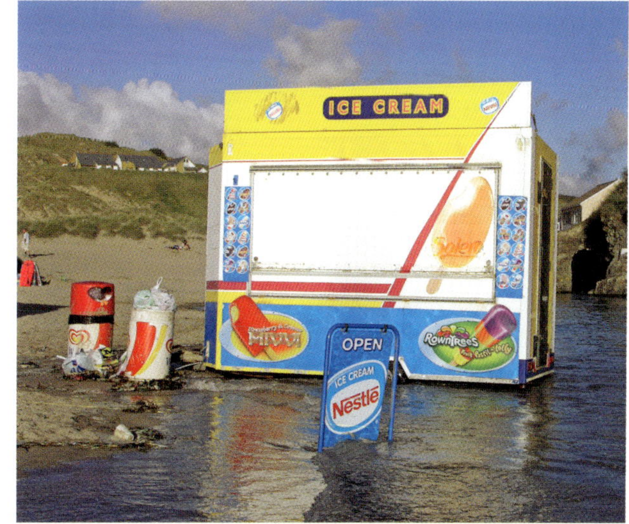

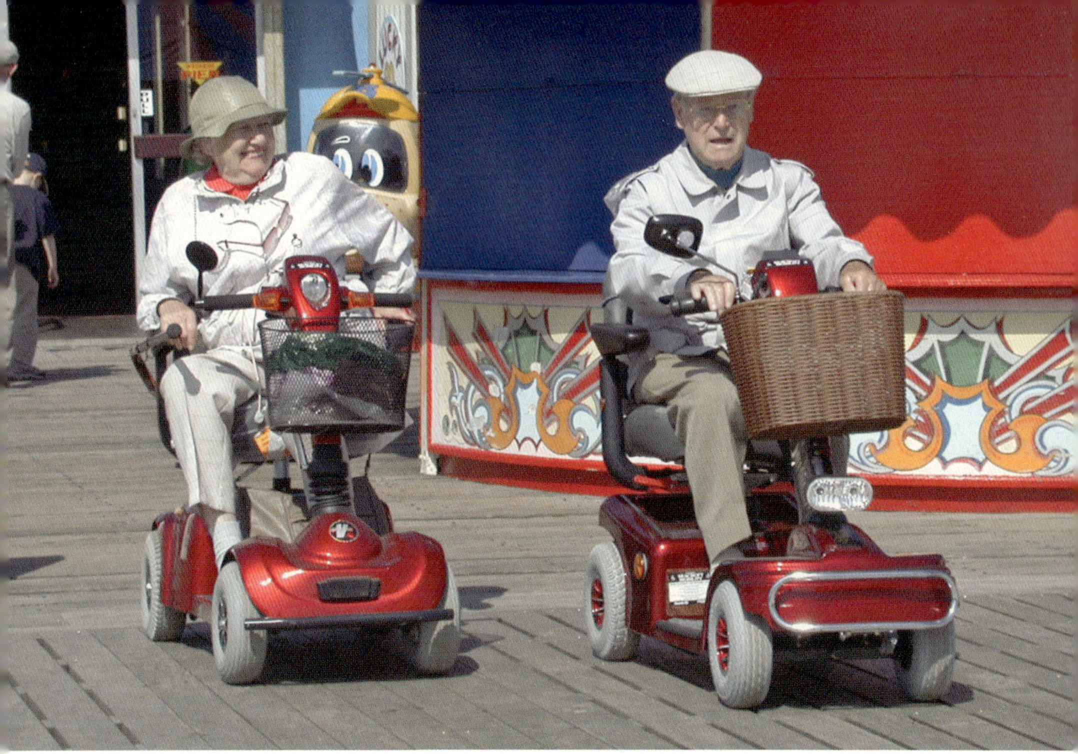

Getting about

With growing congestion on the roads and the scourge of over-zealous traffic wardens and clampers, it might be worth considering other modes of transport. How much more pleasant to relax in a lovingly maintained bus shelter or glide in tandem down the pavement on your scooters.

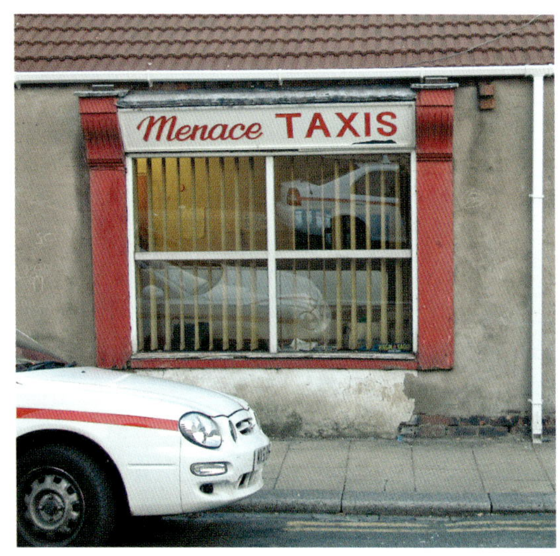

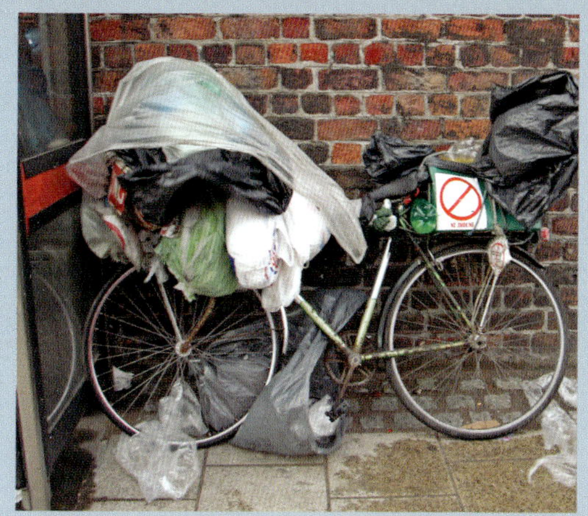

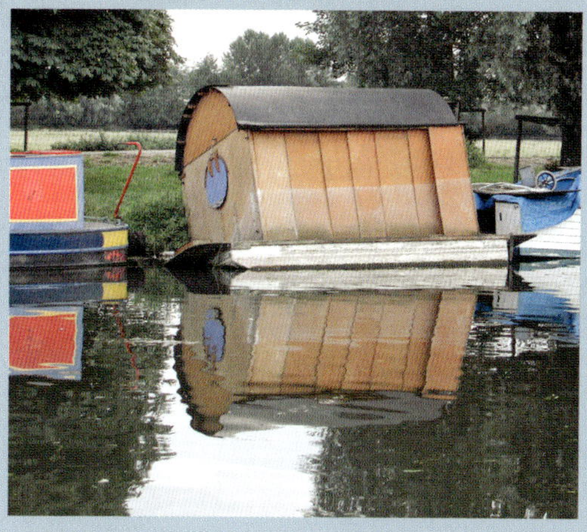

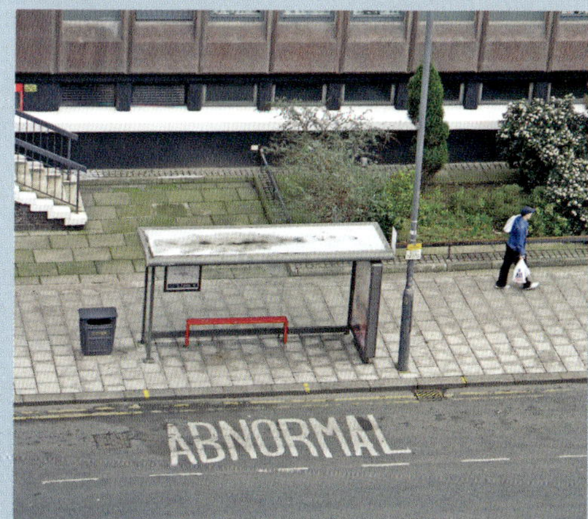
ABNORMAL

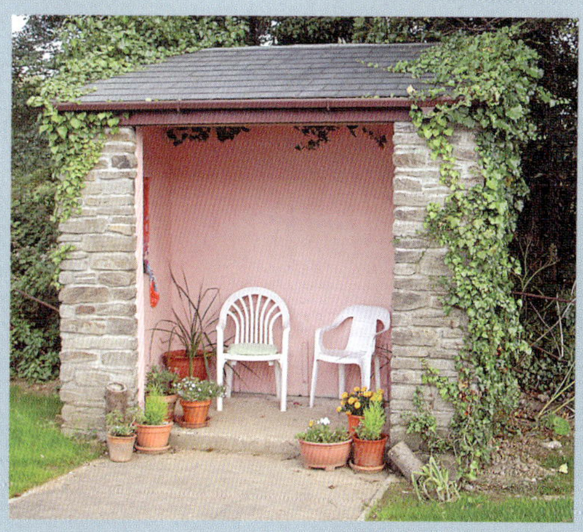

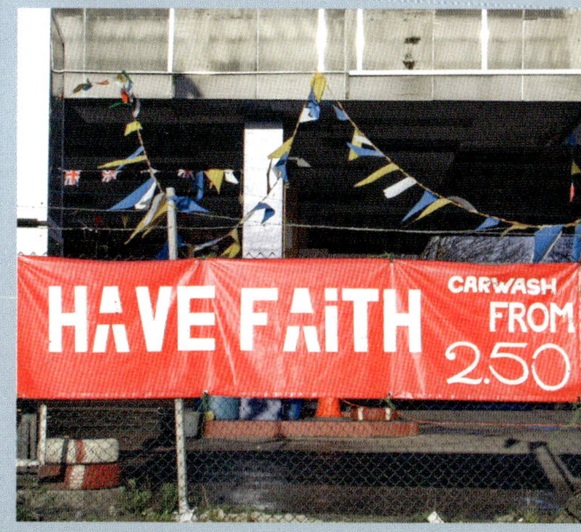
HAVE FAITH
CARWASH
FROM
2.50

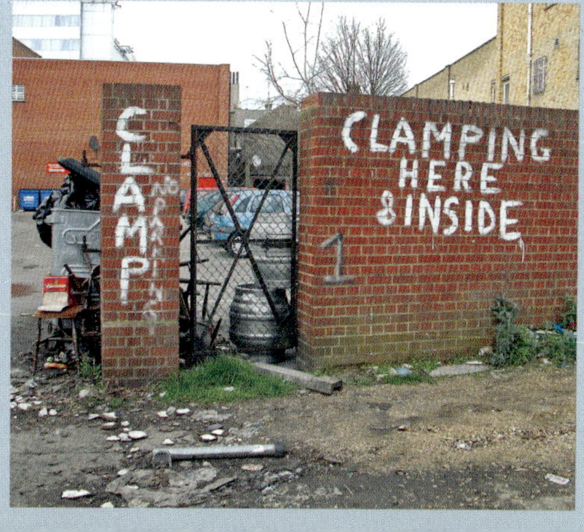
CLAMP
CLAMPING
HERE
& INSIDE
1

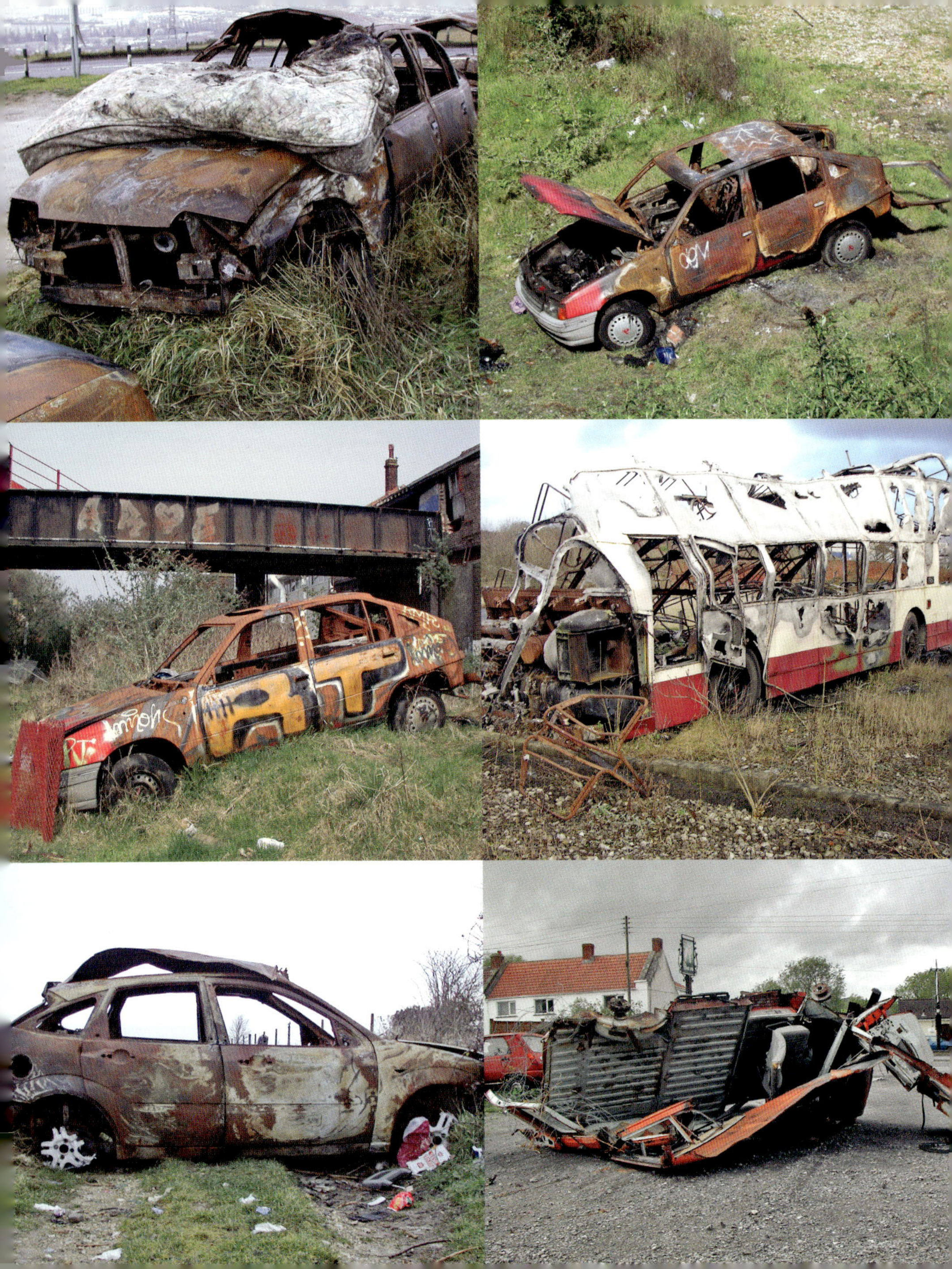

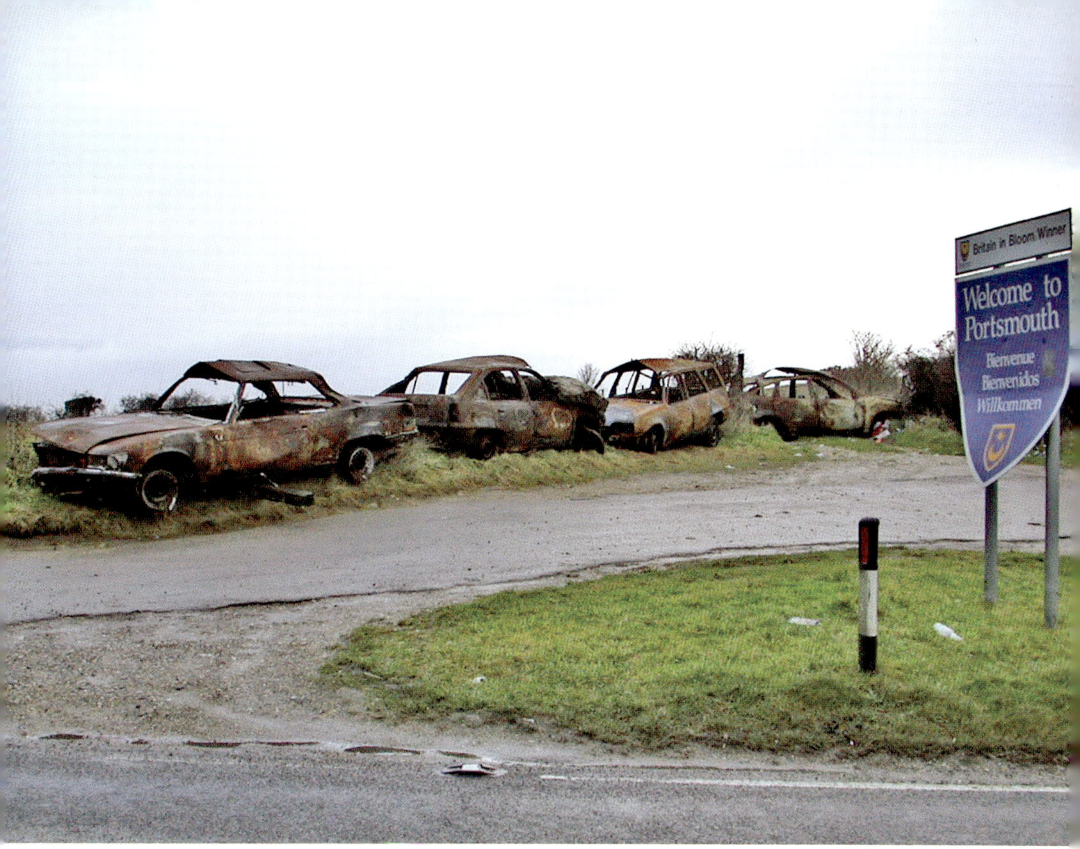

Ex-transport

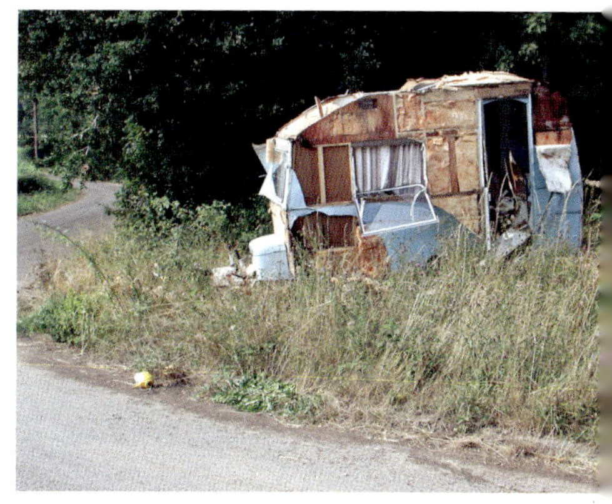

A familiar sight in rural areas, the sculptural presence of burnt-out cars lends the countryside a sinister air. How did they get there? What happened?

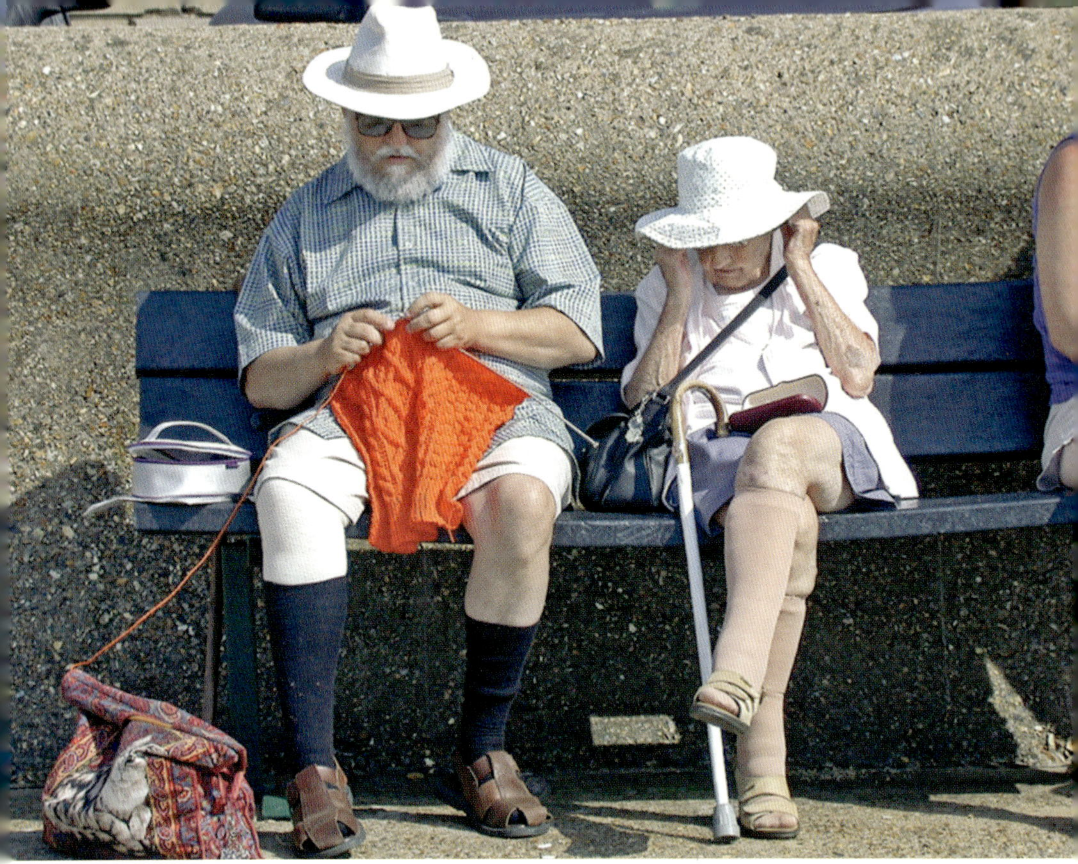

Relaxing

The British have perfected the art of relaxation over centuries. They excel at making themselves at home in any situation, oblivious to the sensibilities of onlookers.

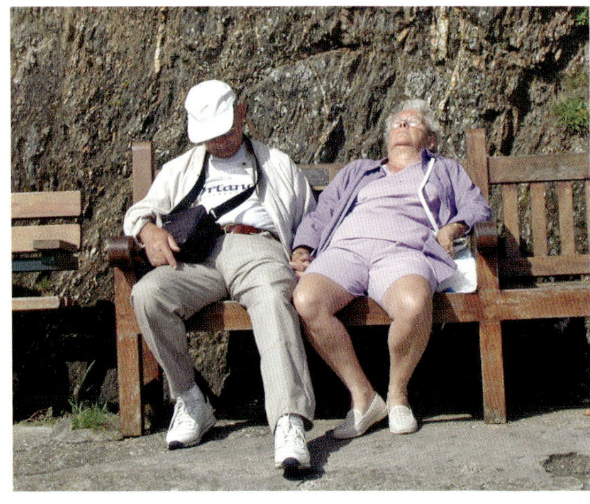

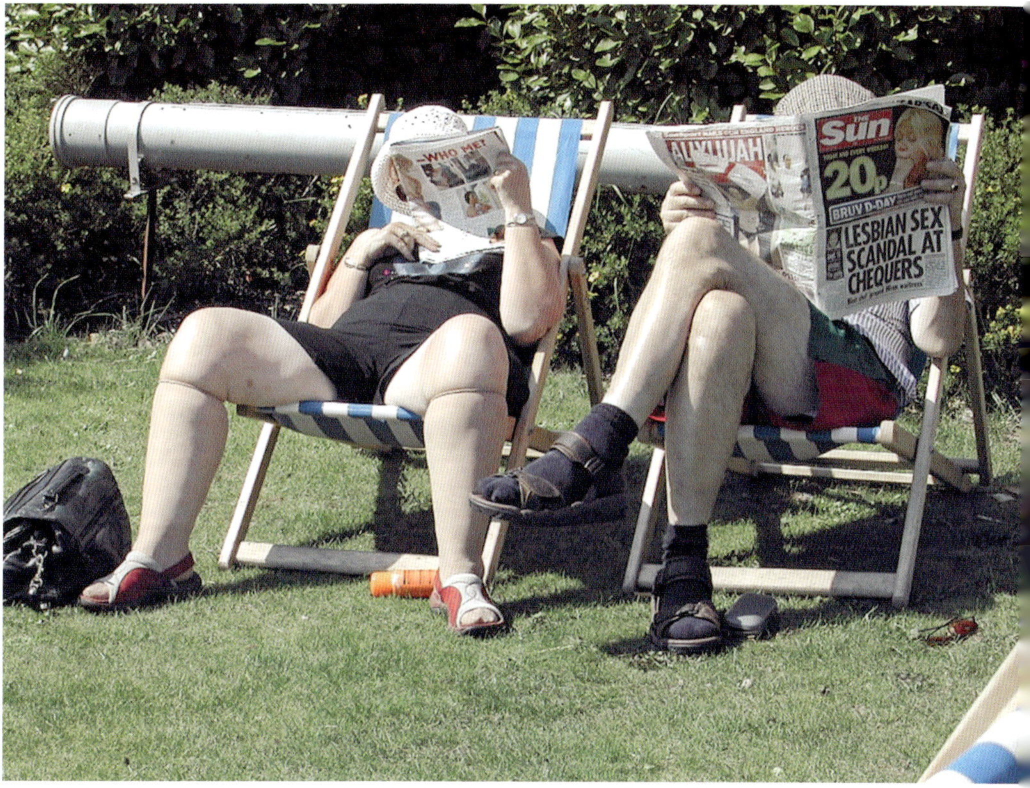

What do you think of as 'typically British'?

A view, a brew and a loo

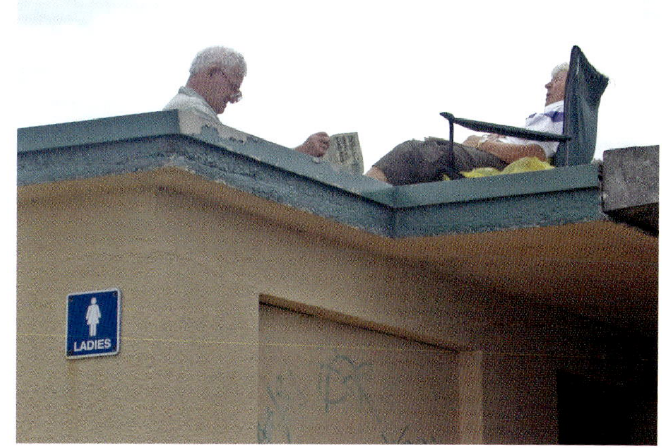

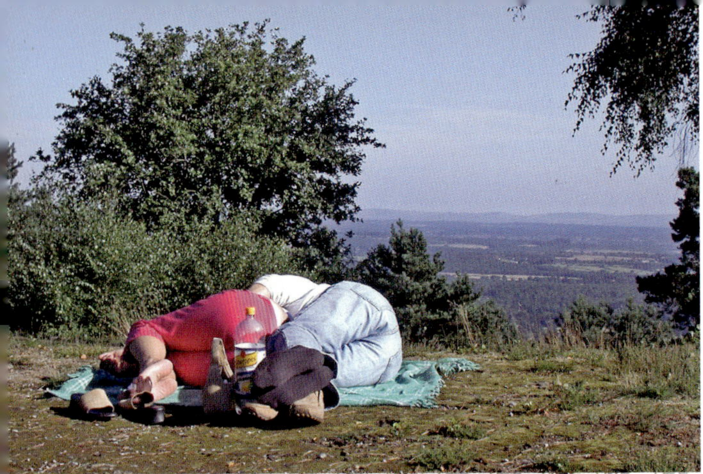

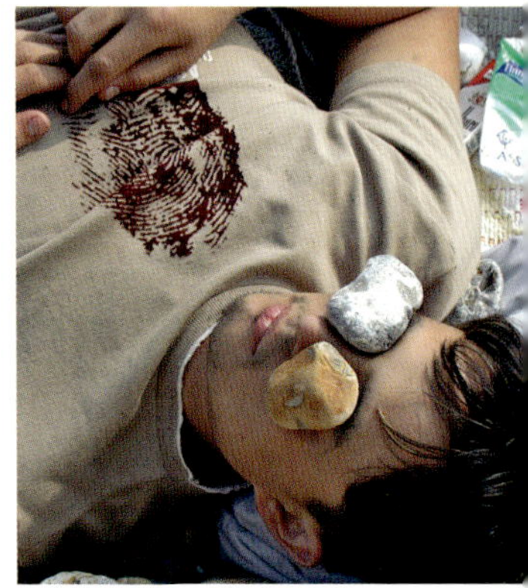

30% of people have never seen their parents naked

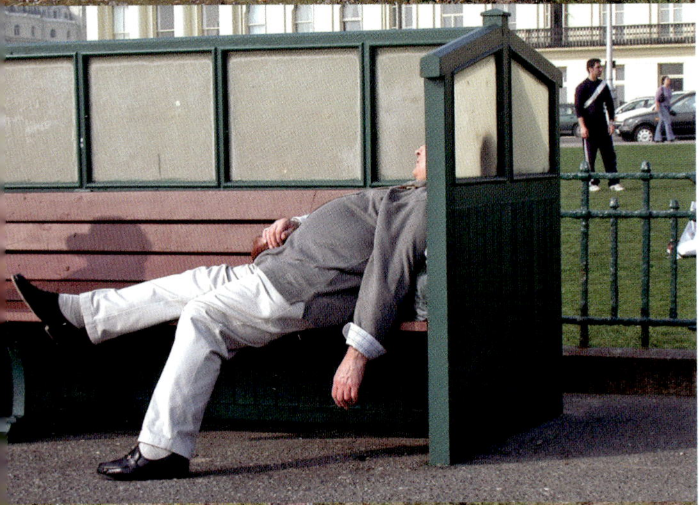

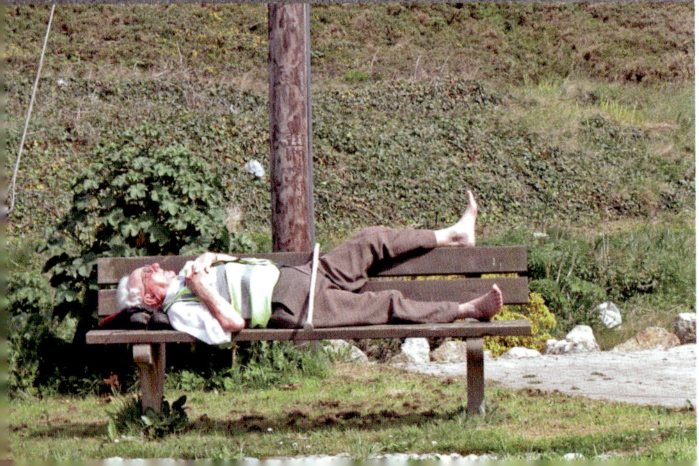

What do you think of as 'typically British'?

Fat people with sunburn

Certain standards

Making the most of it

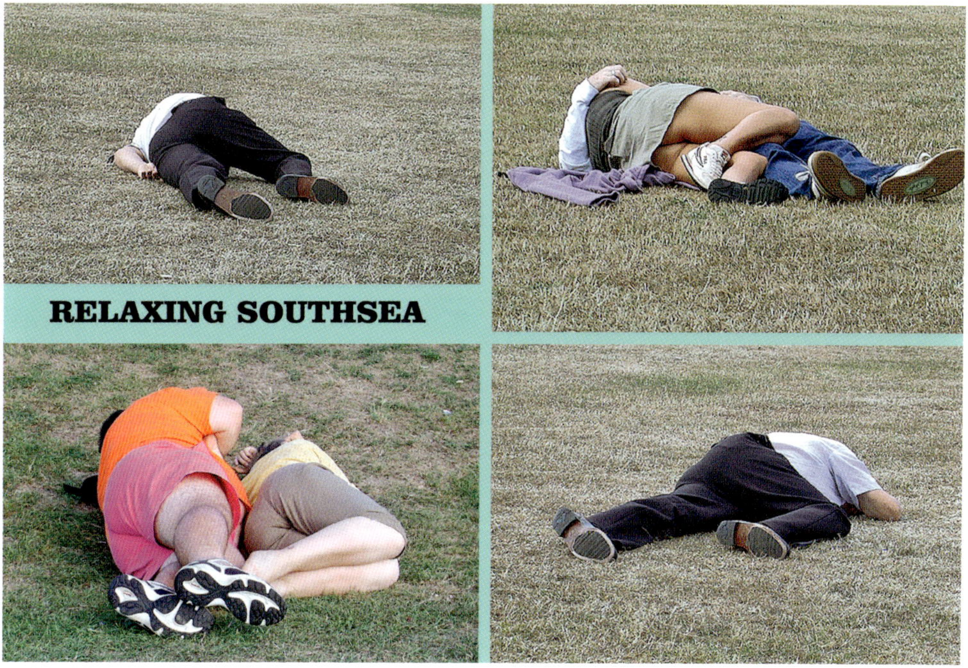

RELAXING SOUTHSEA

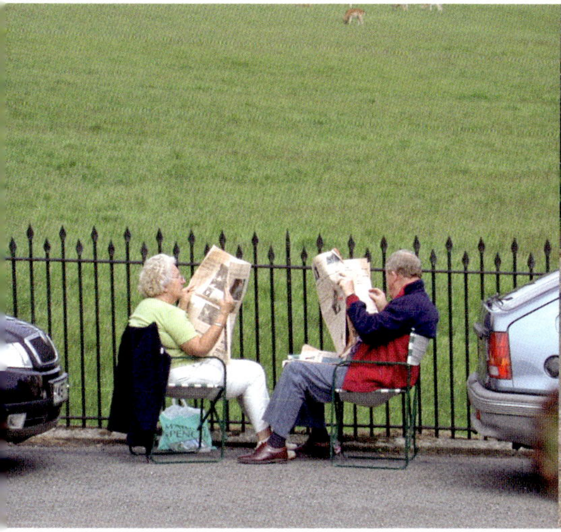

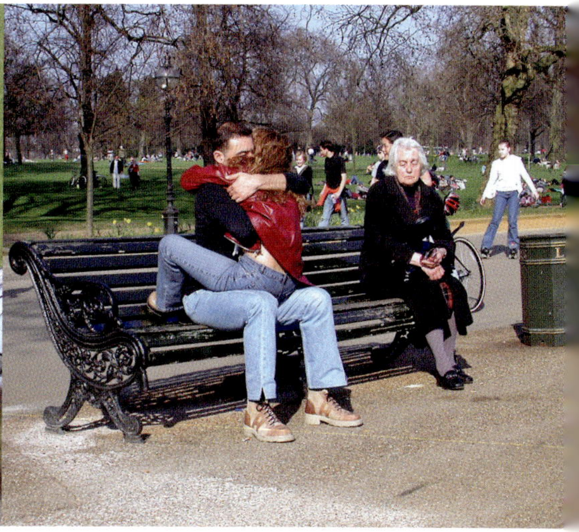

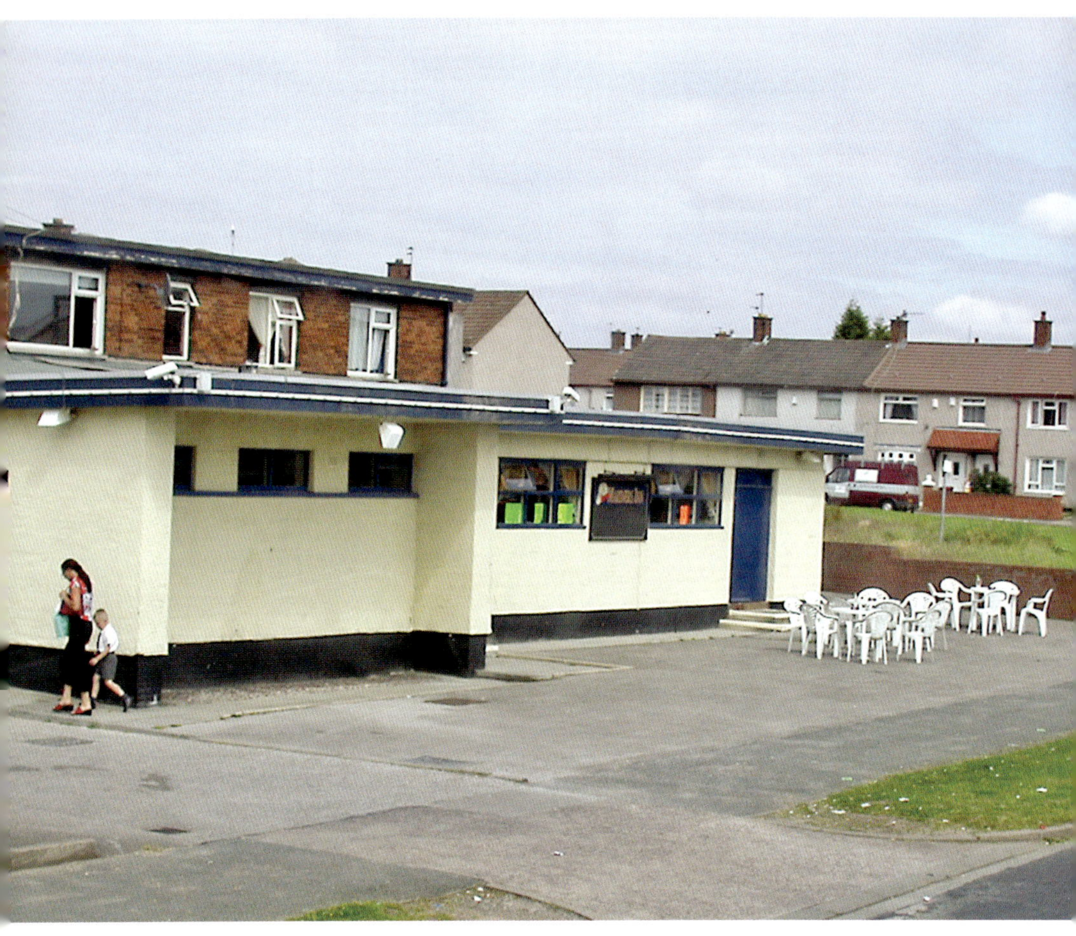

Public houses

Beer and fags, Sky TV, karaoke, exotic dancers, raffles, quizzes, chicken and chips, Phil Collins on the jukebox, patio gardens, fake wood beams, nightmarish carpets, bleak family rooms, that special toilet smell. Marvellous!

What's great about Britain?

Fish and chips and pub gardens, real ale

What's not so great?

Done-up pubs, keg beer, lager louts

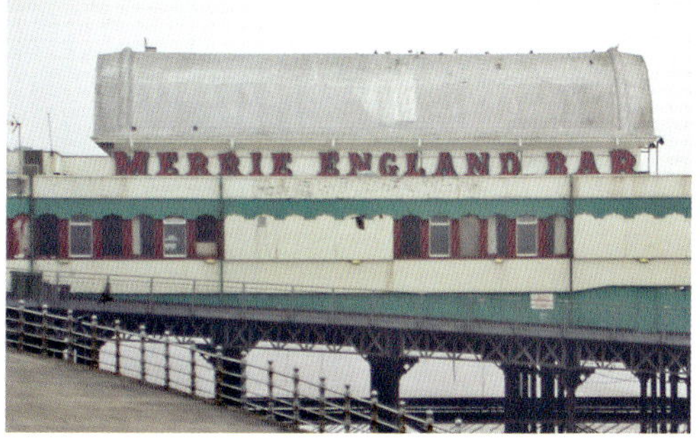

17% of people have won meat in a raffle

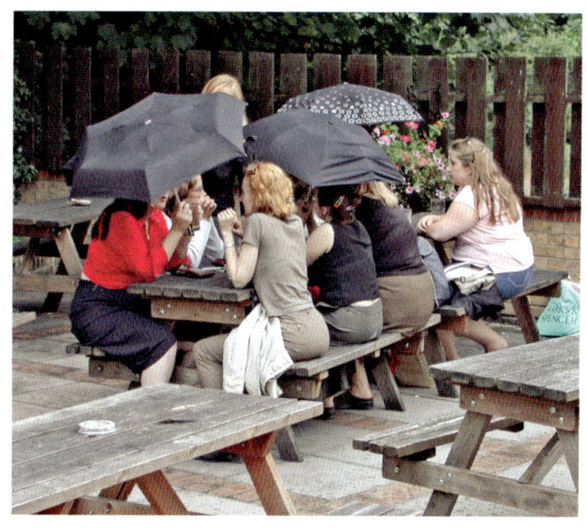

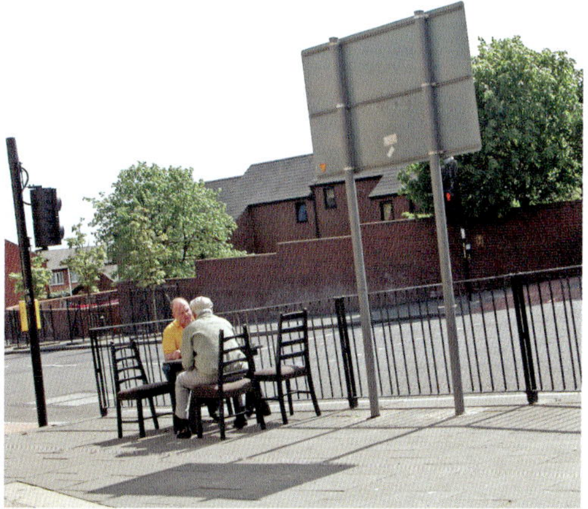

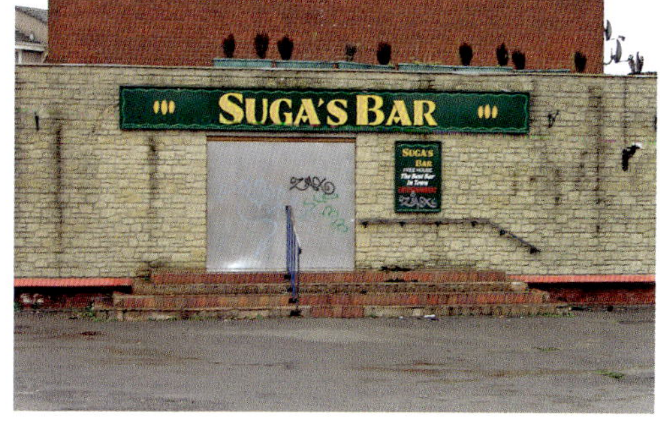

What's your personal motto?

You can't fall off the floor

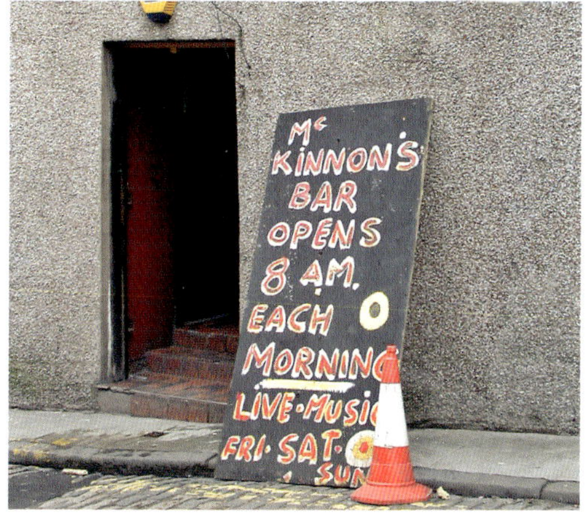

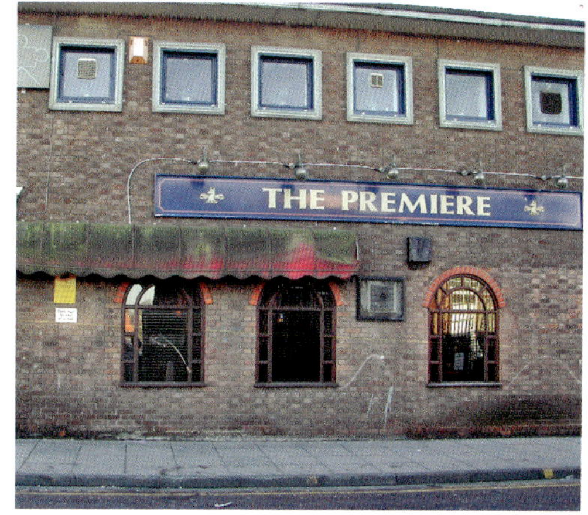

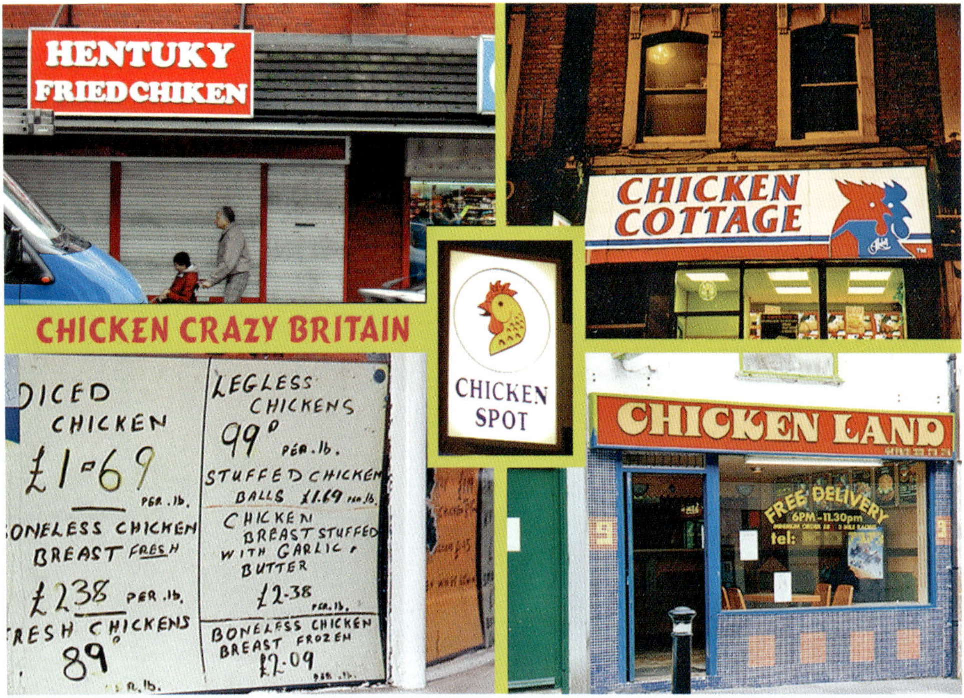

CHICKEN CRAZY BRITAIN

Chicken

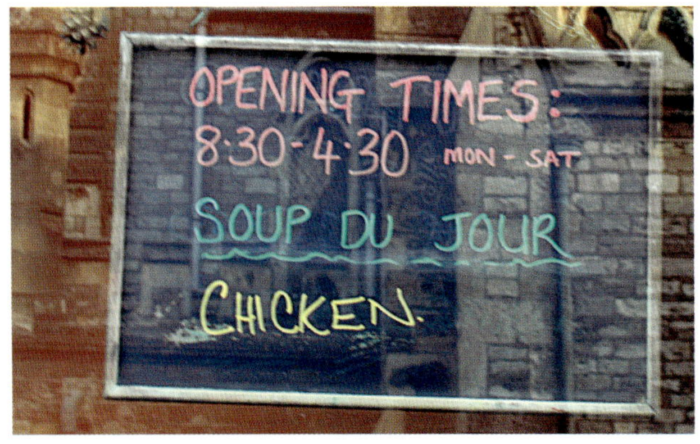

Chicken is storming the nation. Pay attention and during the average British day you will see and hear at least twenty-three references to chicken. A typical example: 'I don't eat meat – just chicken.'

79% of people enjoy chicken

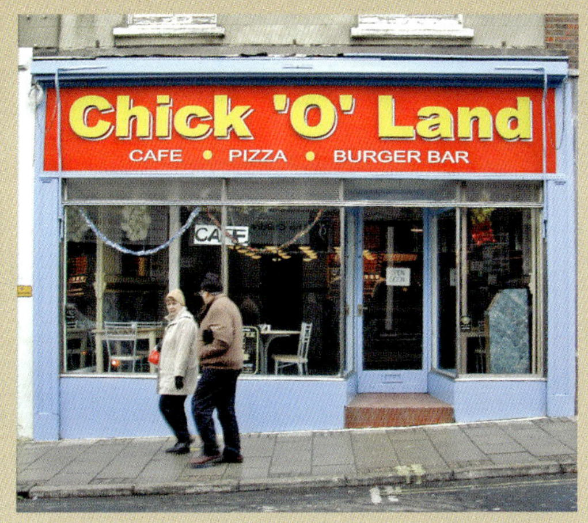
Chick 'O' Land
CAFE • PIZZA • BURGER BAR

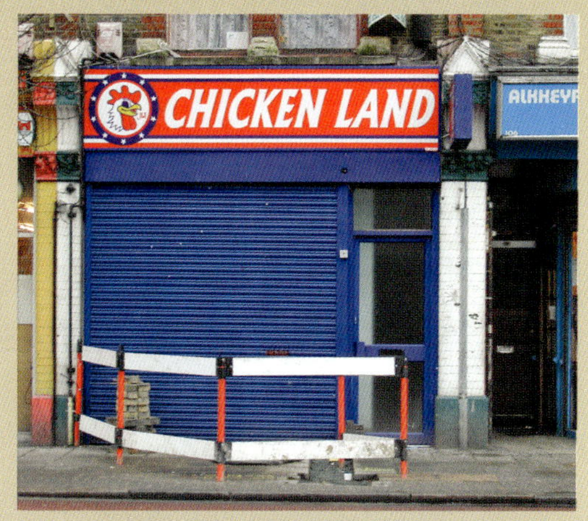
CHICKEN LAND

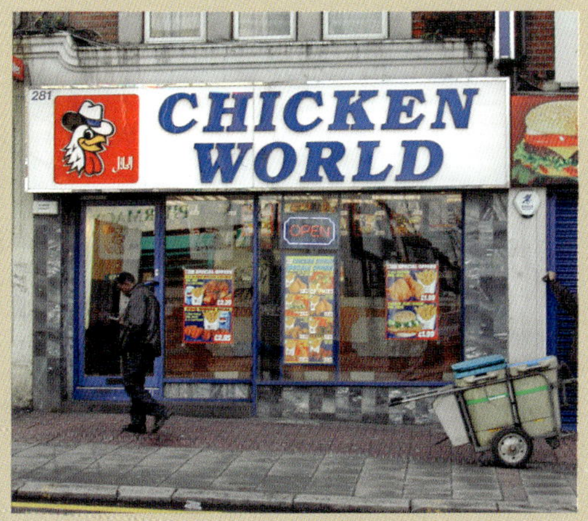
281
CHICKEN
WORLD
OPEN

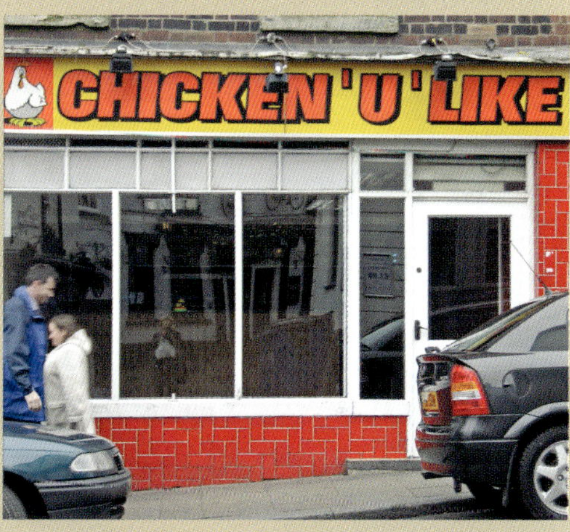
CHICKEN 'U' LIKE

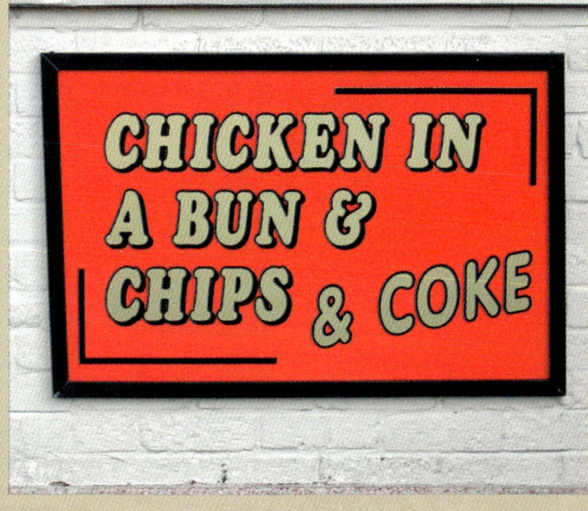
CHICKEN IN
A BUN &
CHIPS & COKE

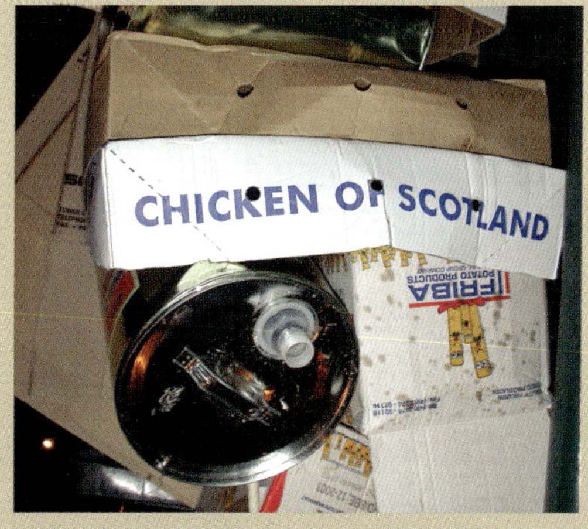
CHICKEN OF SCOTLAND

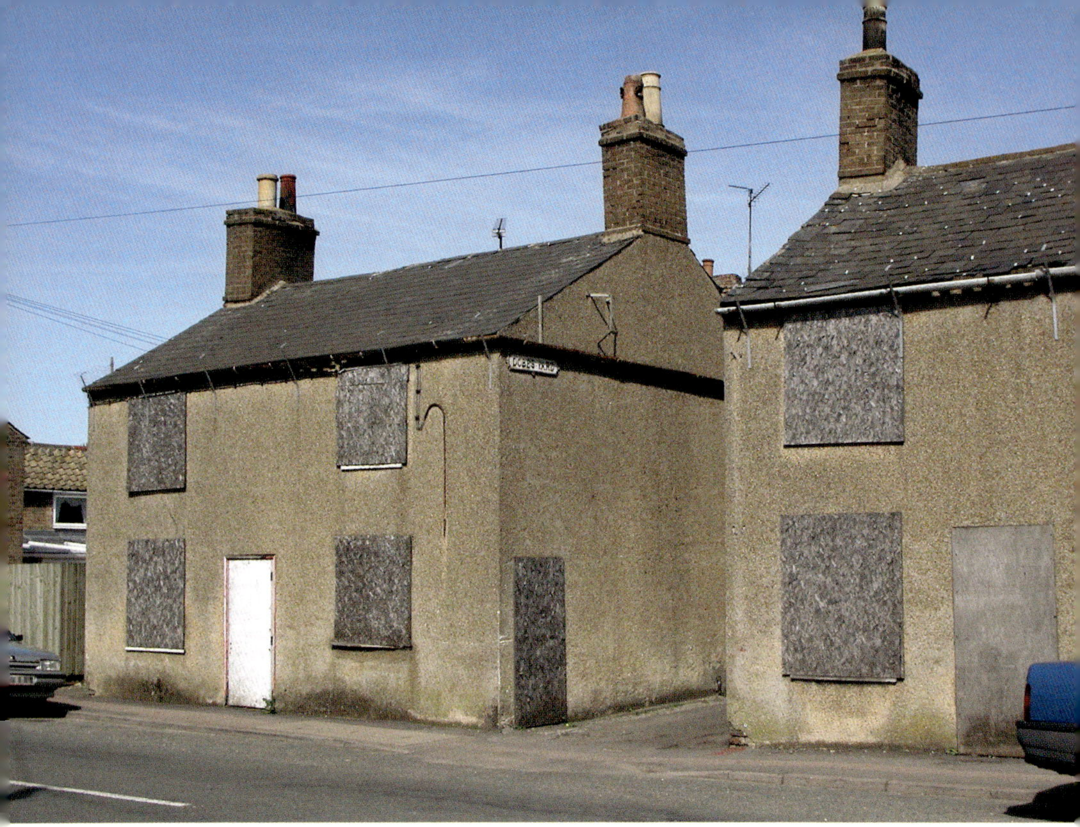

Dereliction

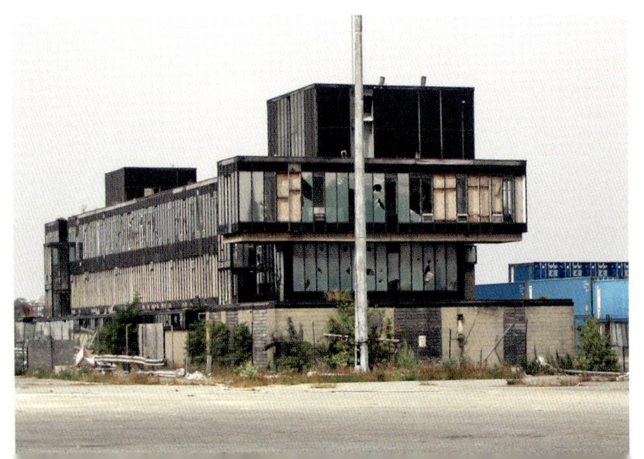

A precursor to regeneration – which may or may not be an improvement.

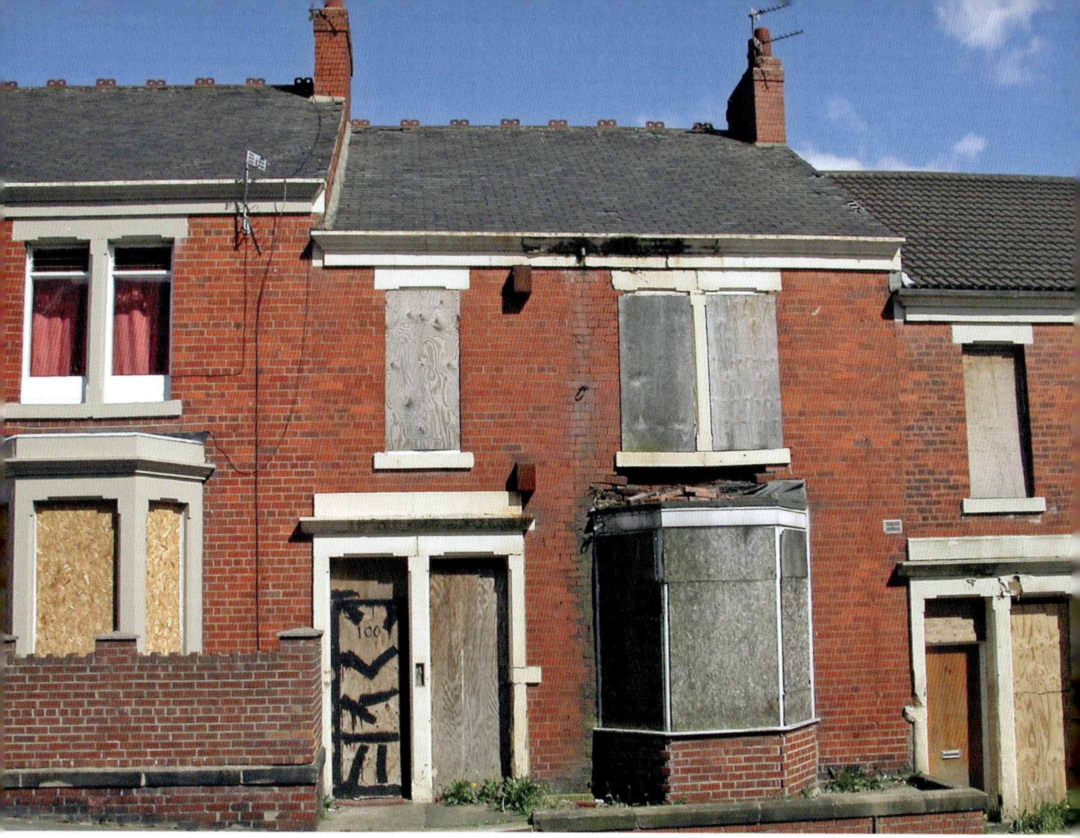

What's not so great about Britain?

Disappearing fields, roadworks and hospital waiting lists

Let's be honest – it's slipping a bit

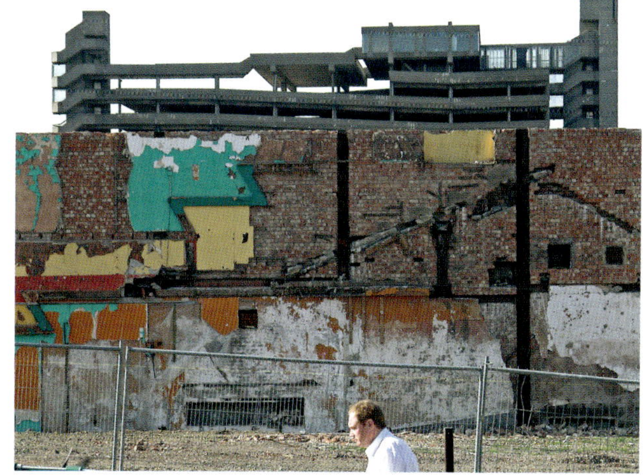

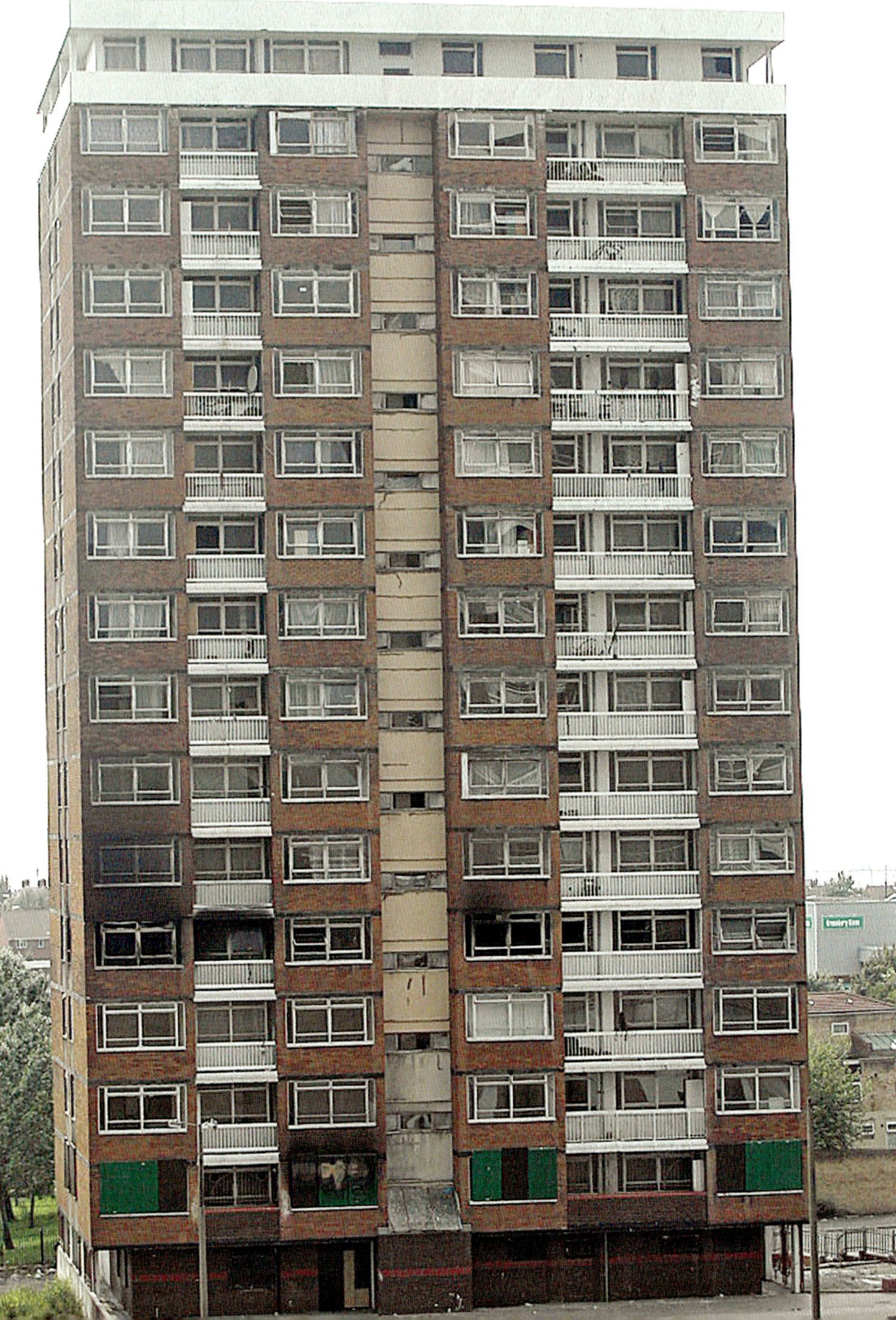

Tower block and ex-tower block in Liverpool – an acre of mud marks the half-way point between dereliction and regeneration. And it looks like poor Glenda needs a new theatre.

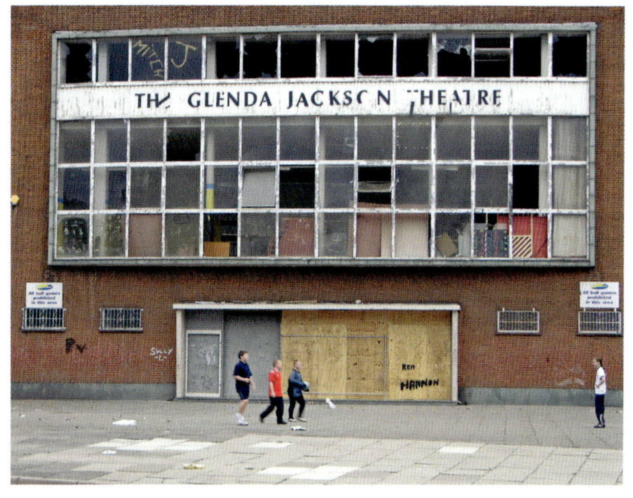

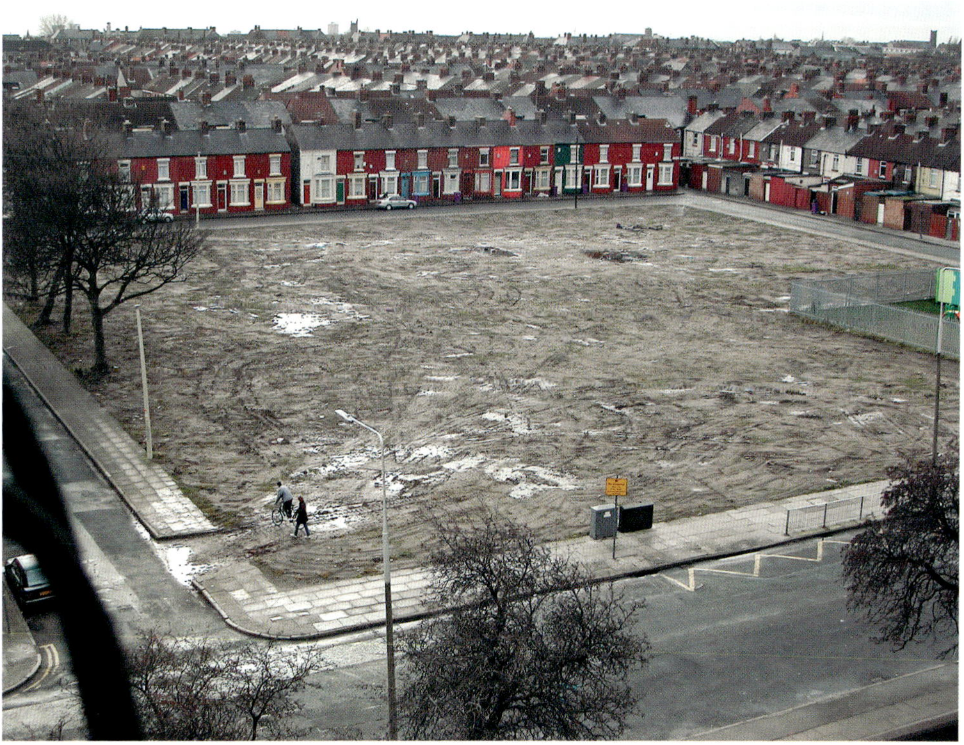

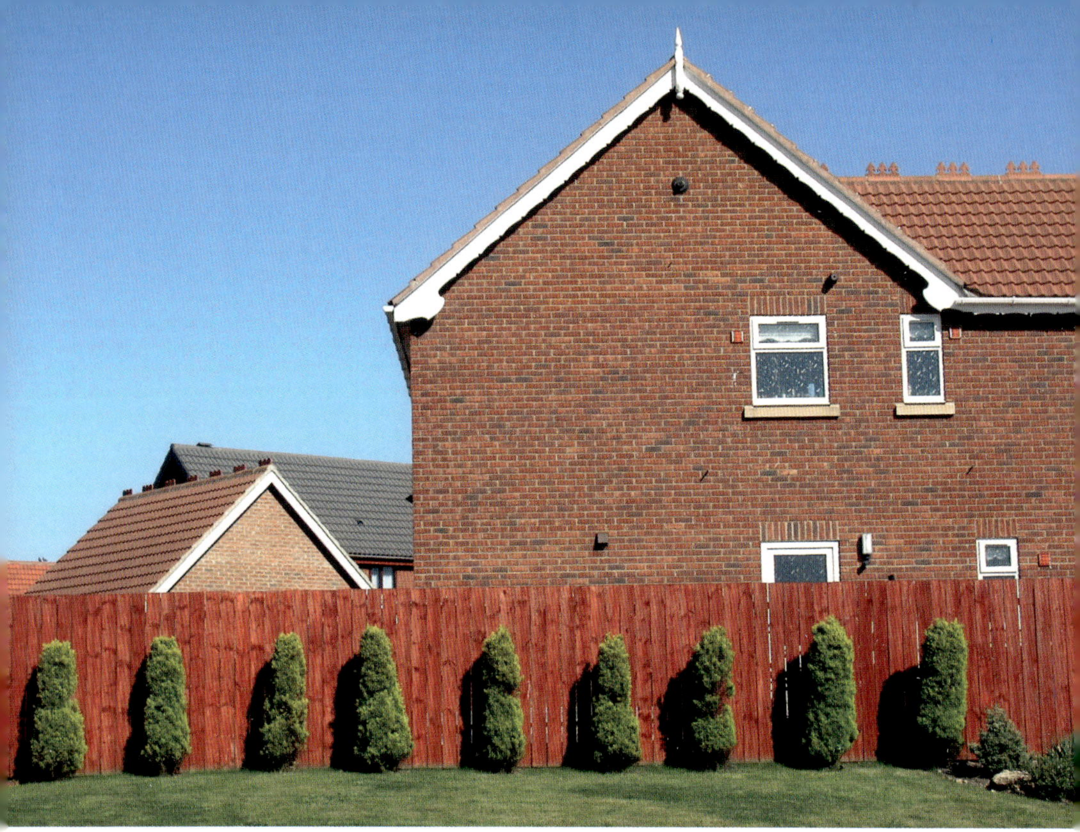

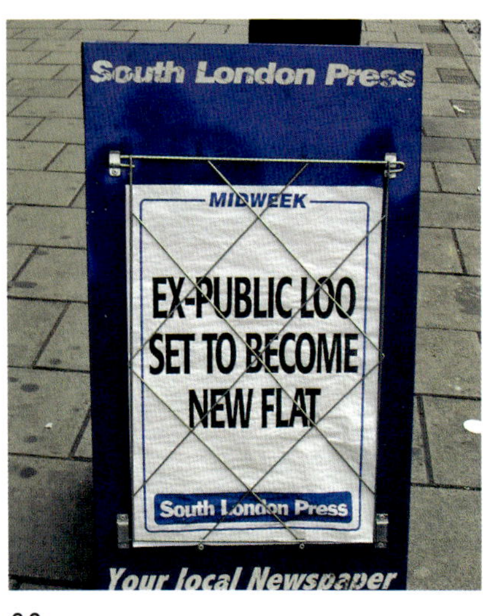

Regeneration

Follows dereliction – which may or may not be an improvement.

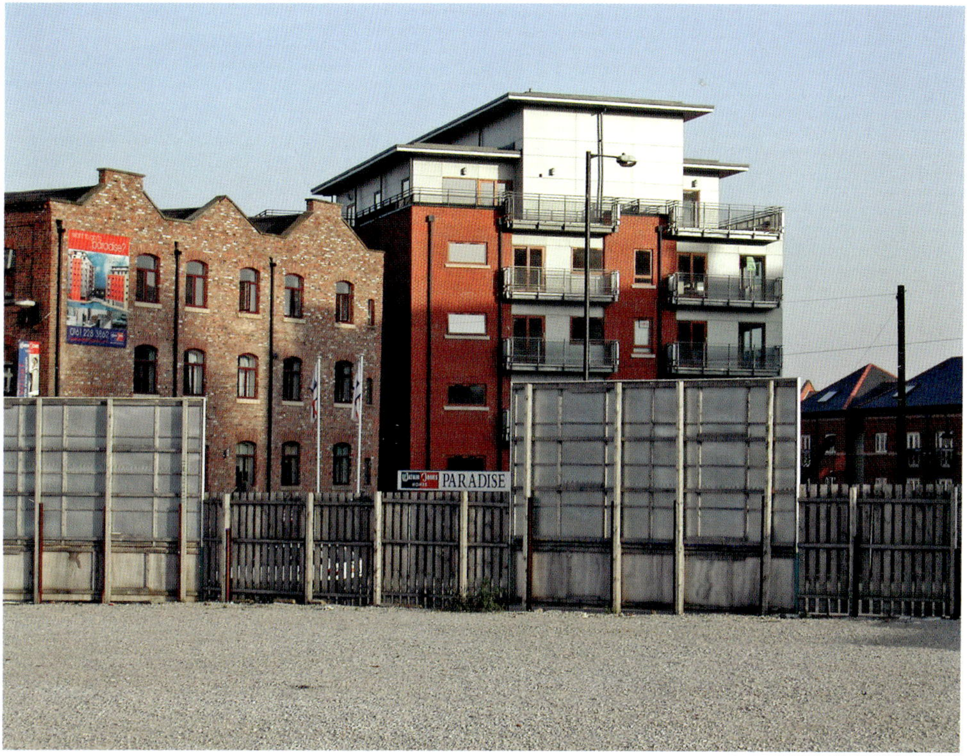

Last week a wasteland, next week a luxury development for those seeking prestigious designer executive lifestyles.

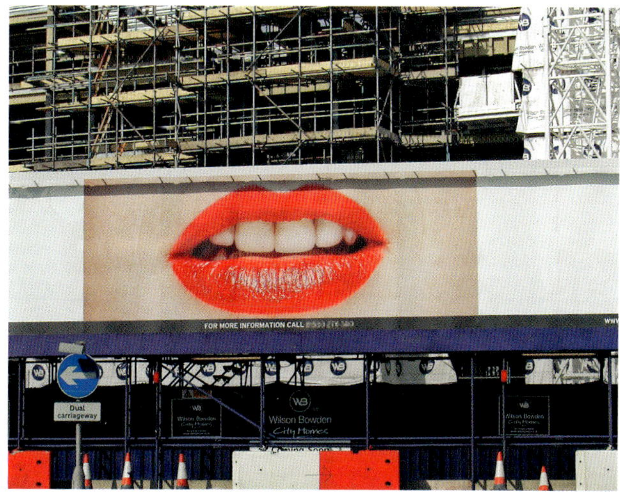

What's your personal motto?

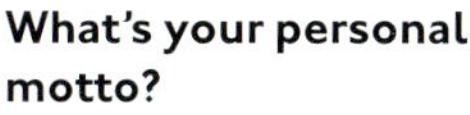

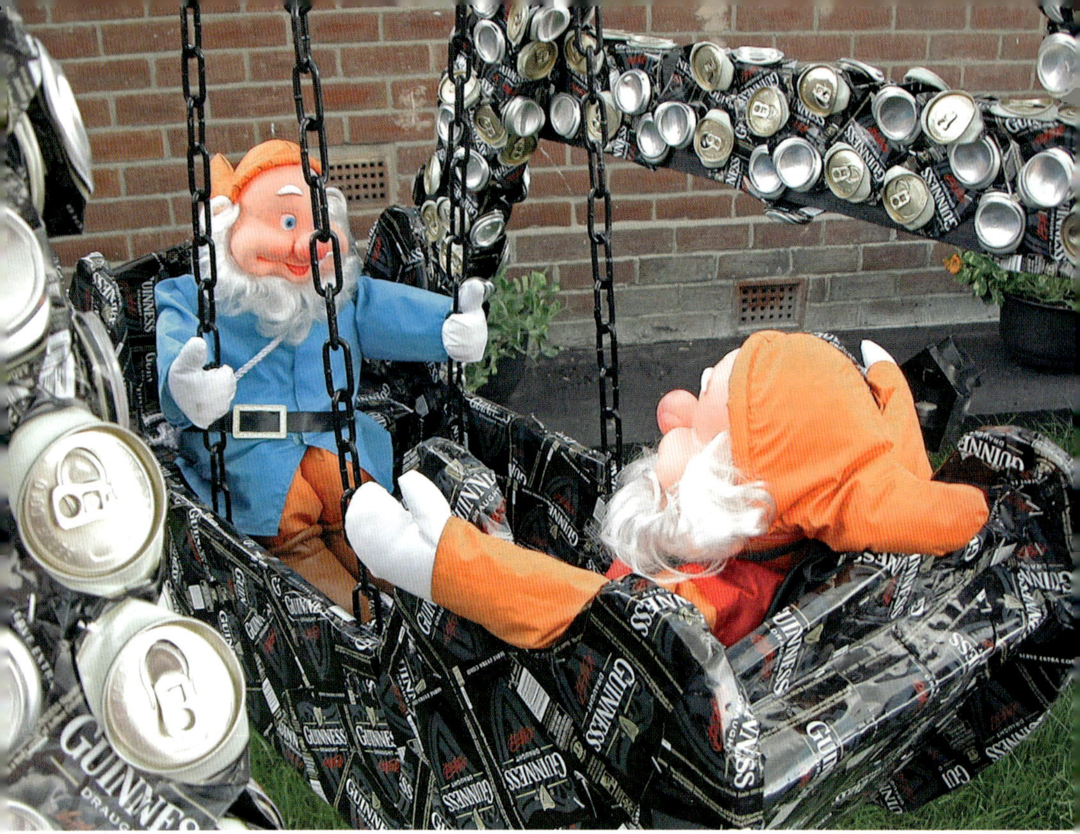

Ornamentation

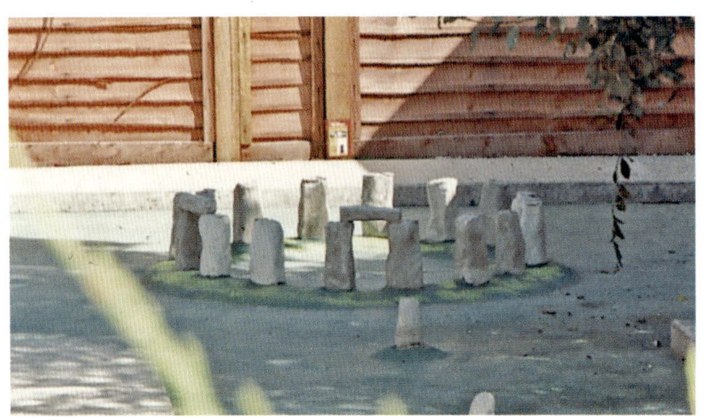

Unleash your creative energies when choosing your garden ornament. A majestic lion or bawdy gnome could be just the thing to perk up your patio. And it's funny how Stonehenge always looks smaller than you expect.

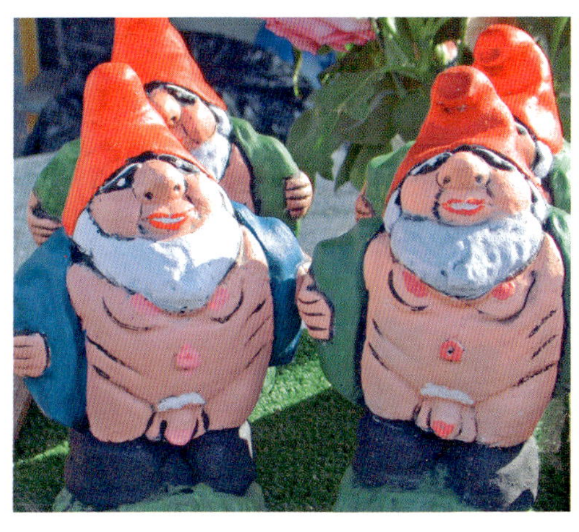

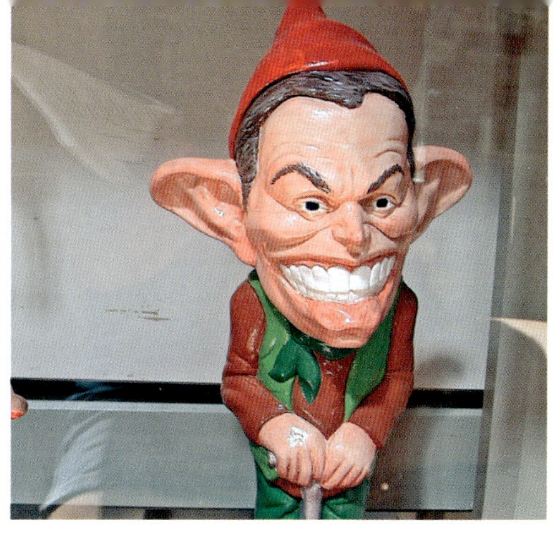

I heard about a Battenburg cake Stonehenge held together with cocktail sticks

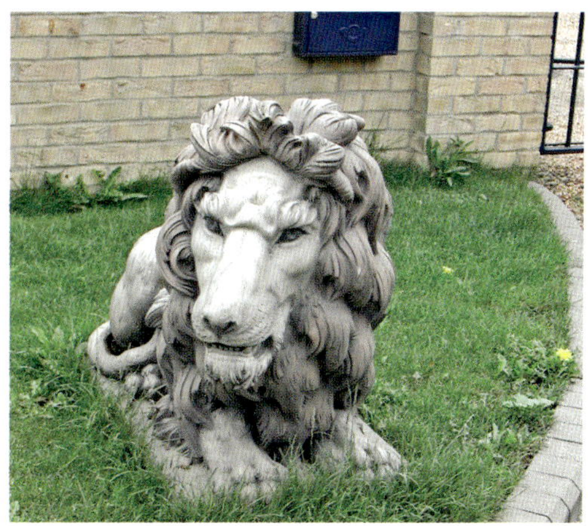

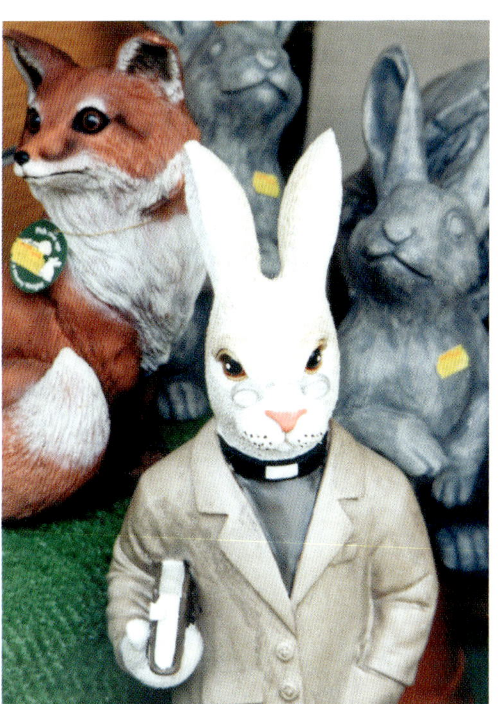

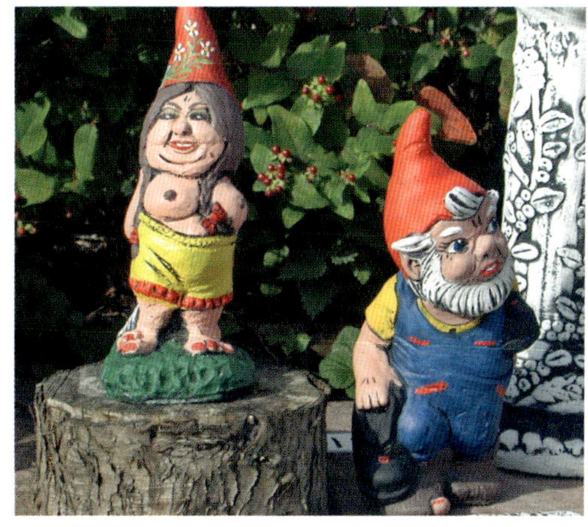

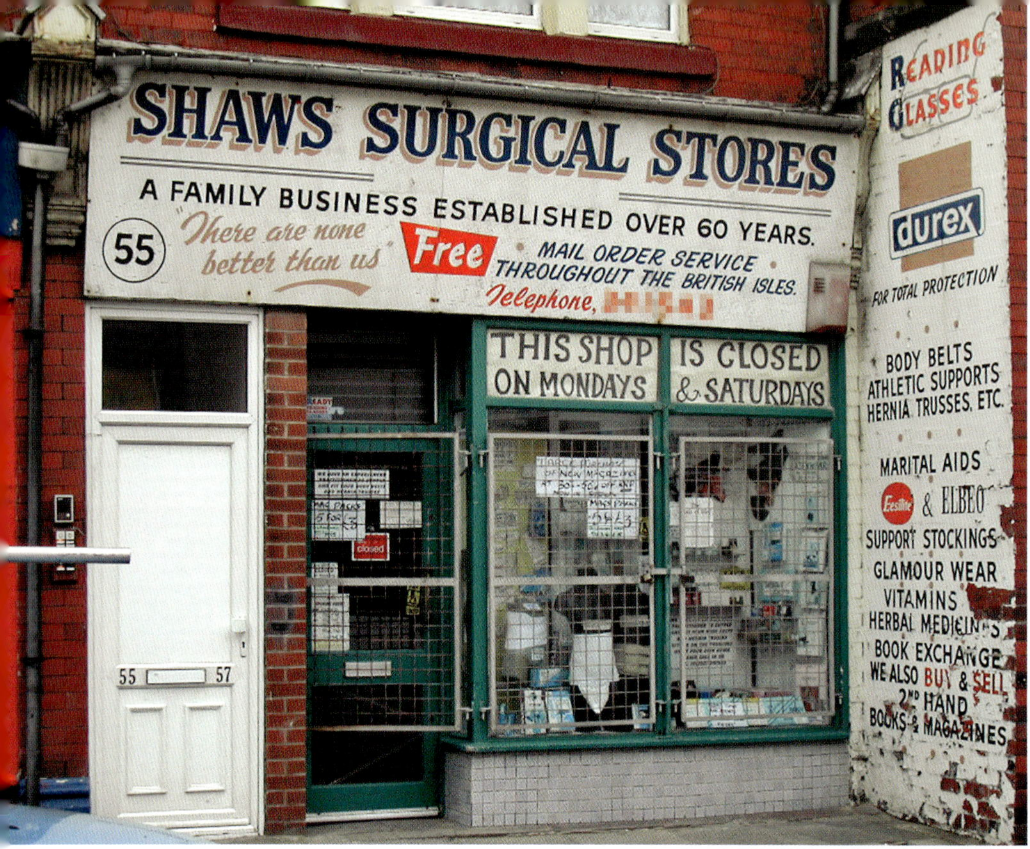

Shops

Shopping is our favourite pastime and there's nothing we like more than a bargain. Buy one, get one free!

18% of people avoid their neighbours while out shopping

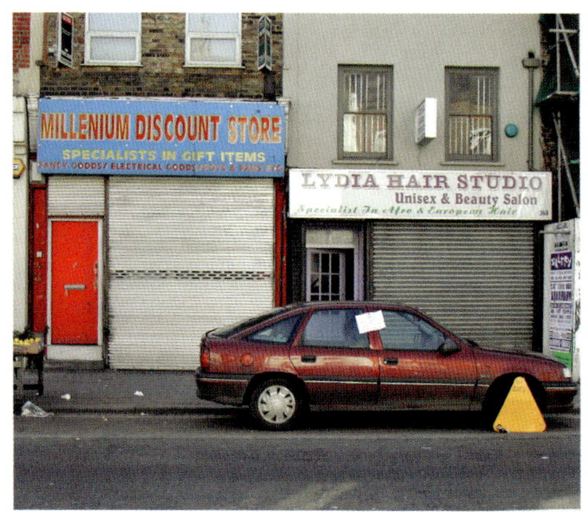

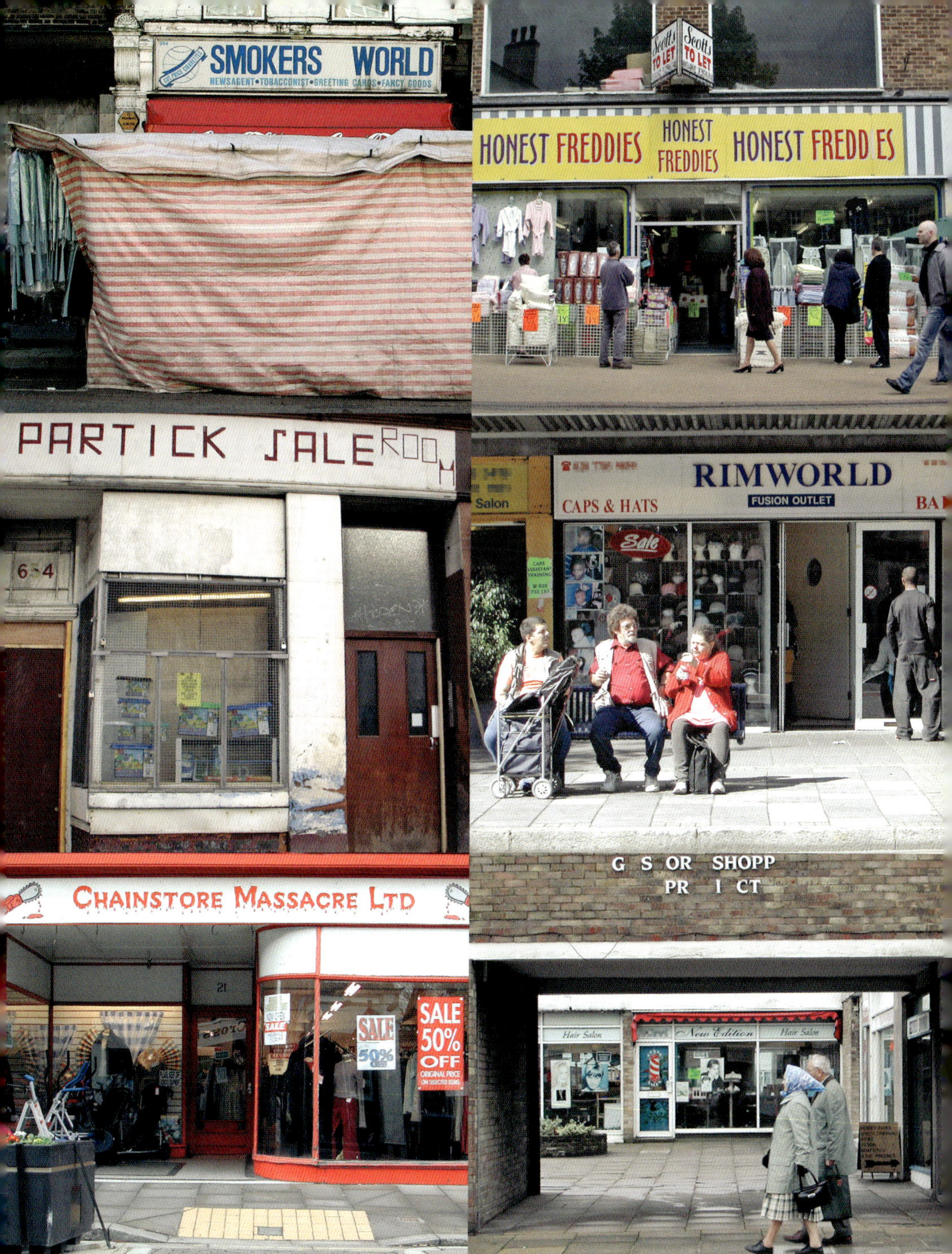

SMOKERS WORLD
NEWSAGENT • TOBACCONIST • GREETING CARDS • FANCY GOODS
HONEST FREDDIES
HONEST FREDDIES
HONEST FREDD ES
PARTICK SALEROOM
RIMWORLD
FUSION OUTLET
CAPS & HATS
Sale
CHAINSTORE MASSACRE LTD
SALE
50%
SALE 50% OFF
ORIGINAL PRICE ON SELECTED ITEMS
G S OR SHOPP
PR I CT
Hair Salon
New Edition
Hair Salon

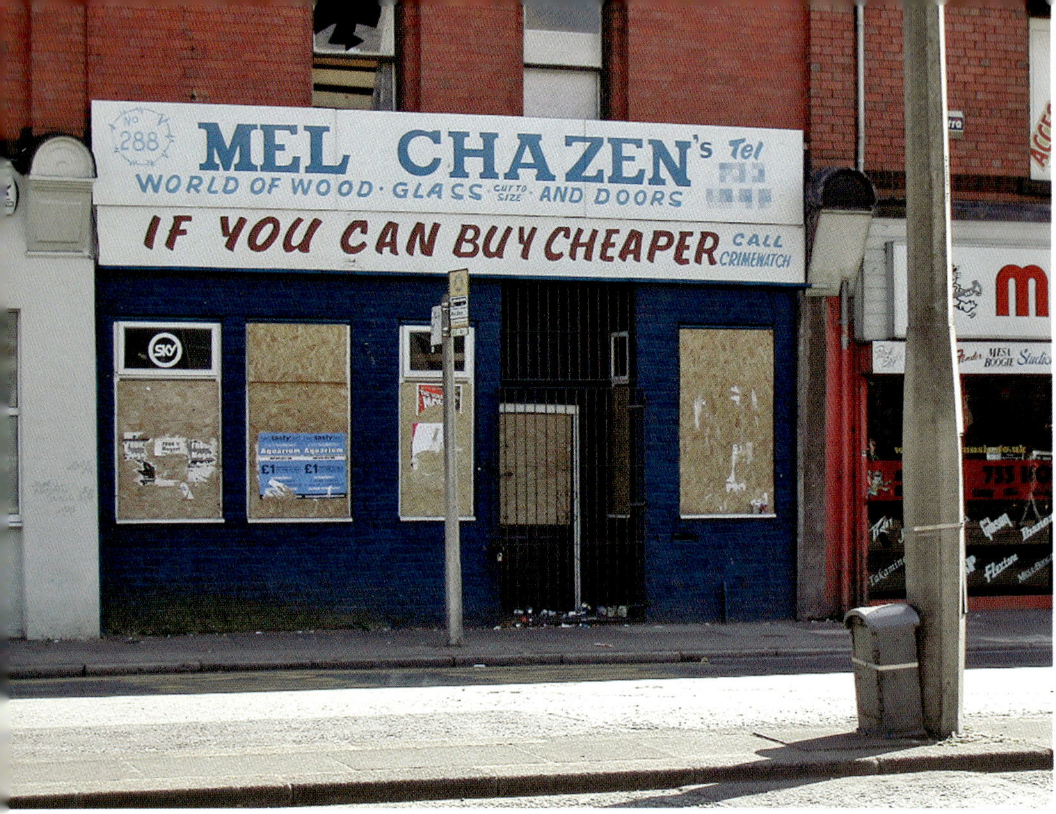

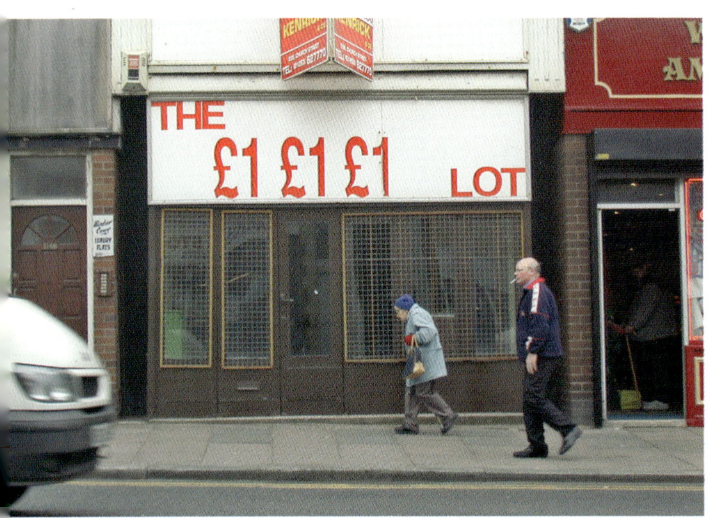

28% of people buy things they don't like because they're cheap

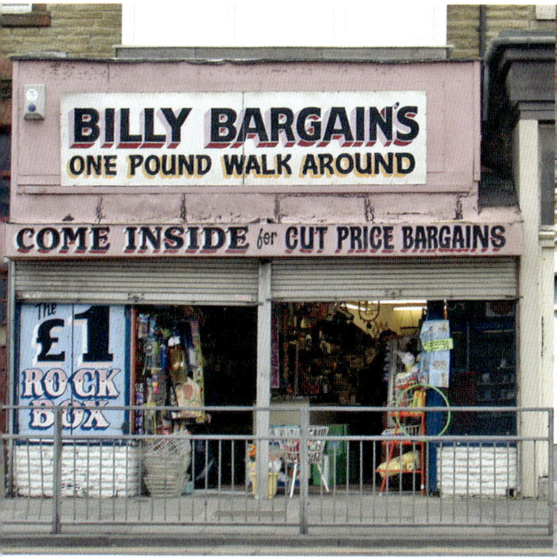

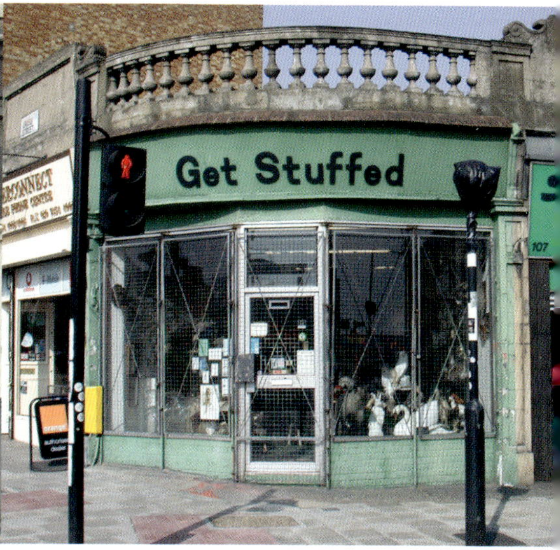

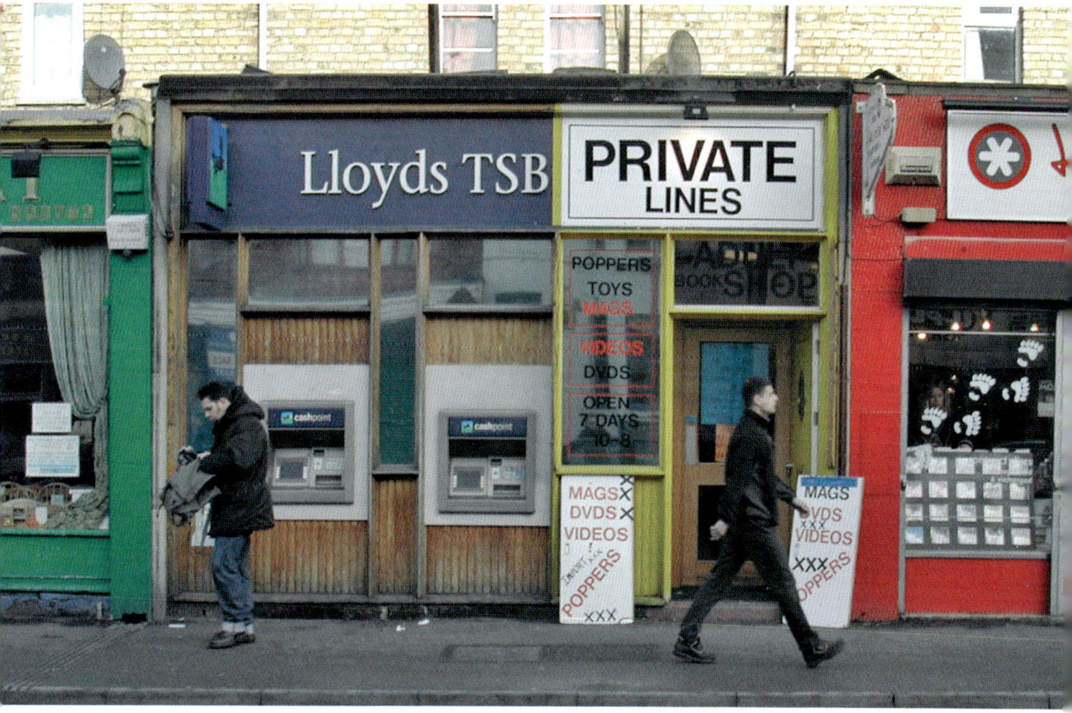

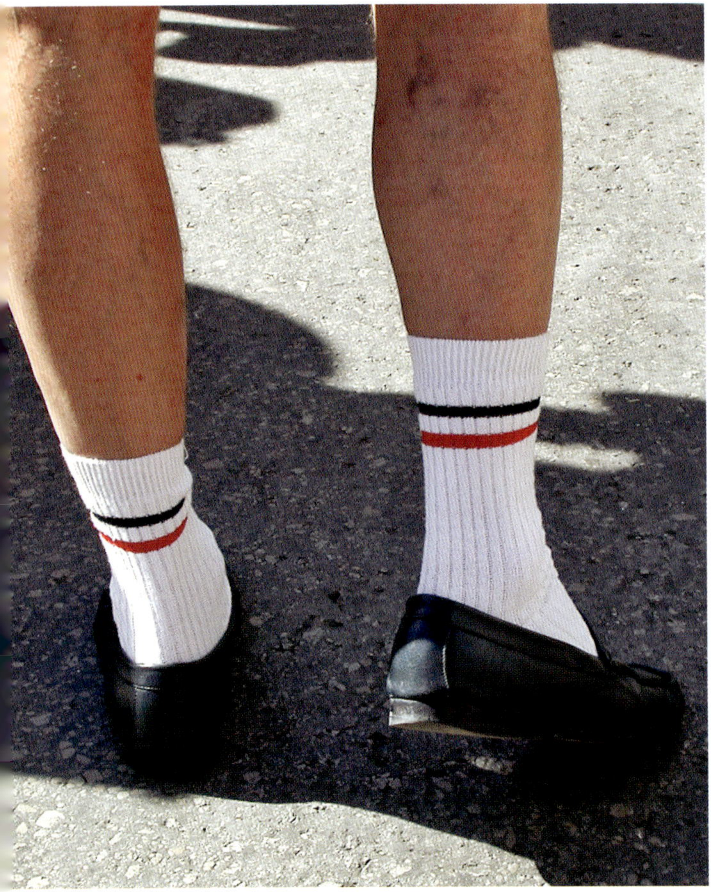

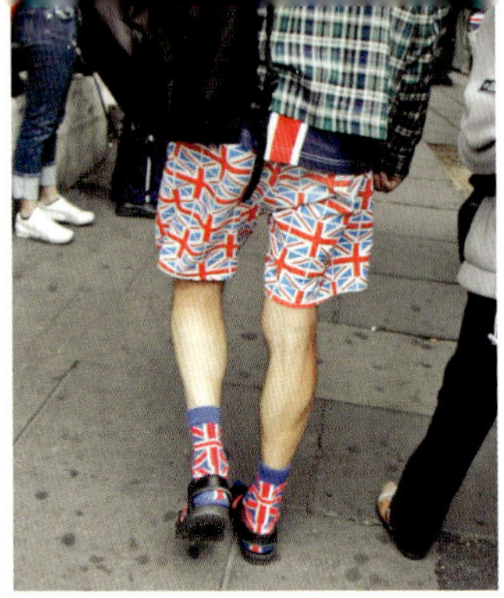

What do the people of Britain wear in summer?

Not enough or anything that is too small for them

There's a man in Huddersfield who has a hat made entirely out of old chewing gum

Fashion

The British like to express their individuality in their choice of clothes. Attention to detail can make all the difference to an outfit.

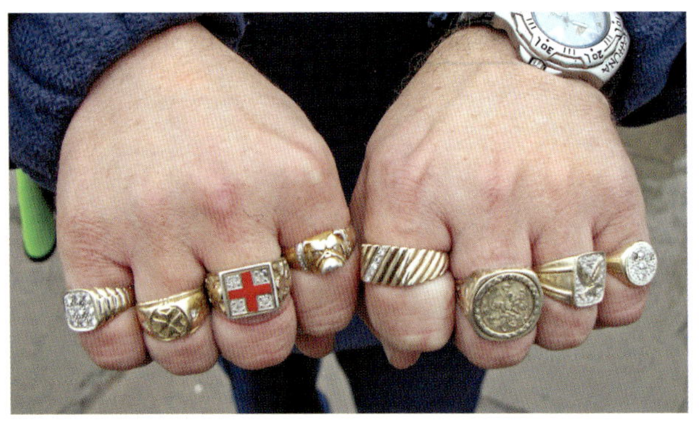

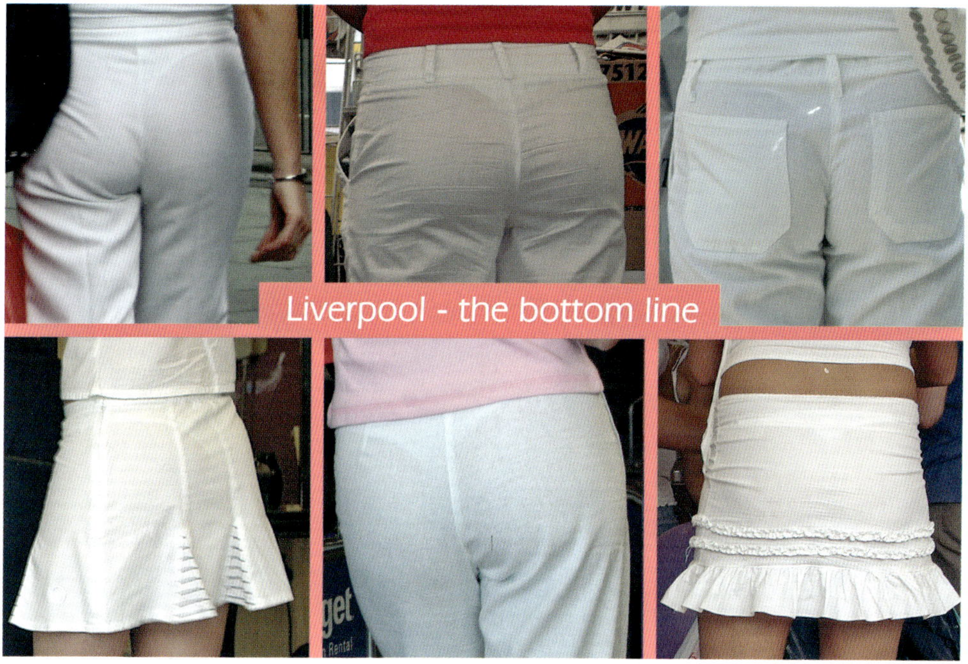

Liverpool - the bottom line

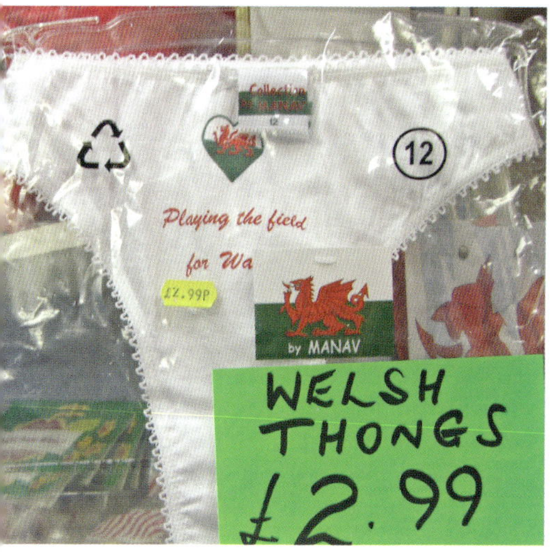

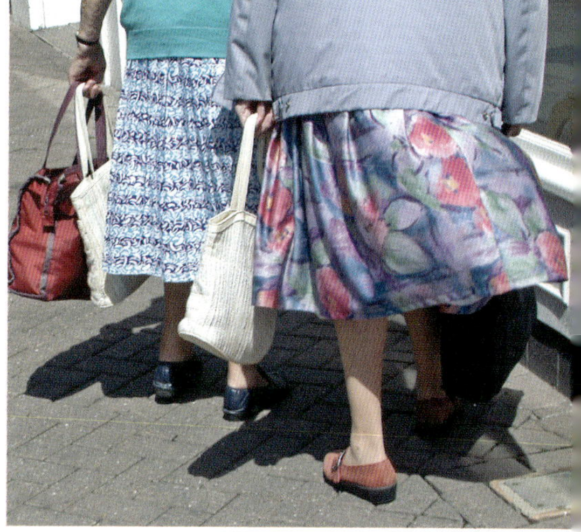

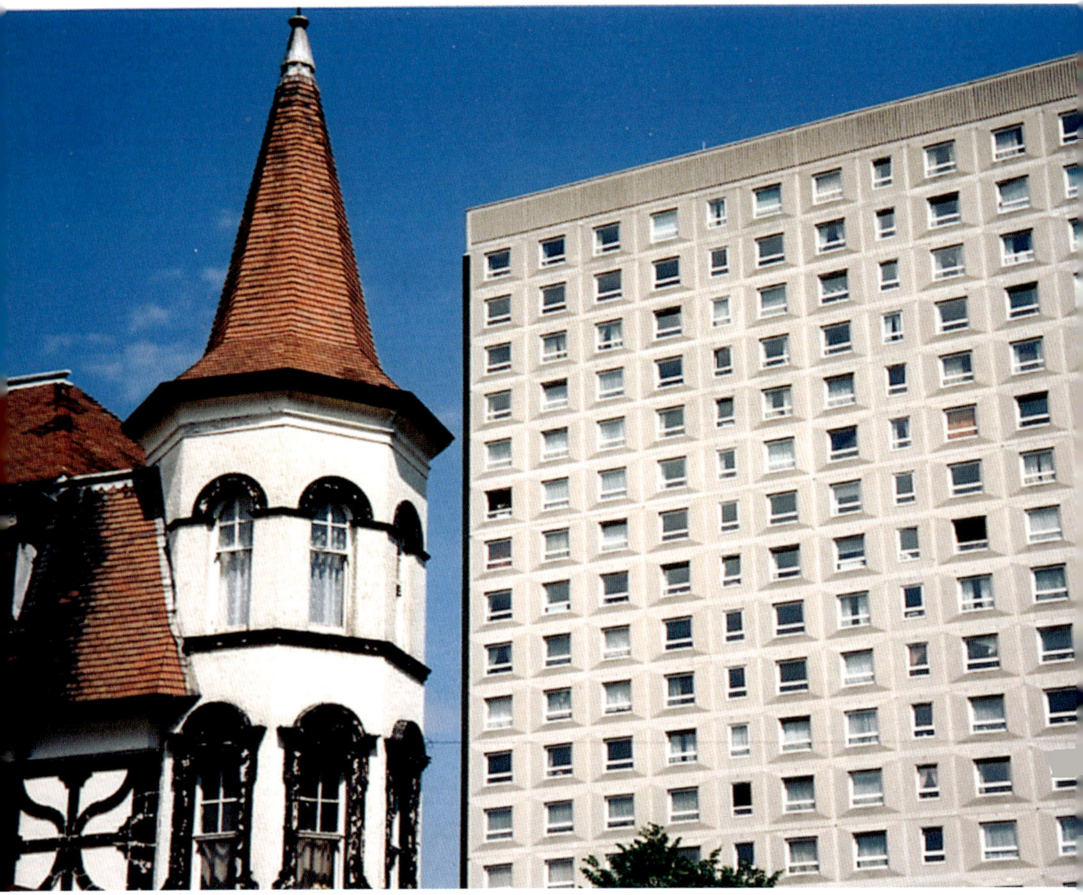

Side by side

Curious juxtapositions – happy accident or bad design? Britain is full of houses neighbouring car parks, pubs tucked under office blocks and fishermens' huts opposite steelworks.

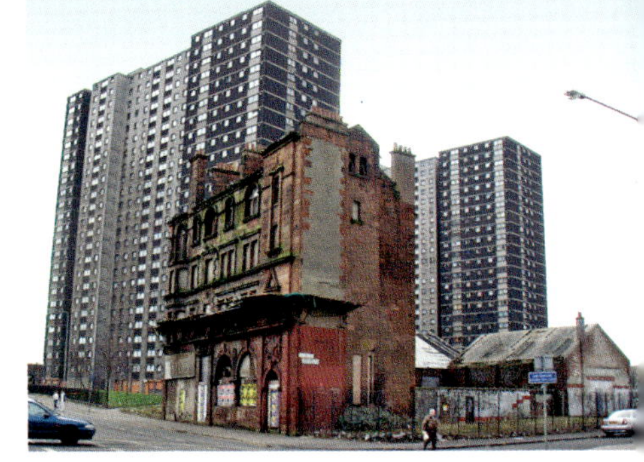

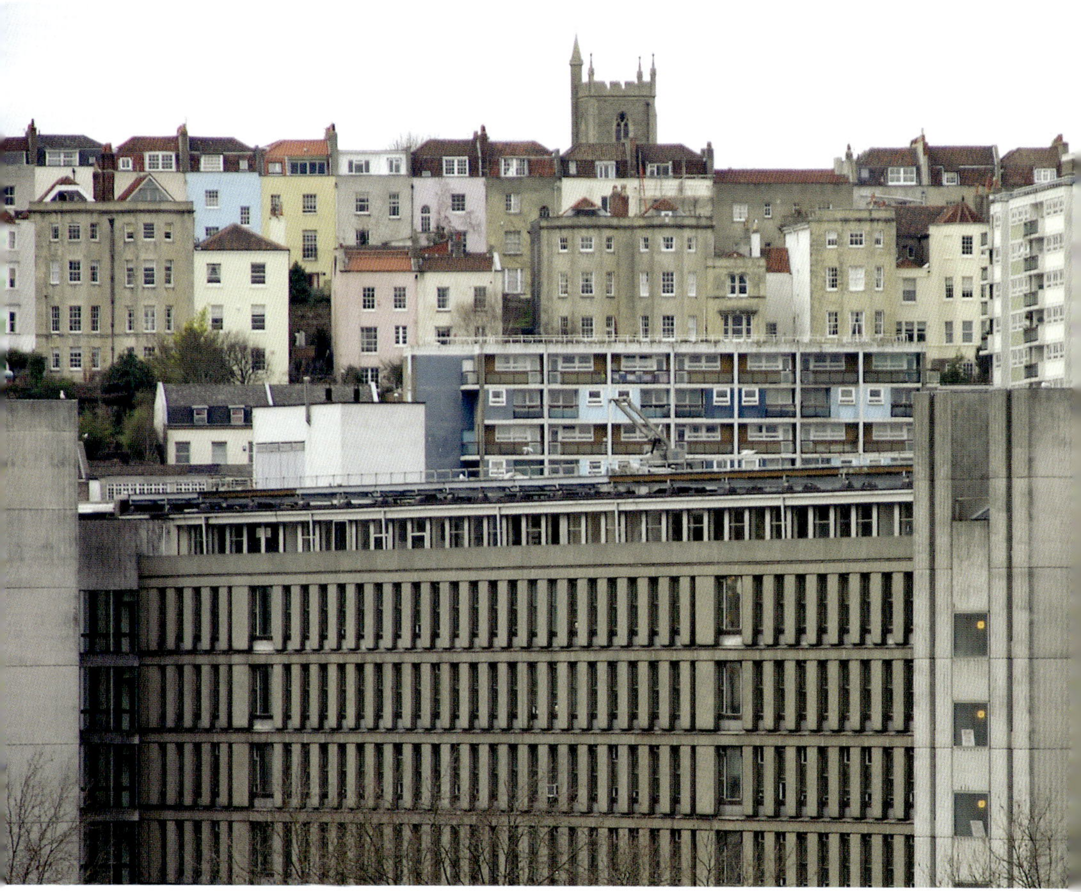

What's great about Britain?

The mixture

What's not so great?

Living in the past

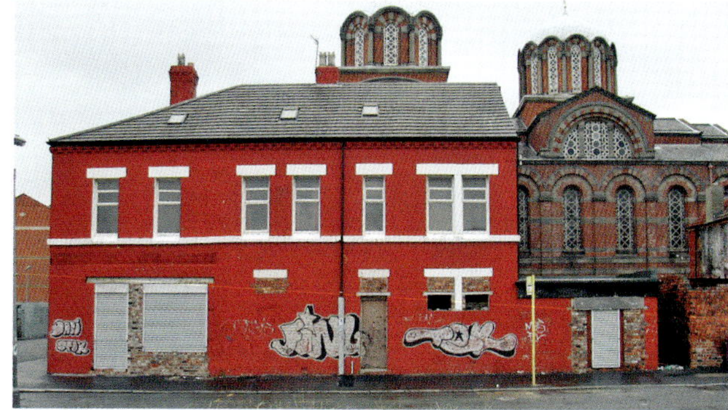

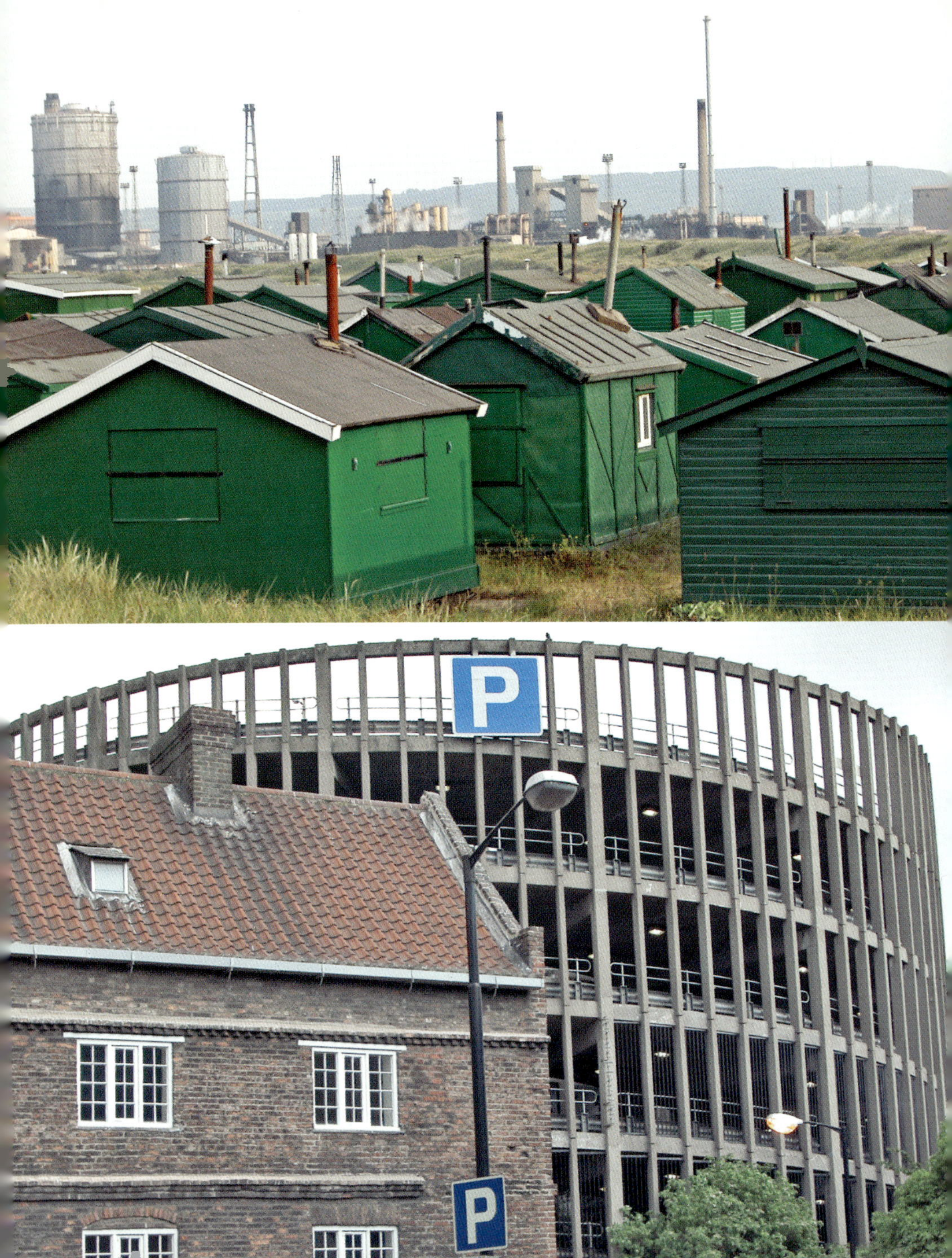
P
P

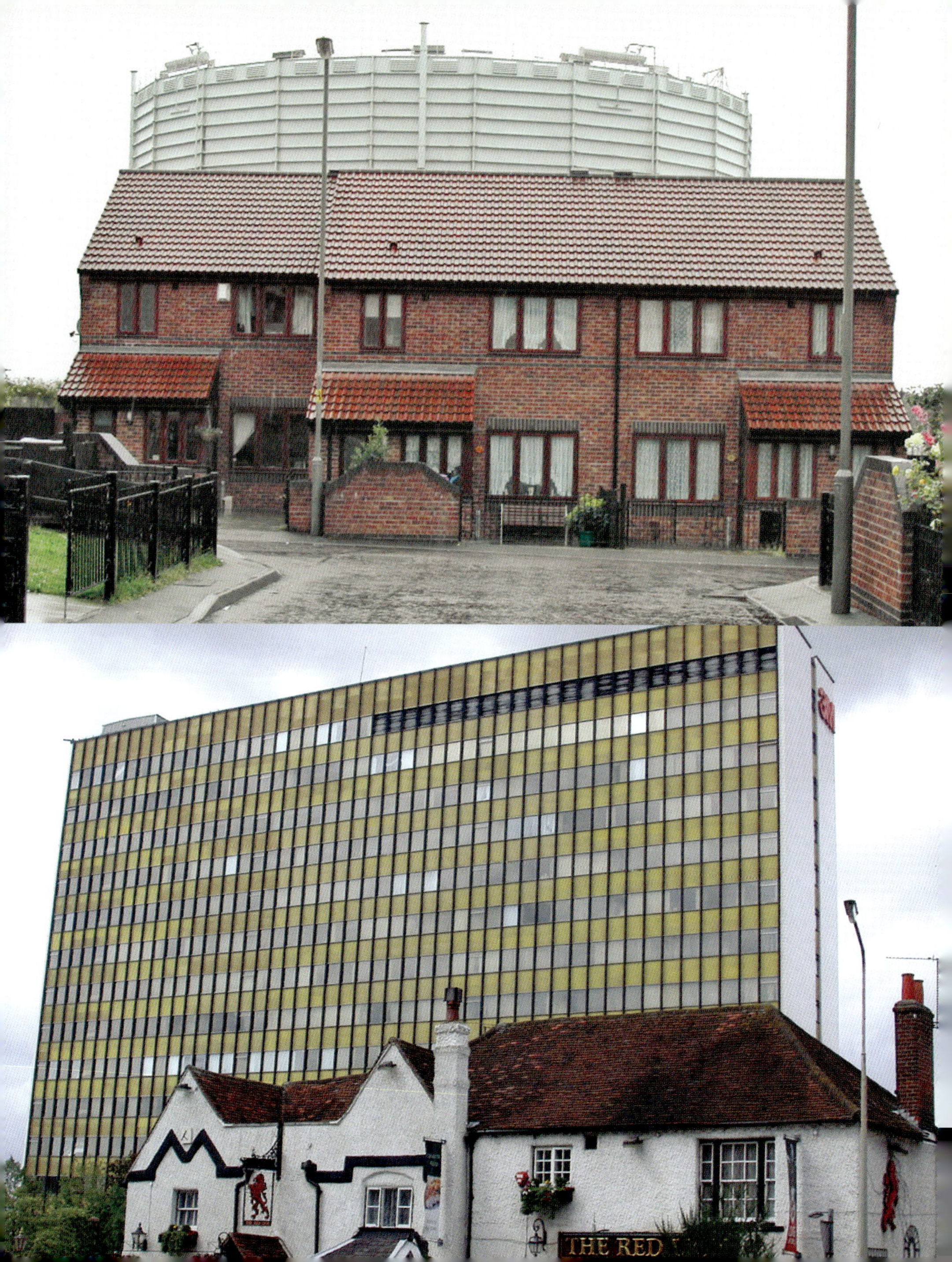
THE RED

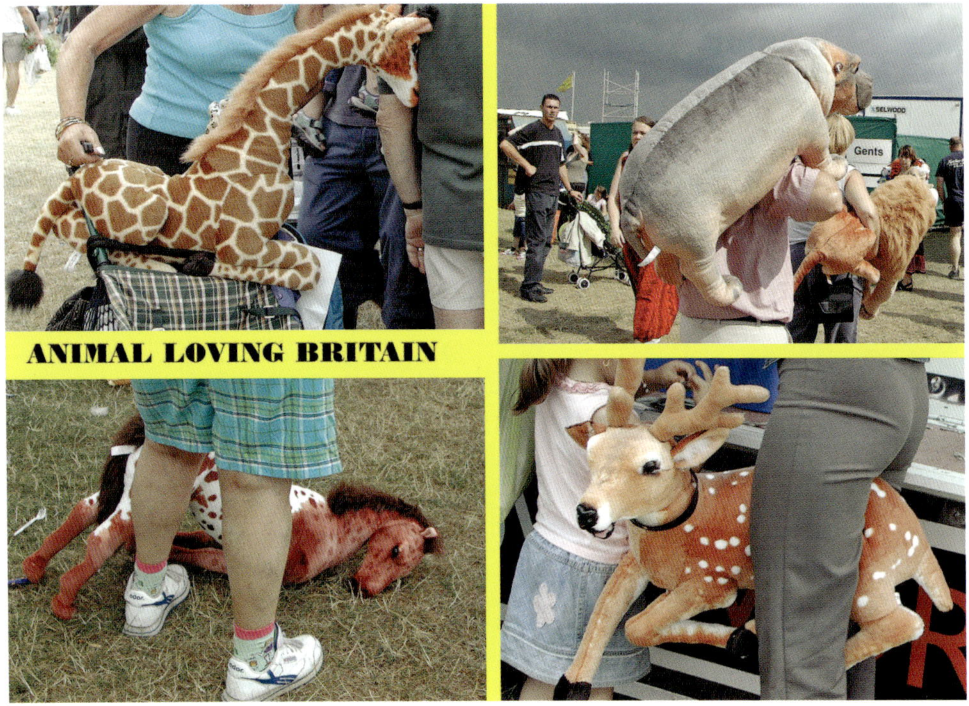

ANIMAL LOVING BRITAIN

Showgrounds

Fun for all the family! Where else can you meet goat lovers, buy a mop, smash a plate, acquire a stuffed hippo, win a coconut, watch a man demonstrate a peeling-slicing thing, purchase fudge, have a beer and use a Portaloo? At one of Britain's many local shows, of course.

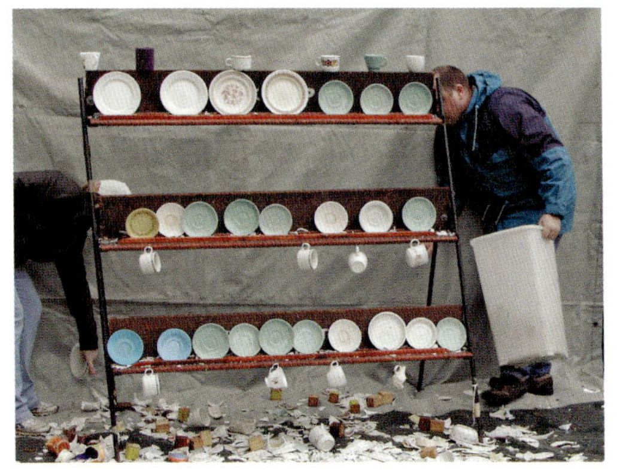

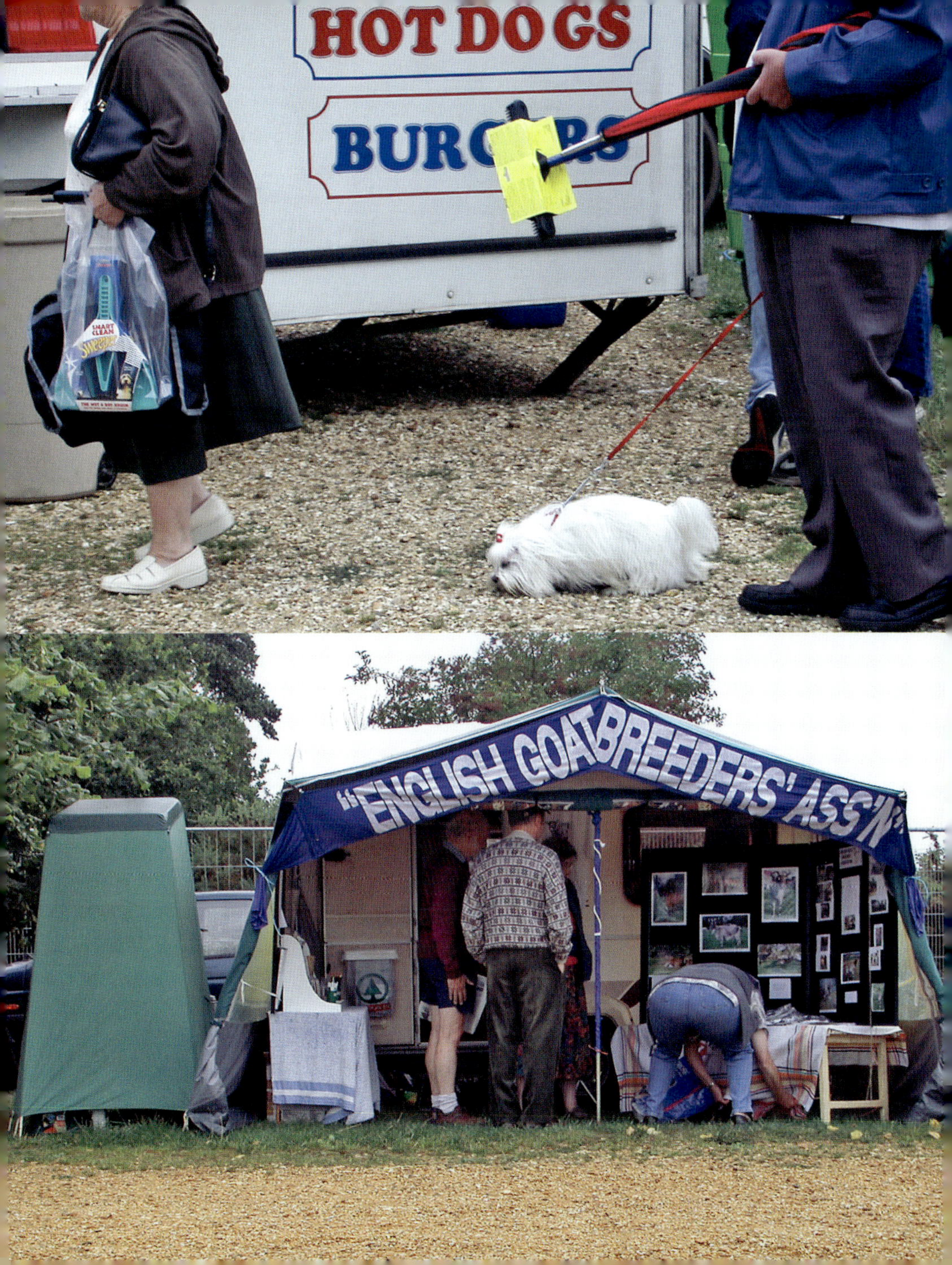
HOT DOGS
"ENGLISH GOATBREEDERS' ASS'N"

Signs

Got something to say? Make a sign. Got something to sell? Make a sign. Got a gripe? Make a sign. Want to know where you are? Look for a sign. Got something to show off about? Make a sign. Has somebody upset you? Make a sign!

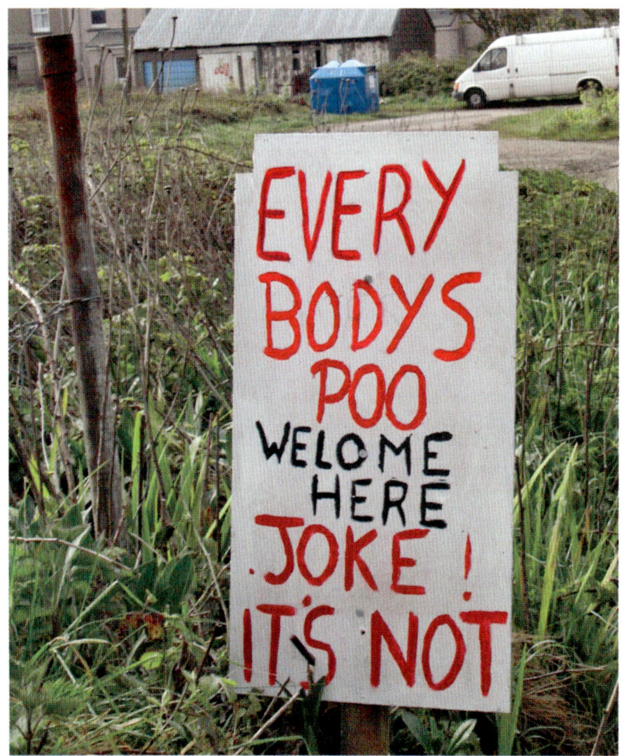

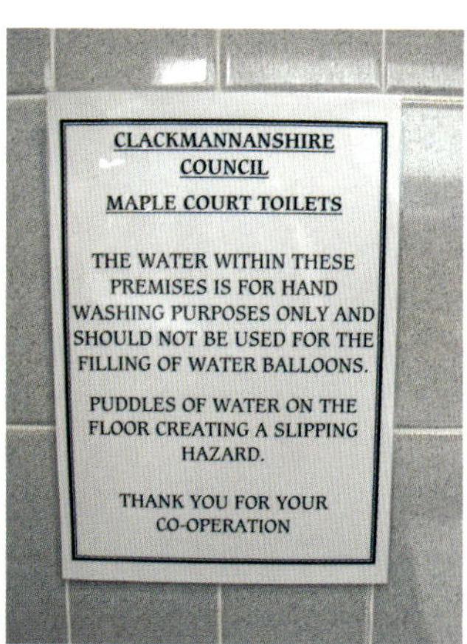

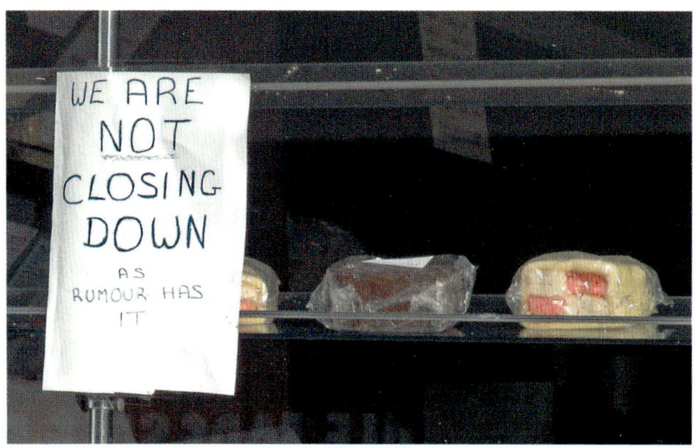

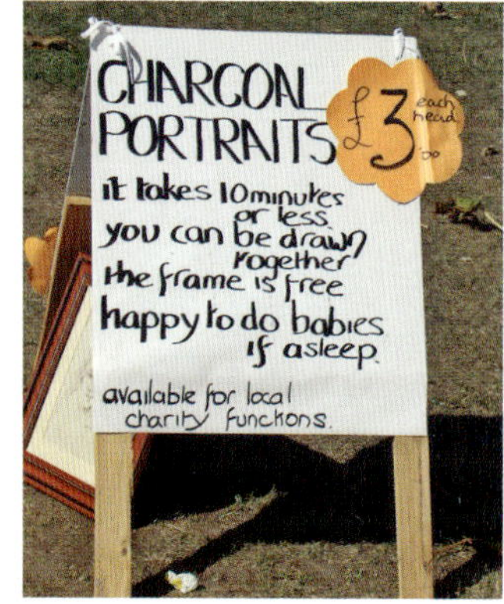

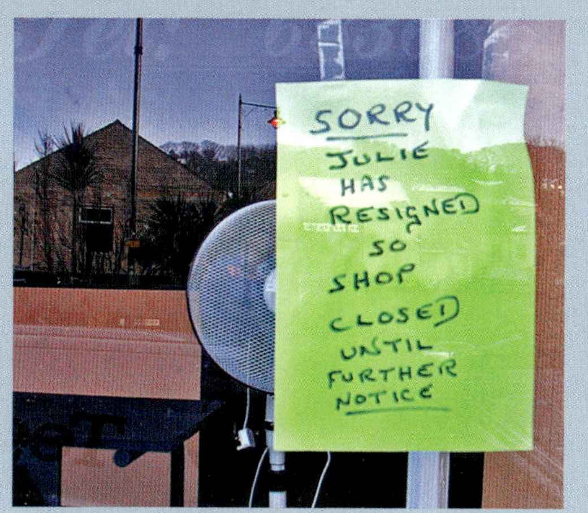
SORRY
JULIE HAS RESIGNED SO SHOP CLOSED UNTIL FURTHER NOTICE

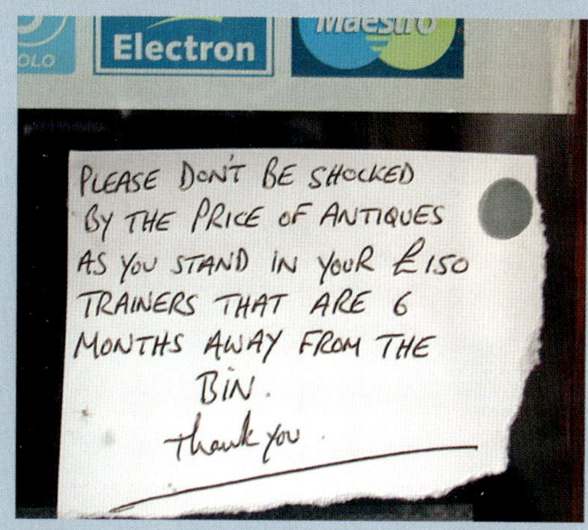
Electron
Maestro
PLEASE DON'T BE SHOCKED BY THE PRICE OF ANTIQUES AS YOU STAND IN YOUR £150 TRAINERS THAT ARE 6 MONTHS AWAY FROM THE BIN.
thank you

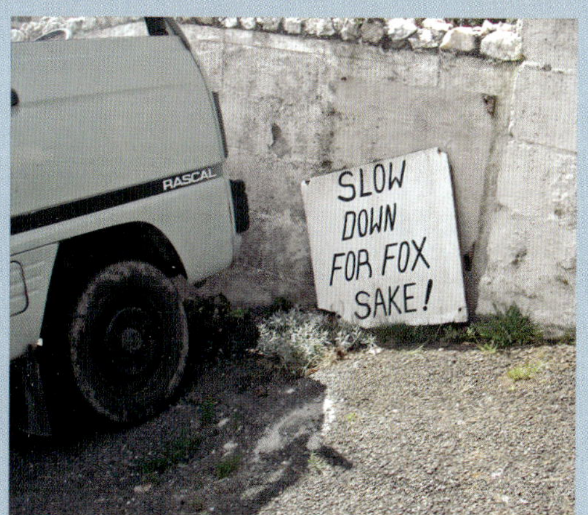
RASCAL
SLOW DOWN FOR FOX SAKE!

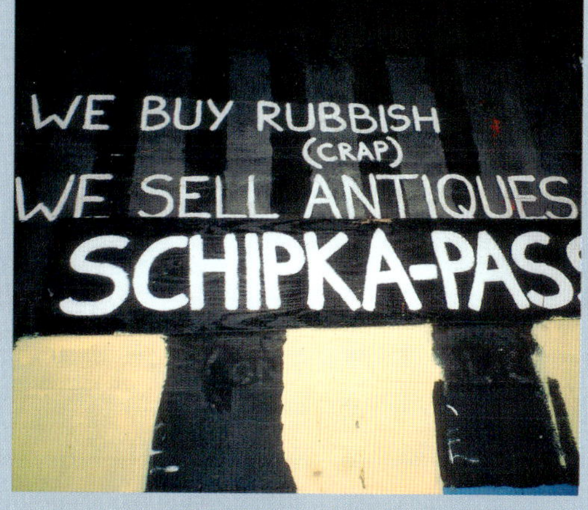
WE BUY RUBBISH
(CRAP)
WE SELL ANTIQUES
SCHIPKA-PAS

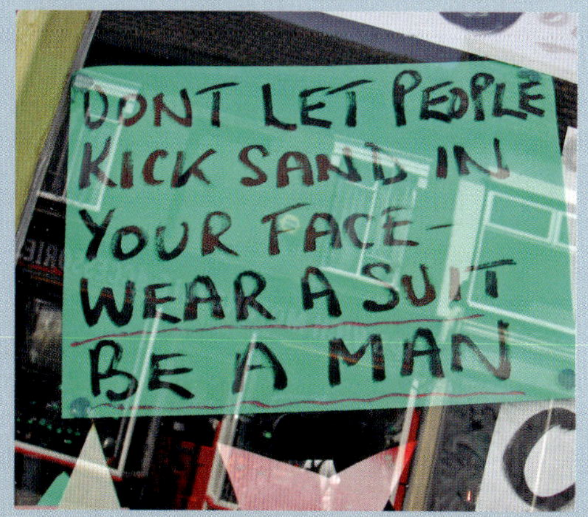
DONT LET PEOPLE KICK SAND IN YOUR FACE - WEAR A SUIT
BE A MAN

FOR SALE
8/7/0
Woven Willow Coffin
Suit 5'9", Medium build - ish.
£100
Make bookcase/storage until needed?!
4/8/04
Beautiful home!

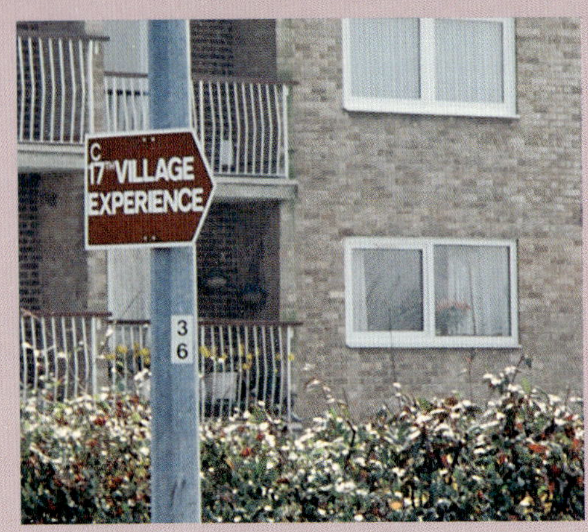
C
17th VILLAGE
EXPERIENCE
36

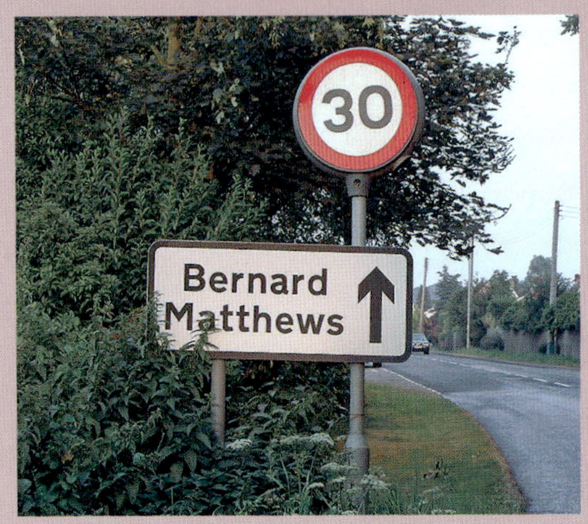
30
Bernard
Matthews

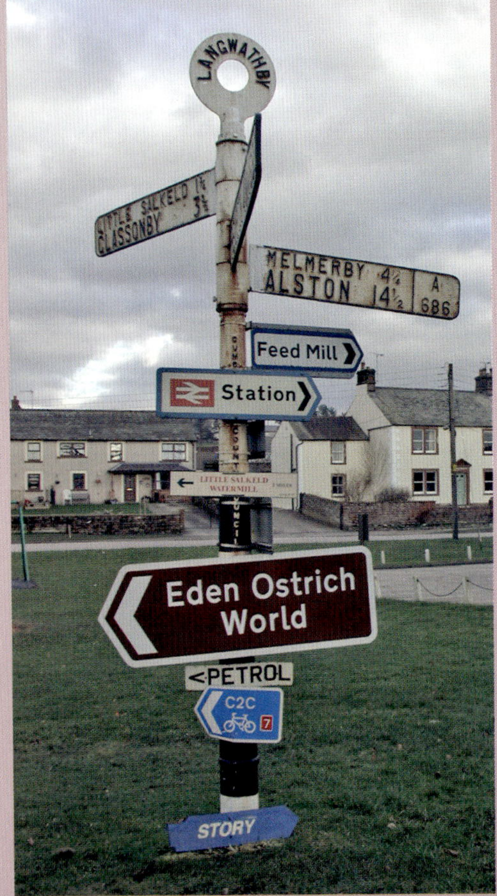
LANGWATHBY
LITTLE SALKELD
GLASSONBY
MELMERBY 4¼
ALSTON 14½
A
686
Feed Mill
Station
Eden Ostrich
World
PETROL
C2C
7
STORY

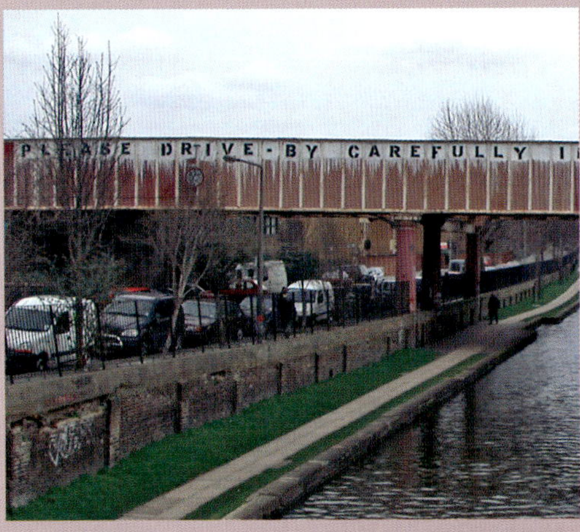
PLEASE DRIVE-BY CAREFULLY

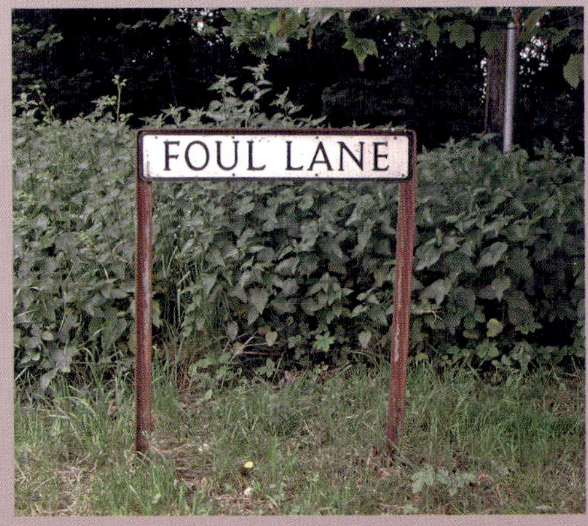
FOUL LANE

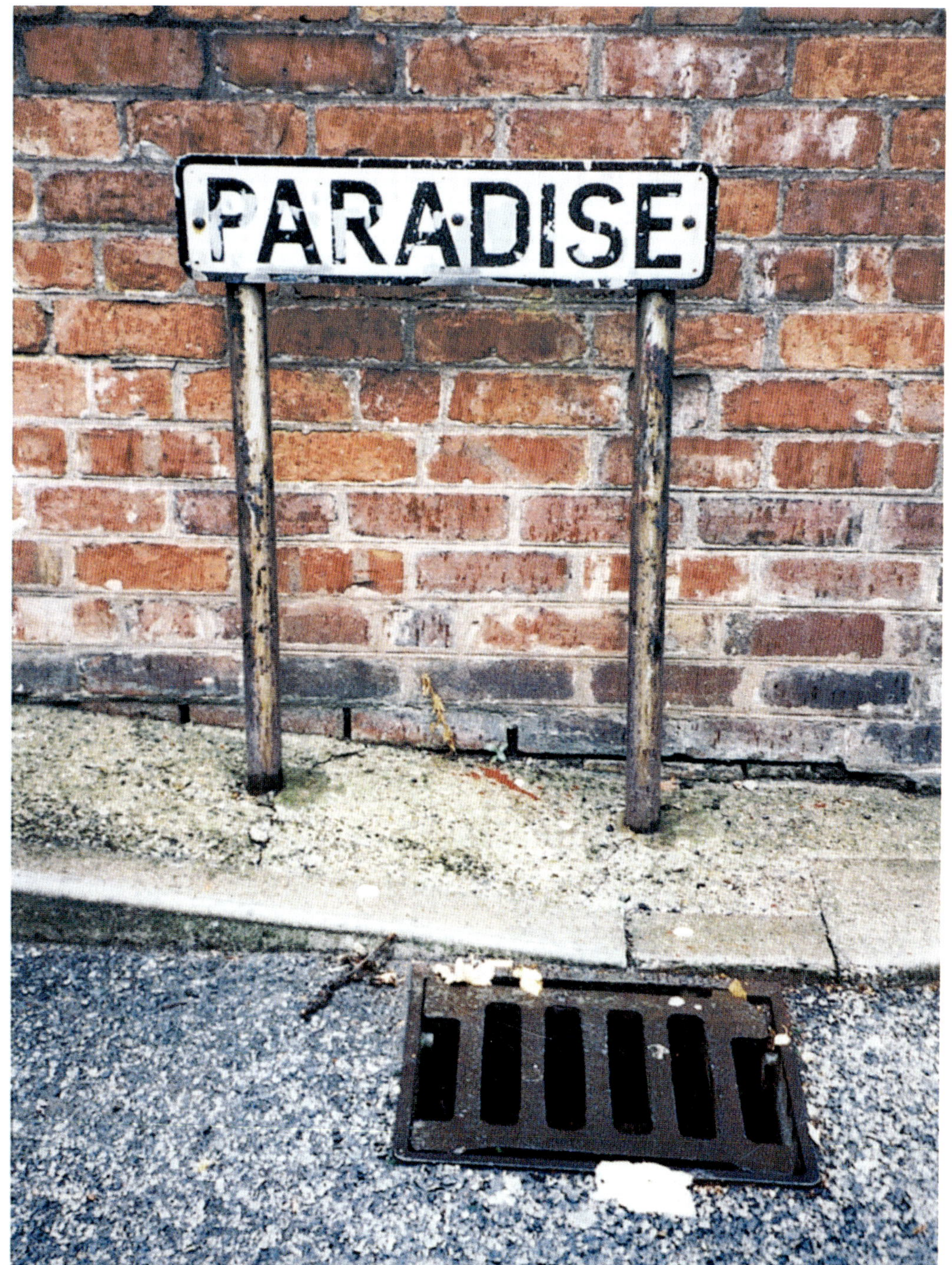
PARADISE

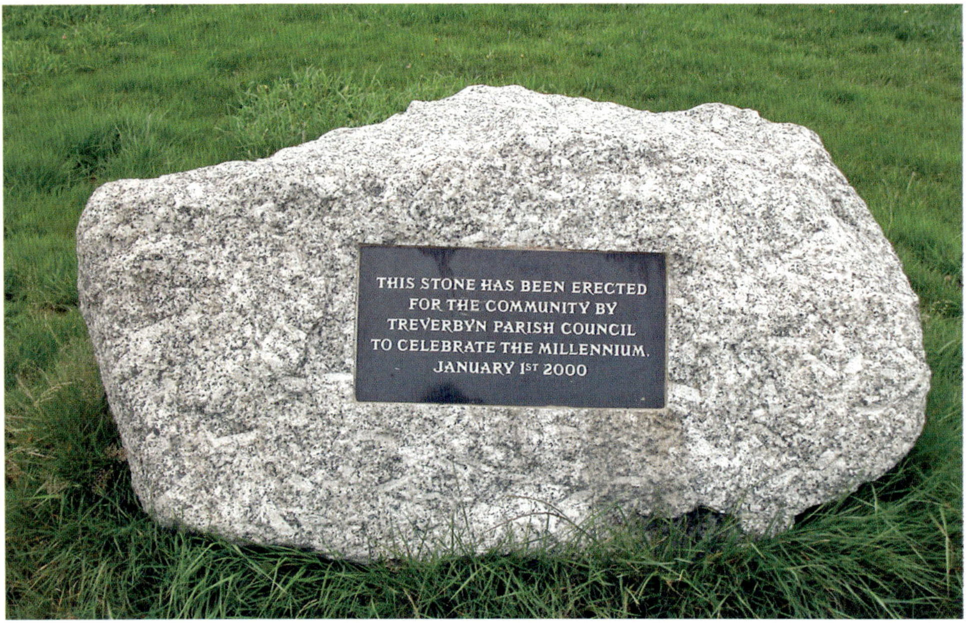

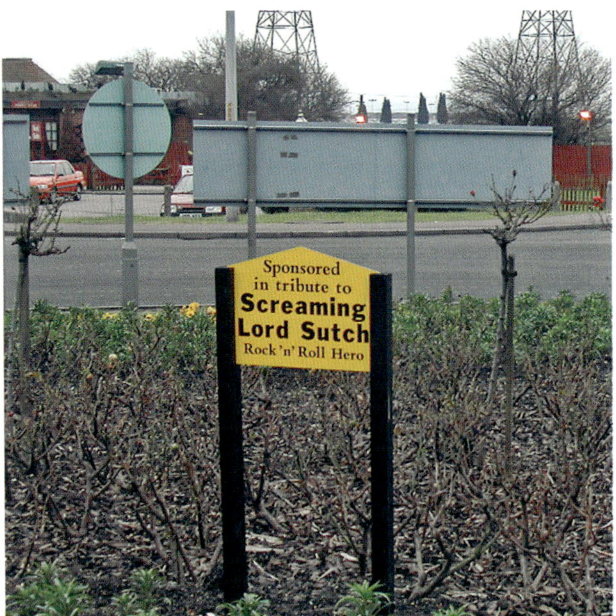

What's great about Britain?

It's old, interesting and strange

What's not so great?

Excessive political correctness

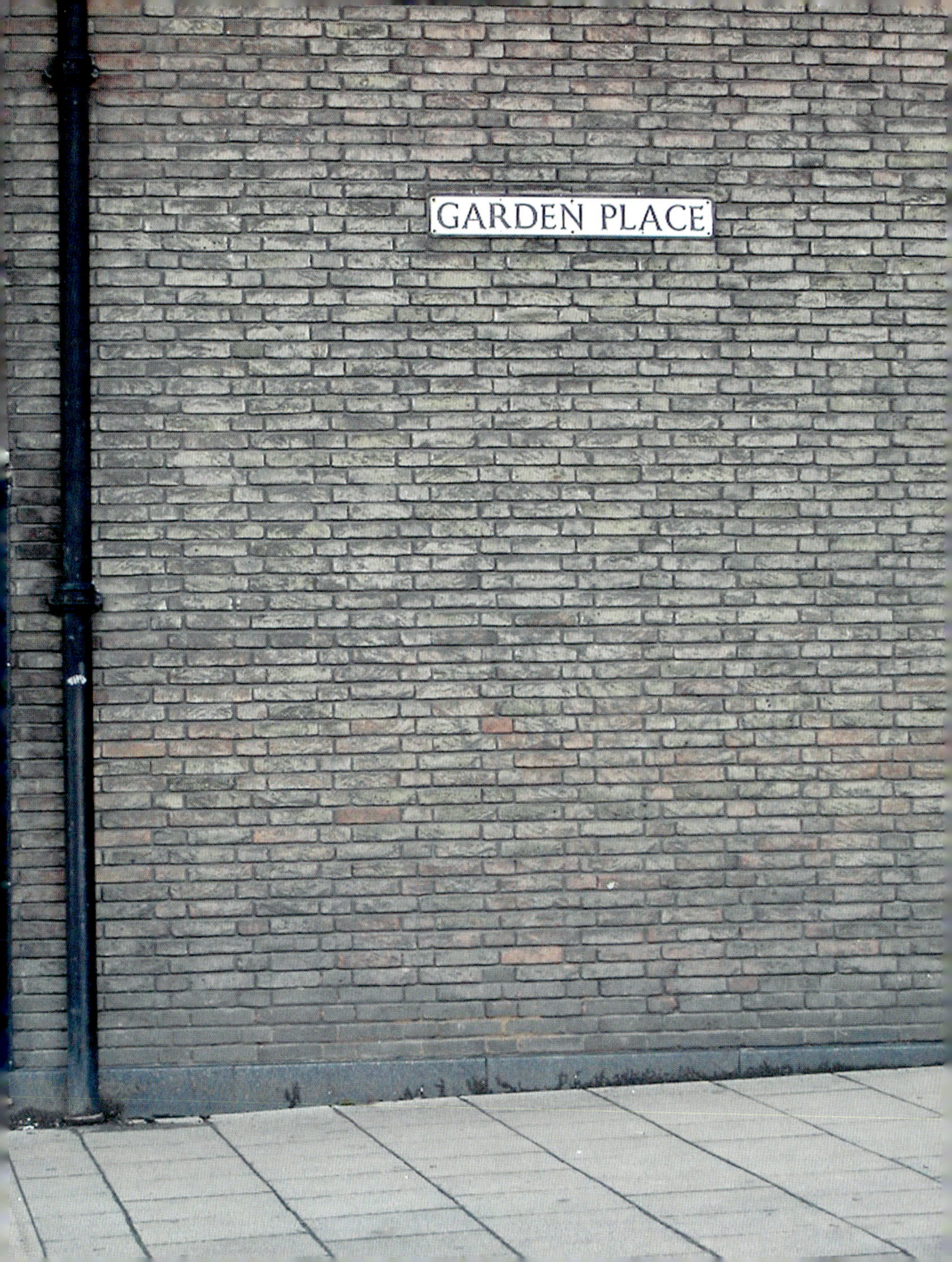
GARDEN PLACE

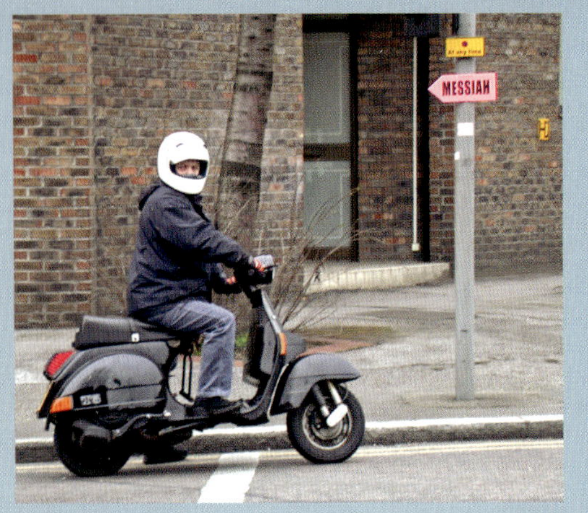

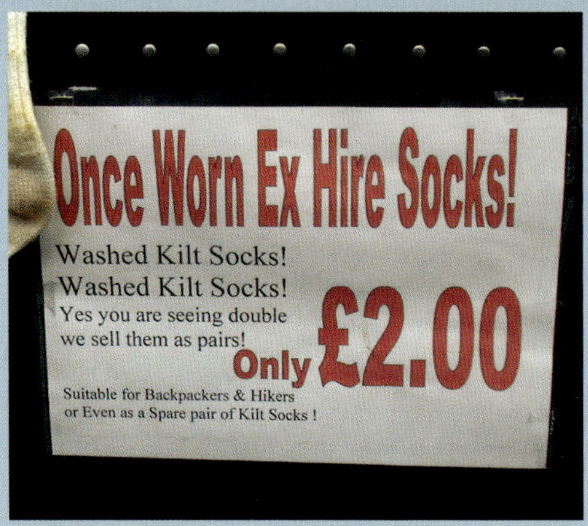

PIE WI PEAS	1/3d	PIE (WITHOOT) PEAS	1/6d
PIE WI BEANS	1/3d	PIE (WITHOOT) BEANS	1/6d
PIE WI ICE CREAM	1/3d	PIE (WITHOOT) ICE CREAM	1/6d
PIE WI SEMOLINA	1/3d	PIE (WITHOOT) SEMOLINA	1/6d
PIE WI IRN-BRU	1/3d	PIE (WITHOOT) IRN-BRU	1/6d
PIE WI JOBBIES	1/3d	PIE (WITHOOT) JOBBIES	1/6d
PIE IN THE HAWN	1/3d	PIE IN THE FACE	1/6d
PIE IN THE SKY	1/3d	PIE OAN THE GRUN	1/6d
PIE 'R' SQUERRED	1/3d	PIE EYED AN LEGLESS	1/6d

"BON APPETITE"
BY RI WAY!

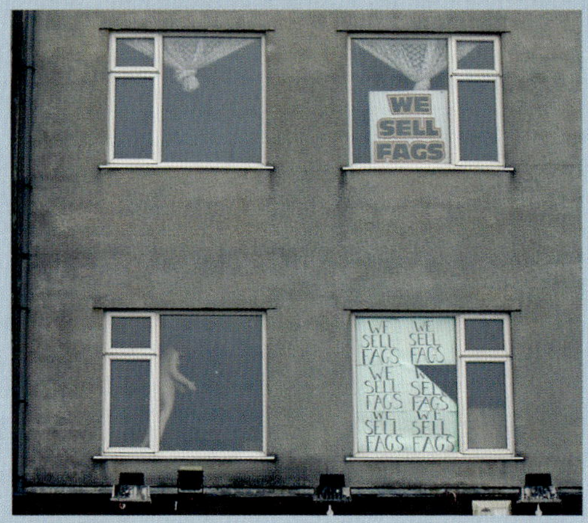

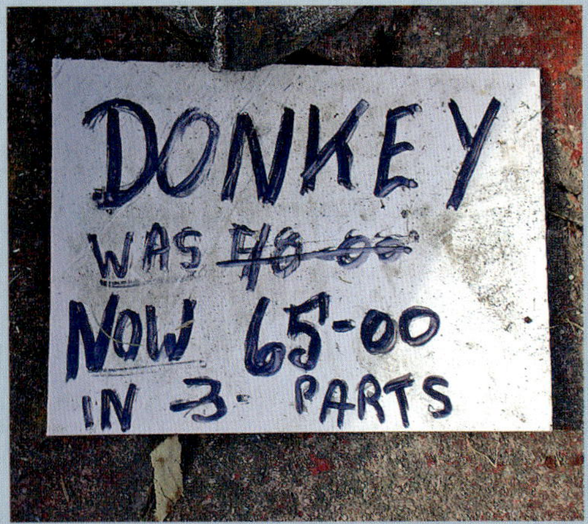

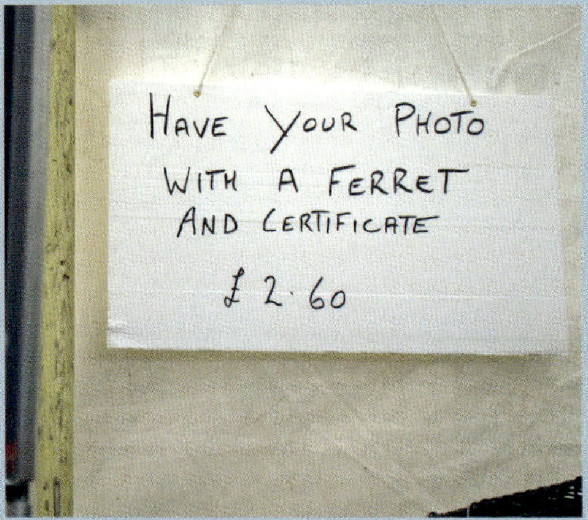

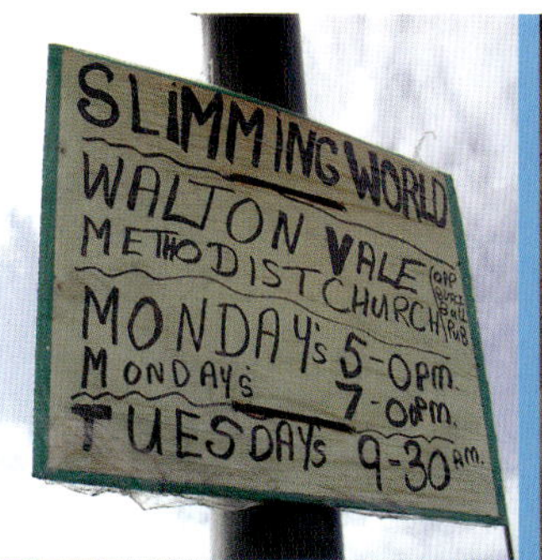
SLIMMING WORLD
WALTON VALE
METHODIST CHURCH
MONDAY's 5-0pm.
MONDAYS 7-0pm.
TUESDAYS 9-30 AM.

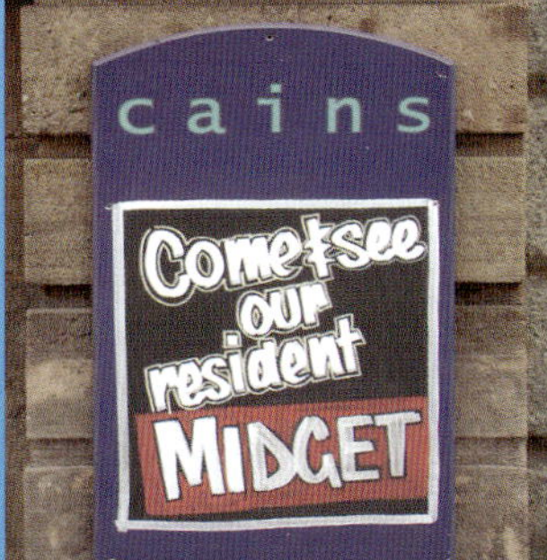
cains
Come & see our resident
MIDGET

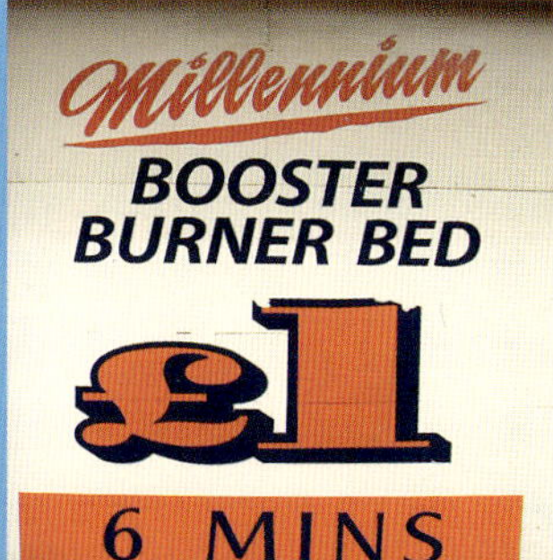
Millennium
BOOSTER
BURNER BED
£1
6 MINS

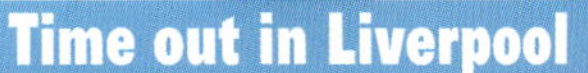
Time out in Liverpool

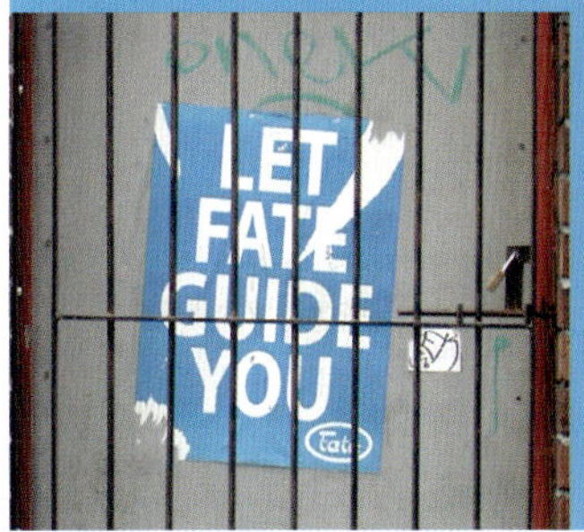
LET
FATE
GUIDE
YOU

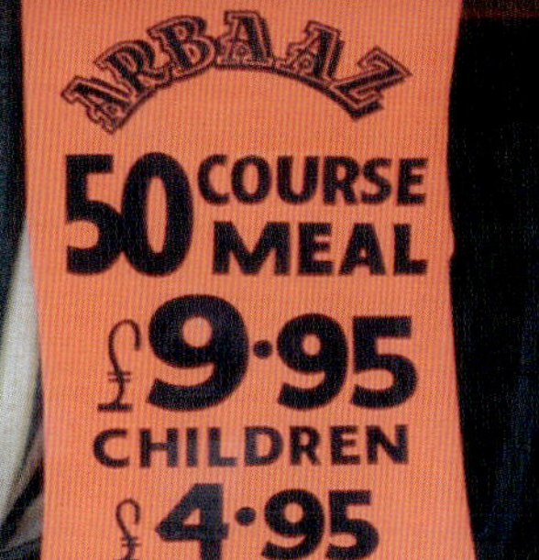
ARBAAZ
50 COURSE MEAL
£9·95
CHILDREN
£4·95

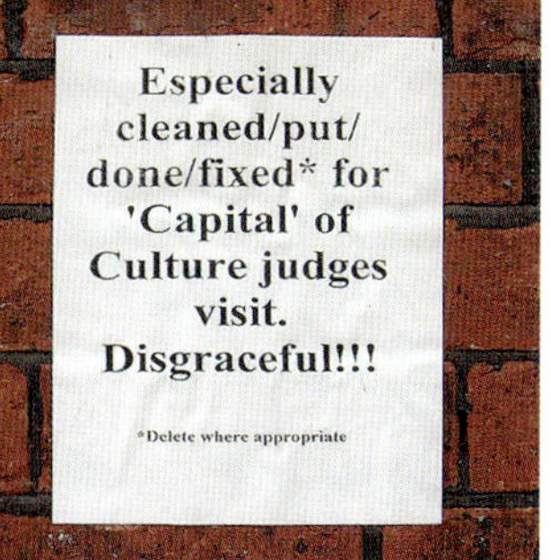
Especially
cleaned/put/
done/fixed* for
'Capital' of
Culture judges
visit.
Disgraceful!!!
*Delete where appropriate

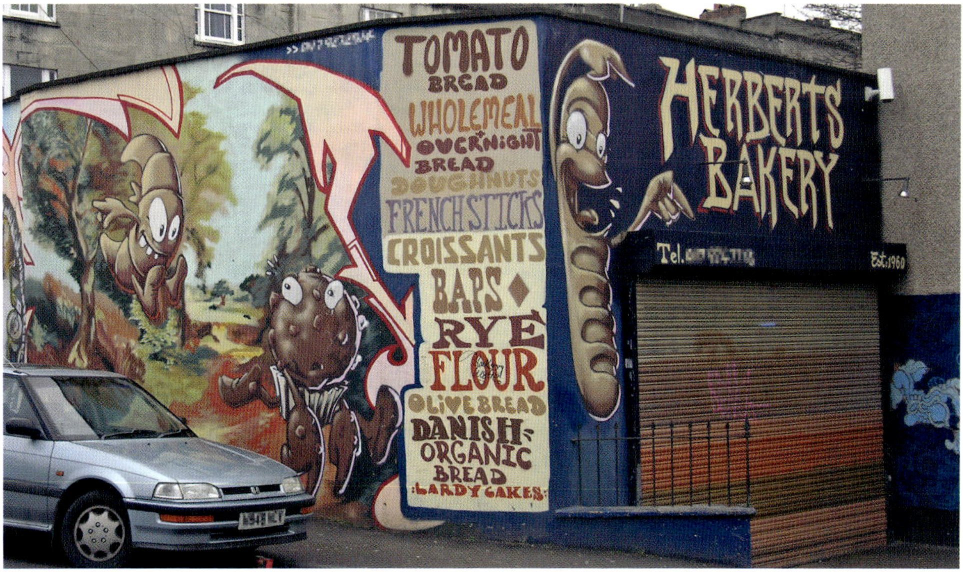

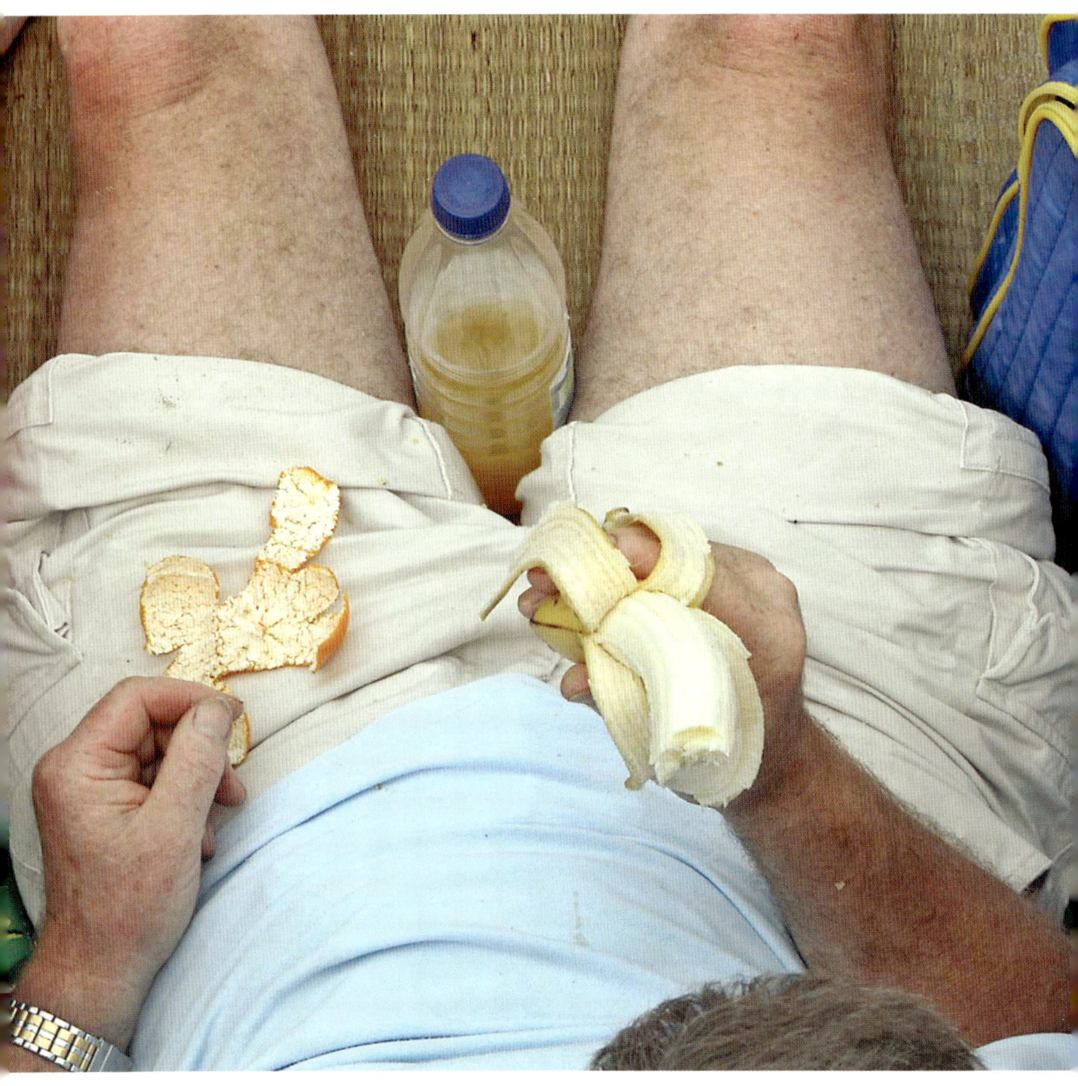

Picnics

As soon as the rain stops the British rush outdoors to enjoy an al fresco feast of sandwiches and a banana. Their choice of location or picnic partners can sometimes seem puzzling.

What do you think of as 'typically British'?

Moaning and roadside picnics

Fish and chips in a bus shelter

Barbecues in the rain

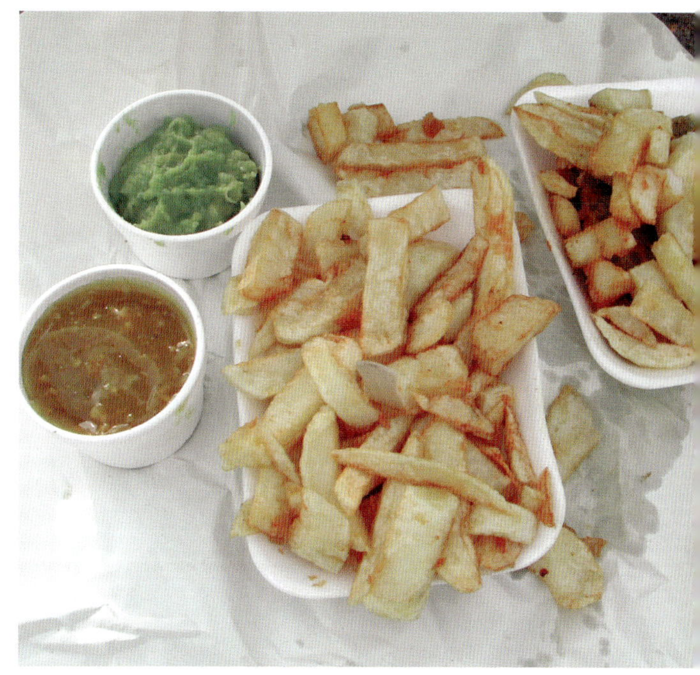

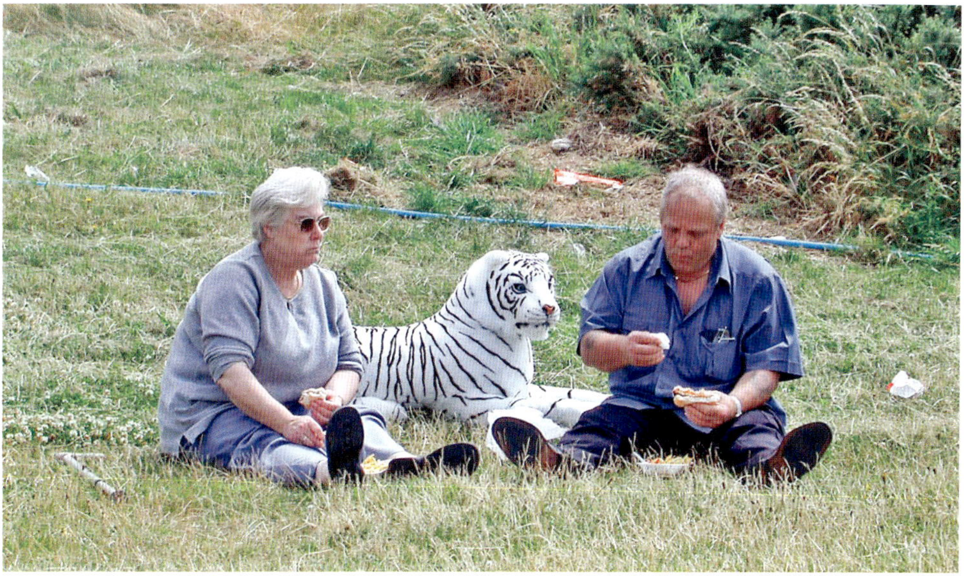

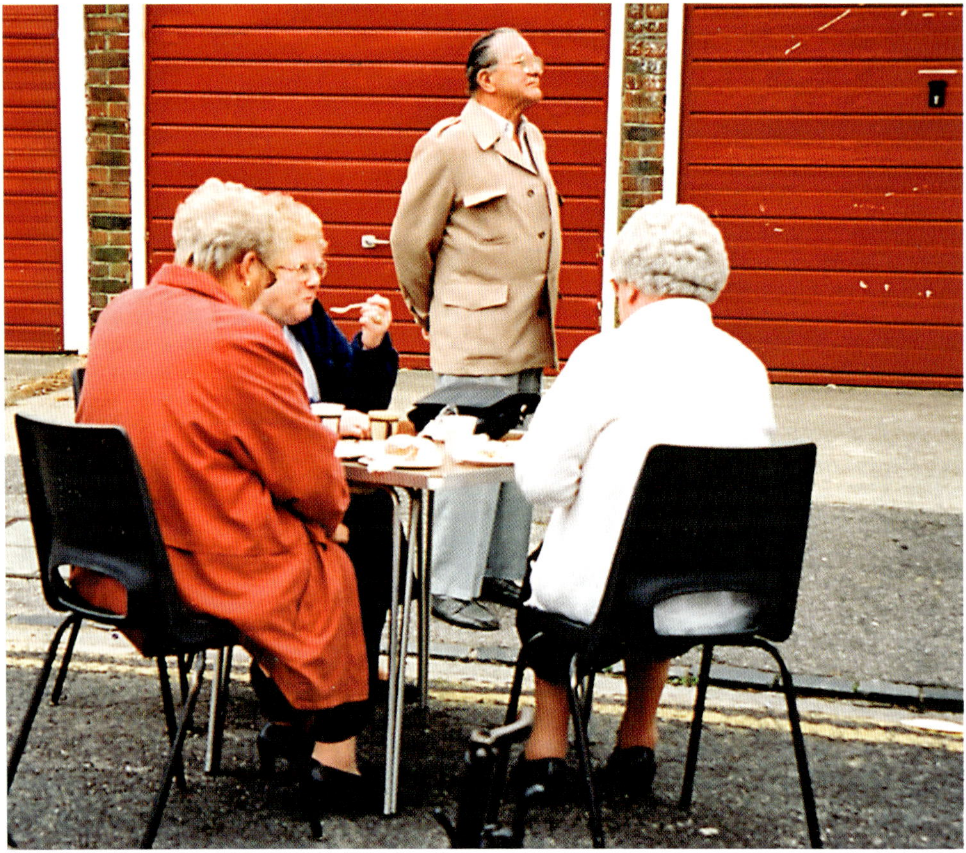

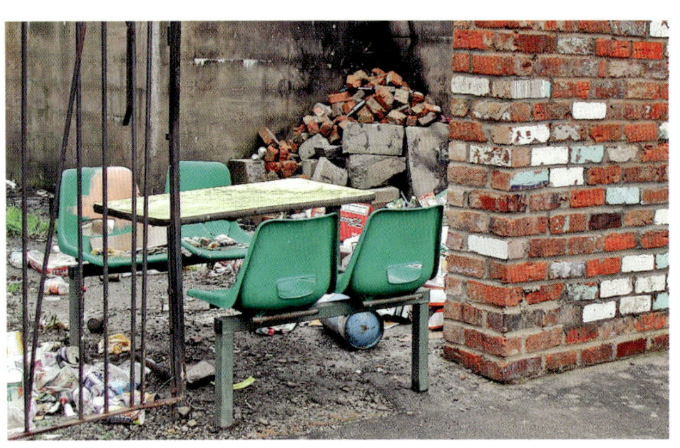

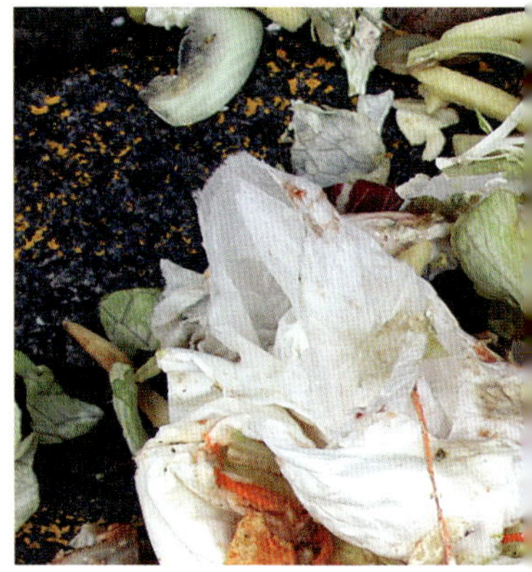

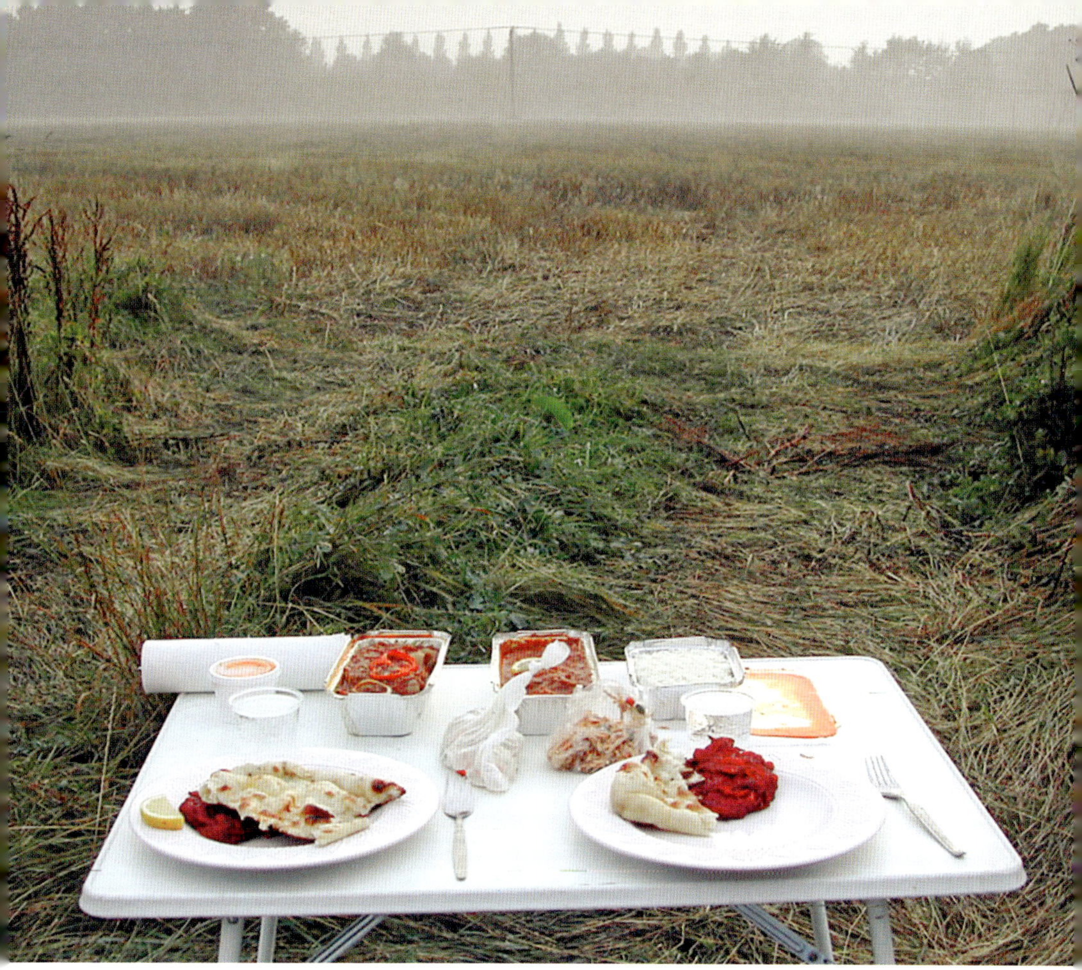

What's great about Britain?

Cornish pasties

What's not so great?

The amount of litter on the floor

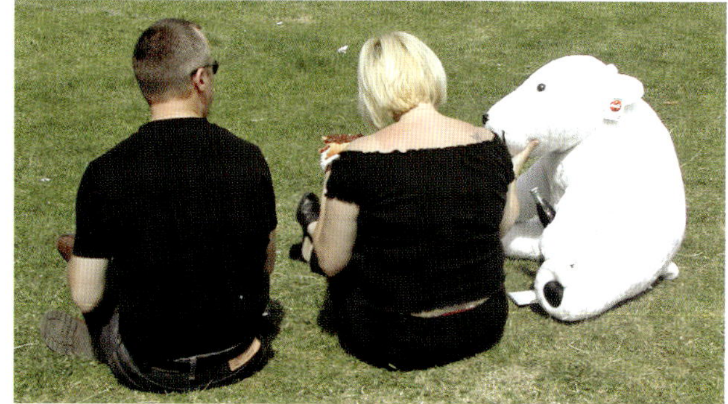

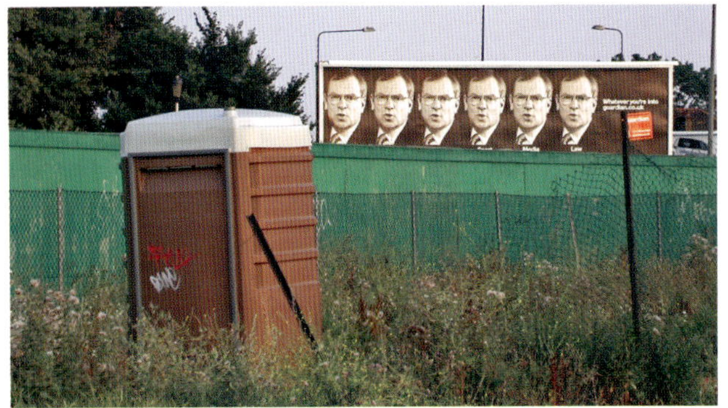

The most important factor when planning a day out in Britain is to make sure that you are never more than five minutes away from a public convenience. Finding one that is open is especially rewarding.

(In)conveniences

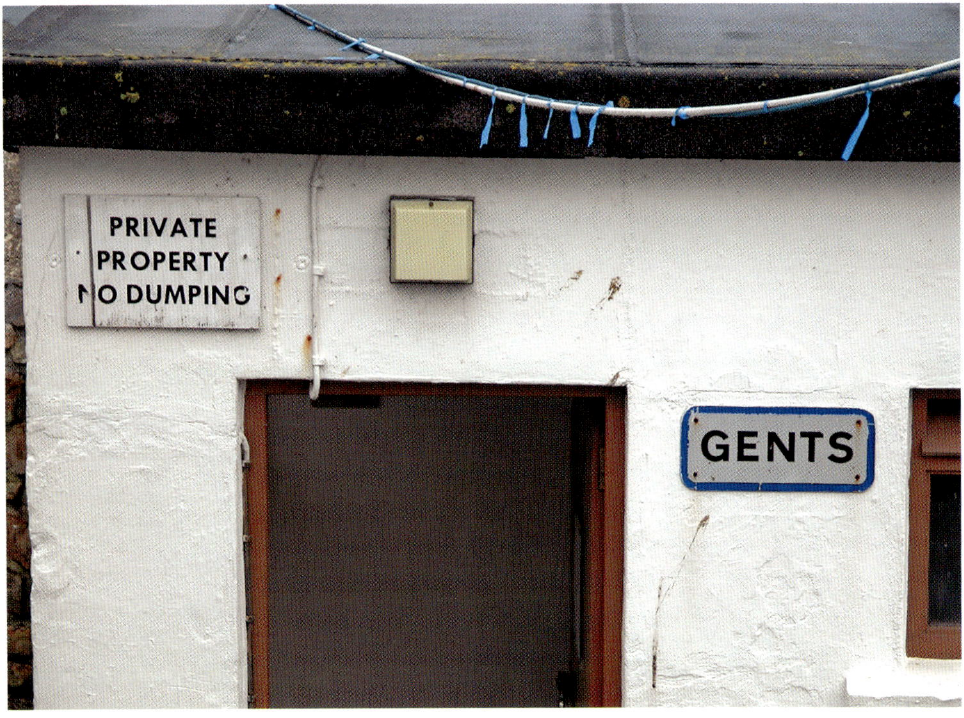

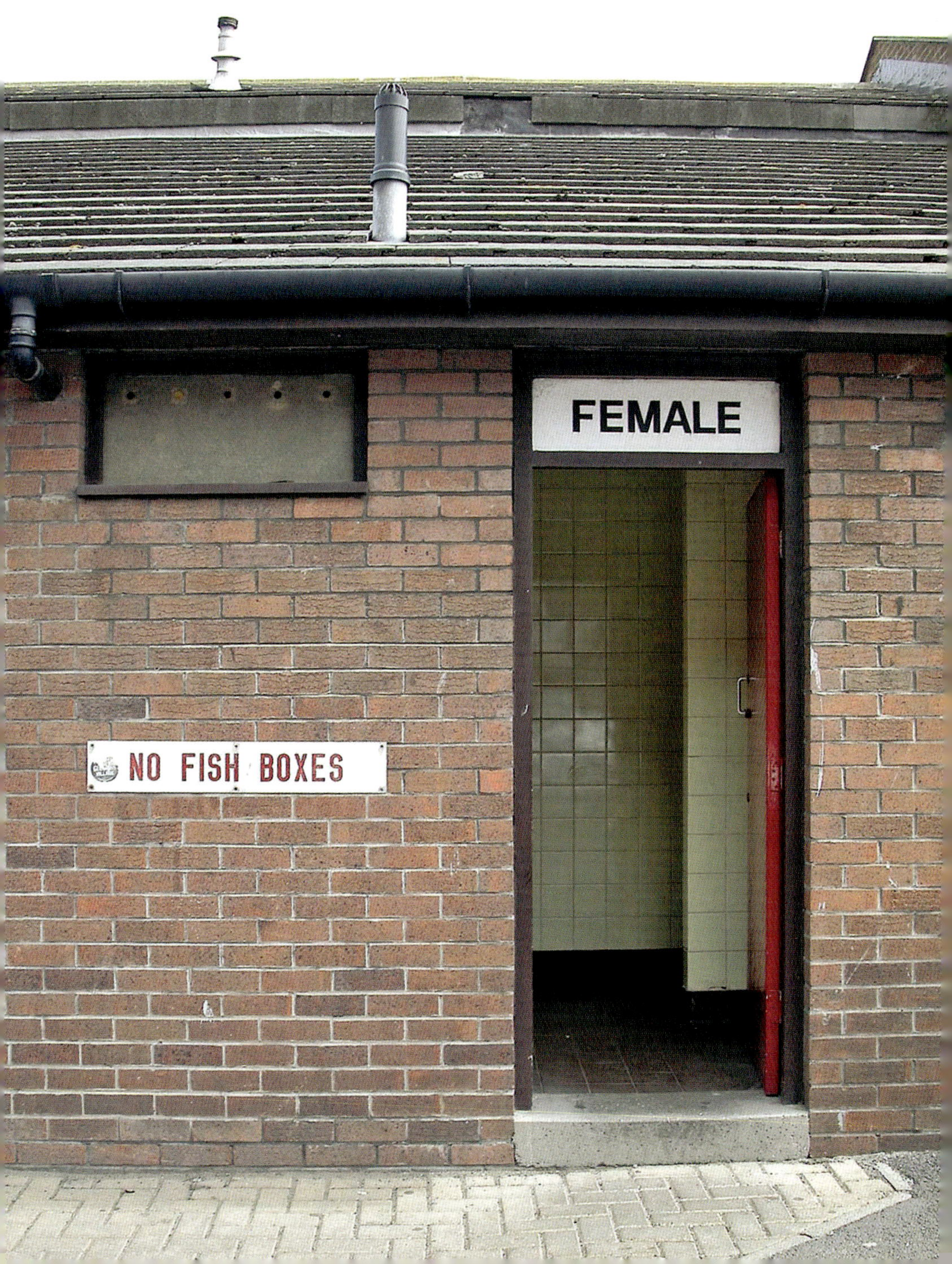
FEMALE
NO FISH BOXES

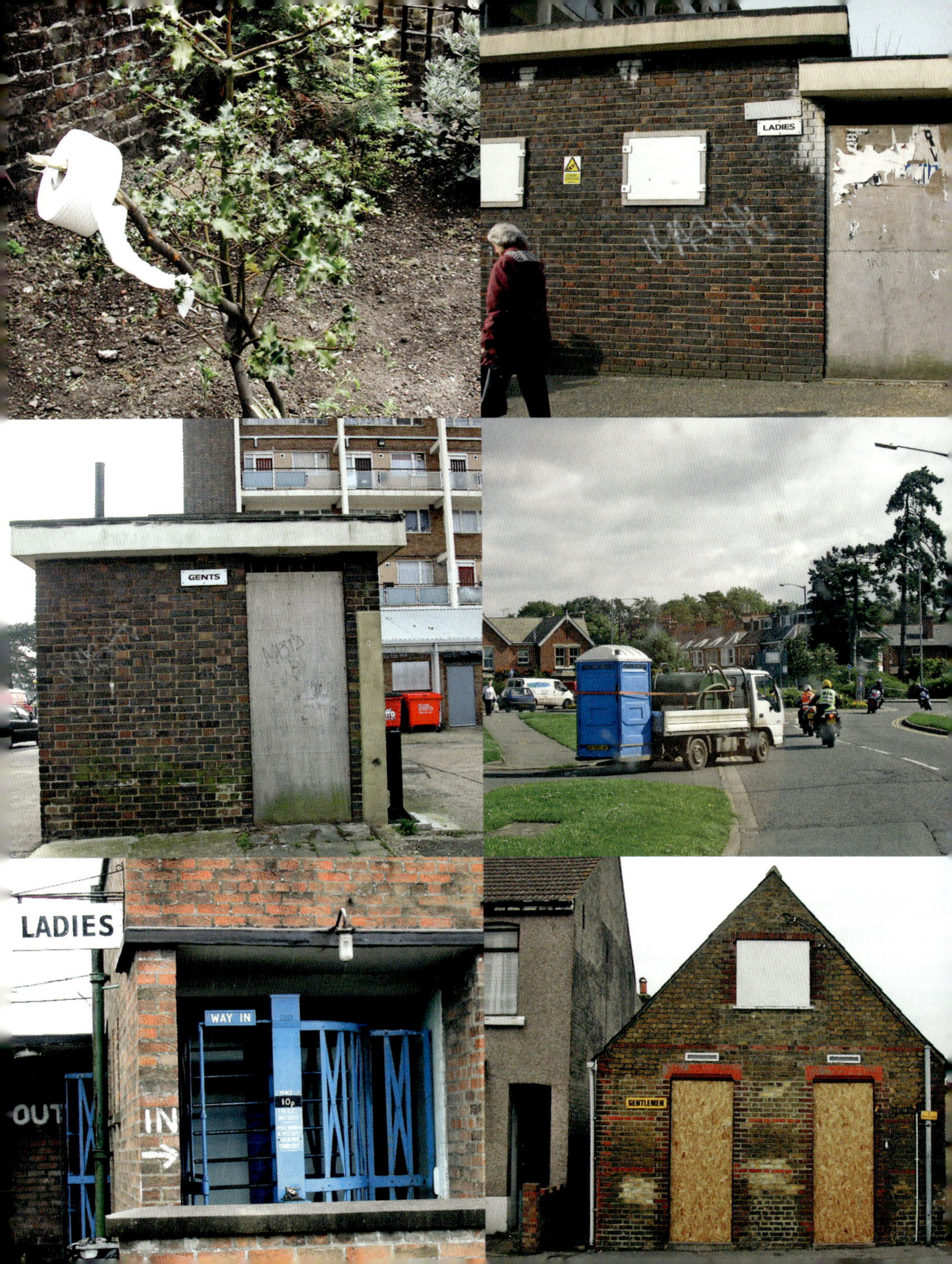
LADIES
GENTS
LADIES
WAY IN
OUT
IN
10p
GENTLEMEN

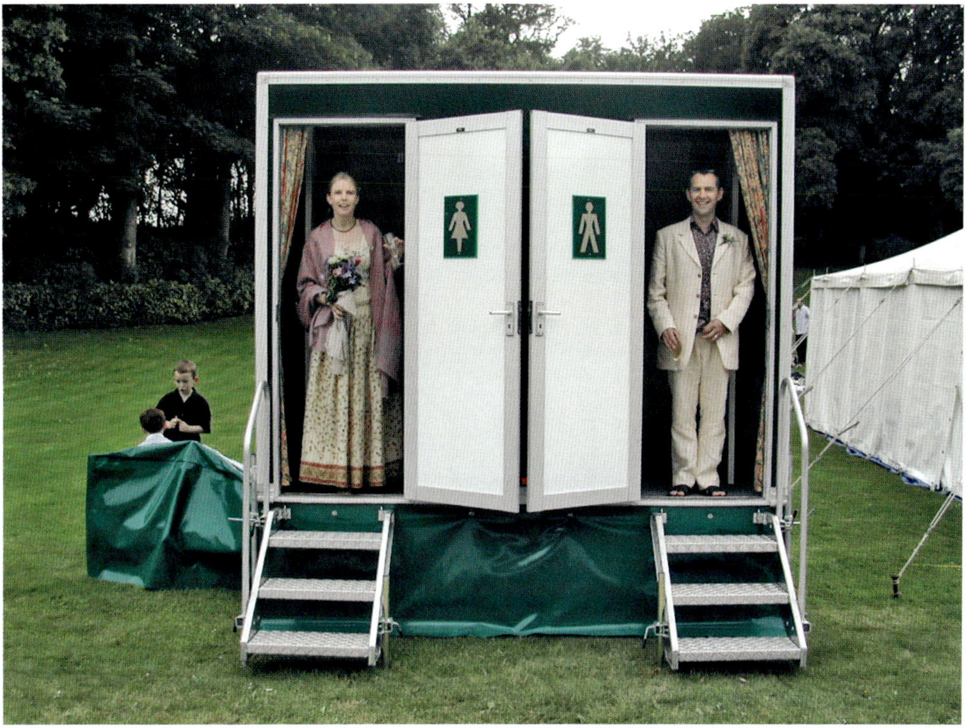

What's your personal motto?

You've already trodden in it

Laugh and the whole world will laugh at you

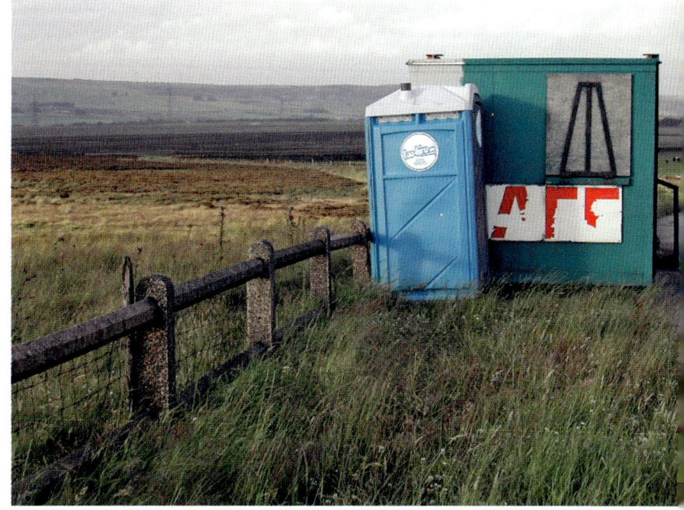

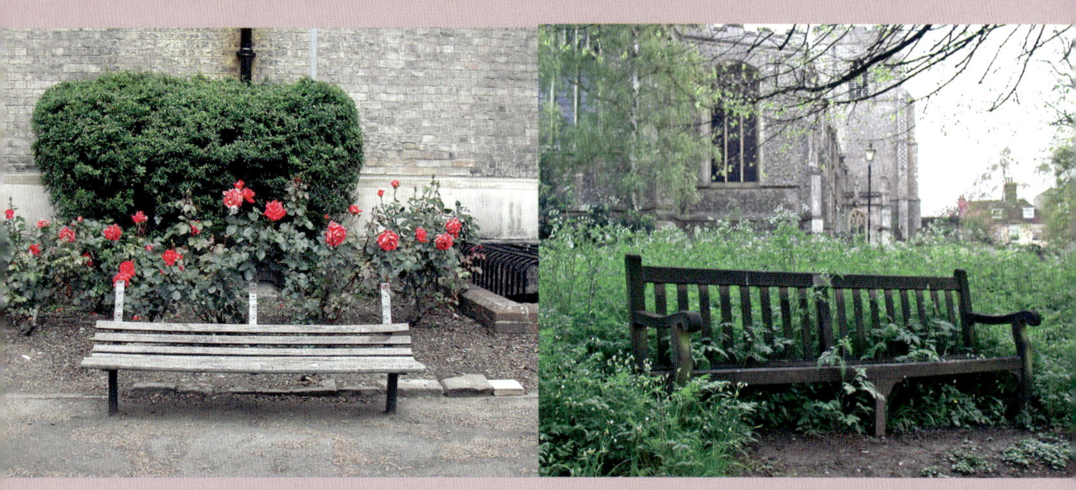

Benches

There is nothing like a nice little sit down in the fresh air to watch the world go by – only sometimes there is precious little to sit on.

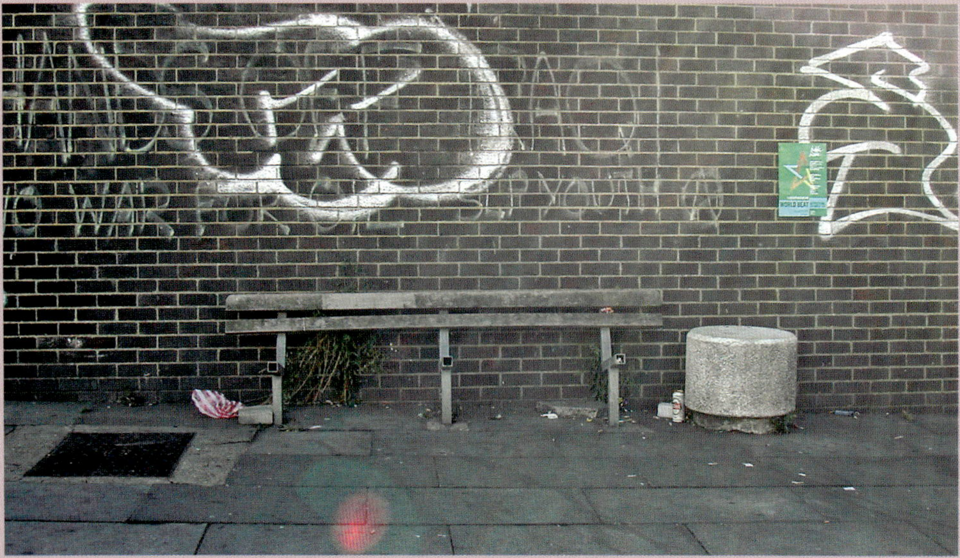

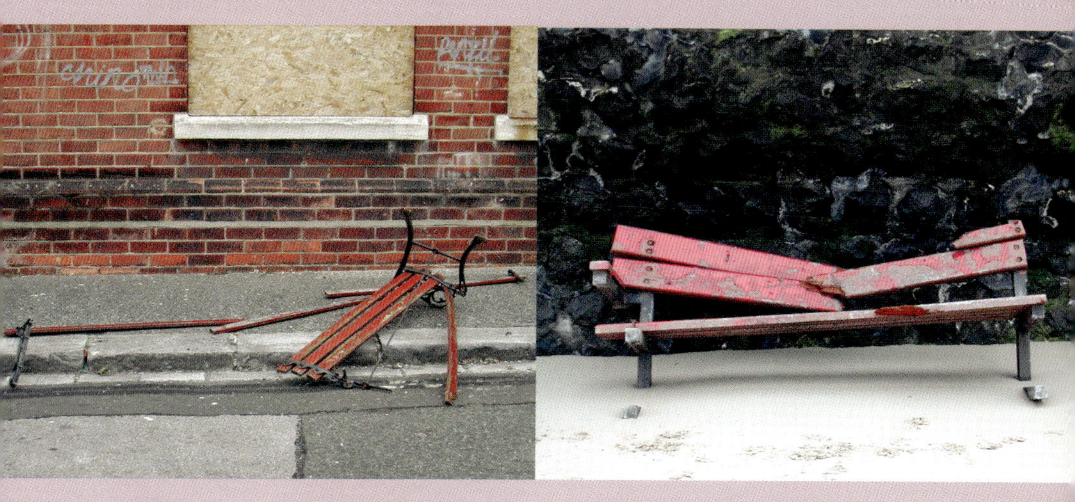

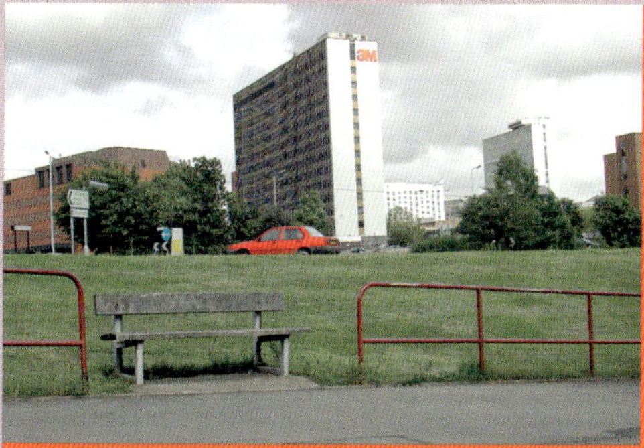

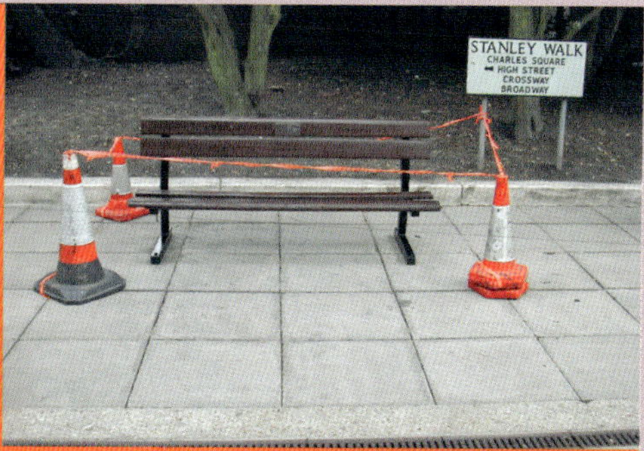

RELAXING BRACKNELL

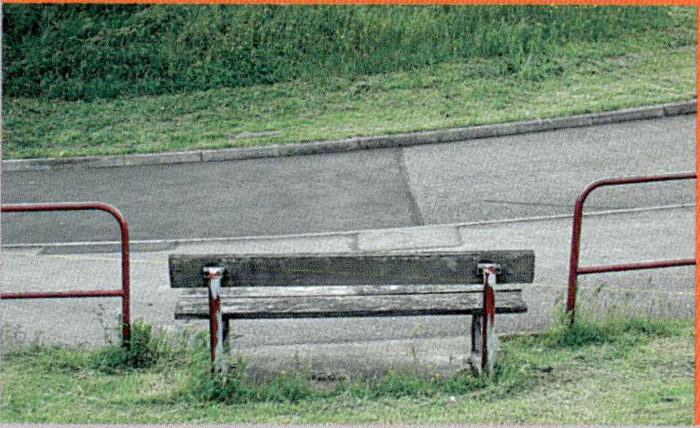

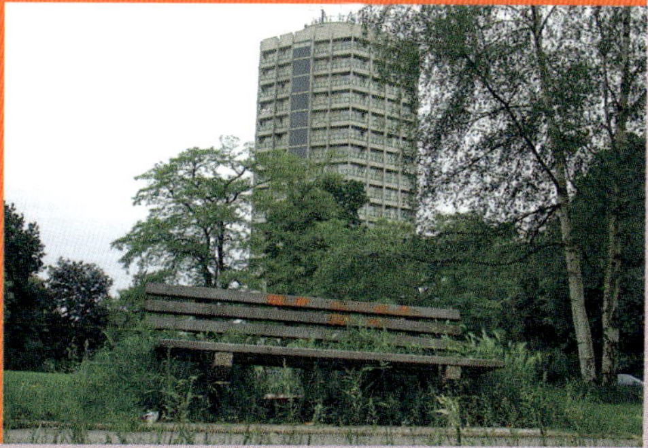

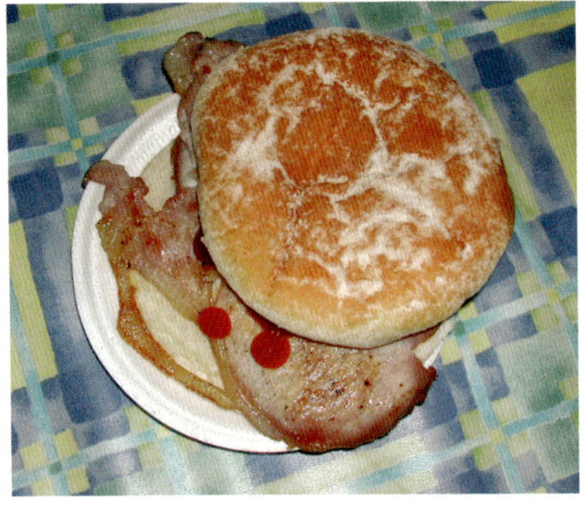

What do you think of as 'typically British'?

A good fry-up after a hangover

What's your personal motto?

Let me eat cake

Never whistle with a mouthful of custard

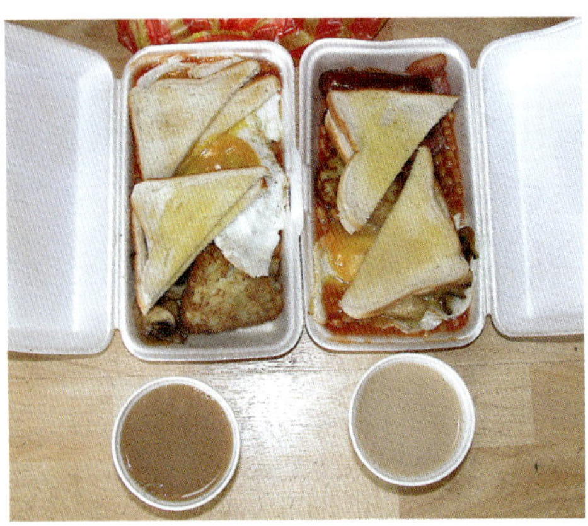

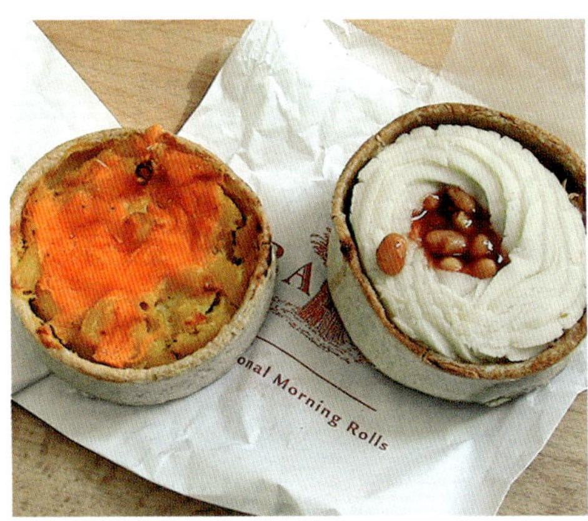

Food

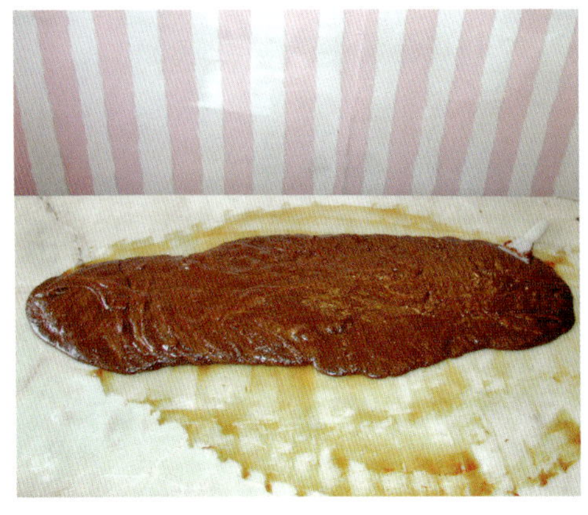

We like good plain food in Britain – nothing fancy. And we'll have chips with that, followed by some traditional handmade fudge. Except after the pub, when we'll have Chicken Vindaloo.

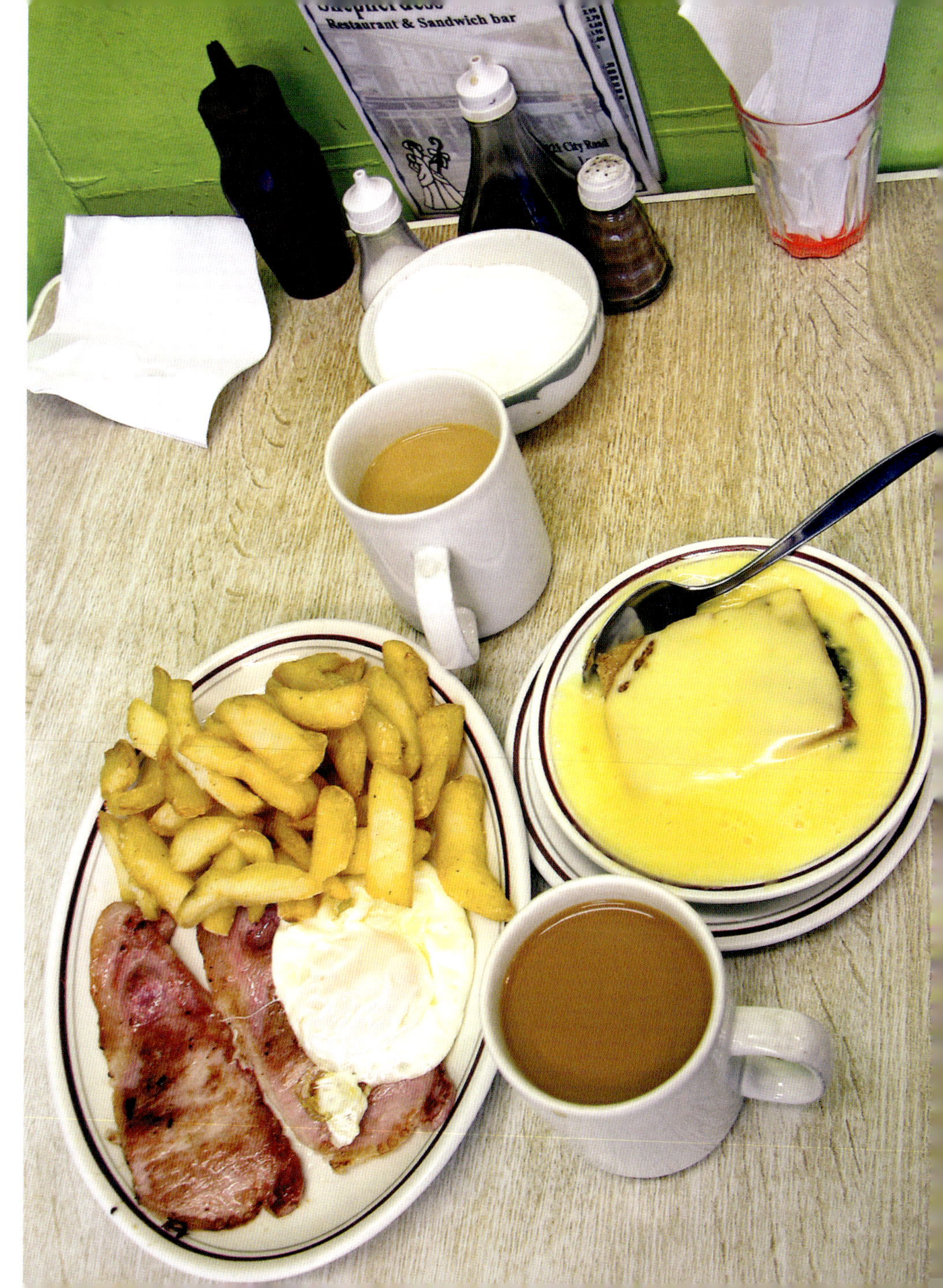
Restaurant & Sandwich bar

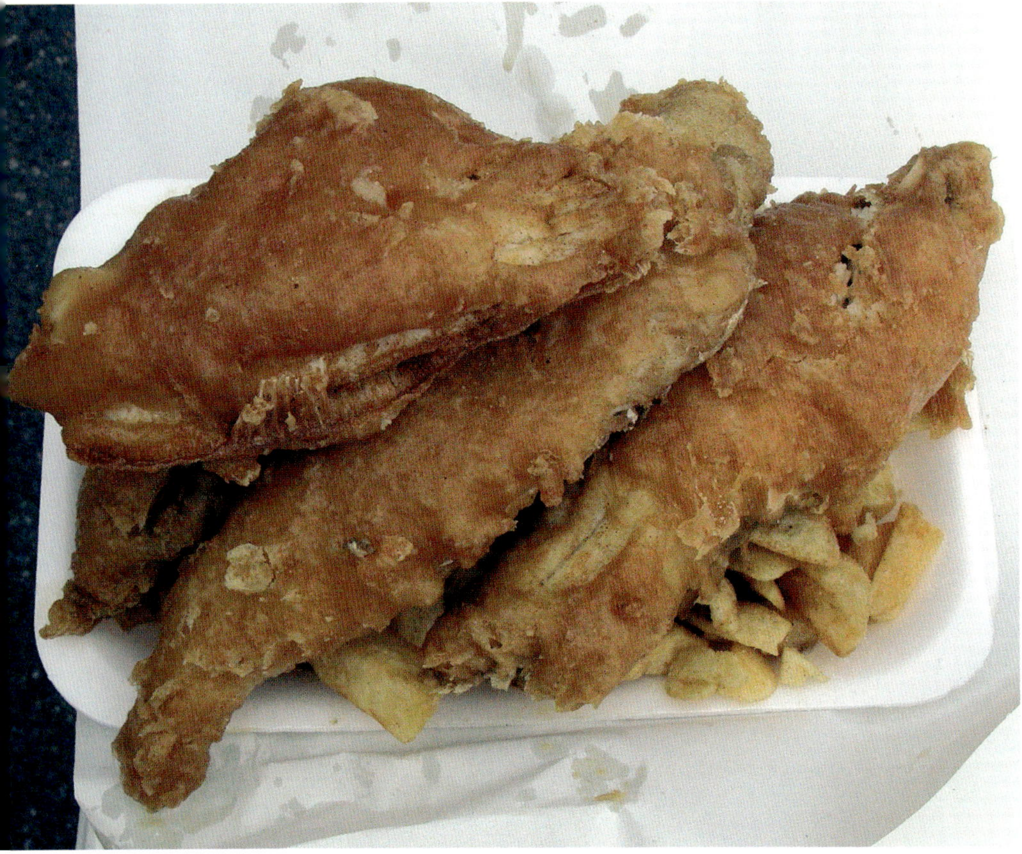

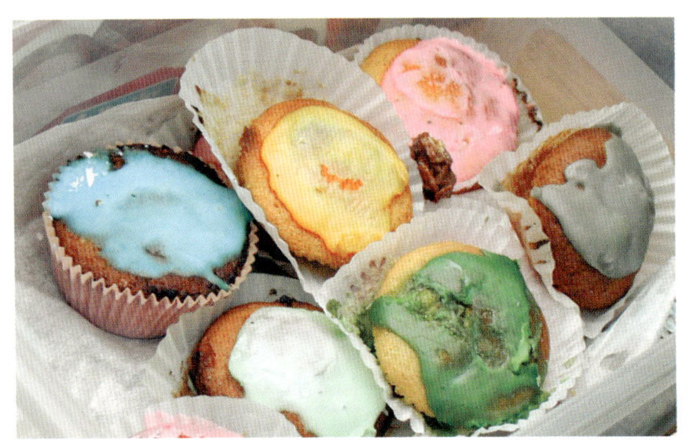

What's great about Britain?

Chips

What do you think of as 'typically British'?

Polite eating

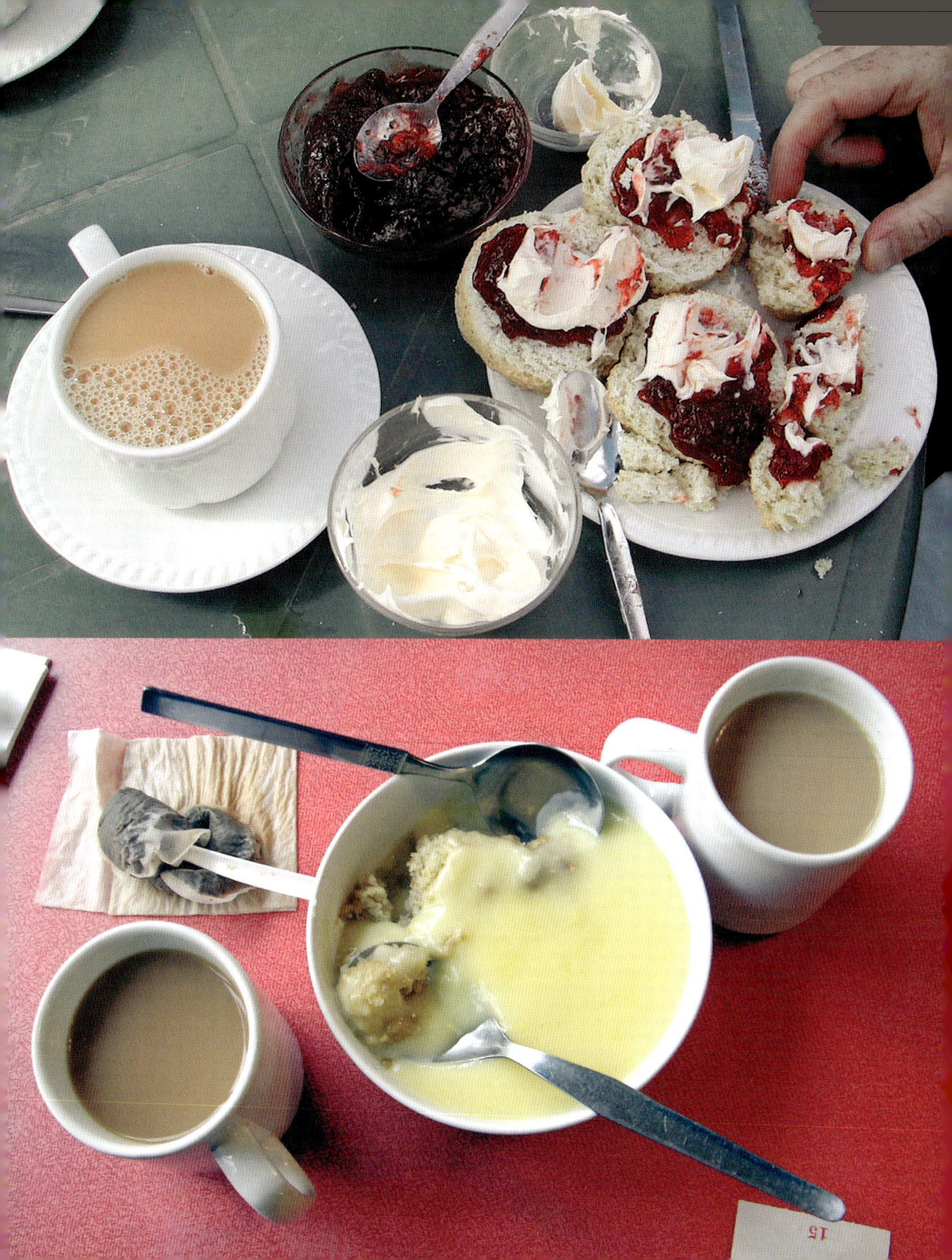
15

Looking good

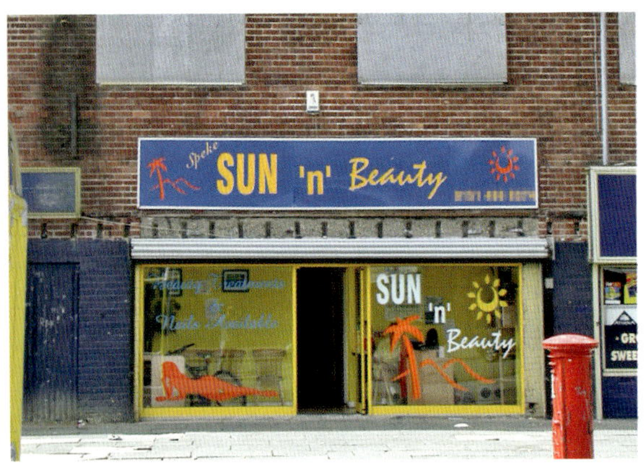

With a bijou salon on every corner, there's no excuse for not looking gorgeous.

What is your personal motto?

Get slim to a size 10

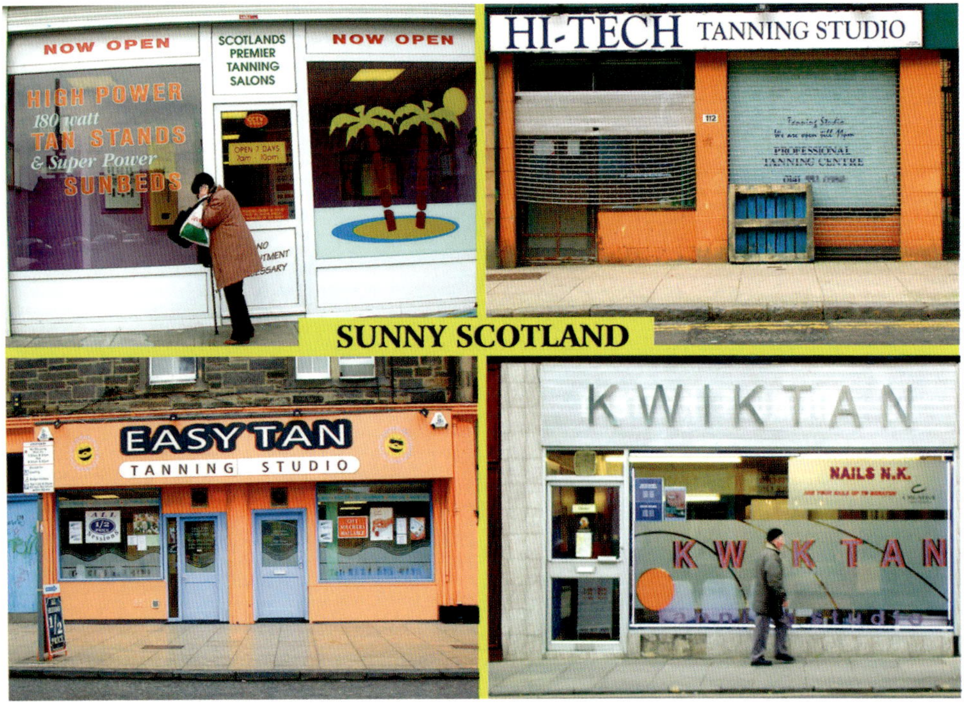

SUNNY SCOTLAND

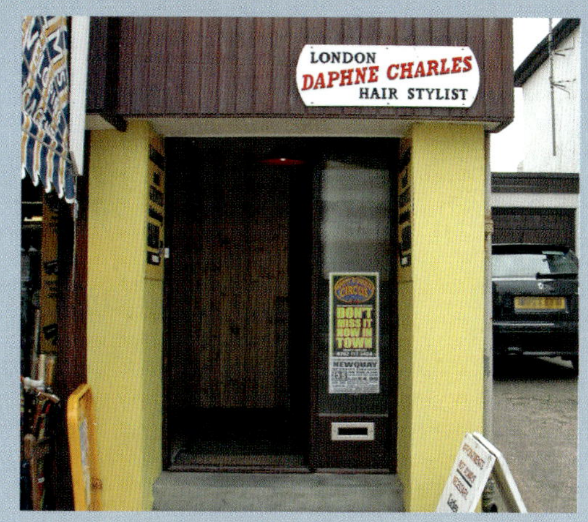
LONDON
DAPHNE CHARLES
HAIR STYLIST

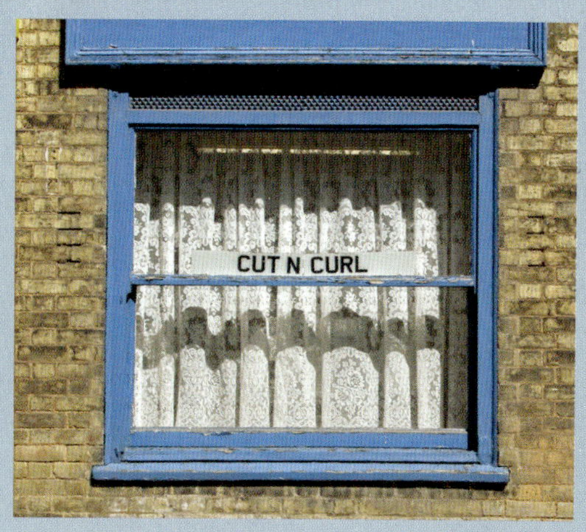
CUT N CURL

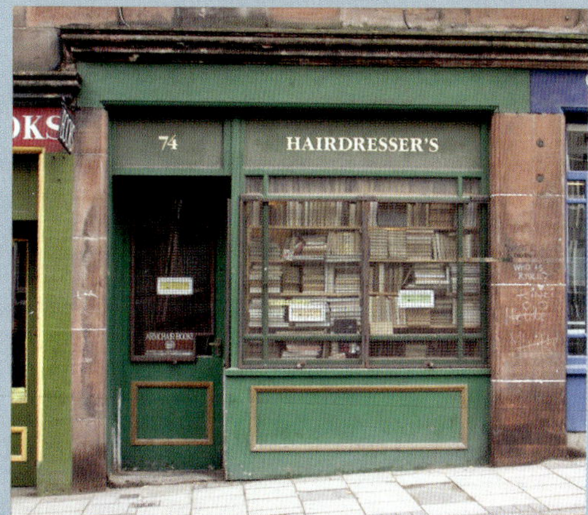
74
HAIRDRESSER'S

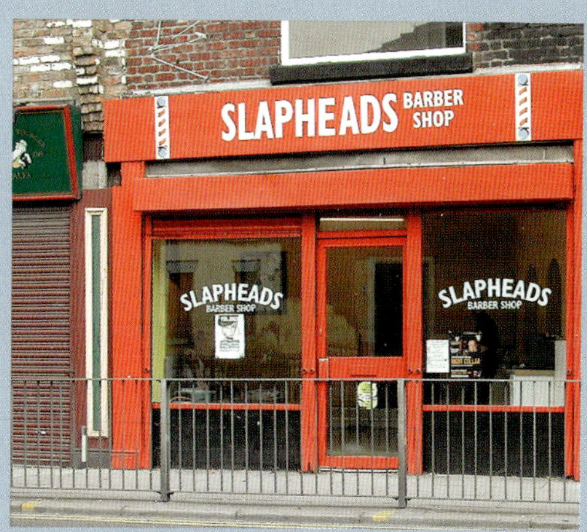
SLAPHEADS BARBER SHOP
SLAPHEADS
BARBER SHOP
SLAPHEADS
BARBER SHOP

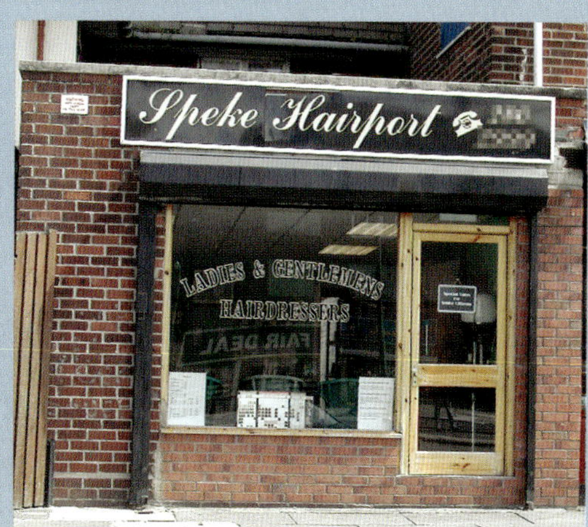
Speke Hairport
LADIES & GENTLEMENS
HAIRDRESSERS

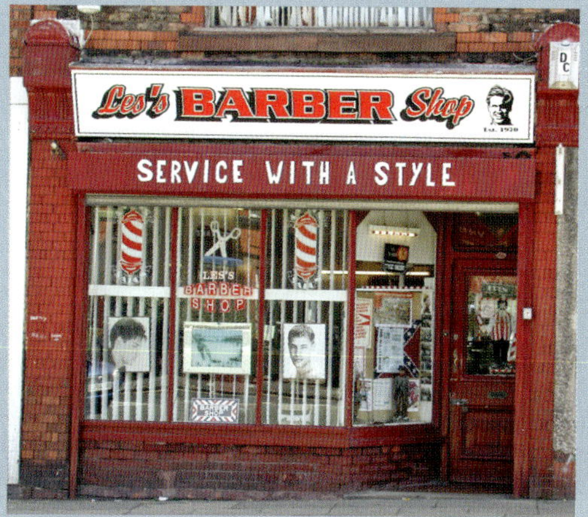
Les's BARBER Shop
SERVICE WITH A STYLE
LES'S
BARBER
SHOP

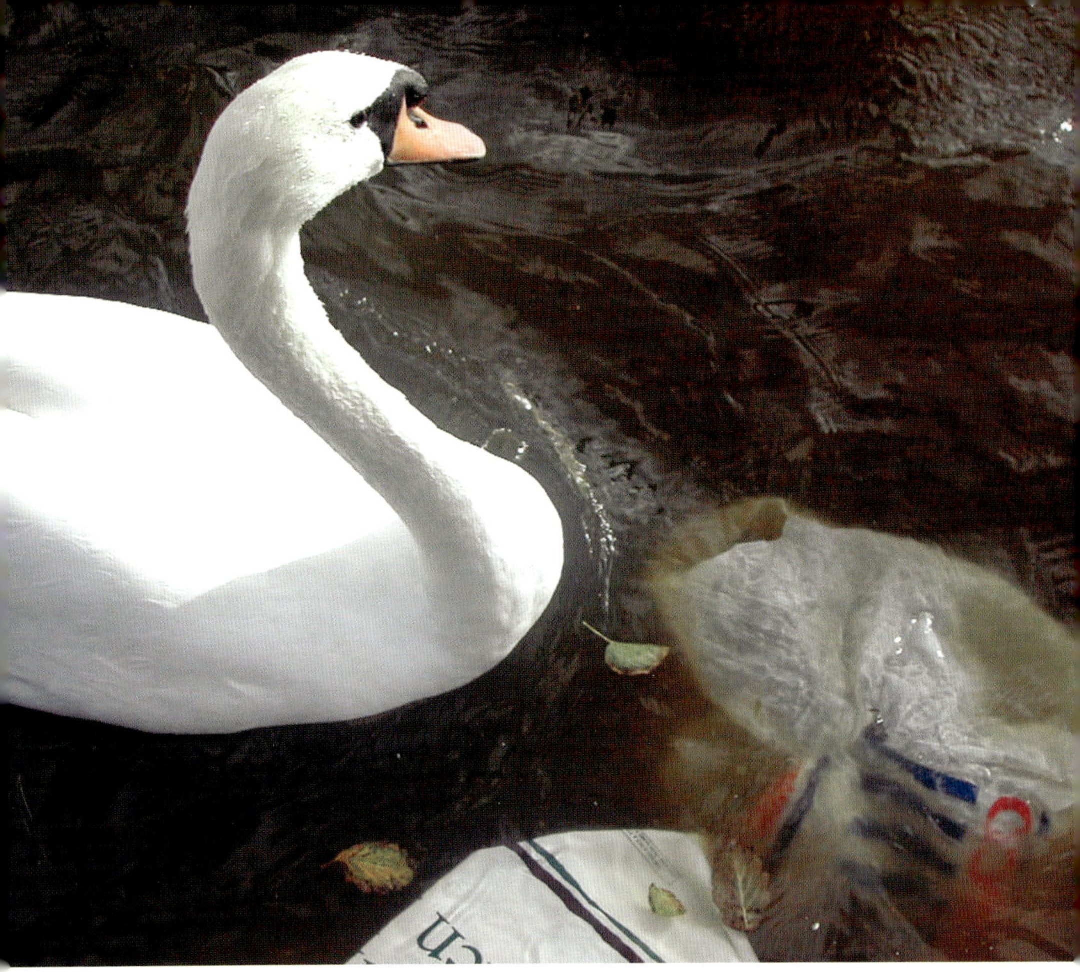

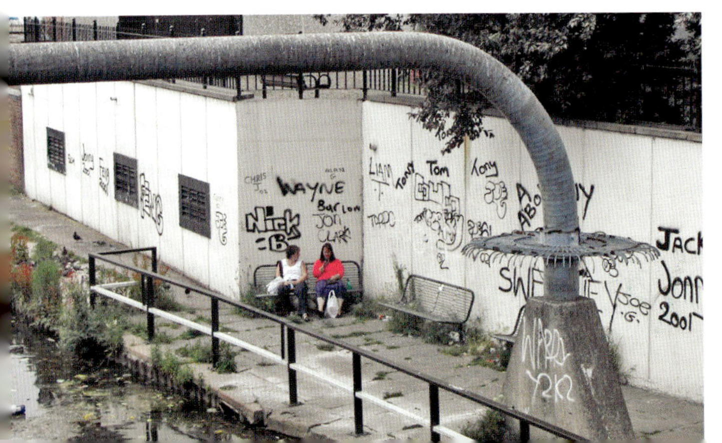

Water

We're surrounded by water, plenty more falls on us and we love a lake, canal or river. It's just a pity we don't always look after them that well.

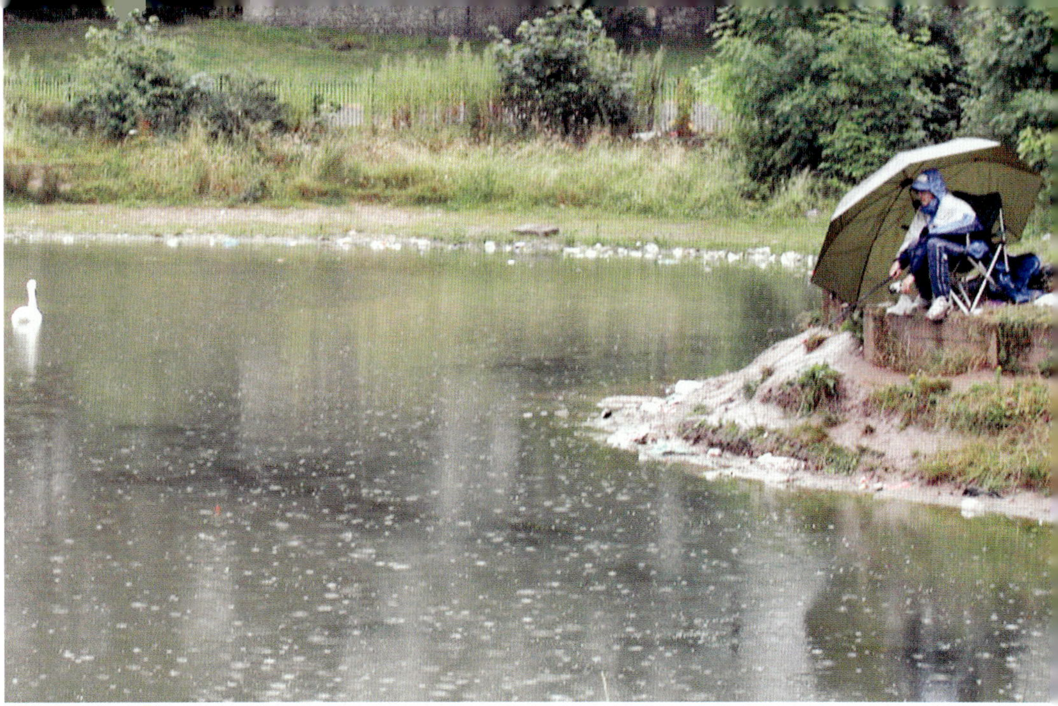

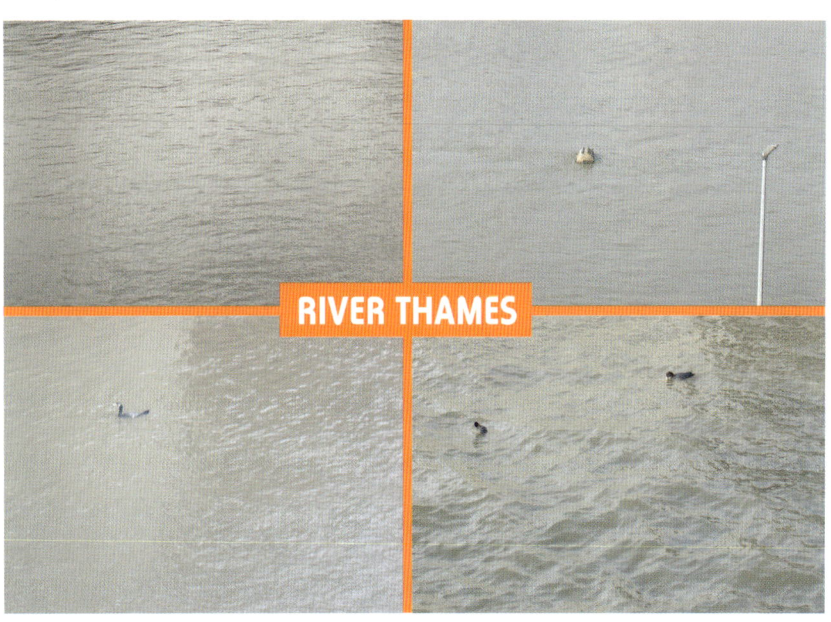
RIVER THAMES

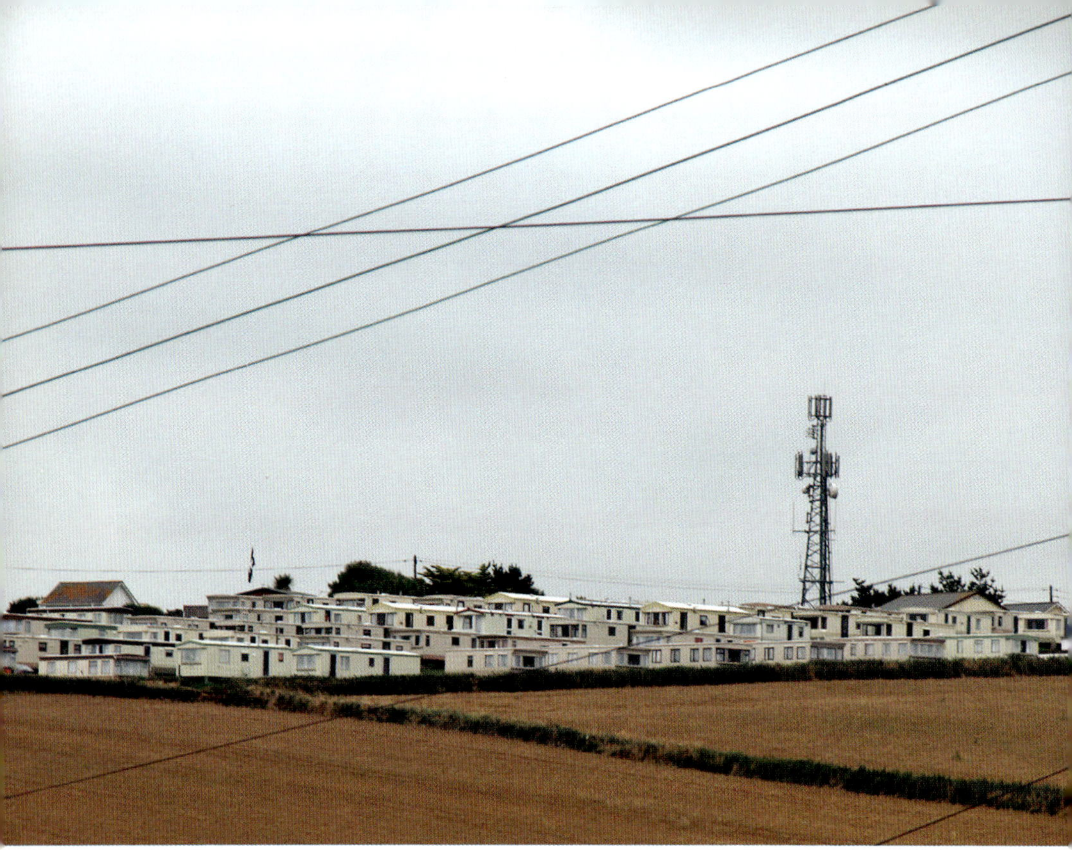

Countryside

The bits between urban areas that city people go to for a run out in the car. It can smell rather pungent, according to townies. Interestingly, people all over Britain – not just in the country – tell us that the residents of nearby neighbourhoods are 'all inbred over there'.

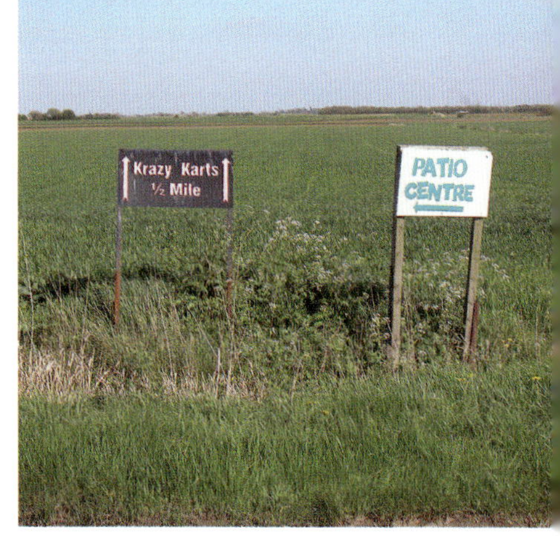

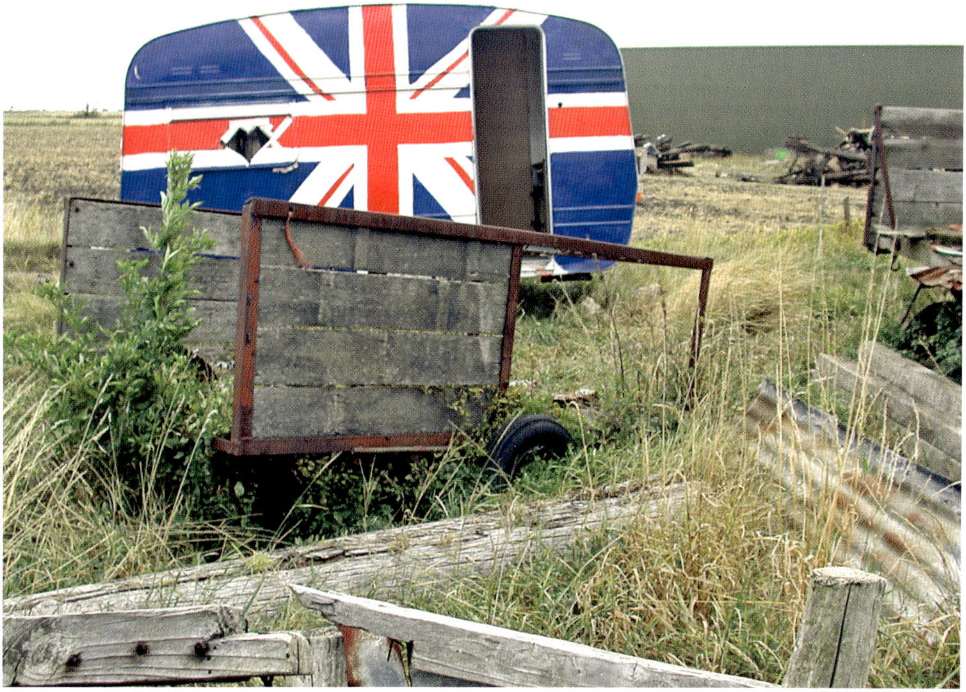

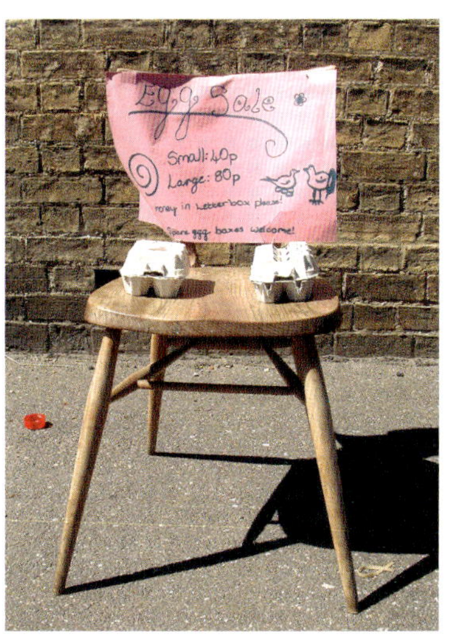
Egg Sale
Small: 40p
Large: 80p
money in Letterbox please!
Spare egg boxes welcome!

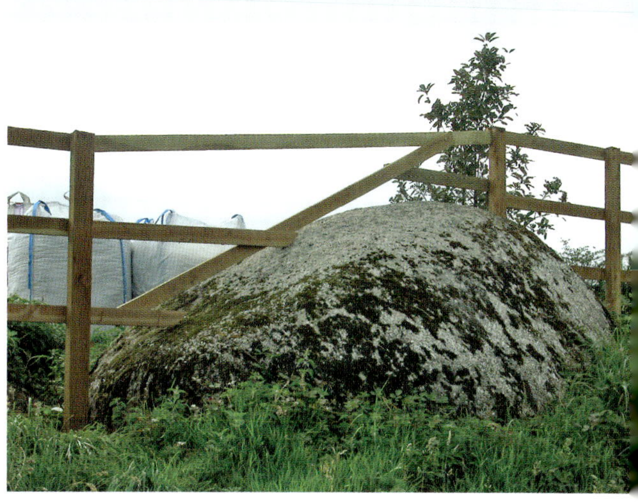

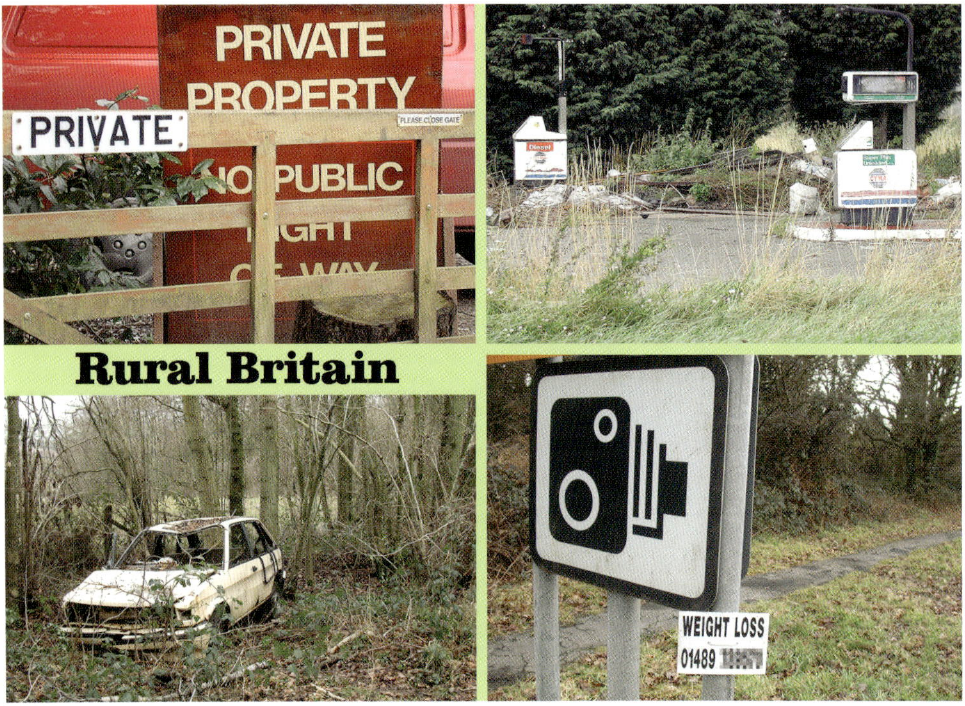

Rural Britain

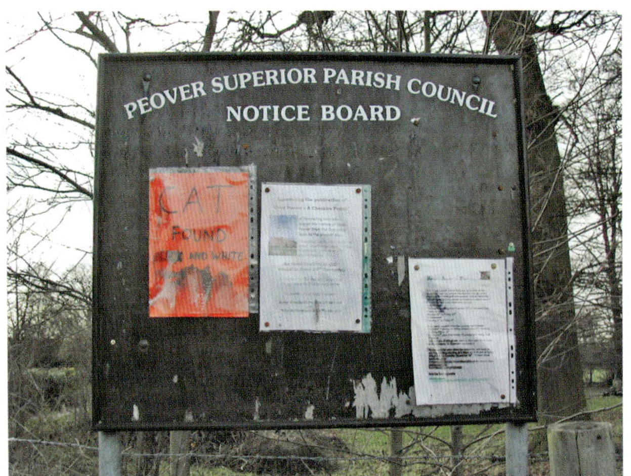

What's great about Britain?

The green parts

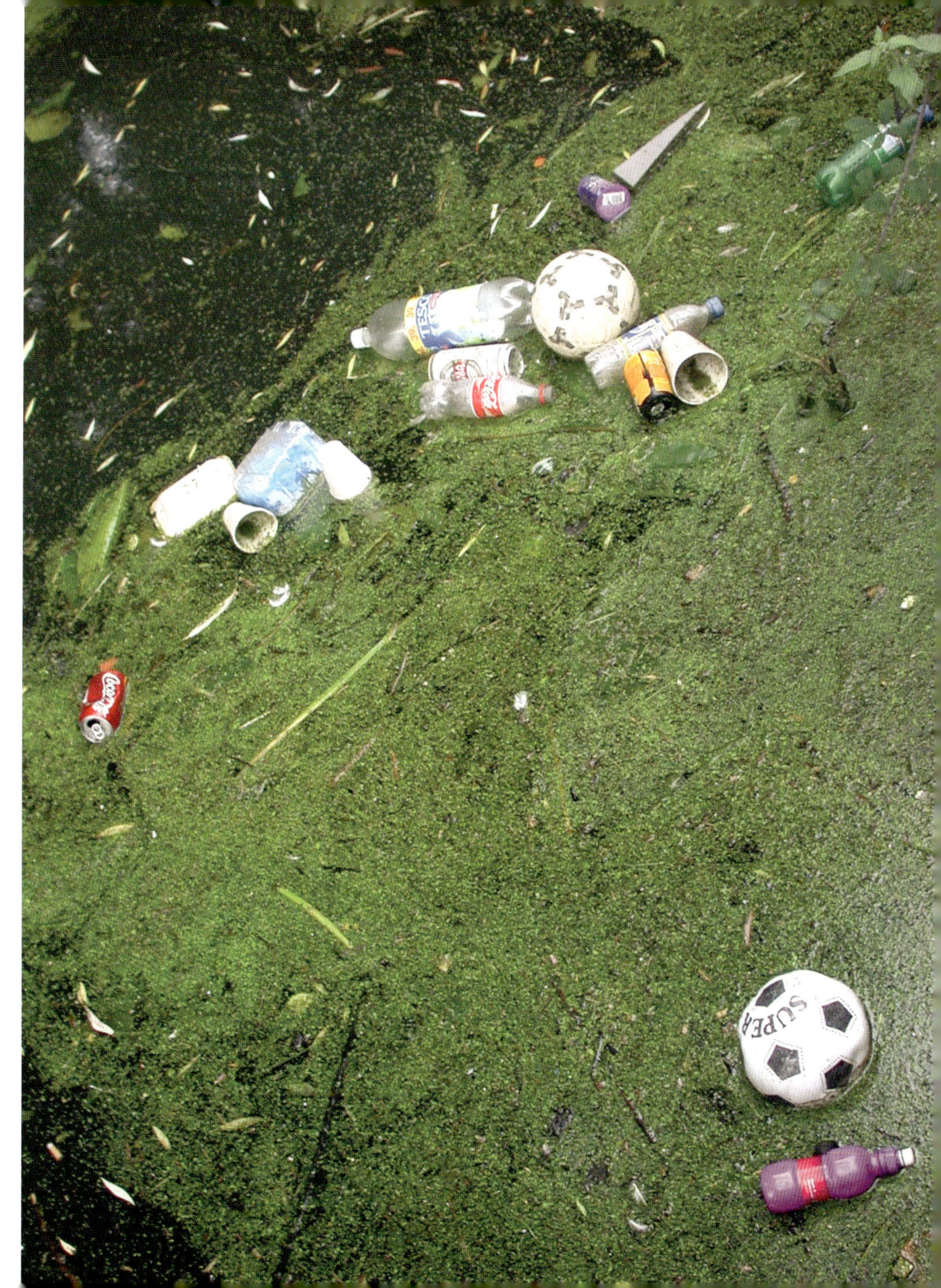
SUPER

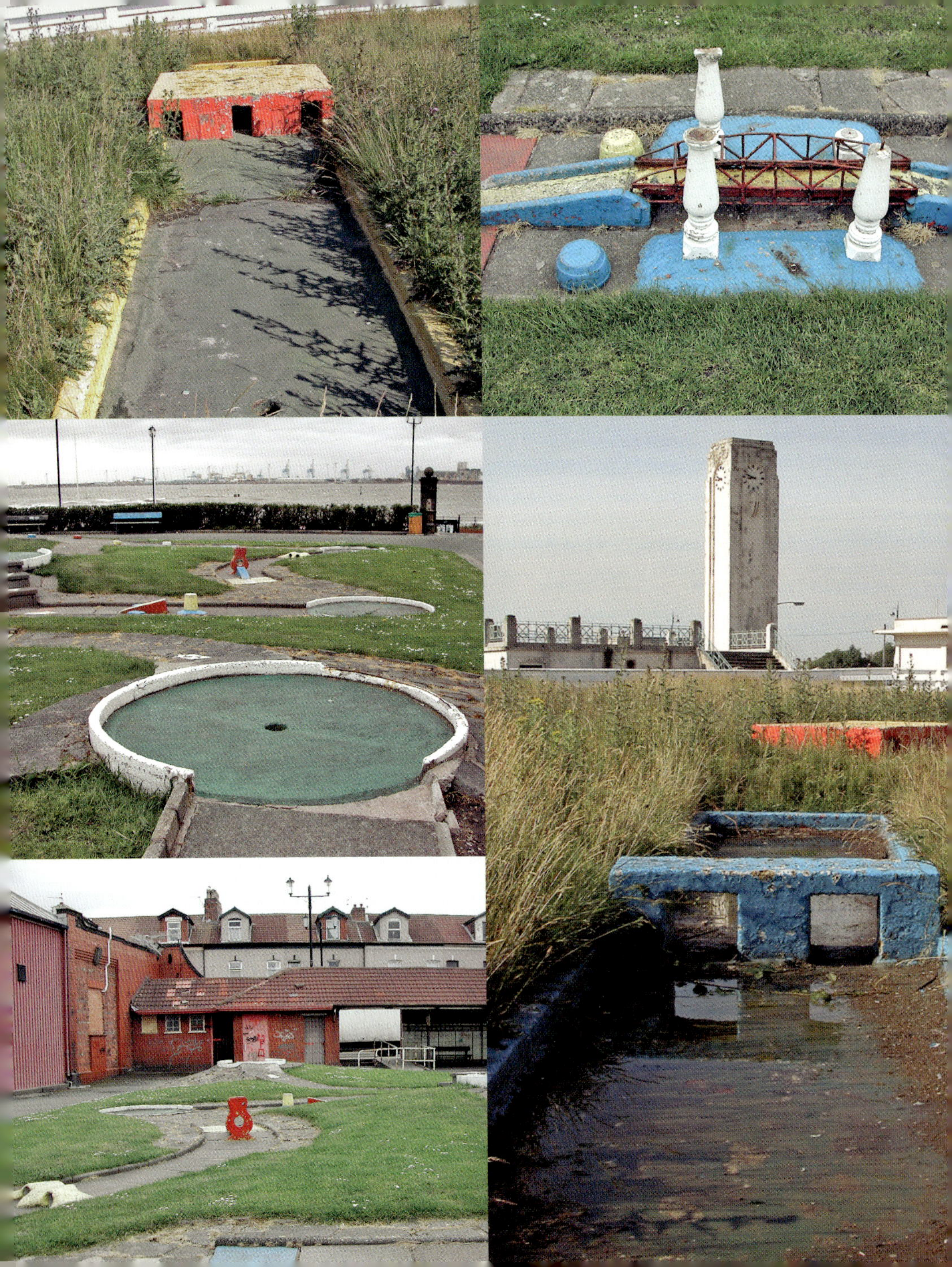

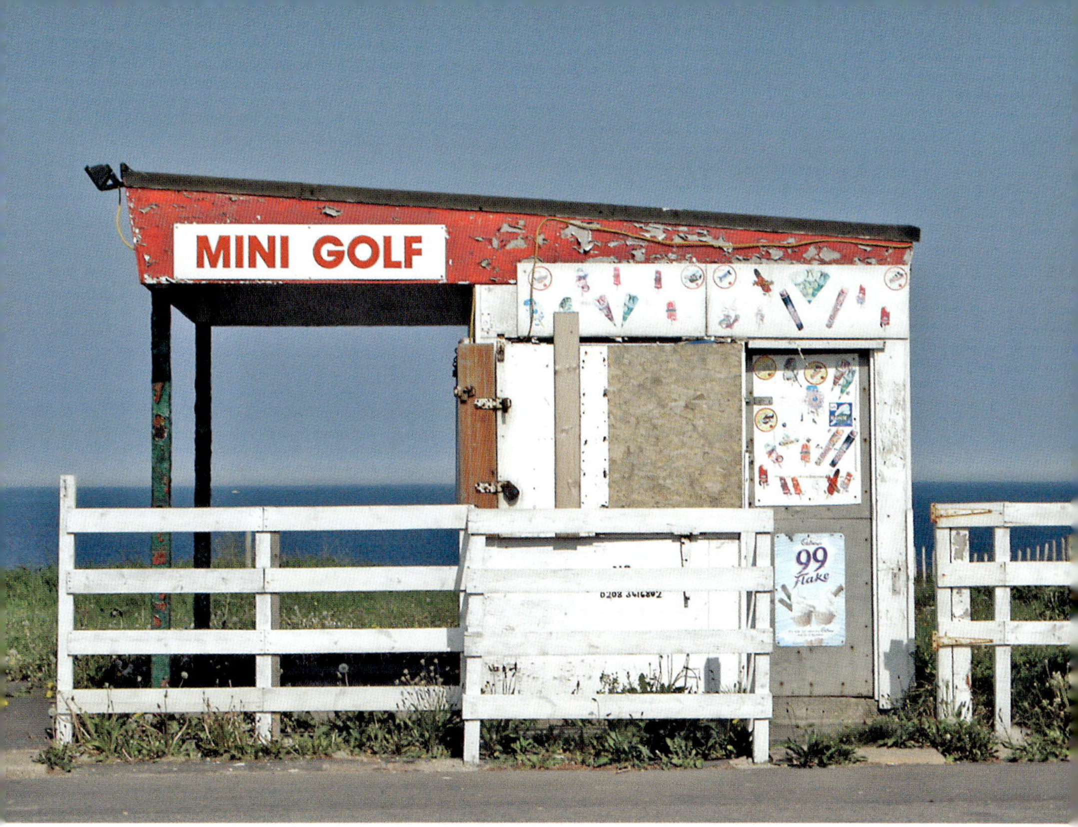

Mini-fun

Crazy Golf was once a popular pastime enjoyed by many a holidaymaker. What happened? Where did it all go wrong? And why was it so appealing in the first place?

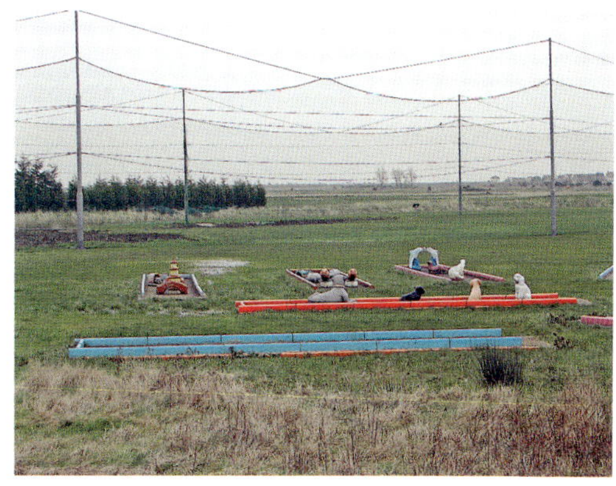

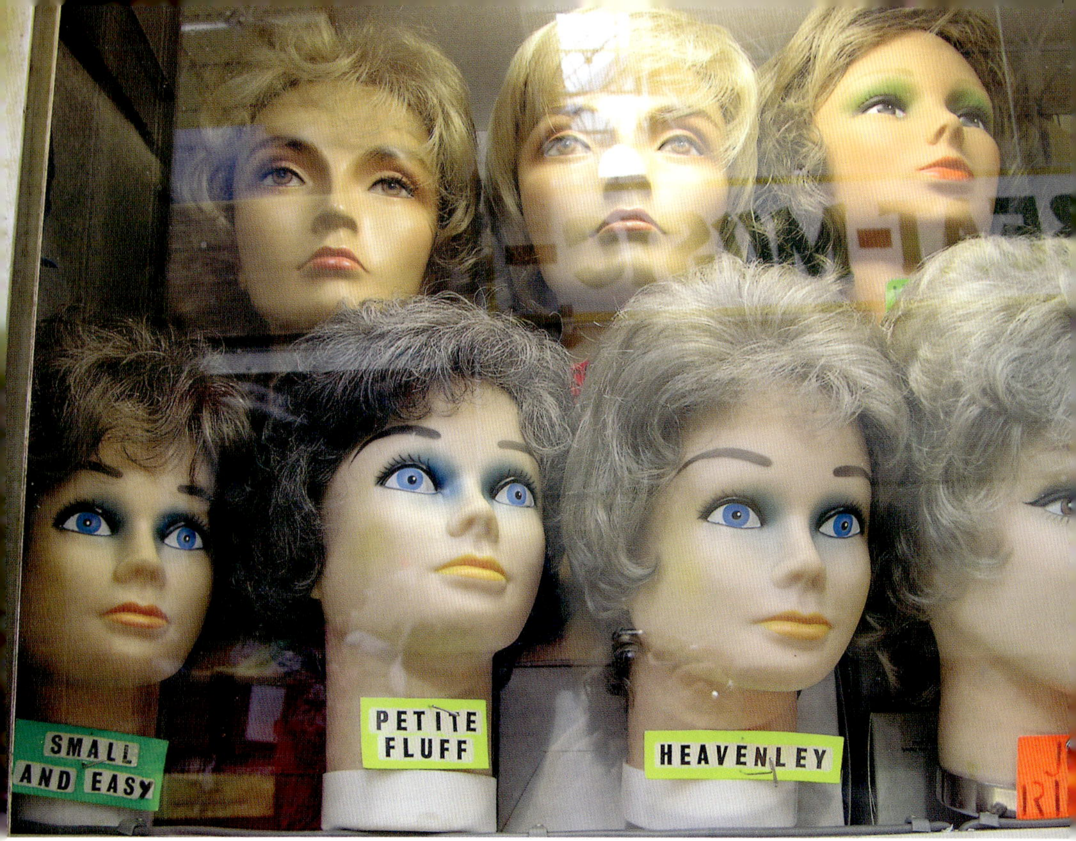

Shop displays

In Britain, we are spoilt for choice when it comes to shopping. From pigs' heads to belly bands, a bewildering array of goods is available on every high street. Lovingly-created displays of items may further enhance the shopping experience.

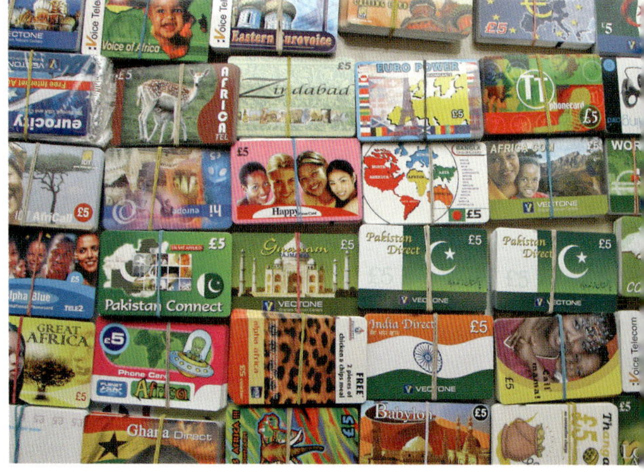

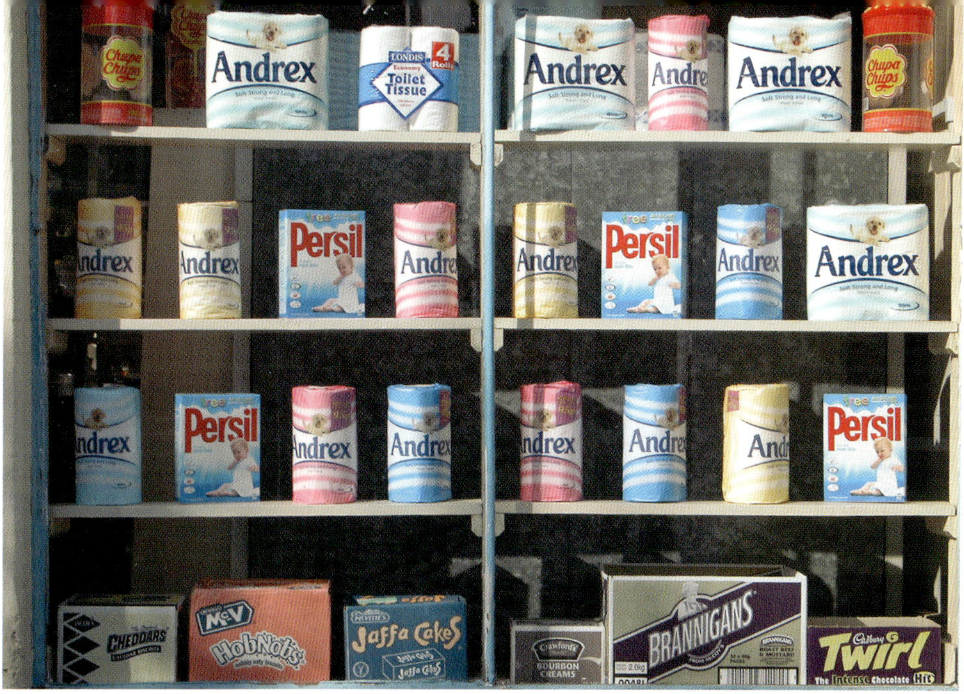

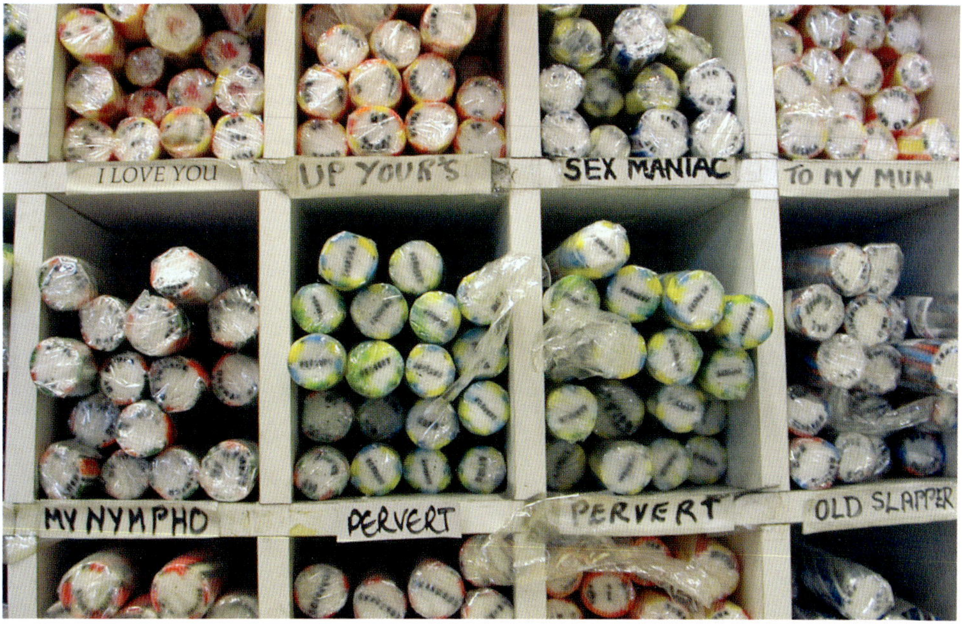

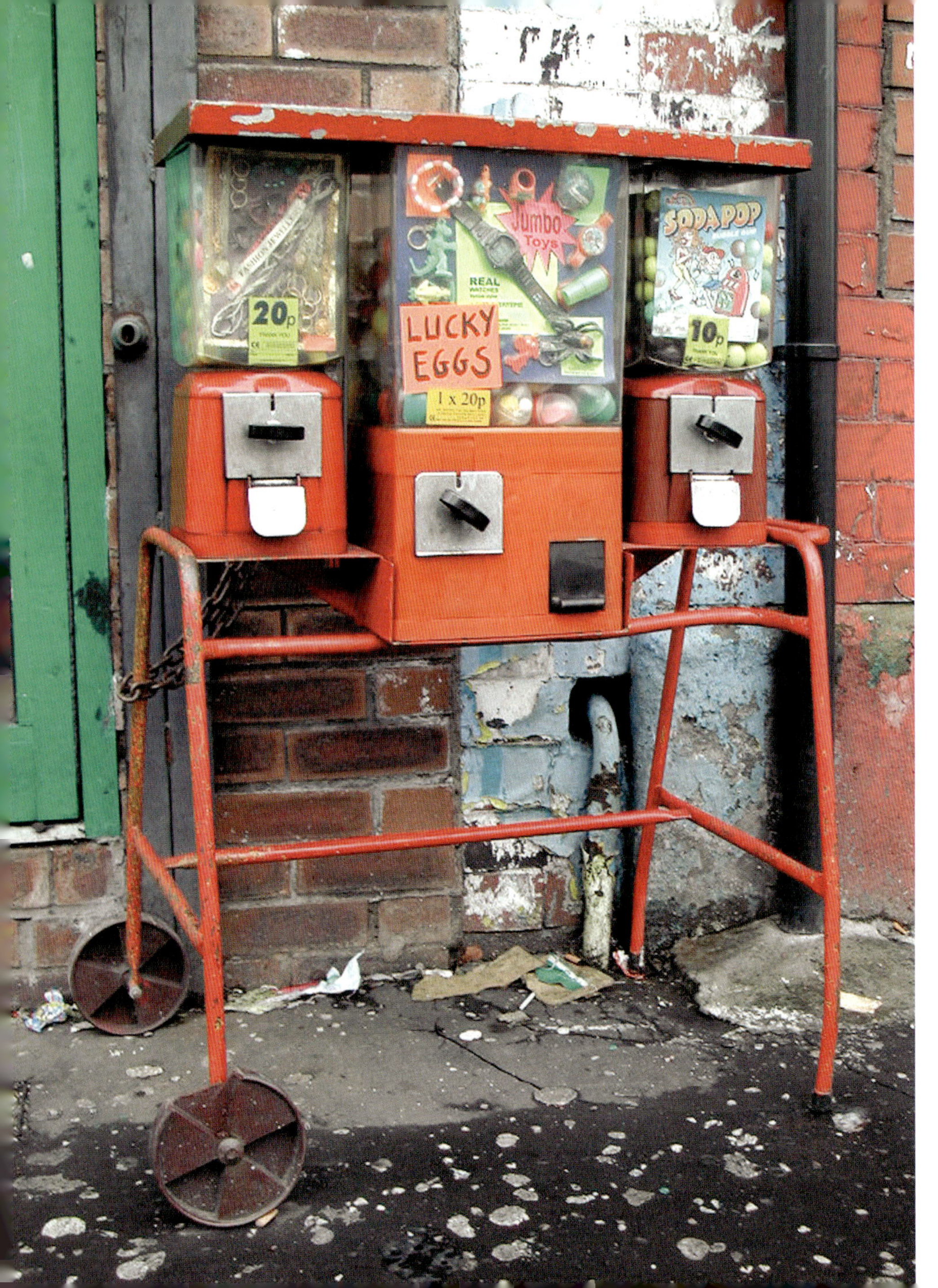
20p
Jumbo Toys
REAL WATCHES
LUCKY EGGS
1 x 20p
SODA POP
10p

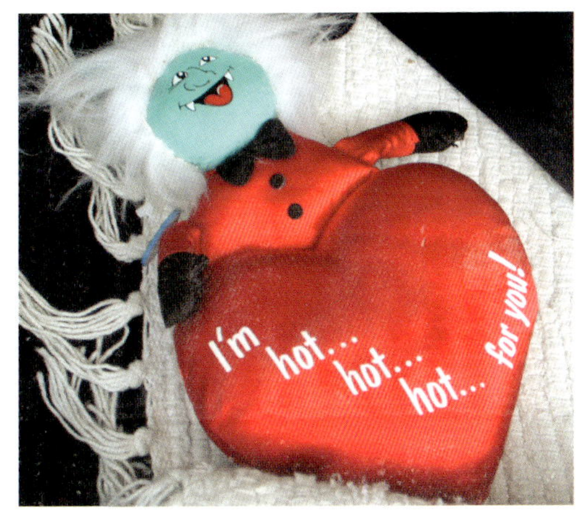
I'm hot... hot... hot... for you!

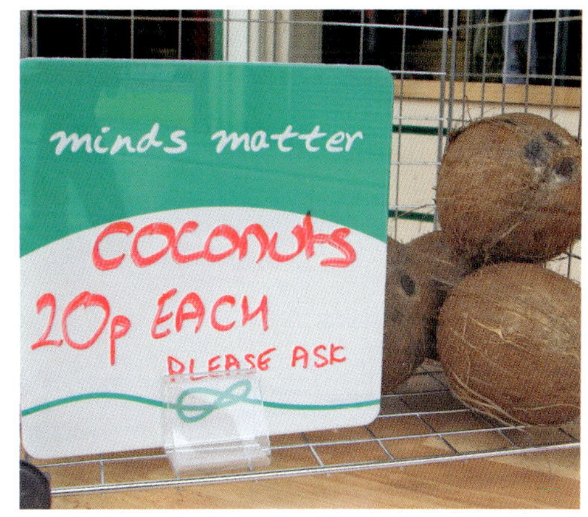
minds matter
COCONUTS
20p EACH
PLEASE ASK

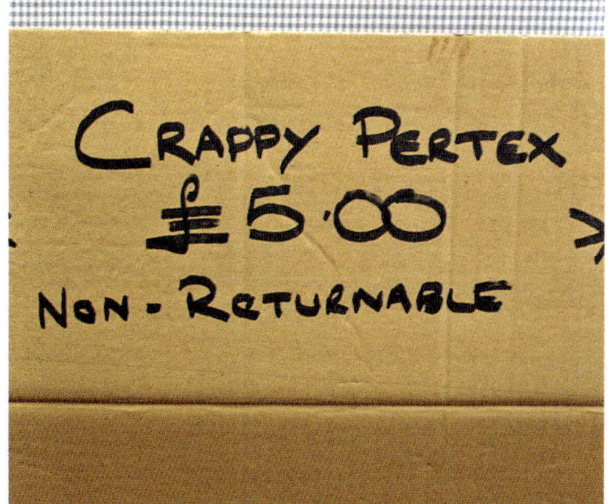
CRAPPY PERTEX
£5.00
NON-RETURNABLE

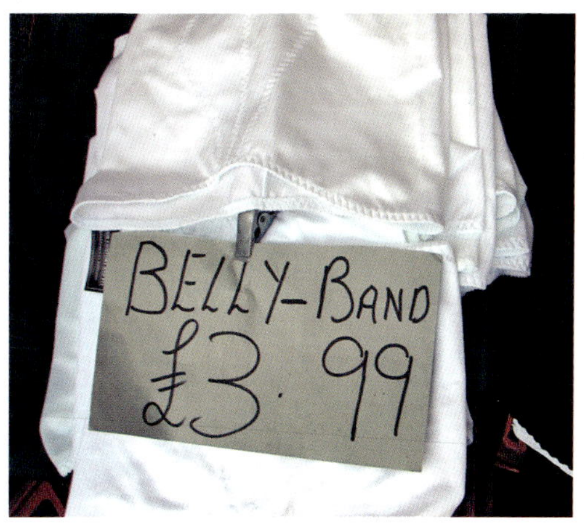
BELLY-BAND
£3.99

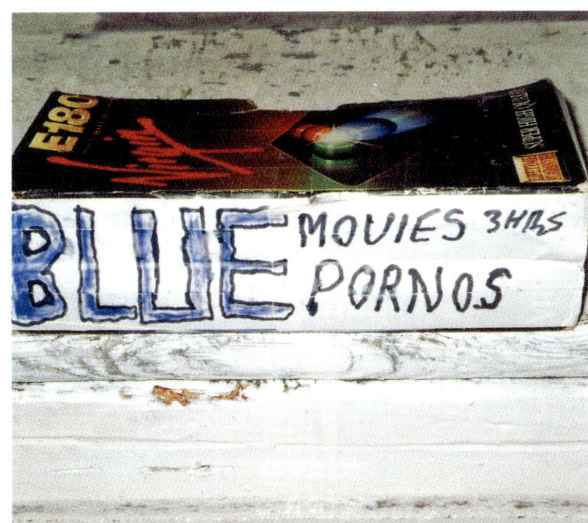
E180
BLUE MOVIES 3HRS
PORNOS

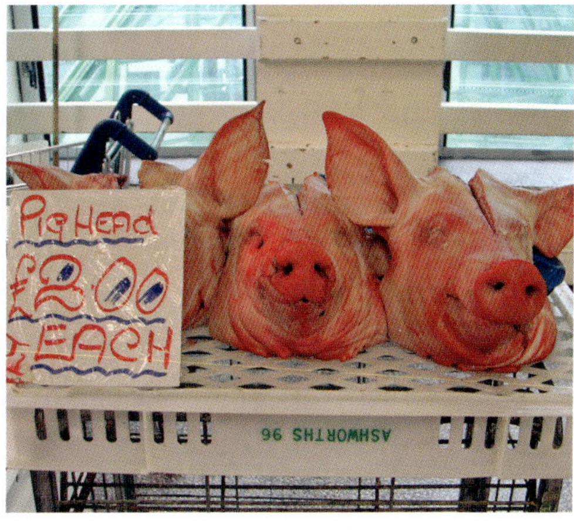
Pig Head
£2.00
EACH

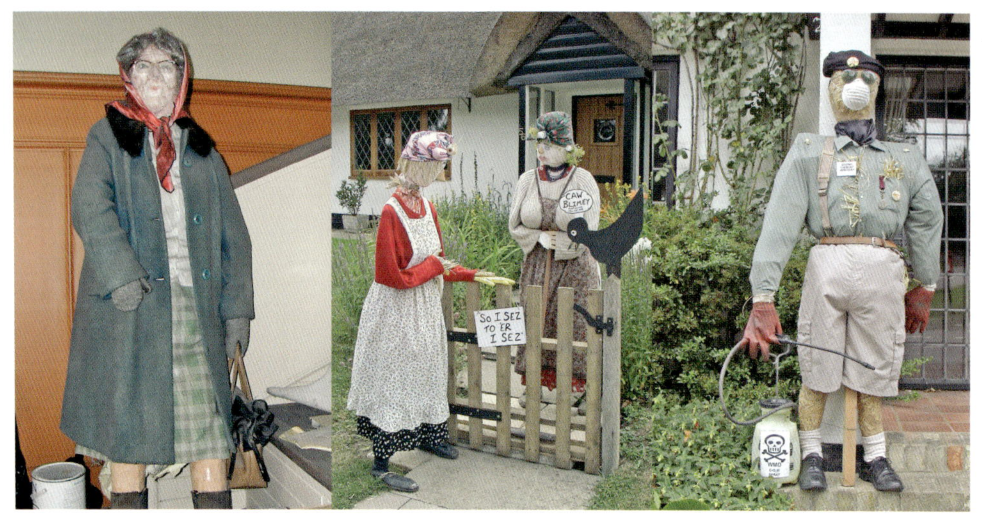

Public art

Little prompting is needed for the British public to get creative in the great outdoors, especially when it involves dressing up or stuffing things.

What do you think of as 'typically British'?

Freedom to be eccentric in a conformist kind of way

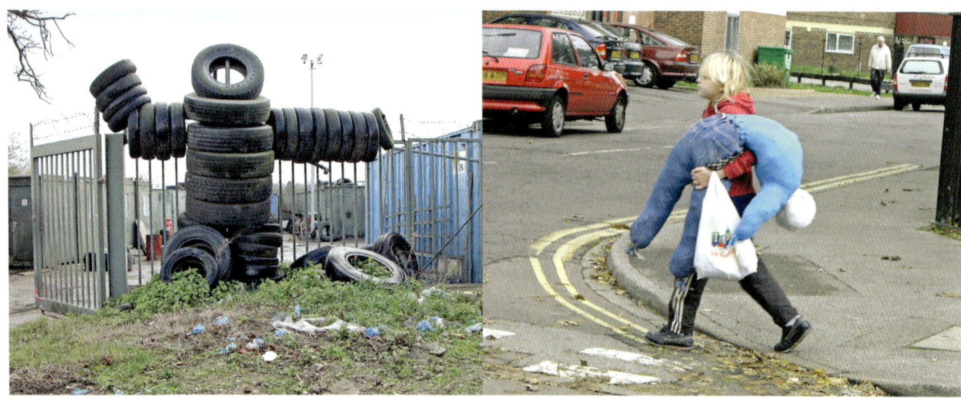

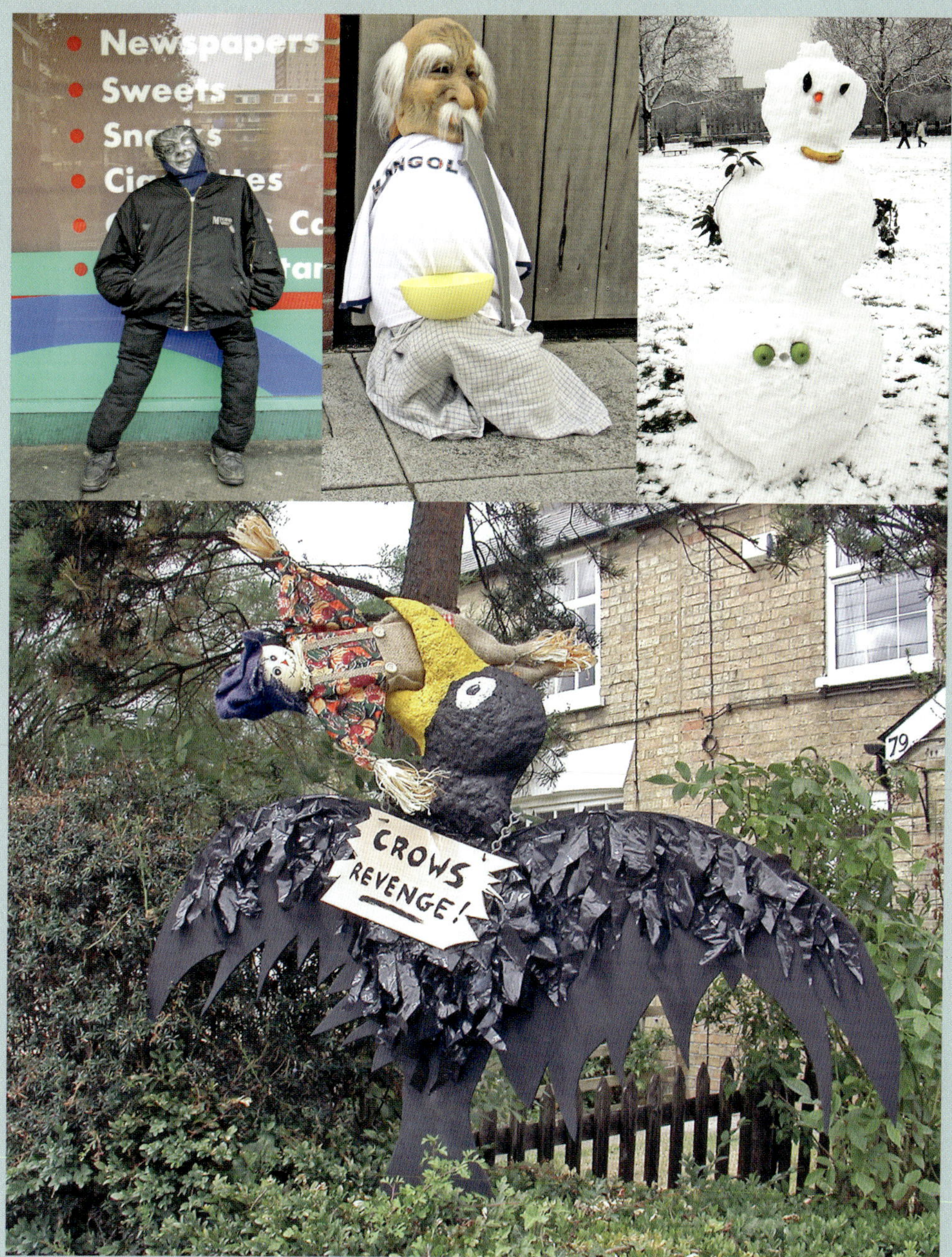
Newspapers
Sweets
CROWS
REVENGE!
79

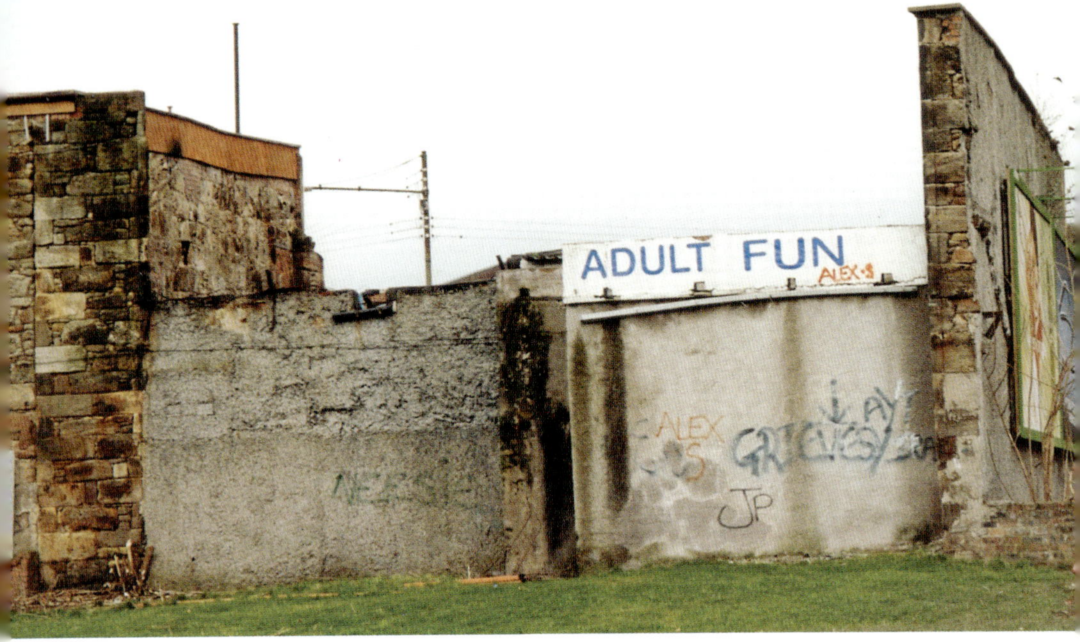

Smut

A play on words here, a missing letter there, an unfortunate pose. Nudge nudge wink wink – there's always an excuse for a bit of innuendo in Carry On Britain. Make mine a large one.

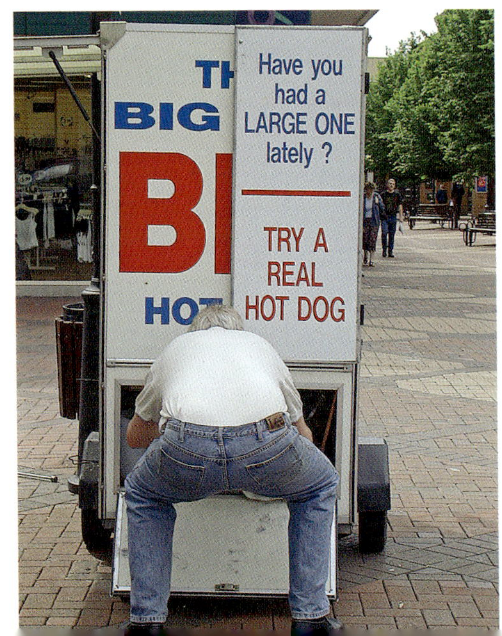

42% of people are looking for love

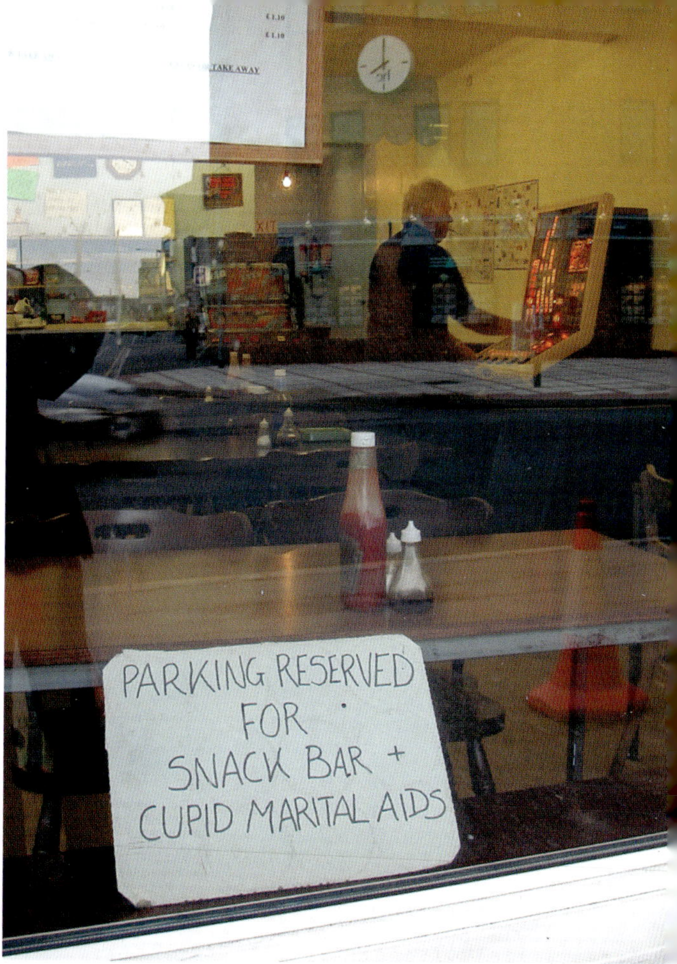

What's great about Britain?

Not sure at the moment

What's not so great?

Uptightness

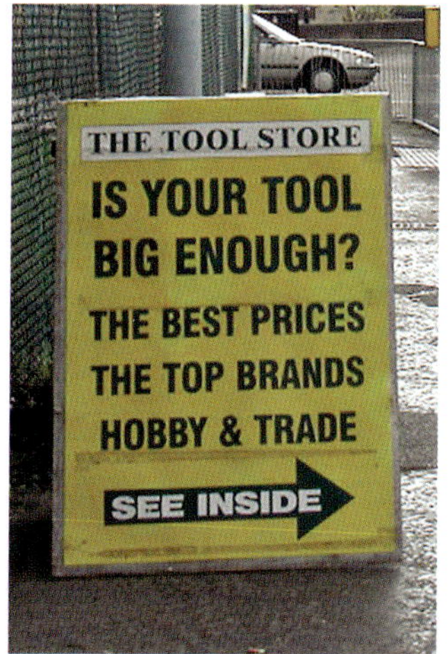

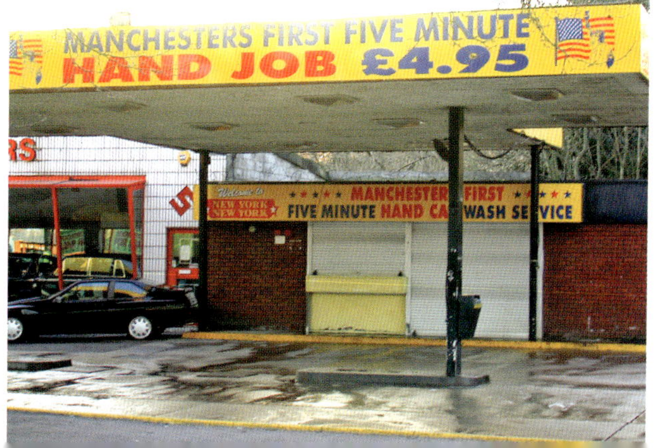

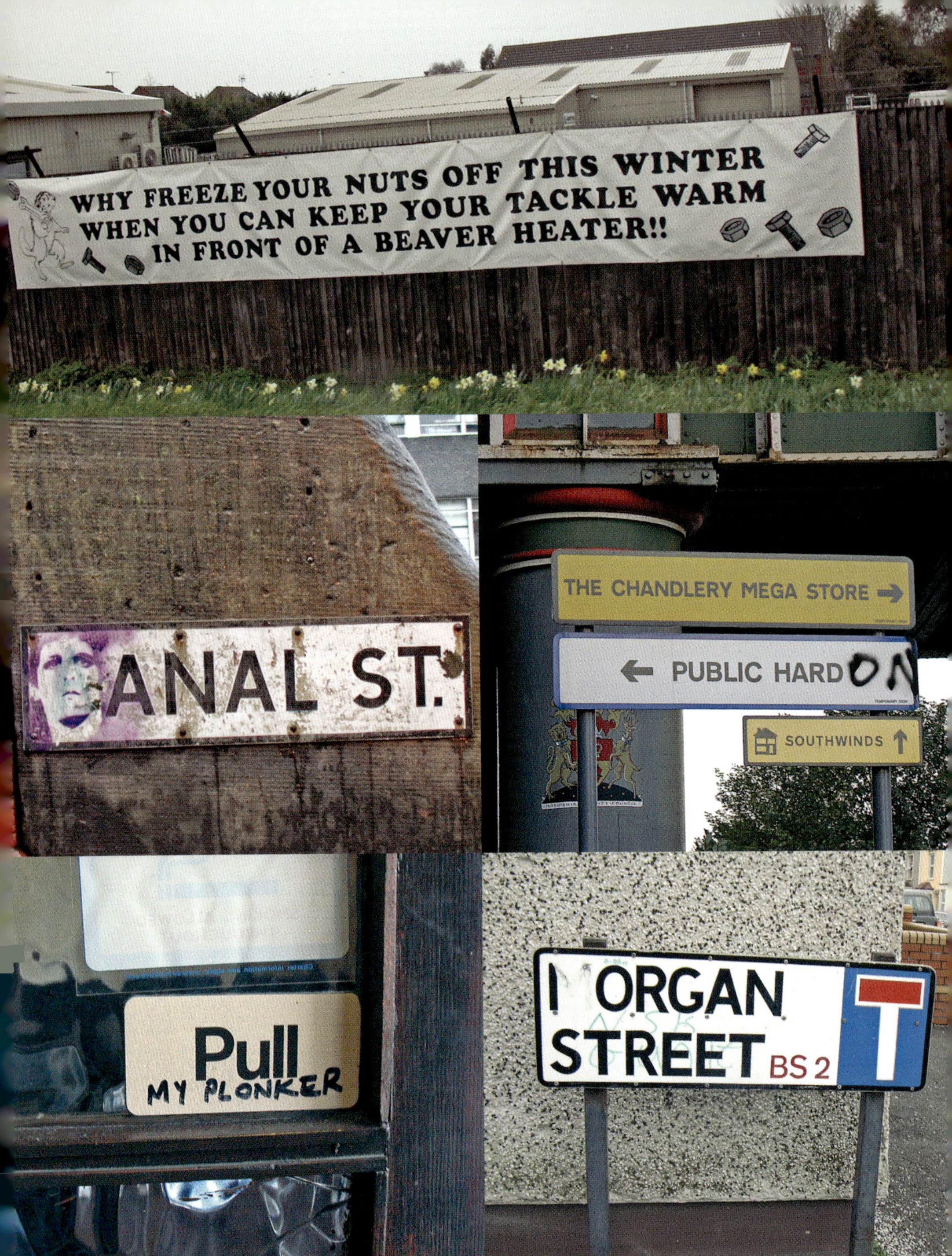
WHY FREEZE YOUR NUTS OFF THIS WINTER
WHEN YOU CAN KEEP YOUR TACKLE WARM
IN FRONT OF A BEAVER HEATER!!
ANAL ST.
THE CHANDLERY MEGA STORE
PUBLIC HARDON
SOUTHWINDS
Pull
MY PLONKER
ORGAN
STREET
BS 2

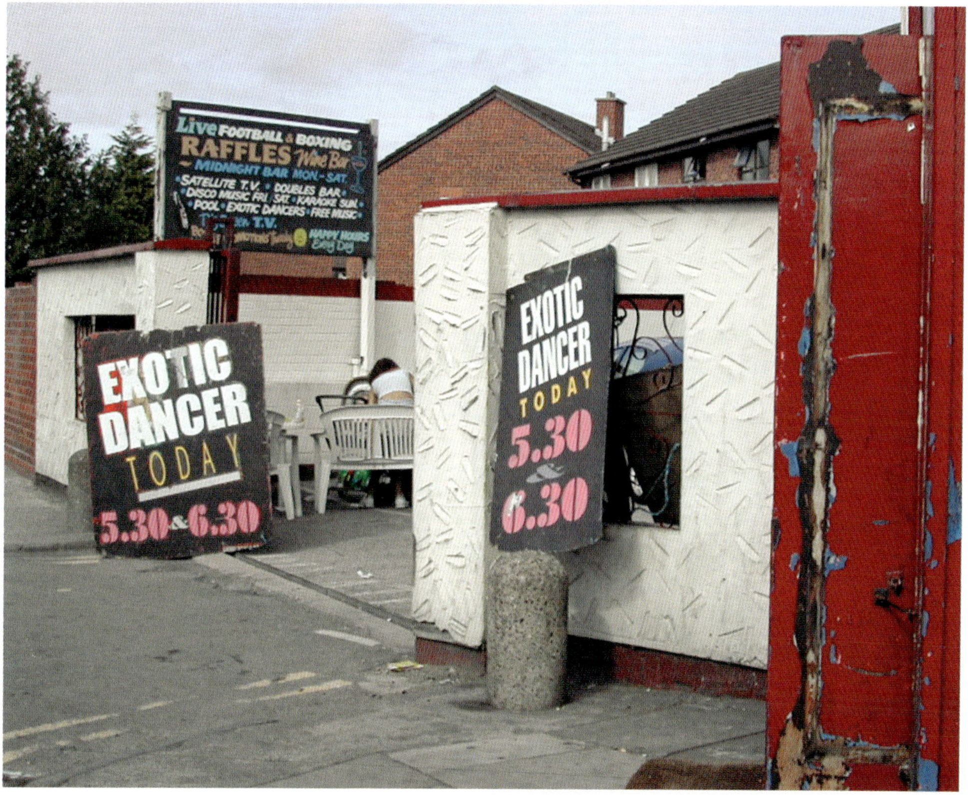

What's your personal motto?

Sex and shopping come first

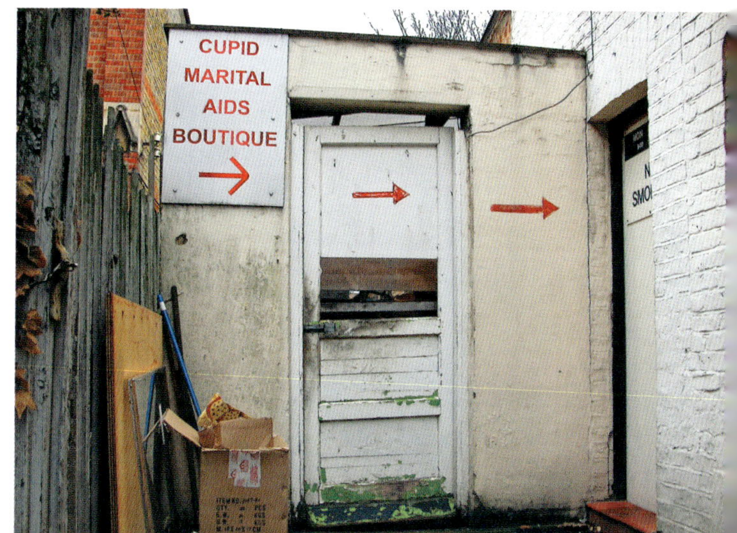

Mis ing lett rs

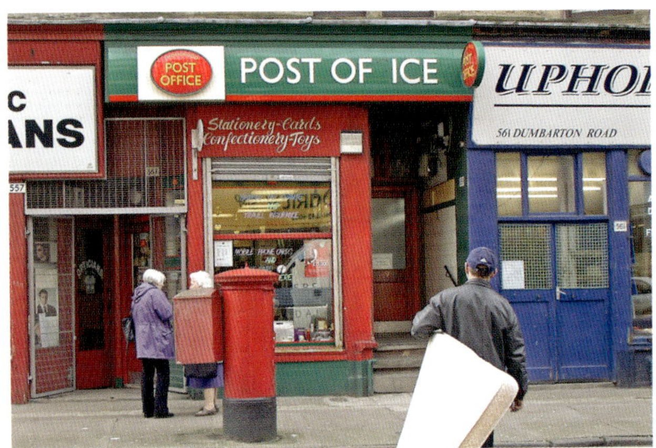

Sometimes less is more.

I was nearly killed by an 'S' from a sign falling on me

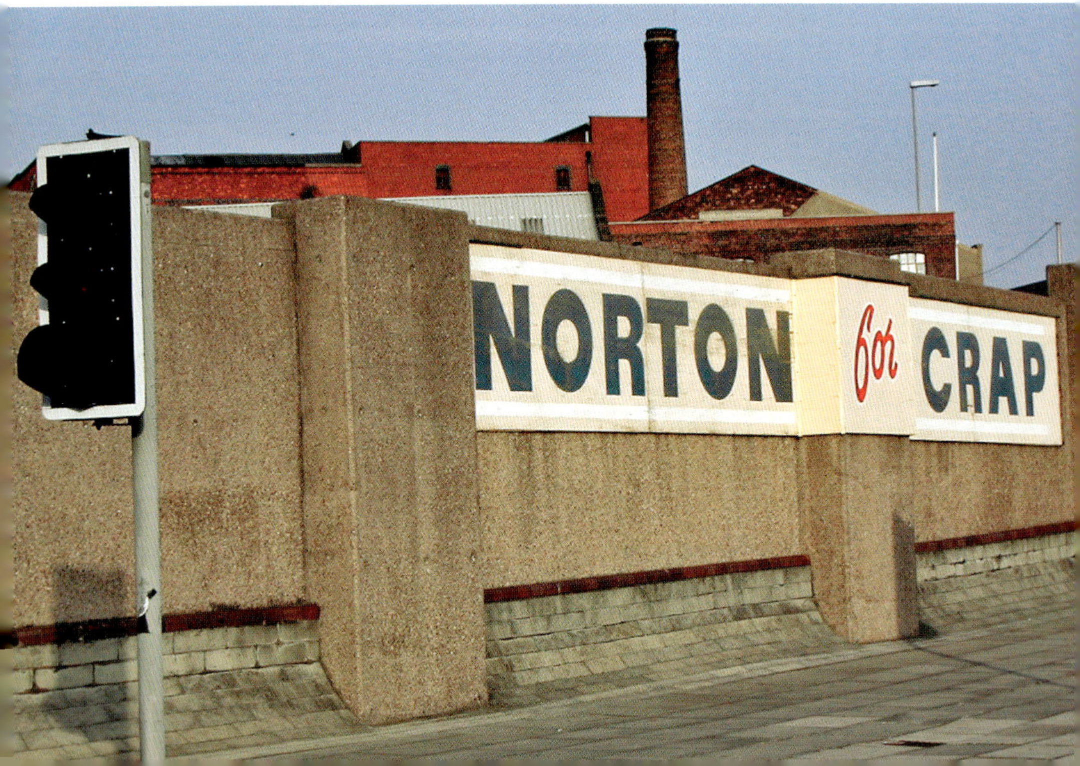

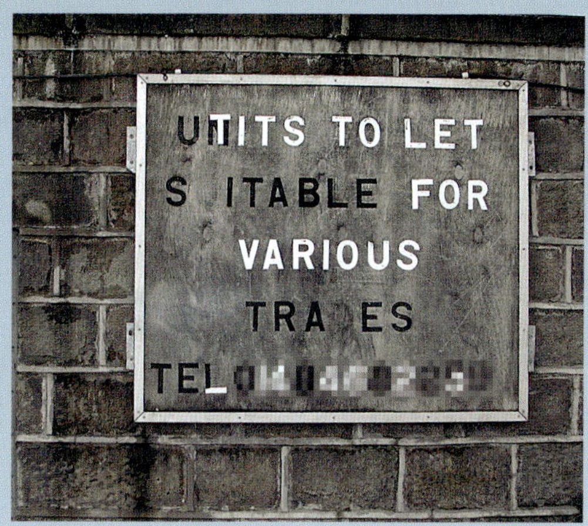
UTITS TO LET
S ITABLE FOR
VARIOUS
TRA ES
TEL

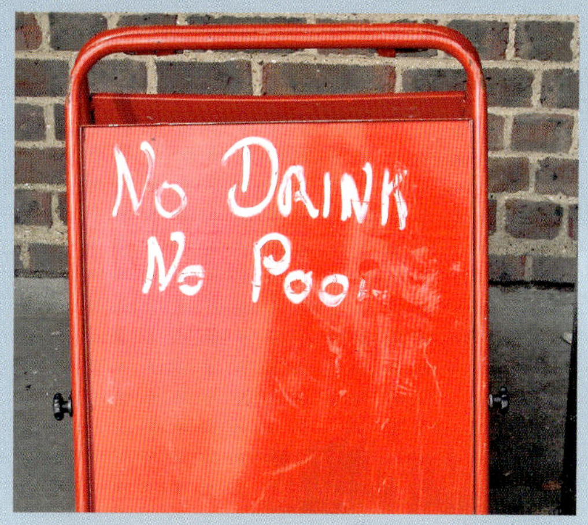
No DAINK
No Poo

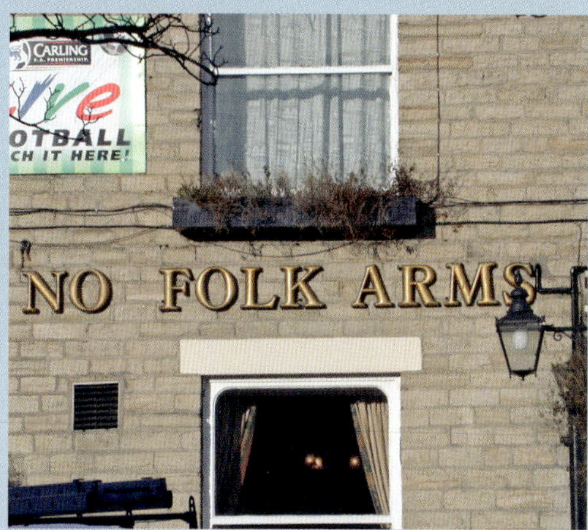
CARLING
NO FOLK ARMS

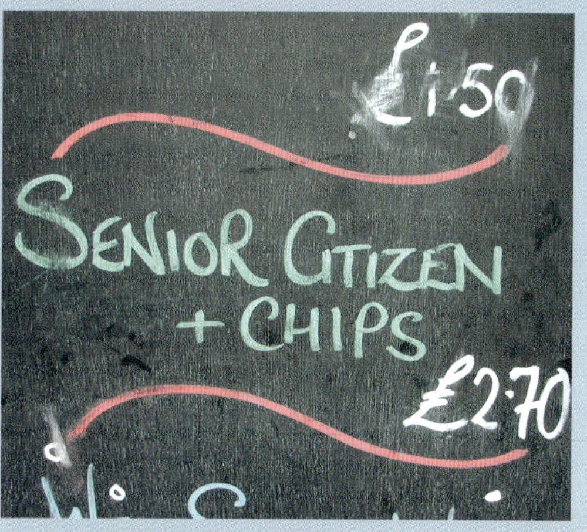
£1.50
SENIOR CITIZEN
+ CHIPS
£2.70

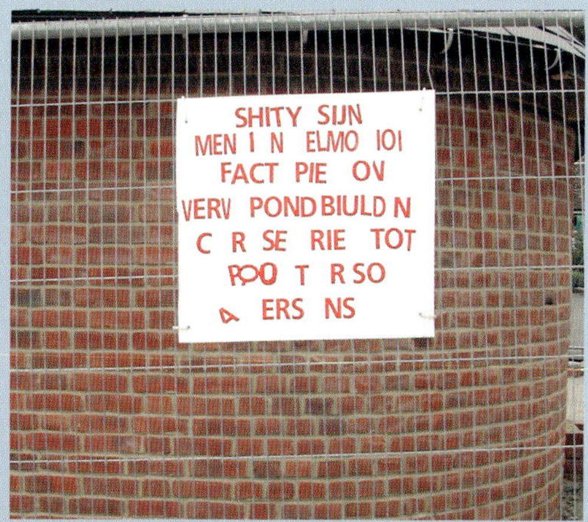
SHITY SIJN
MEN I N ELMO 101
FACT PIE OV
VERV POND BIULD N
C R SE RIE TOT
POO T R SO
ERS NS

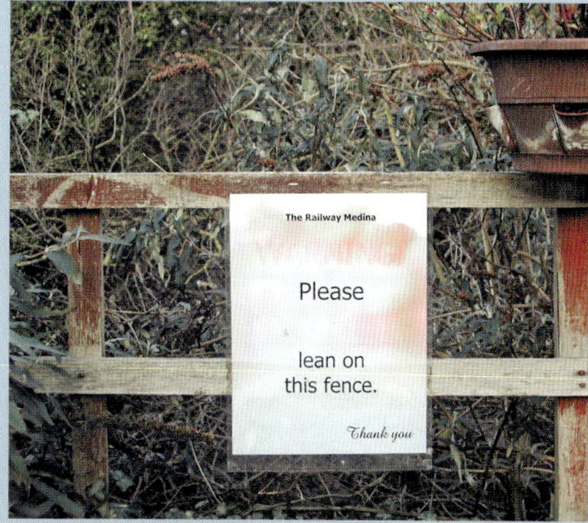
The Railway Medina
Please
lean on
this fence.
Thank you

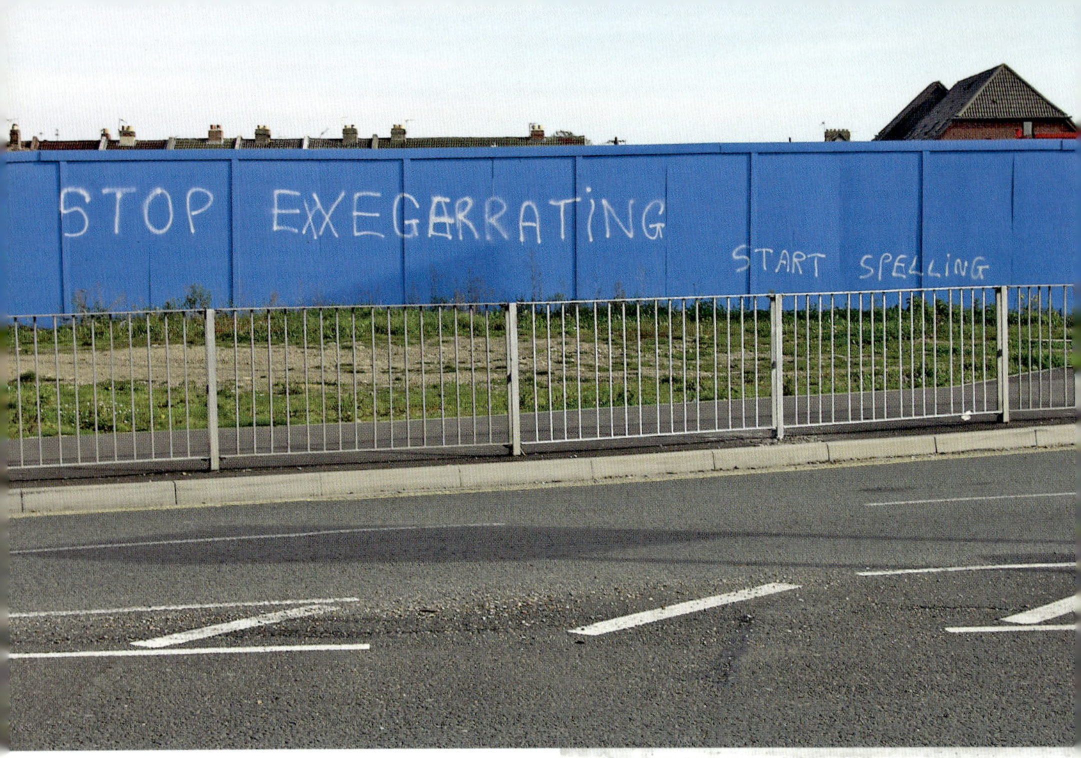

Graffiti

Need to make a public statement? All you need is a big marker pen, a can of spray paint or just a dirty van and a finger.

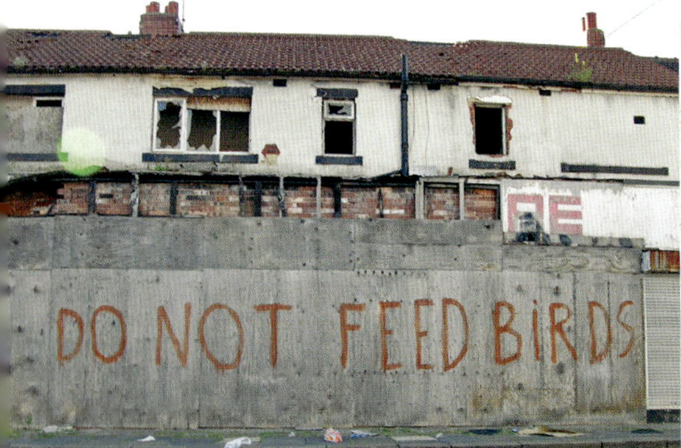

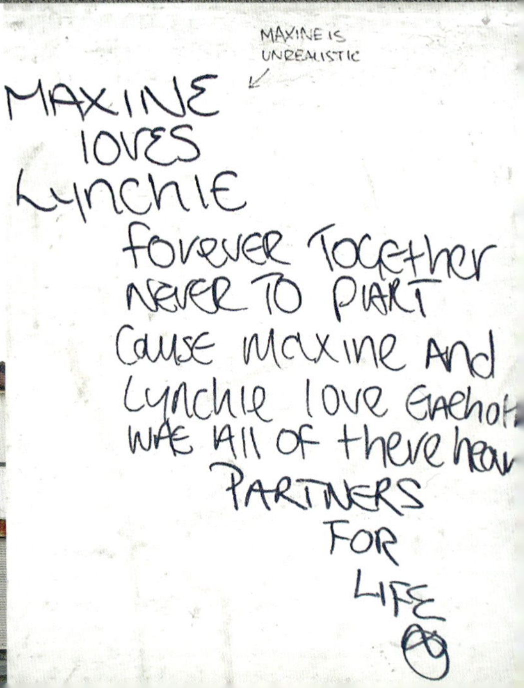

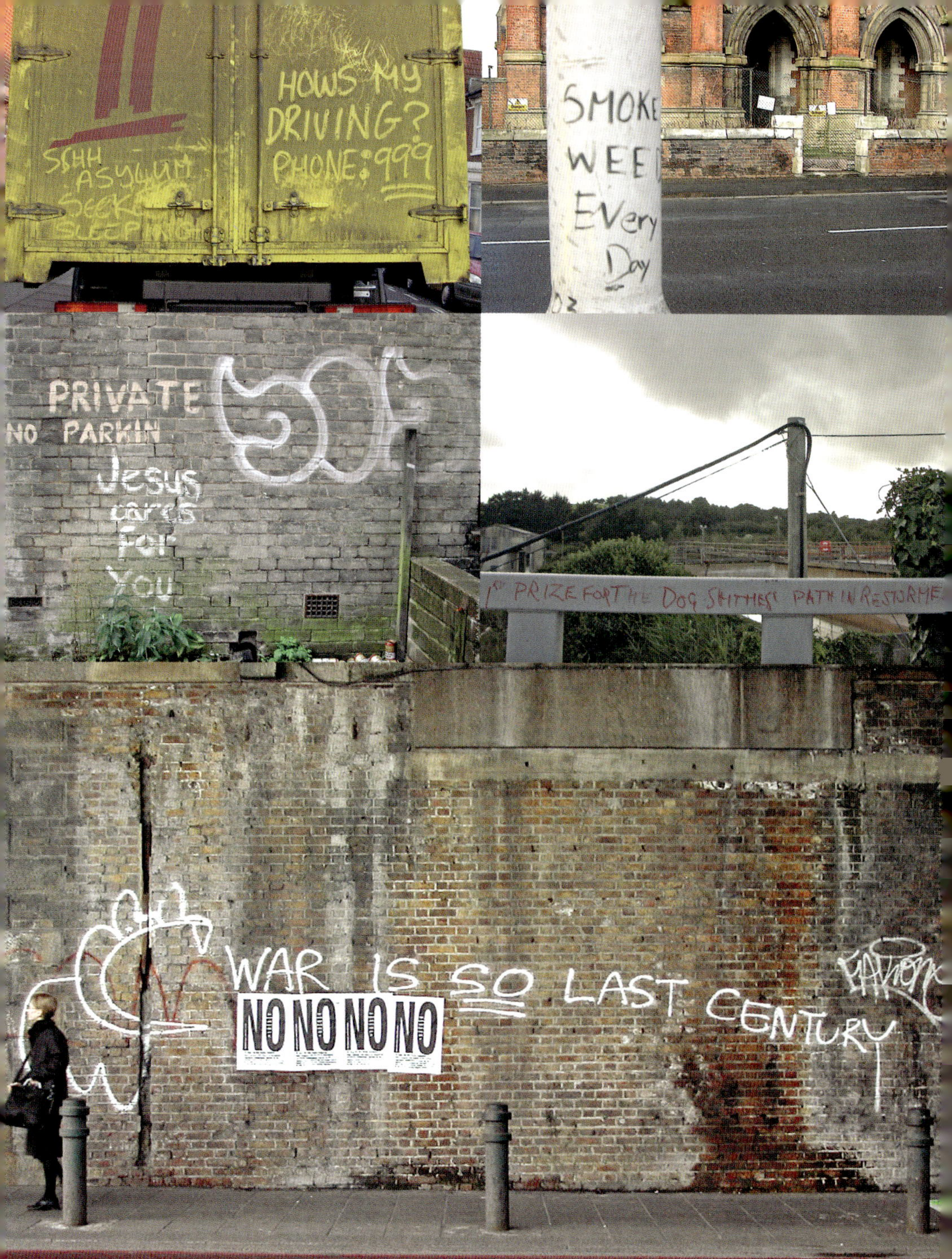
SSHH ASYLUM SEEK SLEEPING
HOWS MY DRIVING? PHONE: 999
SMOKE WEED EVERY DAY
PRIVATE NO PARKIN
Jesus cares for you
1st PRIZE FOR THE DOG SHITTIEST PATH IN RESTORME
WAR IS SO LAST CENTURY
NO NO NO NO

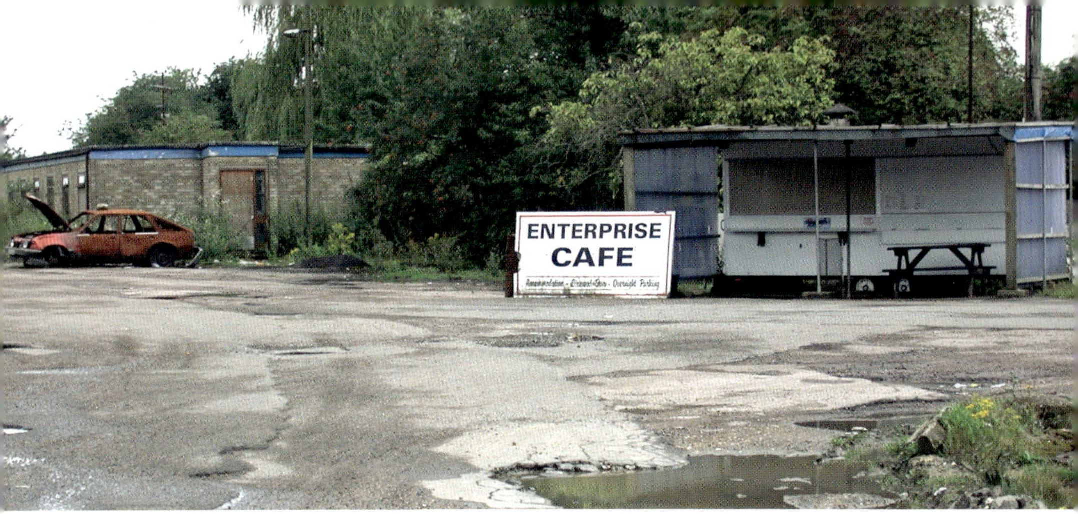

Cafes

A proper mug of tea and an all-day breakfast followed by spotted dick and custard, eaten at a Formica table while sat on a plastic chair. Where else could you be?

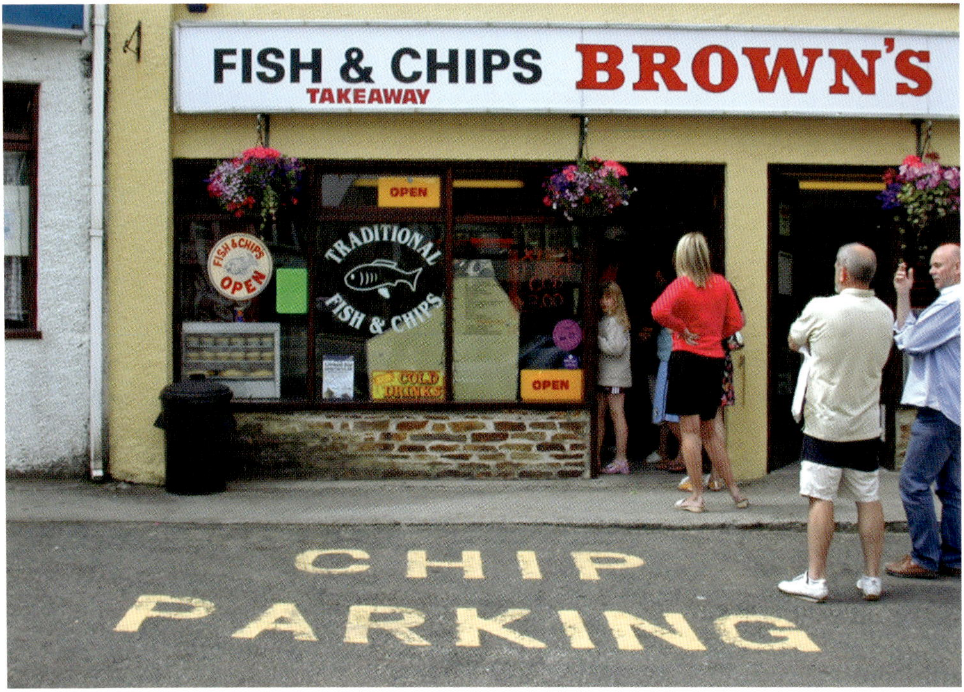

What's your personal motto?

Don't eat anything bigger than your head

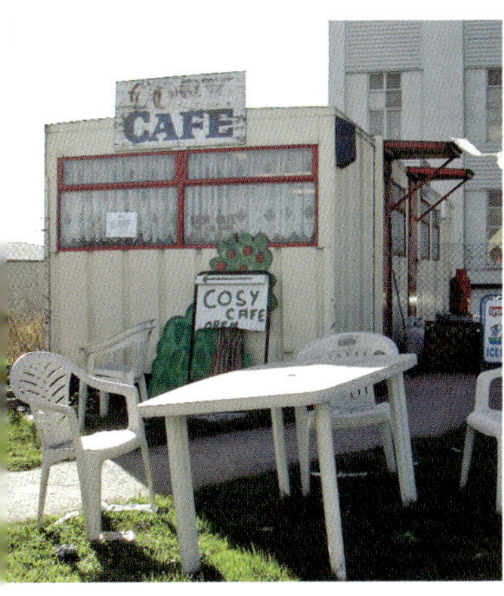

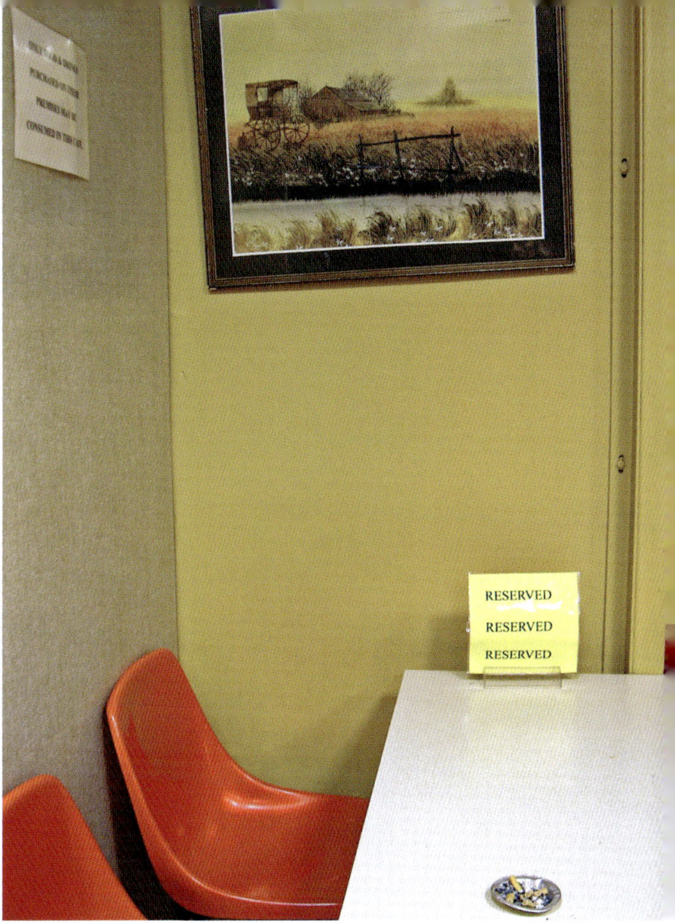

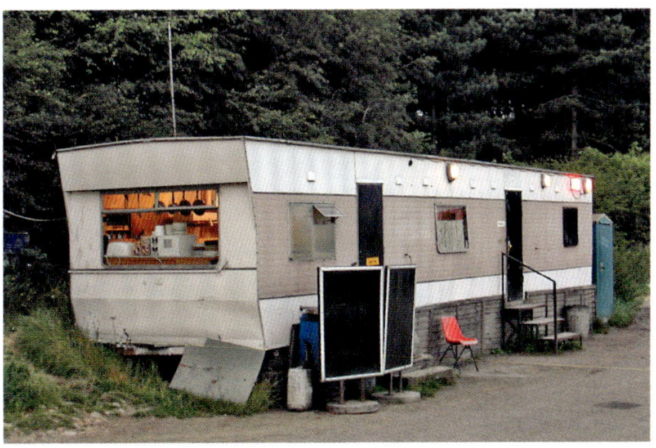

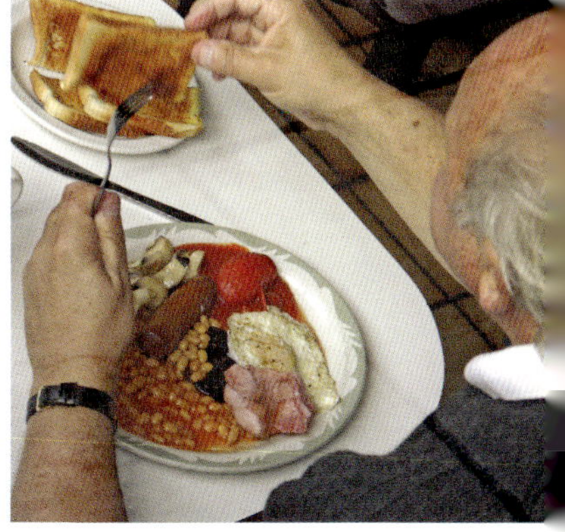

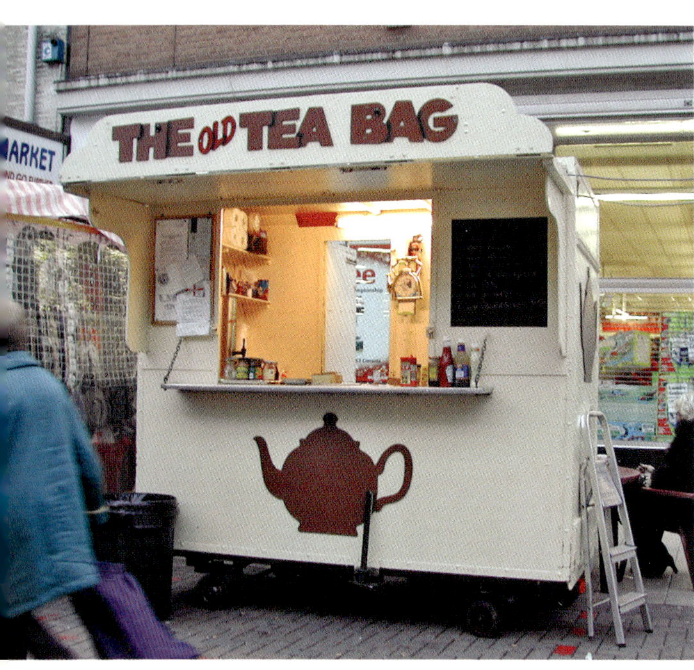

Support your local greasy spoon; it may not be there much longer.

What do you think of as 'typically British'?

Union Jacks, bulldogs, pie and mash

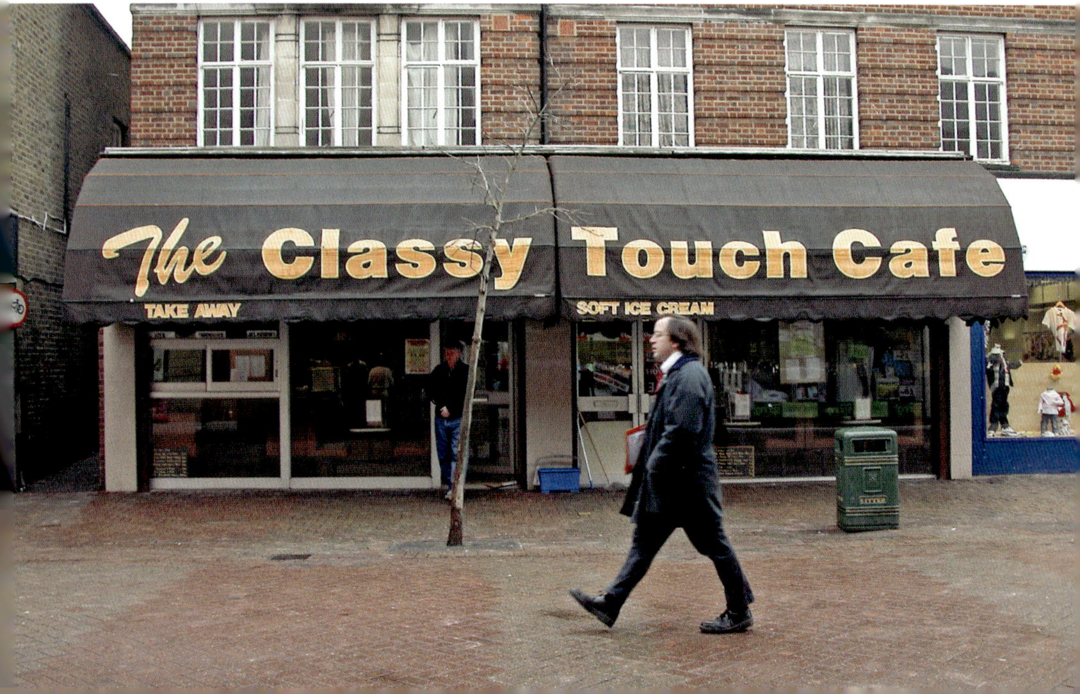

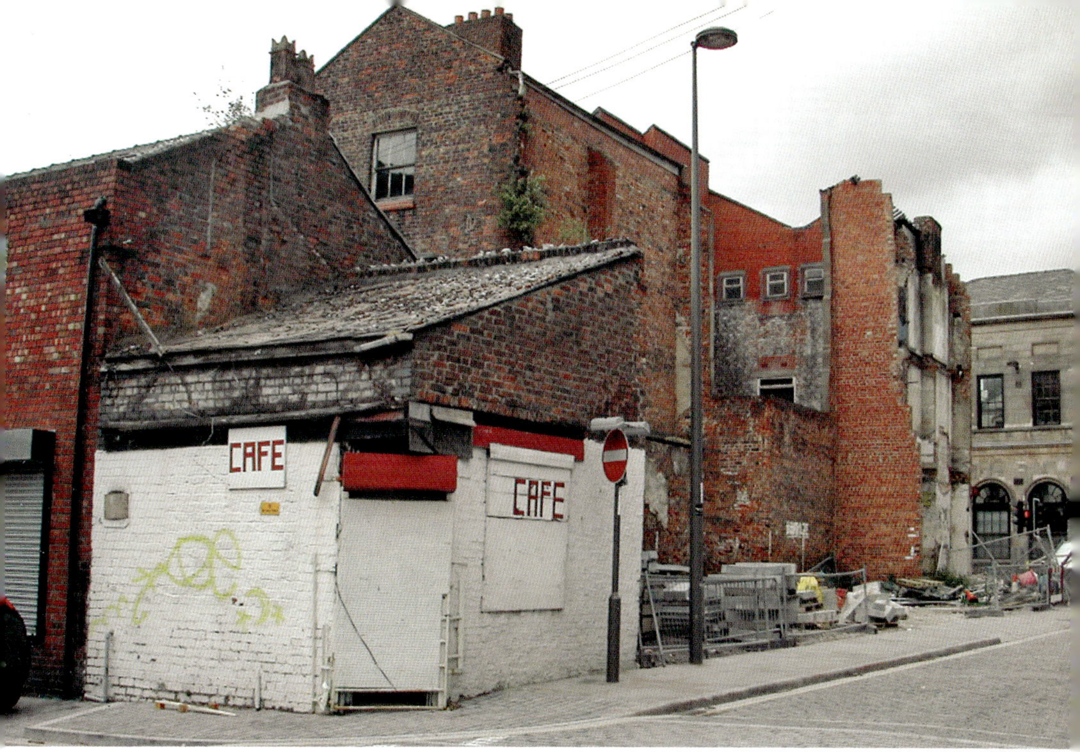

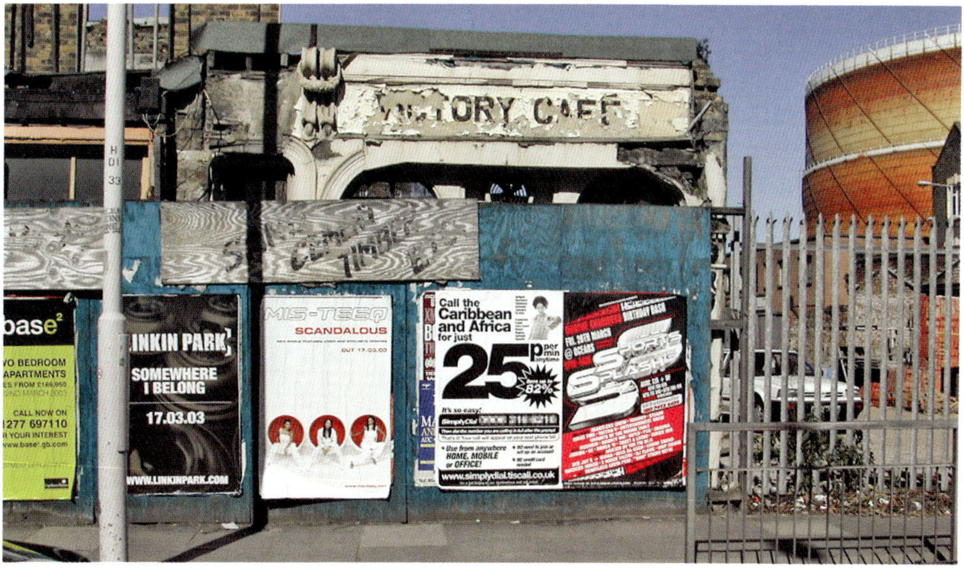

People of Britain

Freedom of expression is highly valued in Britain, even if it means shopping in a crash helmet, brandishing a homemade placard or mowing the pavement. It's a very special place indeed.

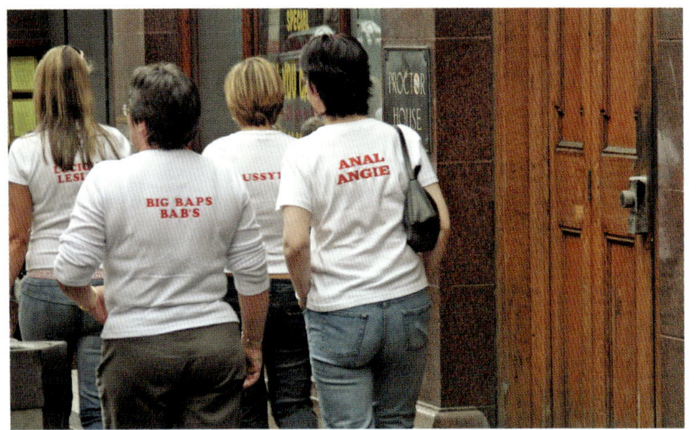

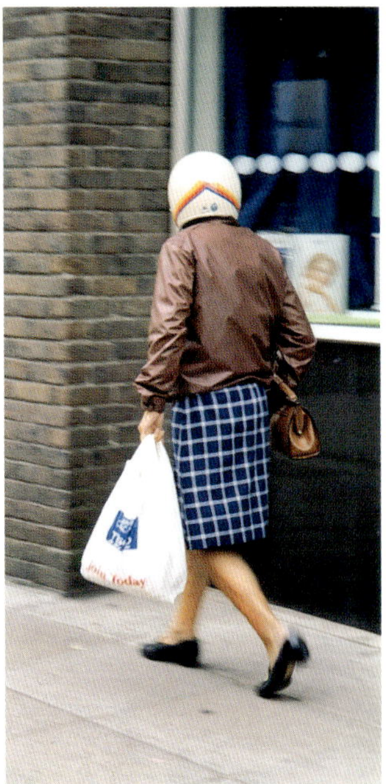

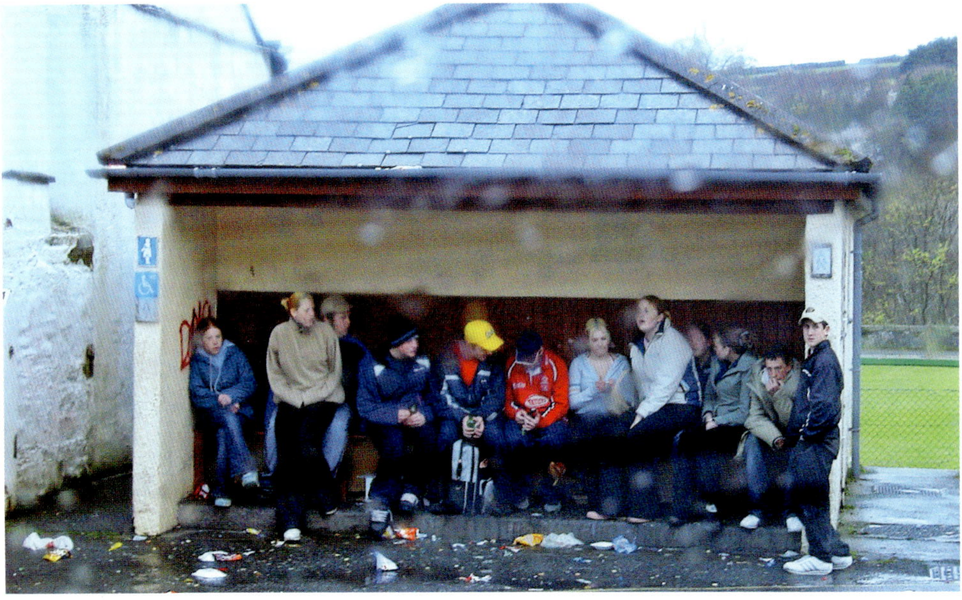

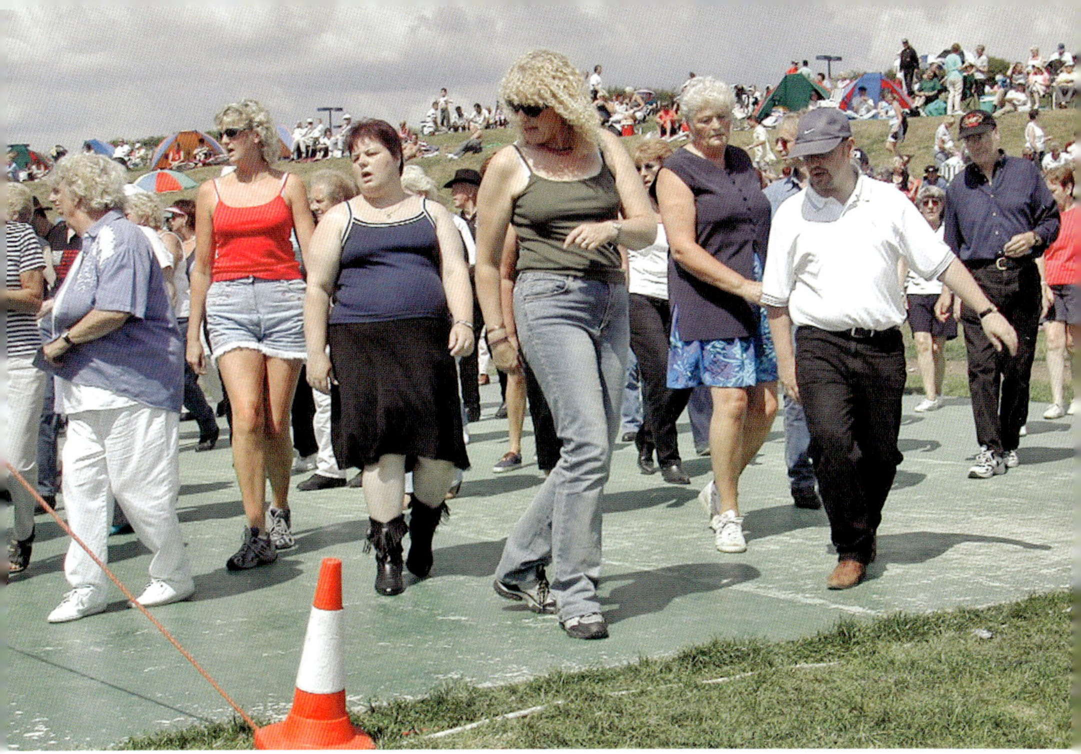

The British have often shown a keen interest in all things Country and Western, and line dancing is particularly popular. Positioned in orderly rows, dancers in Southsea reveal their Achy Breaky Hearts; while other enthusiasts form a breakaway faction of their own.

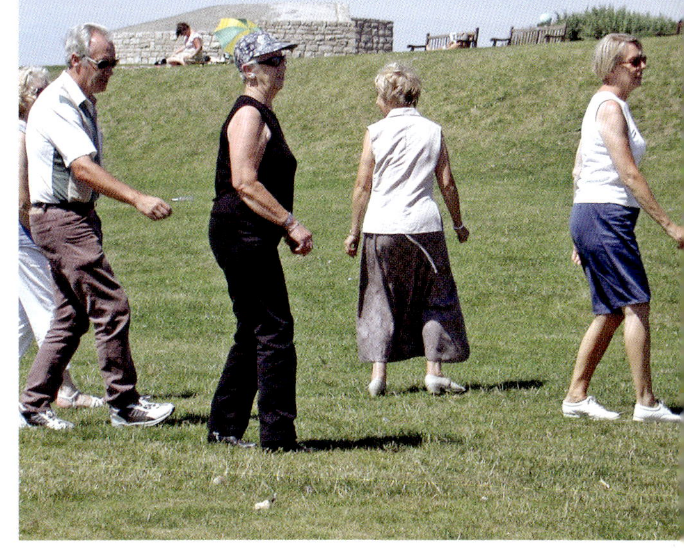

What's great about Britain?

We can laugh at ourselves

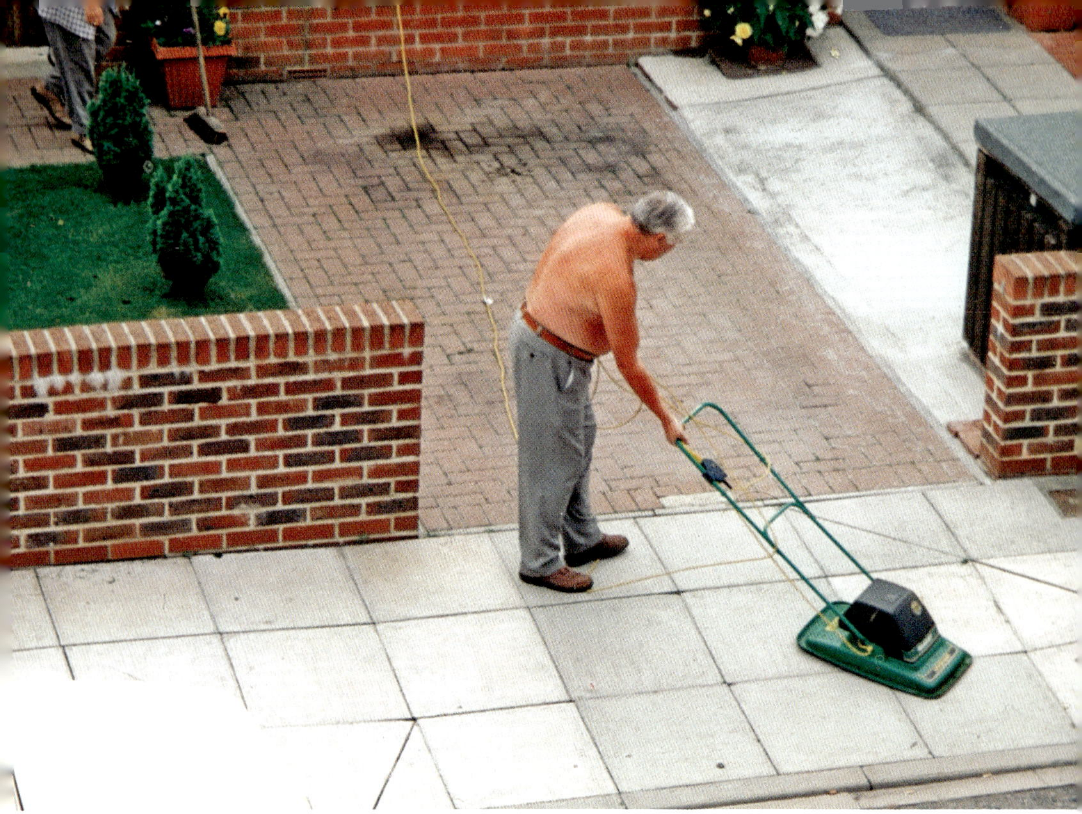

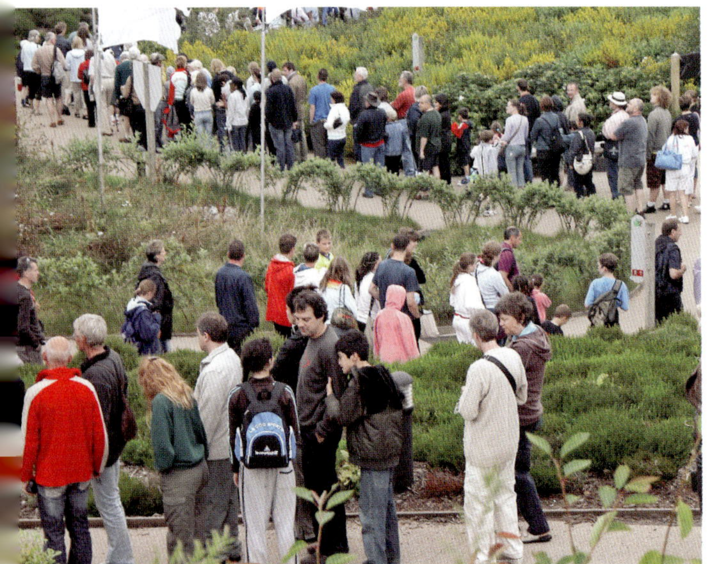

What's great about Britain?

Our ability to queue

We know how to say 'please' and 'thank you'

What's not so great?

People who don't have any manners

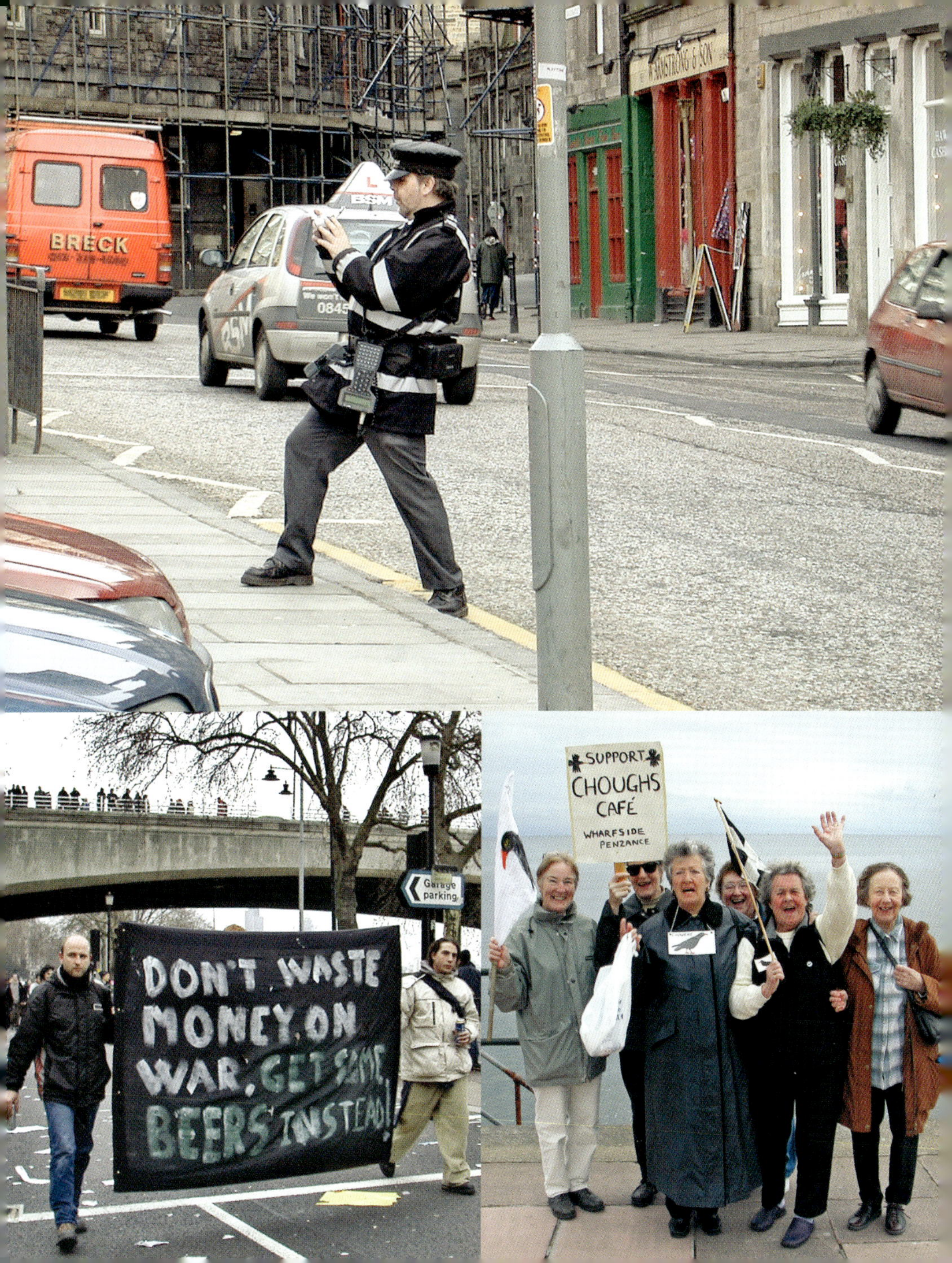
BRECK
DON'T WASTE MONEY ON WAR, GET SOME BEERS INSTEAD!
Garage parking
SUPPORT CHOUGHS CAFÉ
WHARFSIDE PENZANCE

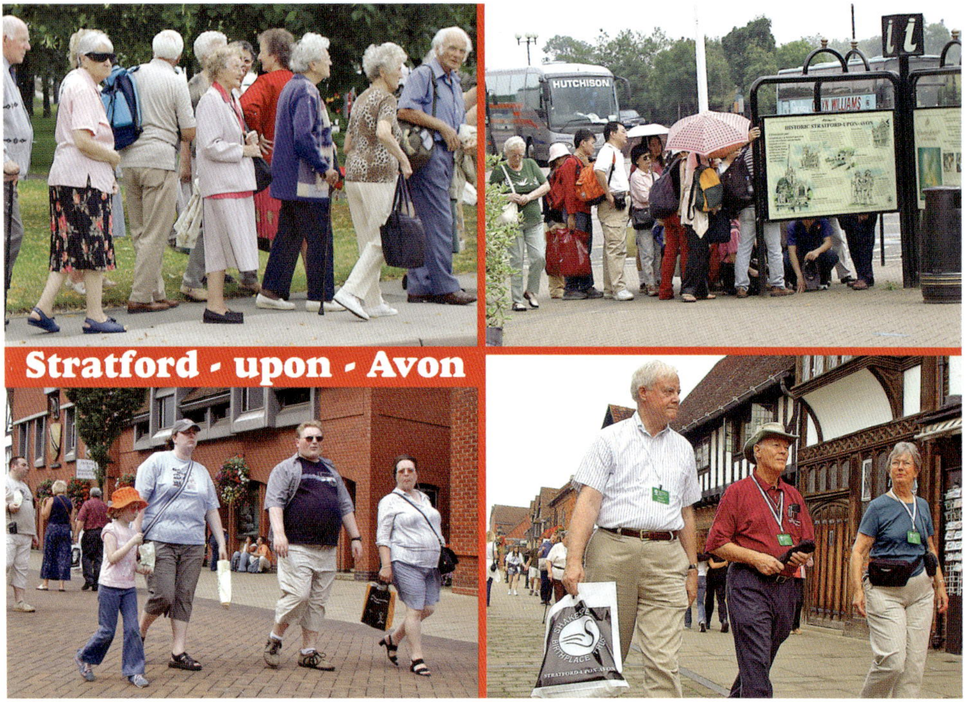

Stratford - upon - Avon

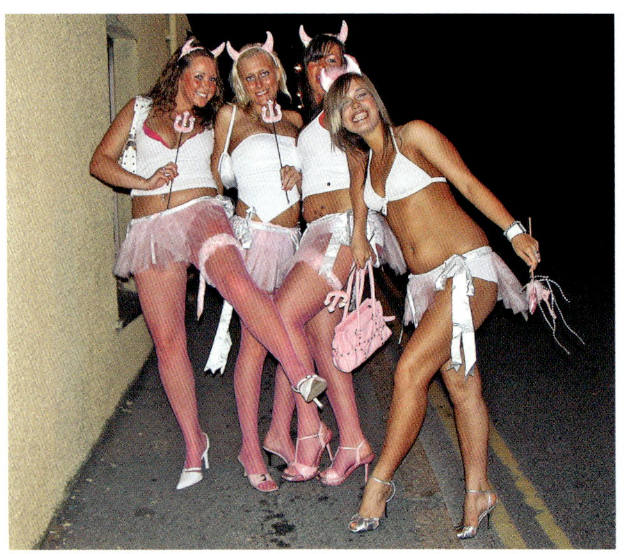

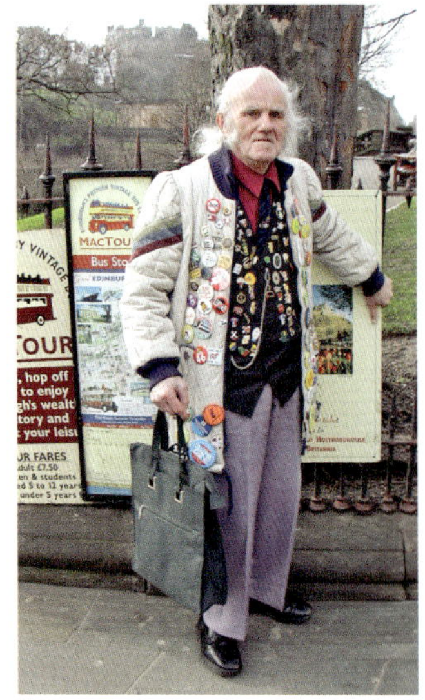

What's your personal motto?

TV is no substitute for real life

Those who say it cannot be done should not get in the way of those doing it

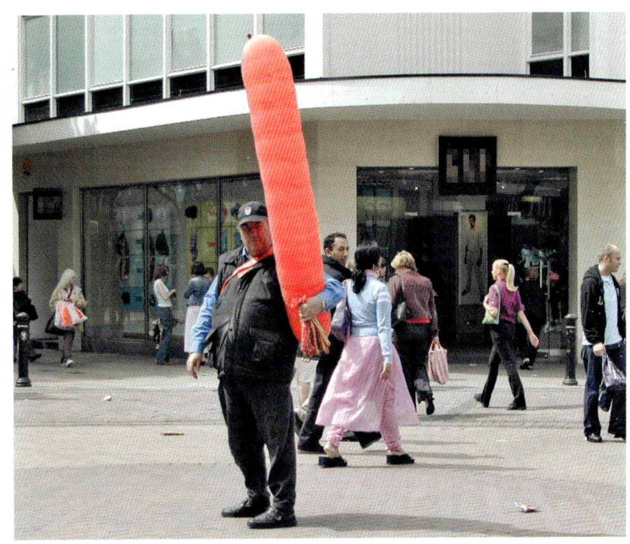

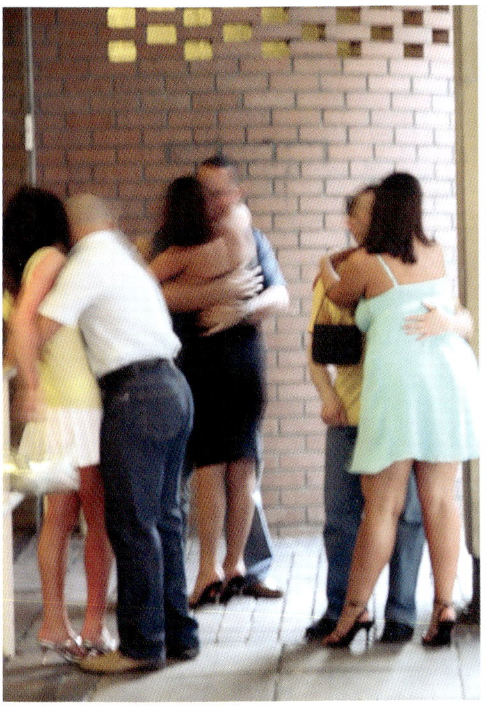

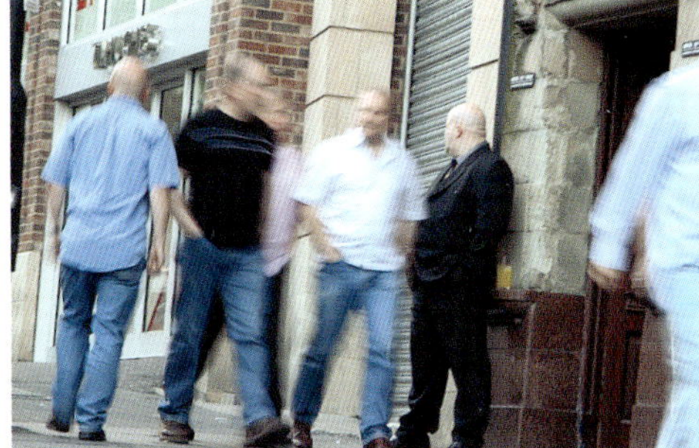

Newcastle Nightlife

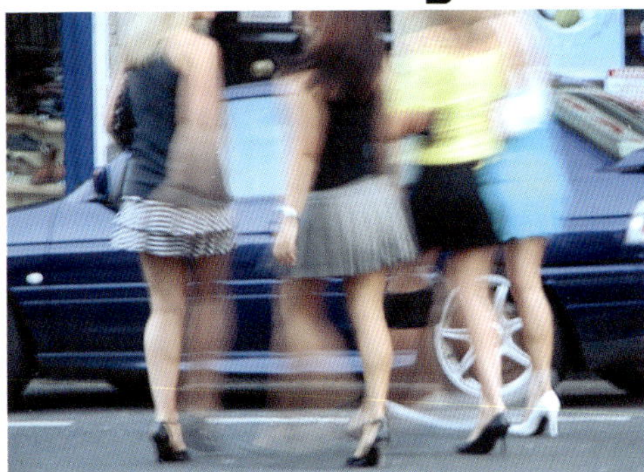

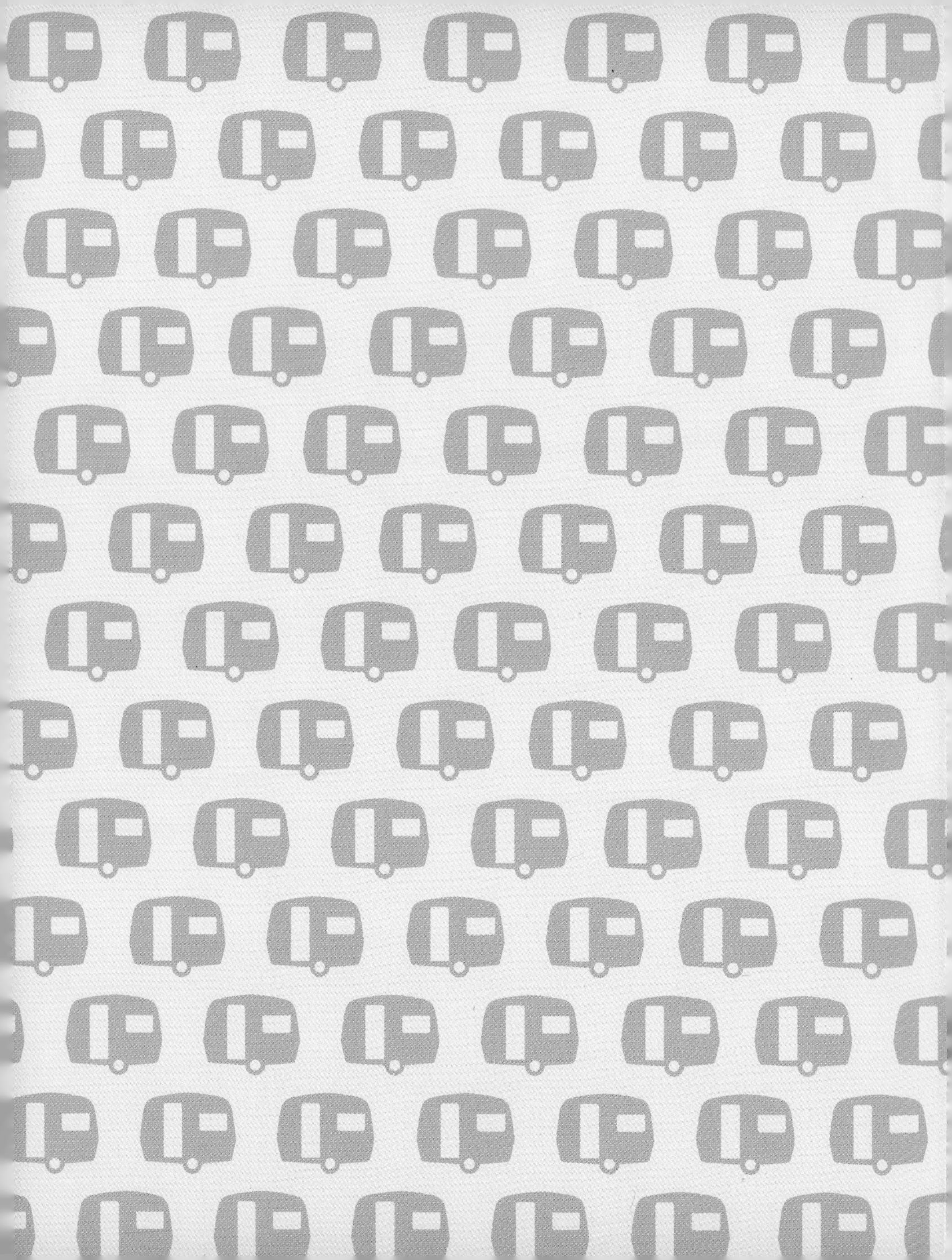